Fighting Computer Crime

A NEW FRAMEWORK FOR PROTECTING INFORMATION

DONN B. PARKER

WILEY COMPUTER PUBLISHING

John Wiley & Sons, Inc.
New York • Chichester • Weinheim • Brisbane • Singapore • Toronto

Publisher: Robert Ipsen
Editor: Robert M. Elliott
Managing Editor: Brian Snapp
Text Design & Composition: North Market Street Graphics

Designations used by companies to distinguish their products are often claimed as trademarks. In all instances where John Wiley & Sons, Inc., is aware of a claim, the product names appear in initial capital or ALL CAPITAL LETTERS. Readers, however, should contact the appropriate companies for more complete information regarding trademarks and registration.

This book is printed on acid-free paper. ∞

Published by John Wiley & Sons, Inc.

Published simultaneously in Canada.

This publication is designed to provide accurate and authoritative information in regard to the subject matter covered. It is sold with the understanding that the publisher is not engaged in professional services. If professional advice or other expert assistance is required, the services of a competent professional person should be sought.

Library of Congress Cataloging-in-Publication Data:
Parker, Donn B.
    Fighting computer crime : a new framework for protecting information / Donn Parker.
        p.   cm.
    "Wiley computer publishing."
    Includes index.
    ISBN 0-471-16378-3 (pbk. : alk. paper)
    1. Computer crimes.   2. Computer crimes—Prevention.   3. Computer security.   I. Title.
    HV6773.P374   1998
    658.4'78—dc21   98-28151
                                                                            CIP

Printed in the United States of America.

10 9 8 7 6 5 4 3 2 1

C O N T E N T S

F O R E W O R D

This is a book of stories. Ostensibly the stories are about computer crimes. At another level the stories are about criminals and their motives. At yet another, they are stories about ourselves, about how we react to the crimes and the criminals. Independent of the crimes the book recounts, it tells stories about our attitudes toward systems, technology, and society. We are the stories we tell ourselves and these stories tell us about ourselves.

One ancient story holds that Donn Parker and Bob Courtney once sat in adjoining seats on an intercontinental flight on their way to speak at an international conference. Donn suggested to Bob that they might want to use the occasion to resolve some of their philosophical differences. Bob responded that was a silly idea for it was just those differences that got them invited to speak at such conferences and in such venues.

I too cherish my philosophical differences with Donn. One colleague likes to recall a philosophical debate between Donn and me during a coffee break at an early Computer Security Institute Conference. He does not exaggerate much when he says that we drew an audience three-deep. Years later CSI formalized that debate and made it into a highlighted general session at several conferences. Perhaps the publication of this book will be an occasion to resurrect the debate.

While our areas of agreement are much greater than our differences, the differences appear to be irreconcilable. Donn has consistently resisted my most persuasive arguments repeated steadfastly over the years. He simply will not consent to my greater wisdom. He listens politely to my rhetoric and then persists in his previous position, unreformed. While I am sure that I am right, I am no longer willing to judge the wisdom or genius of another man by the extent to which he agrees with me and I have never met anyone who agrees with me on everything.

I am not sure that Donn would consent to my description of the differences. Suffice it to say that Donn's view of information security is a forensic one. His justification for the measures on which we agree begins with the prevention of crime. As the title and subtitle of this book suggest, he believes that fighting computer crime is the proper context for protecting information. On the other hand, my context is protecting information from unintended modification, destruction, or disclosure, whether the source be accidental or intentional.

While he might agree that far more damage to information is caused by error than by crime, he contends that appreciating the motives of criminals is essential to good security. His emphasis is on detection, investigation, and punishment of old crime as the principal deterrent to new crime. As I look down the titles on computer crime on my bookshelf, I find that he is far from alone.

He values law and order. For example, he says in this book "Given the choice of criminals abusing my information in absolute secrecy and the FBI eavesdropping on my information, I choose the FBI." Without commenting on the validity of this choice, I identify with Dr. Franklin, who told us that "those who would give up essential liberty for a little temporary safety deserve neither liberty nor safety." Indeed I cherish this difference most of all; while I can rely upon the FBI to protect me from the lawless, I have only the Constitution to protect me from the state.

I too am concerned with order, but not so much with law. Rather, I am concerned with good manners and freedom from error. I believe that trust in our systems is essential if we are to enjoy the benefits that are promised by computers and communications. If we cannot trust the information that comes from our systems, then we might as well not have them.

The differences are subtle and, perhaps, not so much important as instructive. Whatever our differences, we agree on what must be done. While we may not agree on the primary motive or the detail of the content, we agree that there are minimum standards of security that are generally applicable. This book refers to these measures as "baseline controls" and "standards of due care." These are controls that are applicable to all institutions and systems, and standards of care to which all responsible professionals and managers should adhere.

Individually, few of our systems meet these standards. Collectively, they are a disaster. This book helps us to understand why that is so and helps to empower us to do something about it.

Fighting Computer Crime: A New Framework for Protecting Information recognizes that the standard of our success is not the absence of failure, but it does so without sanctioning or condoning failure. It recognizes that balance is the issue and communicates a sense of the equities that must be balanced. It recognizes that there is no such thing as perfect security. It acknowledges that security is always and only achieved at the expense of other values. Under the best of circumstances, it is a balancing act.

We can make our systems completely secure only at the expense of infinite cost or zero utility. They will be completely secure if we unplug them. They will be completely secure if they have no users or uses. They will be more secure if we do not connect them to a network. There is in the world enough work, access, indifference to detection, special knowledge, and time to detection and corrective action (WAIST) to penetrate any system. Fortunately for us, there is not enough to break every system.

How then are we to measure ourselves? How are we to know when we have it right? How do we know that the crime or system failure that we see is not simply necessary noise? Society's attitude toward computer-related crime has been one of tolerance.

On the other hand, society tends to view infrastructure failures with great alarm and often overreacts. Society's tolerance of any such failures is low. Airplanes may hit the ground too hard. Occasionally, they may even collide. However, they may not simply fall out of the sky without explanation. So, while far more people die on the highway than in the air, there is far more public reaction to an unexplained airplane crash than to all highway deaths taken together. While the highway death and accident rate measured per passenger mile dwarfs that for airplanes, many more people are afraid to fly than to drive.

Similarly, while the use of the Internet for credit card transactions is already safer than the same transaction in person and promises to be even more so, the public's perception is that it is much less so. While electronic banking is safer than the same banking done by mail, the perception is the opposite. This misperception is related, in part, to scale. The public tends to react more to the size of an event than to its frequency.

So, the question turns on whether we are dealing with traditional systems or whether we are dealing with infrastructure. Systems fail for some combination of six reasons. They fail because of shoddy fabrication, weak materials, poor maintenance, bad design, misuse by owners and operators, and finally, because of abuse by criminals. While this book focuses on abuse, a careful reading will demonstrate that inadequate design and poor operation contribute more than their fair share to the problem.

While there is no system that cannot be stressed to the point of failure, I argue that infrastructure is built to a different standard than ordinary systems. Infrastructure does not fall of its own weight. It does not fail under normal load or use. It does not fail in the face of accident or even easily anticipated misuse.

This is the standard that seems to apply but it is a different standard than the one to which we have traditionally built information systems. It is not clear exactly what we thought we were doing but the resulting systems have been fragile, not to say that they have frequently collapsed under little more than their own weight. They have not demonstrated the ability to resist easily anticipated abuse of the kind described in this book.

Much of the problem has resulted from a failure to design for the limitations of our materials. These materials have until recently been so expensive that only the most efficient applications could be justified. The most valued features of our materials have been performance, generality, and flexibility. In order to justify expensive hardware, we have needed multi-user and multi-use operating systems. These operating systems were optimized for performance and not security. It was not simply that these systems were not built for security but that the security properties in use have often been compromised away. Indeed, there seems to be no security property that the vendors can build that users cannot compromise, no security function they cannot misuse, no feature they cannot abuse.

Another major error in our designs is the failure to adequately hide the most sensitive controls from (criminals and other) unprivileged users. To do so would require that managers and operators use strong authentication and encryption. One might expect that system managers would like controls that were available to them but not to others. In fact, because they see themselves as evaluated on the basis of responsiveness, they resist controls that might interfere with response.

These design problems are largely problems of attitude. Most IT managers still behave as though computer hardware was expensive and it was their job to conserve it. In their view, while security is desirable, it is certainly not sufficiently important to compromise performance. Even the staff that knows the most about security and is held responsible for it believes that security is a magical expectation. Even when they really believe in it, they blame their materials for their failures. In one dialogue, a security manager implied that any design that was not built with the minimum amount of the cheapest materials was "over-designed." In other words, as a design criterion, security does not rank with cost.

Jim Barksdale of Netscape likes to compare Internet security to safety in commercial aviation; each is essential to the success of its technology. He goes on to point out that with the Internet, we are about where aviation was in 1937 when the DC-3 came on line. He says that if you held aviation safety at the 1937 level but let traffic rise to today's levels, then we would be killing people at the rate of two 747s per day.

Note that we did not get from the 1937 safety level to that of today by reading last week's accident report. We did not get here by looking back over our shoulders. We got here by looking as far out into the future as we could. The buyers and sellers of airliners have worked together to produce the safest form of transportation in history under the least forgiving conditions.

Some of you will have seen the PBS *Nova* series that documented the testing of the Boeing 777. In one of the most dramatic tests, they anchored the plane to the ground so that they could rip the wings off. In order to break the wings off, they had to apply 154 percent of the maximum load that the fuselage could ever put on the wings. However, what made the test really dramatic was that the two wings broke at the same time. It was so stunning that they created a tape loop and played it over and over again in slow motion.

In another test, they loaded the 777 to its maximum allowable take-off weight and accelerated it down the runway. At the point that it was supposed to take off, they chopped the throttles and stomped on the brakes. The plane stopped just short of the end of the runway; all the brakes and most of the tires were on fire. Not to worry; they had anticipated this and so the firemen were mounted in their engines ready to put out the flames. However, since under most accident circumstances, the firemen would not already be mounted, mounting time was simulated by holding them back for five minutes to demonstrate that the fire would not spread to the fuselage (or the fuel) during the time that the firemen would normally take to respond.

Information technology people see the problem that confronts them as much more difficult than the one that confronts aircraft or bridge builders. They argue that they have more degrees of freedom and greater complexity. Therefore, they have a greater propensity to error and failure.

In fact, the engineers began with the same amount of freedom as the information technology people insist on. They systematically gave it up in the name of reliability. And so it must be and so this book argues. In information technology we must be as diligent, rigorous, and disciplined as our colleagues in other professions and other industries. No lower standard will serve.

We are now using our most novel, fragile, and vulnerable infrastructure to operate and coordinate all of the others. There is no part of our social and economic infrastructure that is not operated by our telecommunications infrastructure. I hope that the reader goes away from this book with a renewed sense of commitment to robust design and, more than that, with a sense of urgency.

So, this is a book of stories but it is also a book of lessons. The lessons are timely, useful, and important. They deserve our attention, study, and appreciation.

—William Hugh Murray*
New Canaan, Connecticut

*William Murray is an executive consultant to the information protection practice of Deloitte & Touche LLP.

P R E F A C E

I wrote this book as a culmination of 28 years of studying computer criminals and assisting their victims around the world. The urgency of protecting information and making computers and communications safe has never been greater. The growing commercial and personal use of the Internet and our dependence on fragile interconnected information systems has finally thrust information security into broad public view. Protecting information plays a critically strategic role in maintaining the viability of our society.

In the first half of the book, I describe computer criminals and errant information users and the challenge they pose to information owners. I also describe the terrible state of what I call the information security "folk art," including our often-failed attempts to understand our adversaries and the nature of the information they abuse and misuse. I abandon the current rationale of preserving only the confidentiality, integrity, and availability of information because it is overly simplistic and unworkable. Computer crime and error is a complex problem in perverse and often irrational misbehavior made even more difficult by the incredible complexity of the technology. To address this problem head-on, we need a more detailed, comprehensive, and articulate treatment of information security.

The second half of the book presents my new foundation and framework for the protection of information and its owners. Rather than attempting to reduce risk alone, this new approach achieves the more important objective of meeting standards of due care to avoid claims of negligence for failure to have implemented prudent protection. I explain in simple, complete, and practical terms how to use this new model to achieve improved—and less onerous—security.

This book differs from many others written about the protection of information. It is based on first-hand knowledge that I obtained from real abusers and misusers of information and their victims. Sources of the material and subjects that I present span many years of security research and consulting and come from my collection of computer crime cases, articles, reports, books, and videos. The experience that I document includes interviewing more than 200 computer criminals and their victims and conducting more than 250 security reviews for many diverse organizations during my career at *SRI Consulting*. I address all aspects of information misuse and abuse, not just unintended modification, destruction, or disclosure of information in computers but wherever the information exists and is sent. I cover all types of protection, not just systems and communications security. Too often, the technologists who dominate this field focus on the security of information in computers and ignore the protection of information stored in the minds of people and printed on paper left in unlocked and unguarded offices. These technologists have not directly confronted their real enemies, and this deprives them of important insights to know what security is all about. They start by finding and reducing computer system vulnerabilities; we must start by battling abusers and misusers of information.

I describe real cases of cybercrime in this book. The scenarios may not necessarily be accurate in all details, since they are derived from only limited interviews of perpetrators and victims and from reports, some of which can be difficult to completely verify. However, the scenarios are sufficiently representative and factual to support my descriptions of the abuses and misuses we must stop. A few of the cases are classics, and I described them in more detail in my earlier writings; however, they are still pertinent in the cyberspace security issues of today. I do not reveal the names of perpetrators and victims unless they are already in the public eye, because many of them deserve some anonymity to give them the opportunity to recover from their past mistakes. I also preserve the security of specific information owners in my examples by avoiding the publication of their names.

To present my case clearly and precisely, I have avoided the use of several confusing and inappropriate terms common in technical writings on these subjects. For example, I do not use the words *access* referring to use of computers, *risk* referring to possible information losses, and *professionals* referring to security "folk art" practitioners. *Access* is an acceptable word to describe the ability to enter a room, but it is confusing when applied to using a computer. *Risk* is acceptable for describing business investments, but it is not so for predicting unknowable information losses. As for being professionals, we practitioners of the folk art do not yet deserve, nor are we sufficiently able to assume, the accountability necessary for this title in information security—even though many of us are competent information technology professionals. Using words correctly and with clear meaning is important in information security, because our adversaries are tricky, and so many people must thoroughly understand how to protect their information from them. The words *integrity*, *confidentiality*, *privacy*, *computer hacker*, and *crime* require careful use for our understanding.

I received valuable assistance writing this book. In particular, I appreciate my family's patience, and my daughter-in-law Peggy's practical advice. I owe much to Anne Meadows, a top professional writer in Washington, D.C., who helped me to achieve higher writing quality. Bob Elliott, senior editor at Wiley, encouraged me to write this book and nurtured me through its publication. The Wiley editors did a superb streamlining job. I am grateful to my peers for imparting their knowledge and wisdom, especially Bill Murray (who wrote the Foreword), Dr. Douglas Webb, Wallace Bruschweiler, Susan Nycum, Dr. Bruce Baker, all of the SRIC I-4 members, and the managers at *SRI Consulting* who assisted me. Last, I give thanks to all of the computer criminals and malicious hackers—and their victims—who cooperated with me to reveal their anguishing experience.

To my grandchildren, Scott, Daniel, Rose, Laura, Allison, and Andrew. May your Christian values see you safely through this computer-empowered world.

—Donn B. Parker
June 26, 1998

1

The Myth of Information Security

I hate having to worry about security. Most of us hate to bother with locking our doors and desks. We dislike making backup copies of our files, remembering passwords. And when it comes to securing information, we're often at a loss as to what we need to protect and why.

As it happens, information is both precious and fragile—it can be easily abused and misused in many ways. To protect information, we've developed copyright, trademark, trade secret, and other laws. When we entered the computer age, we passed new laws to protect privacy and the ownership of information. And we developed a host of security measures—like passwords and cryptography—to make it more difficult for criminals to get their hands on this information in the first place.

Today we are concerned about all of cyberspace—the amorphous realm containing printed, spoken, and electronic information, wherever it exists and is communicated. A lot of good things come from cyberspace, but bad things come as well.

This book concerns the abuse and misuse of information in cyberspace—what I loosely call *computer crime* or *cybercrime*. It's probably true that most loss of information occurs by accident rather than intentional acts—though at times it can be difficult to tell whether an incident is accidental or intentional. But over the years I've learned that safeguards against intentionally caused loss also stop accidental loss. That's why I focus on crime in this book.

THE BIG PICTURE

Information security is important for all computer users, but perhaps nowhere is the concern greater than at the White House. The United States has become so dependent on information technology for its operations that it must protect itself against "information warfare"—attacks against the basic information infrastructure of the nation. Recognizing this danger, President Clinton issued an executive order on July 15, 1996 which states, in part:

> Certain infrastructures are so vital that their incapacity or destruction would have a debilitating impact on the defense or economic security of the United States. These critical infrastructures include telecommunications, electrical power systems, gas and oil storage and transportation, banking and finance, transportation, water supply systems, emergency services (including medical, police, fire, and rescue), and continuity of government. Threats to these critical infrastructures fall into two categories: physical threats to tangible property and threats called cyber threats of electronic, radio frequency, or computer-based attacks on the information or communications components that control critical infrastructures.

This executive order established the President's Commission on Critical Infrastructure Protection (PCCIP), comprising about fifty top government and private sector experts and administrators. The commission was tasked to assess the scope and nature of the threats to critical infrastructures, determine legal and policy efforts to address these dangers, and recommend a comprehensive strategy to deal with the problem.

The golden age of information security has, indeed, arrived. We've come a long way since the late 1960s, when I and others first began worrying about the emergence of a few juvenile computer hackers and high-tech embezzlers.

LEARNING FROM EXPERIENCE

Apart from its potential threat to national security, cybercrime endangers businesses and individuals—we are all potential targets. Unfortunately, for the most part, we see half-hearted efforts—the equivalent of locking the door and leaving the window open. Security experts tell computer users to create passwords that are difficult to guess, for example, but malicious computer hackers routinely eavesdrop on computer networks, using powerful automated dictionary searches to deduce passwords. Many of us are reluctant to spend the time and effort needed to prevent crimes, hoping that we will never become the victims of a cybercrime.

It's true that there's no foolproof way to prevent all crimes—with a big enough hammer you can break anything. But this doesn't mean that we should forego protecting information in some ways, just because we can not protect it in all ways. And regardless of the likelihood of becoming

A Case of Self-Inflicted Sabotage

Knowing what we should do is one thing; following through is another matter. A few years ago, for example, I was the victim of self-inflicted sabotage. I had just given a self-satisfying, passionate speech on information security to executives sponsored by Time Incorporated in New York City, stressing the importance of making frequent electronic copies of their information files in case their originals were lost. On the flight back to San Francisco, I realized that I was not following my own advice. It had been four weeks since I backed up the information files in my own home computer, which contained a major part of my life's work.

When I returned home, I staggered to my computer, turned it on, and inserted a diskette in the A drive. But when I started to type *A* to designate the disk drive for reformatting the diskette, my jet-lagged middle finger hit *C* instead. The computer obediently set about reformatting—and destroying—all of the data, not on my diskette, but on the hard drive. I sat there for twenty minutes, staring at that little red light in the darkness, listening to the soft chug-chugging of the disk drive, and envisioning my month's work being wiped away. I could do nothing to stop it. I spent a week re-creating the information—long enough to ensure that I will never make the same mistake again.

victims of cybercrime, we certainly want to avoid negligence. We therefore should act prudently to protect information by meeting a standard of due care. Simply put, this means doing what other prudent owners of information are doing to protect themselves under similar circumstances. Information owners can reasonably adopt the many well-known information security safeguards and practices to achieve the required level of due care. For example, we can use entry passwords, lock our computer room doors, safely store backup copies of important information, and split sensitive duties among different people. (Note that none of this requires performing complex assessments of risk.)

Of course, we can choose to do little or nothing to protect our information if we have prudent reasons for doing so. Some of us may wish to take the chance and pay the price of any losses (assuming that our actions

A Lesson from My Own Backyard

I have been studying Kevin Mitnick, a lonely, addicted computer hacker, for almost twenty years. Kevin started hacking as a teenager—he was a member of the infamous Roscoe group of hackers in Los Angeles in the 1970s. After several convictions, he was caught as a fugitive from a parole violation and convicted again in North Carolina of possession of stolen credit-card numbers. He now awaits trial on additional charges in California.

Kevin victimized me back when Internet users were cyberspace pioneers. One day in 1988 Kevin's voice wafted sincerely through my telephone: "Donn, I think you need some help; how about giving me a job as an information security consultant?" I was looking to expand my staff, but how did he know that? The answer came a year later, when I learned from a friend at a computer company that Kevin had apparently been reading my e-mail. As part of an FBI investigation of Kevin's electronic theft of a million dollars worth of computer programs from the company's computers, they uncovered my e-mail messages stored in a computer at USC. (One of Kevin's signature hacker techniques is using others' computers to store his stolen booty.) Apparently, Kevin had been able to impersonate my company's systems administrator and, using a default superuser password that had never been changed, obtained access to all my e-mail messages. Though I was embarrassed at having had my privacy invaded, this incident helped to convince my employer to tighten security.

would not harm others). This is a decision that we must make in the context of competing objectives. For example, we may eschew caution to achieve an attractive but risky business objective. After all, business is a practice of prudent risk-taking to make a profit.

Negligence, however, is only one facet of the problem. We can exercise due care and still fall prey to the determined criminal—see the accompanying sidebar for a particularly embarrassing example.

WEAKNESSES IN INFORMATION SECURITY CONTROLS

The number of safeguards employed by the intended victims seems to have little to do with whether crimes succeed or fail. The key to effective protection is using the right safeguards effectively and creating relationships among people and systems in which trust is balanced with the constraints imposed by safeguards.

Based on my twenty-eight years of study of real loss experience and on interviews of more than two hundred perpetrators and their victims, I have found that the security practices of most companies are seriously deficient. Take the case of a branch manager who embezzled over $20 million from his bank over the course of eighteen months. He had previously worked in the data processing department and knew that the main computer would notify auditors if more than one million dollars were transferred from an account, or an account balance was left incorrect for more than five days. Such limits are examples of accepted, due-care controls for every bank, but this clever branch manager made sure that no single theft exceeded the transaction limit and no shortage in any single account existed for more than five days. (I call this the "salami" technique—the thief takes small, undetected slices, one at a time, to get the whole salami.) One Friday afternoon, however, he made a mistake in moving a shortage from one account to another to beat the five-day limit, and the amount went over the transaction limit. The auditors visited him the next week to check on it, saw the pattern of activity, and caught him.

The bank caught the branch manager because he became careless. The security controls were ineffective so long as the branch manager took steps to avoid triggering them. The bank's preventative measures slowed the branch manager down and kept him busy every Friday afternoon (which made it difficult for him to take vacations), but the controls were ineffective until he made his mistake.

Another case illustrates a similar flaw. Many companies use a computer called a firewall to filter data traveling between the freewheeling Internet and the company's internal network. By examining data packets traveling in and out and limiting message traffic to acceptable types, content, source addresses, destinations, and frequency, the firewall provides strong security against any hacker who attempts to use the company's computers. If a hacker tried, for example, to keep guessing passwords until he found one that worked, the firewall would detect these attempts and prevent him from succeeding. In this case, however, a wily hacker found out from a friend of a friend that an engineer in the company had attached a personal computer to his office telephone. Because this computer was connected directly to the company's internal network, bypassing the firewall gateway, the malicious hacker was able to dial into the office telephone and connect his computer to the engineer's computer. He gained entry to the internal network by impersonating the engineer and destroyed vast amounts of information in the computers linked to the company's network.

In each of these examples, strong controls were of little use, because the criminals knew they were there and knew how to get around them. In other words, the controls were predictable and avoidable. *When the controls are unpredictable, criminal attacks are much more likely to fail.*

THE HUMAN FACTOR

The human factor can never be underestimated in ensuring security. In the late 1200s, Kublai Khan and his Mongol hordes tried to break through, go under, and go around the Great Wall of China, but it was too solid, too deep, and too long. He finally conquered the obstacle—and most of China—by simply bribing the gatekeeper. Not much has changed in security since then. Indeed, when strong technical controls (and even unpredictable ones) cause criminals to seek out alternative vulnerabilities, organizations may suffer losses greater than those that the controls were designed to prevent.

A case in point comes from the early days of one malicious hacker. He wanted to explore a medical instrument distributor's computer, but the company's security system stymied him. His only hope was to deceive a trusted employee into revealing the key information he needed for the attack. He placed a telephone call to the night operator at the company's center and, using his most official voice, claimed to be a computer maintenance engineer who could solve the company's "short buffer" problem if only he had the right password. (The hacker knew that this computer was currently having a short buffer problem.) This, he explained, would allow him to send the changes directly by telephone into the operating system program that controlled and ran the whole system. The process would correct the problem and make the operator a hero.

The operator readily revealed the password, and the hacker transmitted code that revised the operating system program and actually eliminated the nagging problem. The revision, however, was a Trojan horse: Embedded in it were secret instructions that took control of the computer. Then the same insertion changed the operating system so that changes to the entry passwords in the future would become available to the hacker as well. He then merrily spewed dirty words throughout the product inventory files stored in the computer, and called the operator's mother some not-too-endearing names on the computer console display. His efforts shut down the sales business of the distributor all over the world for several days. They could not replace the operating system, because his code had made the same changes in the only backup copy of the operating system. In this classical hacker attack, the technical safeguards worked fine, but the human controls failed.

How We Got into This Mess

If criminals seem to be beating us right and left, no matter what controls we put into our systems, it is because we have failed to understand the way they think. Operational and technical controls are inadequate because they come from technical experts who do not understand the criminals' ingenuity and perseverance or the weaknesses or the human factors in our systems.

Our current information security foundation is incomplete, inconsistent, incorrect, and, all too often, inadequate. We need more than a list of controls to implement; we need to understand the principles, tactics, and strategies to use the controls effectively.

Shortcomings of the CIA Foundation of Information Security

The current information security foundation is concerned with preserving the confidentiality, integrity, and availability of information. (Security experts refer to this by the acronym CIA.) The CIA foundation reflects a level of knowledge about security akin to the alchemists' belief that the elements comprised merely fire, water, earth, and air. Although we have significantly improved our technical security controls, our underlying concept of information security has not advanced beyond this primitive stage.

Because computer experts were most worried about protecting information confidentiality, early controls were designed primarily to restrict the reading of information. But many computer crimes involve altering, taking, misusing, and/or destroying confidential information—not just observing or disclosing it. And, computer auditors, the gatekeepers originally designated to ensure the safeguarding of computer information, rarely had sufficient knowledge of computer technology to examine for effective controls. (Their approach was to spot-check incoming data and compare them with expected results—auditing around the computers rather than through them or in them.) Business managers ignored some of the most fundamental management controls—separation of duties and dual control in business transactions, and double-entry bookkeeping—because they believed that computers were too complex for people to use effectively for crime.

In 1966, the first federally prosecuted case of computer crime demonstrated the potential implications of misusing information, which go far beyond CIA. It also demonstrated how dramatically computer technology was changing banking: This was the first time that a *non-employee* of a bank was convicted of bank embezzlement.

The perpetrator was a young computer programmer working under contract with a Minneapolis bank to program and maintain its computer system. As it happened, he had a checking account with the same bank. When he experienced a temporary, personal cash-flow problem, he changed the checking account program in the bank's computer so that it would not react to—and would not report—any naturally occurring overdraft condition in his account. He then wrote checks for amounts that exceeded his balance. He expected to be short by no more than thirteen hundred dollars for a few days, after which he would be able to deposit enough to eliminate the overdraft, and nobody would be the wiser. Instead, his financial problems worsened, and the overdraft grew to fourteen thousand dollars.

One day, the computer failed, necessitating manual processing, which revealed the unreported overdraft. The programmer pled guilty to altering bank records, made restitution, and spent a few months in prison. Ironically, the bank desperately needed him to keep the system running, and so the contract for his services continued while he was in prison!

Note that, under the traditional CIA formula, there was no security breach of the data files in this case, given that the bank's information retained its confidentiality, integrity, and availability. The fact that the programmer obviously engaged in a computer crime underscores the inadequacy of the CIA foundation. He violated the authenticity of the computer program by changing it to perform differently than the bank expected, although the program still preserved its integrity by being complete and in good condition. The overdraft reports were authentic as far as they went but suffered from loss of integrity by being incomplete.

Two other cases further illustrate the inadequacy of the CIA security foundation. In the first case, an operator from a computer service company set fire to a competing computer center, destroying most of the center and its information. The perpetrator, who acted in collusion with his employer, was subsequently sentenced to a prison term along with his co-conspirators. In the second case, a group of night-shift computer operators were secretly selling their employer's computer services. When management discovered what the operators were doing and told them that they would be punished, the operators piled the tapes and disks in the middle of the computer room and urinated on them, causing great damage. In both of these cases good backup procedures saved the targeted companies, but the security issues went beyond confidentiality, integrity, and availability. Usefulness of the contaminated media was also an issue, as well as the authenticity of the restored backup data files as being correct duplicates of the original ones.

The CIA security foundation also fails to address two other areas of concern: information possession and unauthorized use. Possession is an issue when, for example, criminals steal all copies of digitized information and hold it for ransom. Because they don't violate either the confidentiality or integrity of the information and are willing to make it available—for a price—there is no breach of security under the principles of the CIA foundation. However, the timeliness of the returned information brings into question its authenticity since it may have become obsolete and didn't conform to current reality. Similarly, computer users who engage in software piracy by making—or using—unauthorized copies of copyrighted commercial software are guilty of theft, but do not necessarily breach the tenets of the CIA foundations. Again, the issue is one of possession rather than a loss of confidentiality, integrity, or availability.

Expanding the Security Foundation

To enhance the effectiveness of our information security measures, we need to extend the scope of those measures and change our priorities.

While security experts have traditionally focused on protecting computer operating systems and networks from attacks, the most serious security breaches occur in the use of these systems rather than in attacks on them. The recent $1.3 billion Barings Bank securities fraud in Singapore and the $21 million bank embezzlement that I mentioned earlier are examples of authorized people committing unauthorized acts.

In short, all too often security practitioners resemble the drunk who has lost his car keys and looks for them under a street lamp half a block away because the light is better there. Instead of focusing so much of our attention on controlling entry into computers and networks, we must broaden our concept of information security to anticipate all types of material losses that may occur and involving all types of information in all locations, not just computer-based data.

THE EXTENT OF CRIME IN CYBERSPACE

Knowing how much crime is committed might help us decide on how much to spend on security. Estimates by security experts of annual losses from computer crime range from $555 million to more than $13 billion, but there are actually no valid statistics on the dollar losses from this type of crime because no one knows how many cases go unreported. (Although the news media quote numbers of cases and total dollar losses fairly often, the numbers are impossible to verify.) Even when the victims of computer crimes are aware of the crimes, they are often reluctant to report their losses—especially if those losses can be easily hidden. Victims can actually lose more from reporting crimes than they lose from the crimes themselves. Embarrassment, key staff diverted to prepare evidence and testify, legal fees, increased insurance premiums, and exposure of vulnerabilities and security failures can all result from reporting computer crime incidents.

Unfortunately, management often demands that we quantify the risks in order to decide appropriate levels of spending for computer security. This is the motivation for conducting risk assessments that weigh past loss experiences and future loss expectancy to determine the allocation of resources for reducing risks to an acceptable level. However, many insightful business risk and security managers agree that security risks cannot be adequately calculated. We can predict financial investment risks because we have complete and valid information on previous experience and are able to test the results of forecasting. But, when it comes to crime, we cannot predict the future unknown misbehavior of unknown perpetrators at unknown times under any and all circumstances. For example, one individual might engage in a single crime that is as costly in terms of dollar losses as the total of many others committed by numerous perpetrators. Businesses and governments have wasted great resources attempting to perform unneeded and impractical risk assessments.

THE CYBERSPACE CRIMOID SYNDROME

The news and trade media are often responsible for giving information owners a distorted perception of cybercrime. Owners may, for example, incorrectly conclude that attacks by malicious hackers represent the greatest threat to information. I call this phenomenon the *cyberspace crimoid syndrome.*

A crimoid is an event that seems to be a serious crime that receives intense media coverage for a short period of time, making it appear to be a monstrous contagion. The first computer crimoid occurred in 1970 when computers were alleged to have destroyed personal privacy; this resulted in the Privacy Act of 1974. Since then, many new crimoids have emerged. Some crimoids, such as malicious hacker attacks, are real and have grown worse. Others, such as eavesdropping on the radio waves that emanate from computers, have never been proven. Reports of computer viruses, including the Michelangelo and the fictitious Good Times viruses, have added to the folklore of computer crimoids.

Of course, every time the news media publicize a new crimoid, executives contact their overworked security managers demanding to know what their companies are doing about the new problem. Information security managers are best advised to attempt to predict what the next crimoids may be in preparation for the onslaughts. It does not matter whether the crimoid threats are valid; it is the perception, created by the news media, that seems to count.

In 1980, for example, some students at the University of California–Berkeley discovered the electronic-letter-bomb technique. An attacker can put secret computer instructions into messages and send them to computer terminals of victims through a computer he shares with them. The terminals then automatically send the secret instructions back into the shared computer for immediate execution as though the instructions were authorized by the victims. The technique is like sending a basketball out of bounds by bouncing it off of the back of an opposing player to blame the out-of-bounds action on the other team. Computer vendors and security experts were aware of the problem for quite some time and worked diligently to resolve it. In the meantime, the technique created a great deal of excitement when a *Los Angeles Times* journalist discovered and reported it, even though there were no documented cases of anyone actually using it in a computer crime. A variation of this technique appeared in 1996 as the Microsoft Word macro virus called Concept, and the news media again gave it massive attention.

On the positive side, the cyberspace crimoid syndrome helps to increase awareness of information security problems and alerts potential victims to potential disasters. But actual security and people's confidence in cyberspace both suffer when organizations respond by imposing new, unpleasant constraints on using computers. We need to focus instead on understanding the nature of the syndrome and learning to predict future crimoids so that we can prepare for them.

Automated Crime

Automated crime may well be the next crimoid. With some trepidation I describe it here, but not in sufficient detail to be a recipe for crime. In my definition, an automated crime is a complete, fully automated crime—from the selection of a victim to the perpetration of the misdeed and the covering of the perpetrator's tracks—that is packaged in a single computer program. When the program is executed, it automatically commits the crime and removes any damning evidence (including itself) before the victim can blink an icon. The creator can package an automated crime and pass it on to any number of perpetrators. The perpetrators can then execute the crime in their computers to attack any number of victims' computers without the creator's—or even the perpetrators'—further involvement. Theoretically, anyone could possess and send a copy of an automated crime program over the Internet for execution in the victims' computers at any time. Because the crime can be designed for total anonymity, the perpetrator need not know who the victim was, what crime occurred, what method was used, or the results of the crime. And, the entire crime could take place in only a few milliseconds.

Expert criminals could package well-conceived crimes and give or sell them to others. In doing so, they would introduce the concept, for the first time in criminal history, of possessing and selling, buying or bartering, or just giving away potentially perfect crimes. Innocent or not-so-innocent users could download them as freeware through the Internet or purchase them in software stores for $39.95 from a shelf of four-color, shrink-

A Hypothetical Automated Crime

While browsing the Internet, you encounter the offer of a freeware program called Fraudster. You copy and load it into your computer and execute it just out of curiosity. The first and only screen displayed to you says, "FRAUDSTER. How much money do you want?" You decide to play the game and key in $34,000. "Where do you want it?" glows out at you from the screen. You enter the name, Internet address, and account number of your bank (very risky, but you do it anyway). After you hit the Start key following the instruction, "press any key to begin," the screen disappears, and nothing more happens. You forget about it until the next day, when you discover that your bank account balance is $34,000 greater than it was yesterday. What a strange coincidence. You try to check the Fraudster program but find it is gone from your computer. When you attempt to download the program again in an attempt to find out what happened, you discover that it is no longer available from the Internet source. End of story, at least from the perpetrator's perspective.

Now consider the automated crime event from the victim's perspective. A small company in Hong Kong is one of the thousands of customers using a well-known commercial accounts-payable software package in their on-line computer. The head accountant comes into work one morning and discovers an out-of-balance debit suspense item of $34,000 in the double-entry bookkeeping system. He looks at the transaction log. Nothing there. He looks at the audit log. Nothing there either. He looks at the payments register. Nothing. He gets desperate and looks for debits in the receivables. Nothing. End of story. (I have purposely omitted one more step required by the program to short-circuit the bank reconciliation.) You can imagine what the Fraudster program did, based on the experience of these two people in different parts of the world, two people who do not know one another and never will. They were associated for only three milliseconds through a phantom computer program execution that, at one time, was called Fraudster.

wrapped boxes. One might be labeled *Accounts Payable Fraud;* another, *Payroll Checks Fraud;* and another, *Quickmail Espionage.* You could now, possibly legally, possess a crime. No law would be broken until you launch one of these programs from your computer, but who is to catch you?

Automated crimes would go far beyond being computer viruses. They will be extensions of the powerful new hacker tools that are proliferating. They could be perfect crimes unless we devise automated security to detect, mitigate, and recover from each possible packaged crime that we know about or anticipate. We must have an adequate information security foundation to anticipate such events. Preserving confidentiality, integrity, and availability would do little to stop automated crime. Possession of an automated crime and not its confidentiality is at issue.

BACK TO BASICS

To deal with future vulnerabilities and create an effective information security foundation, we must identify and understand the problems to be solved, beginning with the nature of information itself. Information differs significantly from tangible assets, which are probably the most common targets of crime. For example, information has no weight or volume (other than the media that contain it). We can create, copy, or destroy electronic information in a mouse click. And, because information often represents an amount of money, the size of a theft may depend merely on the placement of the decimal point, or the number of digits in the account balance. This leaves criminals with a new problem in their attacks on financial systems: how much money to take. They can steal credit if the amount of money actually present is not sufficient, leaving the victim to pay the creditor. When information represents money, its properties differentiate it from tangible assets as an object of crime.

Electronic communication allows information to be misused or abused from a distance, permitting perpetrators for the first time in history to be absent from the site of their crime. Willie Sutton, the great bank robber, when asked why he robbed banks, replied, "because that is where the money is." Now he would not have to go to the bank anymore. Willie could sit in his bedroom with a computer and dial into the distant bank's vault, which is now a computer, to scoop up and carry away the electronic money.

We place different values on the same information at different times and places, and depending on who possesses copies of it, but we need to protect it—at all times and in all forms—from all types of loss. There is little sense in protecting information stored in computers if the same information is left on diskettes or paper in unlocked offices. We must apply clean-desktop and locked-office requirements when these controls make good business sense. In addition, we need to institute good backup practices and data-entry controls to ensure the continued availability and usefulness of information.

Who Commits Cybercrimes?

We also need to understand the individuals who commit computer crimes. People and their roles in crime are exceedingly complex, and we need to remember that information security is an art in a war against criminals, not only a collection of controls to fix vulnerabilities. Security technologists and law enforcement people tell us that there are two kinds of computer criminals: the outside hackers who attack others' computers for pleasure, challenge, curiosity, educational experience, or to warn society of vulnerabilities; and the computer-technologist insiders who are presumably motivated by greed. Unfortunately, these stereotypes are much too simplistic in this age of worldwide computer networks, contract employees, and mergers and acquisitions that continually change the face of our business partners. The threats to our fragile information systems range from juvenile delinquents playing pranks to malicious hackers, white-collar criminals, career criminals, members of organized gangs, terrorists, and unethical businessmen and bureaucrats, with criminals often migrating from one role to another or playing multiple roles.

The one-profile-fits-all view of a hacker presents him as a juvenile, male, delinquent, computer genius who comes from a home with only one parent who ignores him and compensates by buying him a computer and a telephone service. The technologist stereotype includes the miscreant computer programmer or user who tries to steal money or information through computers using exotic techniques such as Trojan horse and logic bomb attacks (see Chapter 4). Unfortunately, successful computer criminals do not generally look or act like stereotypic criminals. The criminals that I've interviewed—often in their prison cells—are quite different from the stereotypes. The white-collar criminals tend to be situation-motivated. They see themselves as personal or business problem solvers, not greedy criminals. While their motives vary widely, they often began their criminal acts in an attempt to recover from errors, get even, beat competitors, eliminate debts, win sympathetic attention, get better jobs, or survive short-term business reversals. One experienced investigator in an insurance company told me that trusted employees who are undergoing divorce are among the people most likely to commit crimes.

Career criminals and terrorists represent another part of the criminal spectrum. Career criminals earn part or all of their income from crime and view computers as "tools of the trade," learning to use the technology to accomplish their goals—just as any dedicated professional does. Terrorists—those individuals and groups dedicated to extreme political, religious, or social agendas—have been relatively slow to operate in cyberspace. Of late, however, they have turned to cyberspace with its vulnerable, predictable, and ubiquitous computers. Some career criminals and terrorists are coercing computer technologists into committing computer crimes for them, because they lack the technical knowledge to do it themselves. This brings up an important point: Overall, the greatest potential threats to our information systems comes from those individuals or groups (i.e., conspiracies) that possess the *skills, knowledge, resources, authority,* and *motives* (SKRAM) to abuse and misuse information.

Except for malicious hackers, criminals often find that using computers in their misbehavior is not very desirable because they don't possess the necessary SKRAM. Computers are unforgiving for the bad guys as well as the good guys, and criminals have learned that one small error in using a computer can cause their crimes to fail. Many criminals are lazy and look for the easy way to accomplish their goals; they stick to what they know with the least danger. Even if criminals perceive cyberspace to be the ideal place for their crimes, if they don't have the SKRAM, they must acquire it in one way or another. So, in identifying the greatest source of threats, we need to focus on those with the SKRAM, rather than on insiders and outsiders, or criminal stereotypes.

Understanding the miscreants' motives can help information owners to avoid, deter, detect, and prevent crimes, and generally protect information assets. Opportunity to engage in crime is not a motive. If it were, we would have had to give up using our computers a long time ago; opportunity is always present for those with the SKRAM. In thoroughly analyzing the threats to our information systems, security specialists should examine the possible motives for misbehavior relative to each organization's business and culture—always considering the human factors along with the technical controls. Such understanding is especially useful in deriving avoidance and deterrence controls such as denying disgruntled workers use of sensitive information. In addition, understanding that misbehavior is often motivated by personal problems may encourage business management to provide confidential counseling services to help employees deal with personal crises—thus avoiding or removing the motivation for crime.

The Roles of Computers in Crime

Computers play four roles in crime: They serve as objects, subjects, tools, and symbols. All too often, however, the prevailing security foundation focuses only on computers' roles as tools or subjects of crime—omitting the additional roles of objects and symbols. We need to expand our views of cybercrime to include the potential threats inherent in all of these roles, and to consider all of the various combinations of criminals, computers, and roles in order to anticipate future threats and out-think the perpetrators.

Computers are the objects of crime when they are sabotaged or stolen. There are numerous cases of computers being shot, blown up, burned, drowned, fried, barbecued, roasted, toasted, boiled, steamed, irradiated, beaten with blunt instruments, kicked, crushed, and contaminated. The damage may be intentional, as in the case of an irate taxpayer who shot a computer four times through the window of the local tax office, or unintentional, as in the case of a couple who engaged in sexual intercourse while sitting on a computer keyboard. But regardless of the motive, physical computer sabotage destroys information, or at least makes it unavailable. In one such case in San Francisco, an electrical transformer in the basement of a building exploded, causing a poisonous liquid coolant to be released. The computers in the building continued to operate, but the fire department would not allow anybody to enter the building to tend to them, which rendered the information unavailable.

Larceny, like sabotage, makes computers and software the objects of crime. The theft of desktop, laptop, and palmtop computers has reached epidemic proportions. The value of the loss often far exceeds the cost of the stolen hardware because of the valuable information the computers contain. As we buy ever-smaller portable devices, and store increasing amounts of information in them, we need to employ the same types of protective measures as we do for our valuable jewelry.

Computers play the role of subjects when they are the environment in which technologists commit crimes. Computer virus attacks fall into this category. When automated crimes take place, computers will be the subjects of attacks. The third role of computers in crime is as tools—enabling criminals to produce false information or plan and control crimes. For example, criminals may use computers, graphics software, and color printers to forge documents. Criminals who create automated crime software and those who purchase and use the software will be using their computers as tools to commit crimes.

Computers are also used as symbols to deceive victims. In a $50 million securities-investment fraud case in Florida, a stockbroker deceived his victims by falsely claiming that he possessed a giant computer and secret software to engage in high-profit arbitrage. In reality, the man had only a desktop computer that he used to print false investment statements. He deceived new investors by paying false profits to early investors with money invested by the new ones. In other cases, several dating services have been convicted of fraudulent advertising, which included using pictures of computers that they falsely claimed they used to match people for social dating.

Keepers of the Gate

Many of the computer technologists who work in security are not equipped to solve the problems that I have identified in this chapter. They rely on their predictable computers and seem to believe that people are predictable as well. Lacking any significant contact with computer criminals, these technologists view them as people much like themselves, who think as they do and play the game by the established rules. This does not work. In addition to the technologists who can design and implement the technical aspects of computer security, information security requires the broad expertise of business, audit, and industrial security experts who can deal with the human factors and business issues. Information security experts must be knowledgeable in a range of subjects and capable of matching wits with the computer criminals.

Today, information security is starting to be recognized as a legitimate art with strategic value to business and government organizations, but this has not always been the case. Some information security specialists, especially the early practitioners, were poorly prepared to address the complexities and subtleties of information security. Many started as password administrators or surplus programmers and had little, if any, security education or experience dealing with misbehavior.

Although information security has not yet attained professional status and remains a folk art, it is attracting some of the brightest people in information technology, and is moving toward a certification procedure for practitioners. In particular, the International Information Systems Security Certification Consortium is struggling to make it a profession by holding examinations, and the Generally Accepted Systems Security Principles (GASSP) task group is developing a common body of knowledge for defining due diligence in the art. In addition, a number of universities, including George Washington University, Georgetown University, George Mason University, Purdue, and University of California–Davis, now offer courses in information security.

Information security specialists are in extremely high positions of trust, whether as employees, consultants, or contractors. They have the keys to the kingdom—knowing about and controlling the safeguards of the information assets in their organizations. Unfortunately, not all security specialists are worthy of such trust; authorities have already convicted and incarcerated at least three specialists for crimes associated with their security work.

One information security specialist stole $10.2 million in a funds-transfer fraud from a bank where he had been a security consultant. He claimed (and there is some evidence to support him) that he intended to demonstrate to the bank that they needed his further consulting services. When the FBI caught him, he claimed that he was in the process of returning the money. At best, he used very poor judgment.

Another information security specialist, who was in a dispute with management, engaged in a sophisticated Trojan-horse attack. He hid secret instructions in his employers' software that damaged sales commission files and changed the programs' names each time they were executed to hide the evidence.

Several information security consultants are currently engaged in "tiger-team" services in which they test the security alertness of their clients' organizations by performing real, covert attacks. Testing systems by attacking them with the informed consent of employees is effective and acceptable. Testing and deceiving employees without their knowledge, however, is dangerous and may harm them while not proving anything that we don't already know, which raises questions about the ethics of the consultants and the prudence of the organizations' management.

FORTIFYING INSTALLED CONTROLS

Authorized individuals who engage in unauthorized activities inside of an organization's perimeter represent a major threat to information security. Such individuals are undaunted by perimeter security because they operate inside of the protected boundaries. We need to control information location and use—whether in a computer, a person's mind, or a filing cabinet—to protect ourselves from internal, as well as external, threats. Limiting the use of information in computers and networks within organizations thwarts many potential threats and is relatively easy to accomplish from a technical standpoint through the judicious use of passwords and/or security smart cards. On the nontechnical side, we can urge people to be cautious about what they say or write and to consistently use locks and keys. However, installing controls willy-nilly is not effective against intelligent criminals, especially those who are operating within the organization.

We need integrated control systems designed by experts—a comprehensive security architecture with well-documented standards and practices.

Information classification, the process of assigning different levels of sensitivity to information, is a common security control that is often misused or ignored. Classification is intended to match the amount of security to the various levels to avoid insufficient or excessive constraints on information use. This is part of an effective control used in military organizations. Unfortunately, non-military organizations often leave out the most important part: assigning clearance (e.g., confidential, secret, or top secret) to the people who use the information to designate who has entry at each level. Classifying and assigning employee clearance are difficult tasks that require significant assistance from the owners of the information—many of whom lack sufficient motivation—and from business managers. All too often, organizations end up adopting a three- or four-level classification scheme with vague definitions of information sensitivity, then fail to apply it consistently or update it as the information sensitivity changes.

However, simplified and flexible information classification can be quite effective when the information owners determine the kind of usage to allow for each authorized user and for each copy of information in each location. Owners may allow some custodians of their information, such as couriers, to possess it but not to know its content. They may allow others, such as auditors, to examine and know, but not to modify the information in their computers. They may also allow some people, such as data entry clerks, to append more data to their information, but not to modify or use it.

Mobile computers and wireless communications have created new vulnerabilities for our information. In the past, electrical cords and cables tethered our computers to one location, but laptop and notebook computers present new locations and opportunities for criminals to steal hardware and/or information. Eavesdroppers may be able to "shoulder surf" (observe over computer users' shoulders) to view confidential information. We must now authenticate the locations as well as the identity of computer users to achieve effective security in some situations.

Because we design computers to be totally predictable, they are often ideal environments for crime. According to perpetrators, it is difficult, if not impossible, to successfully commit crimes in unpredictable environments. We can achieve unpredictability in many ways, but one simple method is to make controls variable so that no one knows the current limits. In the $20 million embezzlement case, for example, the bank could probably have prevented the crime in the way it was perpetrated by varying the limits for sizes of transactions and times allowed before completion of transactions. The perpetrator might have known that the controls were present, but would have no way of knowing the current values.

Although vendors incorporate many technical controls (e.g., virus scanners) in computer products, their efforts are mixed blessings. The complexity of information systems and the range of potential crimes require that we either obtain numerous packaged control products from one or more vendors, or rely on vendors to integrate the controls in their computer and communications products. Integrating the controls can have a negative effect on the product's functionality, inhibit its ease of use, and/or increase its price. On the positive side, the vendor security products tend to be of higher quality and subject to more testing than "home grown" controls. But, two dangers are lurking here: the limited assurance of vendor trustworthiness, and the minimal longevity of some small vendor companies that produce controls. A major corporation's information security may rest—inappropriately—with two guys in a garage who offer a great control product.

Vendors pose another problem when they deliver their products with the controls deactivated because some customers don't want the controls. When a system manager installs a new computer, she may want to attract users and impress management with its user-friendly operation and unconstrained service. When security breaches occur, she may realize that the full complement of controls is necessary, but is likely to face resistance from users who have become accustomed to the service as it is.

Administering the Security Program

Security management experts advise organizations to begin their information security programs with written policies and standards. Organizations should establish requirements for mandatory control objectives supported by guidelines that identify specific mandatory controls to meet the objectives and additional, discretionary controls and implementation policies. Policies, standards, and guidelines are characterized by the use of the words "must," "should," and "could," respectively. For example, a policy may state that you *must* establish classification of information. A standards control objective may describe the levels of classification and the control objectives for each level that *should* be used. A guideline may include examples of classifications that *could* be used for various kinds of information.

While such policies are certainly good practice, the organization is still in danger if the information owners and users fail to comply with the

> ## Controls Are Ineffective Without User Cooperation
>
> At one time I managed a group of COBOL computer language programmers who insisted on using shortcut programming techniques that reduced the self-documenting benefits of COBOL. I sent them warning memos about the dangerous practice, which they duly ignored. Then I instituted a control in the COBOL compiler that prevented programs from being compiled if the unwanted shortcuts were present. The programmers reacted in a typical way by fixing the compiler, so that it gave the false impression that the constraint was working. Defeated, I finally held a meeting with the programmers to explain the many benefits to them of my way of thinking, and I promised rewards for the fruits of their cooperation. After much debate and controversy, I got compliance, except for the few usual holdouts. I told the resisters individually that I would fire them if they did not go along with the others. They finally agreed to cooperate. Then I put the control back into the compiler, fully instrumented, with the help of the programmers, and I periodically tested it. The problem was finally solved. The lesson for us here is: Never install a control that is not supported by those constrained by the control; otherwise, they will beat you every time. We must be able to demonstrate the rewards and benefits of supporting security as well.

policies and standards or implement them in only cosmetic fashion. The most dangerous situation for an organization is when management is deceived into thinking that security controls are in place simply because they are specified in the standards. This leads to a false sense of security that can be worse than having no controls specified.

Organizations also need a process to accommodate not using a standard, or for taking an alternative action to comply with policy if implementation does not make prudent business sense. We should view security standards as baseline practices rather than as absolute requirements, but we need to document the deviations to know the reasons and the true state of compliance.

Standards and guidelines, however, are only part of a successful security administration program. Organizations also need to provide principles for applying the standards to ensure effective implementation. For example, one important principle is to never install a control that cannot be effectively instrumented. This means that it must be possible to tell whether a control is functioning correctly. The principle is especially important for controls that are buried inside systems and precluded from direct observation such as transaction-value-limit and incomplete-transaction-time-limit controls. Similarly, we must be able to determine—in a timely manner—when a control has been violated, triggered, or incapacitated and must be able to safely disable controls for replacement or service. At the same time, we must not allow the criminals to easily disable or bypass the controls.

A motivation and awareness program is also an important part of good information security administration. It should include training, appropriate rewards and penalties for exemplary and negligent security performance, and follow-up reviews to determine compliance with policies and standards. Although organizations sometimes impose penalties for poor security, few—if any—offer rewards for exemplary security. With the possible exception of the military, most organizations fail to sufficiently motivate and train their employees to achieve effective security. Human resources departments are usually not very helpful in security motivation either, claiming that it complicates the annual job appraisal process and is too subjective to measure. Other subjective performance factors, such as ethics and interpersonal skills, are included in appraisals, however, and we should similarly accommodate security compliance, including it as a specific performance requirement in job descriptions and annual performance appraisals. Employees and managers throughout the organization must view security as an integral part of their responsibilities, not a burden that interferes with their productivity or job advancement.

I call security motivation through job performance evaluation "the mother of all security controls." Without appropriate rewards and penalties, security can never be more than a cosmetic artifice. But the constraints of security should not interfere with the rest of our job functions either. To be practical within the mission of the organization, we must ask how little security is acceptable to avoid negligence, not how much constraint we can tolerate.

How Do We Fix Information Security?

Information security is mostly an inarticulate, incomplete, incorrect folk art disguised as an engineering and business discipline. We can rid ourselves of the inarticulateness by correcting our use of the English language in defining confidentiality (limiting knowledge to one or a few people) and integrity (being whole and in sound condition), and by explaining ourselves more clearly. We can extend the CIA foundation to include all elements of security (availability and utility, integrity and authenticity, and confidentiality and possession) and all types of losses, soliciting input from business managers and human factor experts as well as computer technologists. And, we can adopt the well-known, generally accepted controls that are used under similar conditions by other organizations to safeguard their information resources to meet standards of due care and best practice objectives.

The label of art, however, is unlikely to change with regard to information security, since we cannot generally prove the effectiveness of our security measures under real circumstances because of the infrequency of measurable attacks. We must rely on common best practices of due care and prudence as our measure of adequacy. Bob Courtney (the first information security manager at IBM, and one of the originators of the art) advises us to "never spend more for security than you expect to lose without it." This is good advice under ideal circumstances, but since we don't know how much we can lose without security, we must at least avoid negligence by making sure, within prudent business practice, that we have as much security as other well-run organizations under similar circumstances.

Testing information security is not the same as testing information systems performance. Engineers can effectively test computer and communications systems performance because the systems are predictable. Systems that are operating correctly produce exactly the same results when given the same input, and engineers can define and prove success and failure. Security however, deals with constraining and controlling people as well as systems, and we can't effectively predict behavior—especially misbehavior. People are unpredictable in the sense that they never do exactly the same thing with the same input. We cannot, therefore, successfully test the security of information when we're trying to provide protection from unknown, largely unpredictable human actions.

Since we cannot expect to effectively test security against all possible—or even all likely—real threats, we must choose and prioritize security safeguards directed by:

- common sense and organization objectives
- good advice from experienced experts
- the availability of security controls at reasonable cost from trusted vendors
- the practices of other organizations under similar circumstances
- what we know about loss experience

In addition, we should select safeguards from the entire array of avoidance and deterrence, prevention and detection, reward and penalty, loss transference (insurance), and recovery and correction controls. We can improve controls in many cases by making them work transparently with less human intervention, and making them unpredictable, yet acceptable to the people constrained by them. If we are to be successful against computer criminals in the future, we must develop automated security. This will result in a true state of information warfare against criminals, which will be fought in and among information systems removed from human view and awareness. The electronic battles will be completed before we know that they have started, and we will know who won the next morning. The legitimate owners of information, not the criminals, will more likely be the winners if we effectively apply well-motivated, due-care information security.

2

What Are We Protecting?

Good security is based on the premise that we understand the nature of information and its abuse and misuse. For example, we need to understand the differences between a computer program in the language in which a programmer wrote it, and the language in which it is sold and in which a computer executes it. We need to know whether to protect the program as a trade secret—by applying confidentiality controls, or as a commodity—by applying possession controls. In the broadest sense of security, authenticity and integrity controls protect the meaning of information, while availability and utility controls protect the use of information, and confidentiality and possession controls protect the exclusiveness and medium of the information.

Everybody understands information to some extent because we all create and use it, but few people consider it beyond that basic level, and even fewer consider its various characteristics or the ways in which we need to safeguard it. By definition, information is a representation of symbols, facts, concepts, or instructions that is suitable for communication, interpretation, or processing by people or automated systems. It is fluid in

How Data and Information Differ

Although data and information are synonymous according to most dictionaries, some people like to think of data as "raw" information or as collections of symbols that are not structured and labelled for people to use. Data security is usually synonymous with information security. Some organizations, however, use *data security* to mean the administration of computer security, such as password assignment to users, and *information security* to mean the management of information security, such as establishing security policies and control standards.

that we can change, divide, combine, and/or relocate it in many and various ways—all of which require changes in the ways in which we protect it.

When we combine items of information with different meanings and different needs for security, we create a totally new piece of information with a different need for security. For example, a bank account number requires little protection when it is the sole piece of information available. When we combine it with additional pieces, however, like the name of the bank, the account holder's name, and/or the amount of money in the account, we substantially increase the need for protection. (This is why banks may send a stream of account numbers via one communication route and account balances via another route, matching the various pieces up in the processing center to protect the confidentiality of the information.) Each piece of information is of little value without the others, but taken together, in the right order, the pieces form a valuable masterpiece— which is why we refer to this as the mosaic theory of information.

Information security is not about improving or reducing the quality of information. It is about preserving an existing level of quality such as timeliness, or protecting the act of changing the quality of the information such as updating it. Quality is a measure of how good the information is in any of its characteristics, including its security. The following paragraphs describe the characteristics of information that are relevant to information security.

PRIMARY CHARACTERISTICS OF INFORMATION

Information is a complex, somewhat vague concept. Information can be verbal or written, graphic or coded. It may reside in books, on computer disks, or in someone else's mind, and can be acquired in literally thousands of different ways. So, how do we define, let alone manage, this complex concept? All information has four primary characteristics that we use to comprehend it:

Kind.   Information may be knowledge, descriptive, instructive, expository, factual, fictional, monetary, artistic, accounting, or any of hundreds of other types.

Representation.   Information may be presented as graphics, coded symbols (alphabetic or numeric, ASCII code), or sounds.

Form.   Information has some type of structure, such as a format, grammar, coding, tables, or syntax.

Medium.   Information is represented, or materialized, in some physical way that we can sense, such as ink on paper, energized phosphor on a screen, holes in paper or plastic, or states of switches.

These characteristics—kind, representation, form, and medium or materialization—largely define the types of security controls that we choose to safeguard the information. For example, we must materialize information in a tangible form to know that it exists and to protect it appropriately. We reference information by pointing to it or saying its name. We know that a text file exists because we can see its name in the computer's file directory, and we can open the file to display its contents on the computer screen. But, because copies of the same information can be of different types, we may need to apply different security safeguards to the various copies.

Changing the type within one characteristic does not, however, necessarily make the new version of information a copy of the original. A new version with a different printing may indeed be a copy, but changing the kind of information from instructional to poetic verse may make it a different piece of information rather than a copy. These differences are often the basis for copyright disputes. Each new set of information derived from old information, and at a different time, may require totally different security. This is one reason why the process of classifying business information based on its sensitivity to loss and need for security is such a complex task.

We can destroy information only by destroying its kinds, representations, forms, or media. This has important security implications, because preserving information requires safeguarding it, along with any copies, in all of its characteristics. The security of each set of information involves a set of safeguards and processes, such as locks, or backup copies in a specific medium. Thus, an understanding of each of the four main characteristics provides insights into potential threats and losses, and guides us in devising safeguards.

Additional Characteristics Important to Security

In addition to its primary characteristics, all information has a number of other characteristics that help us to determine the need for security and to choose appropriate safeguards.

Availability. Is the information readily accessible or in hand for use?

Utility. Is the information useful?

Integrity. Is the information complete, sound, and unimpaired?

Authenticity. Is the information genuine and accurate? Does it conform to reality and have validity?

Confidentiality. Is there a need to keep the information secret? To, for example, keep it from being known by the general public or to restrict its observation to only a few, chosen individuals.

Possession. Do we have the information in hand? If not, who does own it or control it?

Quantity. How much information are we concerned with? What is the number of its parts, or constituents such as pixels, characters, words, fields, records, files, or pages?

Location. Where does the information reside?

Timeliness. Is the value or applicability of the information linked to a timetable? Does its value or applicability change over time?

Subject. What is the topic or title of the information? What is represented or described?

Effect. What is the consequence or influence of knowing, possessing, or using the information?

Meaning. What is the intention, purpose, or significance of the information?

Security and legal protection. What safeguards are in place to protect the information?

The first six of these characteristics of information are what information security attempts to preserve; they are extensions and corrections of the CIA foundation. The next two characteristics—quantity and location—are associated with the medium of information and, along with the remaining five characteristics—timeliness, subject, effect, meaning, and security—are also important for choosing appropriate safeguards. I haven't included *quality* in the list because quality applies to all of the characteristics (e.g., degree of integrity or weight of paper).

It is important to note that the value of information may be totally independent of its quantity or quality. A two- or three-letter word, such as *yes* or *no,* in the right context and at the right time, such as the acceptance or rejection of a billion-dollar contract, can be far more valuable than the millions of words in the contract itself. Similarly, the value of some information depends on its timeliness. For example, much of the information in yesterday's newspaper is obsolete and, therefore, of little value today.

We need to protect the processes associated with each set of information when we convert the information from one type to another within each characteristic. For example, an owner can use an encryption algorithm and secret key in a computer to change the form of his information from plaintext to cyphertext to protect it in vulnerable environments, then change it back to plaintext for use. While the information is in cyphertext, however, he must protect the confidentiality of encryption and decryption keys and cryptographic processor as well as the cyphertext itself, not necessarily for confidentiality, but for possession of it.

Now that I've introduced the characteristics of information, I'll describe each of the primary characteristics in more detail and explain how they relate to the choice of security measures to protect the information.

KINDS OF INFORMATION

Kinds of information fall into such categories as knowledge, instructional, business, monetary, literary, and artistic. Writers and artists, for example, usually keep their literary and artistic information private during its creation. They share it only with their agents, editors, or publishers until it is finished. The potential threats, sources of threats, and types of losses may differ at each stage of information development and use, and we need to apply appropriate security measures for all of the various situations. Trade secret, trademark, and copyright laws, for example, provide legal protection for different kinds of information. In addition, we apply safeguards such as locks and keys, observation and disclosure constraints, and copy and modification controls. The safeguards employed depend, in part, on the type of legal protection that is applied. For example, for information to be a trade secret, we must protect it according to legal precedence of due care set by the security controls that are absent from, or applied to, other trade secrets that litigants have challenged in court cases.

We can convert information from one kind to another using a process that is described in a separate set of instructional information, often consisting of software or a printed manual. For example, a business can convert monetary transaction information into accounting information, or a teacher can convert artistic information into instructional information by adding, rewriting, or replacing words.

The following sections examine each of the primary kinds of information of most interest to businesses.

Knowledge and Noledge

Knowledge is a kind of information that we gain by study or experience. Knowledge is an important kind of information because it is the subject or object of both acceptable and malicious action that is of concern from a security viewpoint. Businesses, for example, recognize the importance of knowledge as a critical factor in their competitive position. Business managers must have knowledge about their own and their competitors' products, services, and capabilities.

Knowledge management, a relatively new concept derived since the application of total quality management and reengineering theories, requires that we rethink some aspects of information security. As defined by Alan Kantrow, chief knowledge officer at the Monitor Company (www.monitor.com), a consulting firm, this theory consists of capturing knowledge gained by individuals and spreading it to others in the organization. Douglas Cale, National Director, Computer Assurance Services Practice at Deloitte & Touche (www.dttus.com), says, "The first characteristic of sound knowledge management is collaboration as opposed to organizational hierarchies. A second is openness as opposed to separation of functions. A third is continuous and accelerated learning as opposed to training. Traditional structures such as entry controls, data security, and information classification are barriers to creating knowledge and managing it well." Cale goes on to stress the need to keep the confidentiality and availability aspects of security simple.

One major corporation has already simplified their confidentiality classification scheme from five levels to two. This is consistent with the discretionary need-to-withhold principle that gives everyone in an organization all information except for a small amount that must be withheld. It is the antithesis of the mandatory need-to-know principle that withholds all information from everyone except for the small amount that each individual needs to do his or her specific job. While the need-to-know principle is necessary in the military where the objective is security at any cost, it tends to stifle business where the objective is profit, productivity, and growth at lowest cost.

We must also acknowledge information that is not knowledge. This is information that we do not know or that we may never know by study or experience. I use a new word, *noledge*, only for convenience here to mean the kind of information that is not knowledge. Examples include intermediate results of calculations, object computer programs (in computer code form), encrypted information, trigonometric and logarithm tables, mathematical and physical constants such as pi and Planck's constant, and any other information used and stored in computers and communication circuits (even for a short time) that people do not read or know. When you need to use noledge, computers either find it or calculate it and use it for you. For example, as students, we needed to learn the value of pi, and how to calculate it. After that ordeal is finished, however, we use computers to calculate or store it and use it.

In the future, as computers become even more prevalent, more information will become noledge. Memorizing telephone numbers, e-mail addresses, and Internet URLs, for example, is already becoming unnecessary. We store frequently used telephone numbers and URLs in bookmark lists in our Internet Web search engines. Examples of future conversions to noledge include accounting ledgers, our locations and addresses, our likes and dislikes, automated process control information such as machine tool instructions, states of car engines and transmissions, and anything else that will become self-adjusting and self-correcting. Computers will use much of this noledge to derive useful knowledge when we need it.

Although the differences between knowledge and noledge have significant implications for security, few experts have yet acknowledged these differences. The international nuclear physics research facility in Switzerland provides a notable example. Several summers ago, a hacker intruded upon the main computer and, as a prank, changed one digit in the value of pi. That small change, not known by the researchers, resulted in millions of dollars lost from incorrect research results because the computer used the wrong circumferences and diameters of circles in calculations.

Noledge is highly vulnerable to change when it is not explicitly controlled. Keeping knowledge secure requires controls on people, systems, and networks. Keeping noledge secure requires controls only on systems and networks. Security can be accomplished with relative ease by having computers check noledge automatically for integrity and authenticity. In addition, because noledge is stored and used in computer systems, we can lock it away from people, providing it to specific automated processes only when necessary. One way to do this is to encrypt it (not for confidentiality, but for integrity and authenticity) and then decrypt it only in the location it is needed for a very limited amount of time.

Instructional Information in Cyberspace

Instructional information has taken on new importance because of its use in computers. Information in the form of computer programs (software) instructs machines. Rolls of perforated paper that ran through player pianos and punch cards that controlled Jacquard looms were the simple beginnings of today's computer programs and the multi-billion-dollar commercial software market. Because computer programs process much of the financial information in our society, they are the sources, tools, and inspiration for untold amounts of crime. Thus, we need to focus much of our security effort on instructional information, most notably on software.

Source programs, and the object programs that are compiled from them, are the subjects, objects, tools, and sometimes-deceptive symbols of crime. An embezzler can modify either a source program or the associated object program to engage in fraud. If she modified the source code, however, she would have to take the additional step of compiling the source program into an object program for a theft within a computer to take place. Investigators of the suspected fraud could easily identify modification of the source code, but detecting a modification of the object code would require a painstaking comparison with a trusted copy of the object program.

Business Information

We need to protect several kinds of information that have strategic value in business:

MARKET-SENSITIVE PROPRIETARY INFORMATION

Securities traders, journalists, and business competitors pose the major threat to this type of information. They are particularly interested in the business volume and customer list. Security in this context focuses on confidentiality, including protection from unauthorized disclosures by employees and eavesdropping by others. Even businesses with much to lose in the event of espionage or theft are sometimes guilty of imprudent disclosure. In one large computer manufacturing company, for example, the systems engineers complained that "it is a strange ship that leaks from the top," when their top executives bragged prematurely about their new product plans.

FINANCIAL INFORMATION

The loss of the integrity and authenticity of financial information is usually more serious than the loss of confidentiality. Because this type of

Source and Object Computer Programs

A source computer program consists of thousands or hundreds of thousands of highly interrelated instructions and data (also called source code) that are written by programmers. The source-code instruction that a programmer writes, $X = A + B$, for example, indicates that he wants the numbers stored in computer memory locations with addresses A and B to be added and the sum placed in the computer memory location with the address X. For a computer to execute a program, it must first use a compiler program to translate the source program into its own language, called an object program, which consists of millions of coded simple computer instructions combined with data. Object code is in a machine language that consists of many detailed instructions—like one that sends the contents of memory at address A to the computer's accumulator as the first instruction in the source-code instruction $X = A + B$.

We treat source programs as human-readable knowledge and object programs as computer-readable data that are not meant to be knowledge. A person can, with great difficulty, study an object program, thereby making it knowledge. The task is, however, seldom necessary or worth the trouble.

Average people are unlikely to need to understand the concepts of source programs and object programs, but sometimes crime thrusts the details of computer technology onto the public consciousness. For example, in a California case involving the theft of a trade-secret source program, defense lawyers tried to convince a jury that the defendant could have independently programmed an identical version of the allegedly stolen source computer program found in his office. All he would have needed to know was what function the program was to perform in a computer for it to compile into the same object program. The jurors found against the defendant—they did not believe that he could have independently created the identical source computer program, because it would not have the same dirty words embedded in the descriptive comments.

information is usually widely known, its validity is crucial. Government requires most businesses to report financial information to the public, as well as to a variety of governmental agencies—making secrecy nearly impossible. Prudent businesspeople need to ensure that widely dissemi-

because it can be misused in a variety of ways. Too many security specialists are divulging details about their organizations' security practices and/or their losses; this represents a gross violation of security.

Money in Cyberspace

Some information has distinct monetary value. This is a unique kind of information that requires great security. Indeed, the threats to monetary information encompass the full spectrum of crime: Fraud, larceny, extortion, sabotage, forgery, and espionage focus on it. On the Internet, for example, we encounter real, negotiable money in bank account balances or as *e-cash* or *cybercash* (i.e., credit recorded by a third party that can be traded through the Internet for goods and services). Each amount of money consists of (optionally) the name of a country and its currency symbol, numeric characters, and a decimal point (a comma is used in some parts of the world). An ordered set of these symbols and characters represents an amount of monetary credit in an account. You may, for example, own US$432.28 or UK£267.33, either of which you can exchange for goods or services, or use to reduce a debt. When you spend some of this money electronically, the balance in the computer account or smart card is debited by the appropriate amount, and the balance in the merchant's account in another computer is credited with that amount. Your bank and the merchant's bank then log and reconcile the transaction in their computers.

In "The Emperor's Old Armor," published in the *1997 ACM New Paradigm Workshop* (Lake Arrowhead, CA, © 1997 ACM, reprinted by permission), Dr. Bob Blakley proposes a fanciful means of protecting information that represents money:

> A back-of-the-envelope calculation suggests that $1 billion US, in $100 bills, occupies perhaps 15 cubic yards. At current prices (as this is written), $1 billion US, in gold weighs about 80 tons. $1 Billion US, in electronic cash, on the other hand, is 32 bits plus some application-dependent headers. This is madness—surely a prescription for fraud on a breathtaking scale. . . .
>
> The size and weight of cash is inconvenient. It was *designed* to be inconvenient—precisely so that there would be inherent limits to the scale on which fraud, smuggling, and theft are feasible. Our value-bearing instruments are built with these secrets of intrinsic limitations. A check's amount field is small—in part to limit the amount which can conveniently be represented in it. This is one of the reasons business checks are often printed on

A Flawed System for Protecting the Transfer of Funds

In the 1980s, British banks proposed a new security measure for electronic funds transfers. The measure, called the Standard Test Key (STK), treated monetary values only as series of three-digit groups—which resulted in major problems. The banks planned to use the technique to check the authenticity and integrity of messages that authorized the transfer of money from one bank to another. In these messages, the sending bank would replace each unit of information, such as the name of a bank, the date, and the amount of money to be transferred, with a code number obtained from a codebook. The bank's computer would sum these numbers to yield a number—called the Test Key—that it placed at the end of the message. Any error in transmission or change in the message after it left the sending bank would produce a different Test Key, which would warn the receiving bank not to act until the discrepancy was resolved.

Designed to reduce the number of codes that the banks had to keep track of, the STK system used standardized (and easily obtainable) tables of four-digit code numbers for the words that were transmitted. Since monetary amounts usually exceeded four digits, they needed to be broken up into three-digit groups. For example, if Bank A had an account at Bank B and instructed Bank B to transfer sums totaling $191,975 from that account to three other accounts in Bank B, the total would have been coded by checking the STK tables for the code for 191 (5580) and 975 (5359). Adding the two code numbers would produce a sum of 10,939, which, with other code numbers, would yield the STK.

Unfortunately, the same STK would result from a transfer of $975,191, an amount created by transposing the first and last three digits. An enterprising criminal could tap into the transmission line and send an additional message to transfer the surplus $783,216—the difference between $975,191 and $191,975—to an account that the thief had set up under a fictitious name at Bank B. The STK code would be unchanged, and the bank would remain unsuspecting until it reconciled its account with the sending bank—but presumably long after the thief had emptied and closed her account. The thief would not need to know what amounts were being transferred. With the transmissions between the banks routed through her computer, she could simply program it to calculate whatever additional amounts would result in the same code

(continued)

numbers as those in the genuine messages. Of course, if a thief went to the trouble of tapping a bank communications line and spliced in her own computer, she could engage in any number of additional interesting thefts.

Fortunately, the banks dropped the STK idea before it was adopted when a London security consultant revealed this vulnerability in *Time* magazine. Today we have encrypted message authentication codes (MAC), which are used throughout the world to perform the same function as the STK. This makes the job of the thief with her spliced computer considerably more difficult, but not necessarily impossible; if the job can be done, some criminal will eventually do it.

bigger stock than personal checks—businesses legitimately engage in bigger transactions. The temptation to make electronic cash better (than physical cash) by removing the inconvenient relationship between value and size is natural—and it should be resisted. . . .

If we wanted to make electronic cash secure, a good start would be to give it *physicality* by making its size more proportional to its value. A sensible approach to electronic representation of cash amounts might be to take the dollar value and square it to arrive at the desired number of representation bits. Note that by making value inherent in the representation of electronic cash, we can make all implementations more secure, without imposing an assurance burden on implementation code—if your machine doesn't have 1 billion terabits of storage, you can't steal a billion dollars, no matter how flaky the owner's e-cash implementation is.

Owners may require different degrees of security for monetary information, depending on differences in its values, representations, and media. For example, the monetary information in trading records on the stock exchange or in investment ledgers may have different values if packaged in different media because of who could or would see it and when they might see it. Thus, we need to consider the information's value to various individuals to identify where and how to apply security. Consider the vulnerabilities of graphic text (e.g., a faxed funds transfer message) compared to the same information in coded text (e.g., in an e-mail message), or the vulnerabilities of an accounting ledger in a bulky hard-cover journal as opposed to a compact disk. The choices of security controls may depend on these differences as well as on the means of converting from one representation or medium to another.

REPRESENTATIONS OF INFORMATION

Representations of information include graphic images, coded symbols (digital text), and digital sound or speech, as well as other representations, such as analog, that we won't cover in this discussion. Multimedia information systems facilitate representations of the same information in pictures or symbols. For example, a newsletter may contain both pictures (as patterns of pixels) and text (a series of coded symbols). We can scan, write, speak, or type words into a computer using a process in the computer to translate from one representation to another.

Different representations of the same information expose it to different threats, which may require different safeguards. (Safeguards are usually specified relative to the media that each representation requires.) From a security standpoint, modifying one bit or character in graphical data does not necessarily destroy the information content—even though it may slightly degrade its quality of authenticity. Modifying a single bit in a digital text file, however, is likely to change or destroy the meaning of the information represented. This can have significant security implications for both the integrity and the authenticity of the information.

One vexing computer virus, for example, affects the representation of information in dramatic ways. It causes characters in lines of text on a display screen to visually tumble down to the bottom of the screen, one at a time with increasing speed, until they all land there in a heap. The screen still displays the data, but the data have lost their integrity and are useless as knowledge until we can restore them (hopefully) from a backup copy in the original order and positions. The virus also modifies the data file containing the information in the computer memory into a scrambled collection of characters. The information is still there, but we can not use it without reversing the modification process. The information has lost integrity, authenticity, and utility but retains its availability and possession—for what little good that might do without the reversing process.

Security requires that we protect information in each representation in which the owner or user needs it, as well as protect the computer programs that may be necessary to do the required conversions from one representation to another. We must also protect the means of representation, such as display screens, and limit who may observe them.

FORMS OF INFORMATION

Forms of information include style, font, language, syntax, encoding (encryption with a secret key), format, size, and spacing. There are several security considerations related to forms; changing the form of information can alter the meaning of the information. We may, for example, lose information if an act of sabotage converts it from one form into another, useless one. This was the case when a disgruntled employee encrypted all copies of a personnel file and destroyed the key. In fact, encrypted information involves some unique security considerations: We may need to protect weakly encrypted information from being taken, whereas strongly encrypted information may require no acquisition controls at all.

Preventing the manipulation of forms of information may involve distinguishing parts of the information for acquisition and specifying the privileges that individuals, groups, or computer programs (sometimes called processes) have to view or change it. Although we typically assign acquisition privileges on a file basis, there is sometimes a need to differentiate individual records or fields for acquisition. For example, personnel systems usually assign each employee's record to a master personnel file containing all employee records. In some cases, management gives human resources clerks the privilege to view or change certain employees' records within a file, or to modify certain fields within the records (e.g., fields containing addresses, or health, job performance, or compensation information). Large companies commonly achieve additional security by separating executives' personnel files from those of other employees, often storing and processing them in an entirely separate computer.

Maintaining the integrity and authenticity of forms of information can be critical to security. Programmers who work with fixed-length fields can cause serious vulnerabilities if they fail to test for the lengths of data being entered into the fields. This failure can allow excessive lengths of data strings to run over into other fields, opening the possibility for unauthorized activities. For example, a hacker may enter a double-length fictitious password (such as *q;/2hkq;/2hk*) that replaces the master copy of a valid password with the first half of the fictitious password (*q;/2hk*) in an adjacent field that is used for comparison with the second half (*q;/2hk*) of the entered one. The hacker attack success is assured if the programmer has failed to include a field-length test to stop the overflow into the next field. Programmers are also guilty of lax security if they do not prevent numeric data from entering alphabetic fields and vice versa.

Organization of Information in Cyberspace

Traditionally, information has been organized into libraries, books, chapters, documents, sections, paragraphs, sentences, phrases, words, and characters. Information is organized in similar units in computers. Word processing application software organizes it into folders of documents. Computer operating systems organize it into files of records, each record containing fields of bytes, each made up of bits. We use groups (bytes) of eight bits at a time in codes, such as the American Standard Code for Information Exchange (ASCII), to represent the punctuation symbols, alphabetic and special characters, and decimal digits.

Bits and pixels are fundamental units of information. A pixel is rendered as a dab of phosphor on a monochrome video screen or as three dabs of different colored phosphors grouped together on a color screen. A computer user may turn on or off each pixel to change the graphic being displayed. A bit is a symbol in the binary number system, which uses only two symbols (0 or 1) to count. The binary numbers 00, 01, 10, 11, 100 . . . are the counterparts of the numbers 0, 1, 2, 3, 4 . . . in the decimal system. Computers render a binary digit, or *bit* for short, in many simple ways. Electrically, a bit may be a pulse or lack of a pulse of energy; one of two possible states of an electronic, acoustic, or optical switch; or the north-south orientation of a magnetized region of a ferrite coating on a plastic surface (magnetic disk). Mechanically, it may be the position of a switch, a hole or no hole in paper (punch card or paper tape), or a pitting or lack of pitting of a plastic surface (CD).

The Millennium Problem

As we approach the year 2000, we face another multifaceted security problem regarding forms of information. At present, the date fields representing years have a capacity of only two digits in most computer programs. In 2000, computers will interpret going from 99 (1999) to 00 (2000) as going from 1999 to 1900. However, the problem will not begin on the first of January, 2000; it will begin when the first computer applications start using dates in 2000. This will occur in such applications as spreadsheets and loan amortization, planning and budget systems, and is likely to begin at any time. The U.S. government's fiscal year 2000 starts on September 1, 1999.

The security issue, which few experts have recognized, is that organizations—in their haste to convert existing software to the new format—may hire untested and even untrustworthy contractors to do the job for them. The opportunities for crime are likely to be widespread, especially if programmers eliminate important security controls to simplify the conversion.

At the same time, however, the millennium conversion efforts may uncover some crimes that otherwise would go unnoticed. Victims sometimes discover ongoing crimes when they revamp their software, systems, and/or procedures because many crimes require unchanging, predictable environments for continued success. Conversely, the millennium conversion efforts may provide opportunities to improve existing security controls or add new ones. Finally, failure to successfully solve the millennium conversion problem in commercial software may be considered a significant crime in terms of negligence and liability. As we approach the year 2000, beleaguered business managers and angry shareholders are likely to bombard the courts with lawsuits claiming negligence. Produce Palace International in Warren, Michigan has already filed suit against Tec-America in Atlanta because it is alleged that cash registers in the produce store freeze when customers use credit cards with year 2000 expiration dates.

MEDIA

All information is stored in one medium or another—even if the medium is the human brain or air. Other examples of media include ink or paint on paper (i.e., hard-copy documents), electromagnetic pulses in space (i.e., radio waves), and electronic switches in computers (i.e., digital signals). Damage, modification, and misrepresentation of media pose substantial threats to information, as do theft and denial of use. The security measures we take to protect media often focus on controlling their storage, use, and backing up the information content on another set of media.

Copies of Information

As the value and availability of information copies change, so too do their security requirements. For example, the cost of printed copies decreased dramatically after Gutenburg invented the printing press. A microfilm copy of the Gutenburg Bible, for example, has far less commercial value—

and need for security—than the priceless original. Backup copies may or may not be practical depending on the media in use and the time and cost involved in creating backup copies. In some cases, a copy has minimal value—as in the case of copying original art works. In other cases, the copy's value may be equal to the original—especially if it uses the same medium. The typewriter, printing press, xerography, photography, carbon paper, computer displays, scanners, and computer printers have all changed the number of copies that we can produce in a practical, cost-efficient manner. These technologies and devices have changed the cost of producing copies and altered the security value of backups.

In cyberspace, we store copies of information in many places (e.g., the source computer, communications gateway, switching and receiving computers, printer storage buffers, and backup facilities) and on a variety of media (e.g., disks, diskettes, tape, and paper). For example, I use both diskettes and Iomega (www.iomega.com) Zip disks to store information from my own computer, and store the disks and diskettes in a separate location. These storage facilities supplement the computer hard disk, which contains twenty-eight hundred million bytes, in which multitudes of erased (but not overwritten) copies have life cycles of their own. To put this in perspective, this book contains only about one million bytes, half of the capacity of a typical diskette. I have draft chapters of the book, backup copies, shadow copies, copies under different names, obsolete copies, copies in temporary files, and who knows how much more mysterious information. In addition, many of the files and backup files are duplicated on the publisher's and editor's computers. If I wanted to destroy the manuscript totally and securely, I would have to know the names and locations of every copy of every file and document. Fortunately, this proliferation of copies and media causes problems for the criminals as well. When a disgruntled computer operations manager held all of his employer's master data files for extortion, for example, he had to be sure to take all of the electronic and backup copies, as well. He succeeded, but it was a challenge.

Money Instruments

In his book *The History of Money* (Crown, 1997), anthropologist Jack Weatherford says that we are at the beginning of the third monetary revolution. The first occurred 2500 years ago when people started using coins instead of shells; the second came in the fifteenth century with the development of paper money. In this, the third revolution, the use of electronic monetary instruments (e.g., e-cash and cybercash) will become the norm.

Weatherford predicts that electronic money will supplement, rather than replace, coins and paper and plastic money. This is largely because there is a huge amount of tangible money (i.e., paper and coins) in circulation throughout the world, despite the growing use of credit cards and electronic cash transfer. It is, however, unlikely that tangible money will prevail for very much longer. Our growing trust of electronic information leads me to believe that the widespread use of such a convenient—and potentially more secure—form of money is inevitable. A few nostalgia stores and retail bank branches with human tellers may survive, but we may have to go to Disney World to find them.

The electronic money medium is as real as any monetary instrument can be. Money is now a kind of intangible information retained in fragile electronic media in computers. Banks squeeze money through telephone lines. It rides radio waves and resides on computer disks and in electronic memory. As a kind of information, US$432.28 typed in an e-mail message may have no value at all, or it may have far greater value than $432.28 if, for instance, it creates a strong emotion in the person reading it. The context and medium of the monetary amount makes the difference. The e-mail message itself may become a negotiable monetary instrument worth US$432.28. Opportunities for monetary instrument crime are endless, but so are the opportunities for security—if we are sufficiently motivated to exercise due care. Unfortunately, far more crime, and losses far greater than the few billions we are now losing, will probably have to occur before we are willing to make material efforts to achieve more than cosmetic security of whole systems and networks.

The potential security of electronic book entry for negotiable stocks and bonds far exceeds that for paper certificates. Note that I cautiously use the word *potential* because we have a long way to go to fully implement due-care controls to more than a superficial level of security. But, as the last generation of paper-committed investors passes away and our awareness of information security increases, we are likely to see the demise of paper certificates. Can the demise of paper money and checks be far behind? Security plays a key roll in the success of these transitions.

The Variety of Information Media

Physical objects contain implicit information such as constituency, color, shape, size, weight, and marks. These objects also have extrinsic information associated with them, including their locations in space and in relation to other objects, their purposes, and their sensitivity to various actions (i.e., the effects of use or loss). For example, scuffed-up old shoes at a

Stock and Bond Certificates

A great political battle erupted in the 1980s when the director of the U.S. Securities and Exchange Commission (SEC) proposed to convert the securities industry's use of paper stock and bond certificates to electronic book entry (in which certificates are replaced with ownership information stored in computer media). Investors wanted to retain their paper certificates, not trusting brokerages in New York City to maintain them only as electronic records.

The companies that print the certificates also resisted total conversion to electronic book entry. Their businesses depended on owners retaining that pretty paper. In some cases, owners and their heirs have been keeping stock and bond certificates for more than a century. They did not believe that computers could store information electronically on magnetic disks and tape for long periods. Technically speaking, they were right. Information stored in magnetic media fades away in tens of years, and the computer equipment necessary to read old forms of media becomes obsolete and disappears long before that. Investors would have to depend on computer operations staffs in brokerages to transfer the data files to new media using new, constantly evolving systems and media.

Several European countries, including France, converted to book entry many years ago—perhaps because Europeans have traditionally trusted their institutions to a greater extent than have Americans. In the United States, the certificate-printing companies and long-time investors won the paper certificate war in 1990. Congress agreed to let natural attrition take its course as people discovered the convenience of electronic book entry and increased their trust in the book entry recorders.

garage sale exude the information that they are well used, and a sign in front of them stating, "Used Shoes For Sale" agrees with the observable information. Thus, we can have information in the form of the characteristics of physical objects. Similarly, you have probably seen computer-generated pictures created from thousands of characters where a dense character, such as *W*, creates a dark region, and a period creates a lighter region. There is information expressed by the meaning of the characters and also by the pattern they create. Security requires that we recognize this information within information and protect both. This leads to the concept of hiding information within information (called steganography), and raises additional concerns for security. Discovering covert information and covert channels of communicating it is difficult, if not impossible in some cases. For example, a criminal may be able to create covert information and bury it in other information in a computer, then create covert means of leaking the information from the computer. Information security researchers generally agree that it is impossible to prove that a computer is "clean" and does not contain such covert information or output channels.

We buy, sell, barter, and trade information about objects and convert it to a tangible asset when we materialize it into physical media, such as books, art works, or software packages. Purchasers pay for both the intangible information and the tangible medium. Of course, the leather and

Covert Channel

Spies and thieves could theoretically use covert channels to secretly remove information from computer systems. A spy risks detection if he prints or displays information that he plans to steal from a computer because the victims may see his efforts and stop him, or the computer may create an audit record of his actions. He might, however, find other ways to get the information from computers. He could, for example, create a covert channel by secretly writing and executing a program in the victim's computer to examine each bit of data that is to be retrieved. If the bit were a *0,* a brief use of a disk drive would cause the usage light on the control panel to briefly blink. If the bit were a *1,* use would be longer and the light would remain on for a longer time. The espionage agent could make a video recording of the blinking light from a hidden location, play it back slowly, and manually record the bits as the light blinks. This covert channel would be very slow, and the spy would be well advised to get the information in a variety of other ways, such as bribing an operator or dumpster diving (also called *trashing*) for discarded computer listings. However, it could work and be worth the effort in a highly secure facility.

Many other covert channels easily come to mind; spies could give coded meanings to variable lengths of printed lines (less than forty characters could represent a *0,* and more could represent a *1*). They could use the rhythm of the noise that a printer makes, use the motion of a tape reel in a tape drive, or receive the radio frequency emanations that radiate from high voltage electronic circuits.

paper pages of a rare volume of Shakespeare's works are more costly than the information that the book contains. The information alone has no monetary value because it is in the public domain, and the leather binding and paper separately would have little value. To provide security against threats to such information, we must recognize these differences. For example, we must protect the possession value of the tangible medium from theft and the authenticity and integrity value of the content from plagiarism.

We also need to recognize the difference in security requirements for information that we store and information that we communicate. Information is usually more vulnerable in a transmission medium, such as a wire, than in a storage medium at the end of the wire. In terms of computer time, information that is transmitted electronically through the public switched telephone network or the Internet is in the transmission medium for a relatively long time. It is, therefore, exposed to threats as it passes through long, uncontrolled areas that are often in the public domain. This is why cryptographic protection is so important for communications, but relatively less important for information stored in isolated computers in secure buildings. We have numerous, cost-efficient means for protecting information that is stored in computers, but cryptography is the primary practical protection for information that is being communicated.

The security of information on paper, regardless of its location, is usually increased when we physically mark the paper to indicate the sensitivity of the information (e.g., SECRET, CLASSIFIED, PRIVATE, etc.). Such marking lets the information users know what security measures are required to protect it. Unfortunately, computer operating systems rarely allow us to indelibly mark the information in electronic media in the same way. With a few exceptions, we identify the sensitivity of much computer-stored information only implicitly through access control lists (ACLs) that indicate to the operating systems which computer users are authorized to use the information and what functions they are allowed to perform. One of the exceptions, IBM's *RACF* entry control software provides a security label (tagging) feature in which the label accompanies each information file, even as its location changes. Unfortunately, however, I suspect few IBM customers use the label feature for security. Encrypted marking embedded in the document and digital watermarking are additional techniques.

We can also tag computer information manually, but must do so explicitly if the tagging is to be effective for security. This means that users must be aware of information's security classification as well as the appropriate controls to apply. Aside from the military and intelligence agencies, few organizations follow this policy on any formal basis. For example, when employees who are entrusted with sensitive information go to conferences, document tagging should remind them what they are and are not allowed to discuss with their peers or present in their talks.

The quantity of information also affects its security requirements. Information printed on paper is sensitive to weight and volume, whereas the quantity of information in a computer causes no change in weight and physical volume. Criminals may need to exert greater efforts to steal large quantities of printed paper (e.g., using trucks rather than cars), but contend only with minimal differences in timing (e.g., a few milliseconds) or storage facilities (e.g., sufficient disk or memory space) when they attempt to manipulate or steal huge quantities of computer information. We often need extensive security controls for such quantities of printed information, such as sturdy doors or large vaults, but locked cabinets and safes may be sufficient for protecting disks or tape cartridges containing an equal or greater amount of information.

OWNERS OF INFORMATION

Ownership of information is a complex issue with many variables. Everyone owns information, including personal information that is protected by privacy rights. Business, religious, and political organizations also own information, including information about the organizations themselves, and, although these organizations have rights to privacy, their privacy is not protected by law to the same degree as personal privacy. Instead, their privacy is largely protected in terms of trade secrets. Public figures should have the same privacy rights as other individuals, but the law allows less of their personal information to be private.

Thus, privacy protection depends largely on ownership—but it is sometimes difficult to determine ownership. When, for example, does a sender of information lose ownership or exclusive ownership of information? And when does the receiver attain ownership? We often possess information that is owned by others, or that exists in the public domain. Similarly, copies of information that we own may be in the public domain, either by our choice or inadvertently, or others may illegally possess (own?) copies of our information. Such possession may dramatically change the value of our information. If, for example, you own an original painting, its value may be greatest if nobody else has a copy, or it may be more valuable if many others have copies and wish they had the original. All of these factors play roles in determining the threats, vulnerabilities, and value of information, as well as the extent of security required. This is one reason that it is so difficult to put a value on information for security purposes.

Information owners assign ownership and/or give possession of information (original or copies) to other individuals or groups. They also grant permission to act on or with the information (e.g., view, copy, or modify it). We identify these other individuals or groups as new owners, co-owners, custodians, service providers, and users of the information. Each possessor or user has a security role in protecting the rights of the other stakeholders in these complex, oft-changing relationships. For example, information owners often require non-owner possessors to protect the information. In organizations, we identify "owners" who do not legally own the organization's information in their custody but we hold them accountable for its use and protection. As advisors to the information owners, security practitioners are not accountable for the protection of information that is assigned to employee owners. The subjects of information (i.e., the individuals and organizations identified and discussed in the information) also have some rights with regard to information that is owned by others, most notably the right to have their privacy protected.

Government information involves some unique issues with regard to ownership. The U.S. government protects its information with copyrights, but universally assigns them to the public domain. This is to signify that citizens are the owners of government, and therefore, own the information. The government is the custodian, and has legally established secrecy classifications, in the best interests of its citizens, concerning the confidentiality and possession of the information. While the U.S. Privacy Act of 1967 covers personal information in the government's custody and that of its contractors, it does not apply to others outside of government. Other laws protect personal information in the banking, health, and credit-reporting industries.

The rights concerning information and its value are even more complex in the private sector. Courts in some jurisdictions have ruled that personal financial information about customers that is possessed by banks belongs to the banks, but the banks are constrained by the banking laws to protect their customers' privacy. In the United States, an employer who pays for employees' creative efforts—including software development—owns the results of those efforts. (In other countries, this ownership is shared, and employees have certain rights to take their creative works with them when they move on to other employment.) The significant differences in information ownership and possession between governmental and private organizations, as well as among various countries and legal jurisdictions, should caution against relying blindly on the security concepts and practices of others.

Legal Protection for Information Owners

Owned information may be subject to several kinds of legal protection, including trade secret, copyright, patent, or trademark regulations, but many of these regulations are in a state of flux. Many countries are scrutinizing their trade secret and copyright legislation to protect their indigenous industries from industrial espionage, plagiarism, and piracy. The World Intellectual Property Organization has agreed on guidelines to achieve uniform laws, and the U.S. Department of Justice has convinced the Congress and President to adopt federal legislation to protect trade secrets, which were previously under the exclusive jurisdiction of individual states. This national and international legislative activity is spurred by the increasing commercialization of the Internet and our increasingly global economy.

Ownership versus Possession

In the early days of computing, management did not generally understand the value of software as a commodity and did not assert ownership of the software written by its employees. Understandably, employees often assumed that they owned the software they wrote. When I was a programmer in the 1950s, I freely shared my employer's software with anybody. Calling our IBM computer users' association *SHARE* epitomized this system of values.

In the 1960s, software became recognized as a valuable intellectual property, and management began to assert its ownership rights. Today, some programmers still do not understand the proprietary nature of software, and get into trouble when they take copies of their programs with them to new jobs.

We need clear and complete information security policies to sort out these issues of ownership and possession. Considerable grief can be avoided by spelling these policies out in software development contracts and by sharing agreements. Again, we need to recognize the differences between confidentiality and possession, and treat these issues as distinct elements of information security.

The dual nature of software, as functional and literary as well as utilitarian and creative, raises some significant legislative issues and security concerns. In an article about software protection ("A New View of Intellectual Property and Software" in *The Communications of the ACM*, March 1996; © 1996, paraphrased by permission), authors Randall Davis, Pamela Samuelson, Mitchell Kapor, and Jerome Reichman assert that computer programs should be viewed as machines whose medium of construction happens to be text. Programs behave and are written to *do* something, albeit in computers. The behavior and text are only loosely connected: For example, subroutines, or parts of programs, can be reordered without having any effect on the behavior. Also, two programs with different text can have the same behavior. The know-how that is easily visible when software is run is immediately observable and, hence, cannot be kept secret. Steve Jobs, of Apple Computers (www.apple.com), was shown the graphical user interface (GUI) at the Xerox Palo Alto Research Center (www.parc.xerox.com) in 1979. According to the lab director, "Once he saw it, the damage was done; he just had to know it was doable."

In their article, the authors identified key elements of legal protection related to intellectual property. One essential element of copyright is that the work be expressive, or artistic, rather than functional. An essential element of patent protection is that the advance be non-obvious, and an essential element of trade secret protection is that the trade secret remain secret. Although Congress has modified the copyright laws to accommodate the protection of computer programs, significant questions remain. For example, should a new program that performs in exactly the same way as another commercial program, but which looks entirely different, instruction by instruction, be considered a copy for purposes of prosecuting plagiarism or criminal pirating? Some individuals and organizations are arguing for a completely new form of protection for commercial computer programs. Until this happens, however, or until we refine our existing copyright and patent laws to provide sufficient protection for computer software, we'll have to rely on ethics and information security to safeguard our valuable programs.

Legal protection for owners and possessors of information is an important aspect of information security. The security controls that we choose to apply depend, in part, on the legal protection that the owners choose. Trade secrets subject to threats of espionage require confidentiality controls, while copyrighted and patented works that are not trade secrets may require possession, integrity, authenticity, and availability controls.

Debate on Intellectual Property

Some people argue that traditional intellectual property rights do not apply in cyberspace. They claim that ownership of information requires a physical object that serves as a medium for the expression or application of information. An author can have copyrights for a book, for instance, because the book is a physical object but not copyright protection for the ideas contained in the book. These individuals claim that because cyberspace removes the physical medium and leaves only ideas behind, traditional forms of intellectual property become irrelevant. According to them, copyright protections do not, therefore, apply to digitized information, such as computer software, e-mail messages, and Web pages.

Other people (including myself), however, believe that ownership of information is independent of the medium. That is why an author can own the information printed in a book, as well as the same information on a diskette or stored in a computer. Authors receive copyright protection for each rendering of their work. Ownership is an ethical and contractual issue; it is not limited to what the copyright law states. Information in electronic form is still information in a medium. There is no doubt, however, that the electronic medium—in which information can so easily and quickly be copied, modified, destroyed, and transmitted—is different than other more tangible media.

The anti-regulators say that any serious attempt to enforce traditional notions of copyright would wreck cyberspace, because enforcement would require a high degree of censorship, regulation, and control over the Internet and Worldwide Web. Property rights would exert too much control over the free flow of information that is vital to the Internet and Web. They cite the failure to control software piracy as an example of the failure to control intellectual property rights and maintain that it is best to handle misrepresentations of works in terms of plagiarism, libel, deception, or other moral notions, instead of trying to enforce copyrights.

Again, I disagree. Automobile speed limits are frequently violated, but that does not detract from their value or the value of enforcing them. Both copyright and speeding laws have a confrontational moral value. Law-abiding people will not exceed them by very much most of the time if they have too much to lose by widespread violations. As software industries develop in third-world countries, widespread piracy is likely to diminish out of self-interest. Outlaw pirates will continue to violate copyrights and other laws designed to protect writers, but we must adapt copyright to electronic information so that protection will fall into place in our value system.

Software piracy is a serious worldwide problem, but the software industry is alive and well in spite of piracy. Copyright bureaucrats from 160 countries in the World Intellectual Property Organization (WIPO) agree. When people in countries that violate the copyright protection of software realize that it is in their own best interests to prevent piracy, they will make the software market viable in their countries as well. WIPO recently adopted several new treaties, to be approved by each government, to bring the world into harmony with common kinds of copyright protections.

CONCLUSIONS

We are continually confronted with information; it is so pervasive, eclectic, and embedded in our minds that it is difficult to stand back and examine it objectively. Yet to protect information and its stakeholders, we must understand its pertinent characteristics. Information is like both a liquid and a gas, combining and flowing to fill available space. It also assumes many of the properties of its media. It changes from having no value (like a blank check) to having great monetary value (the face value of a freshly written, signed check). It goes on to become the realized value of an endorsed check, and once cancelled, becomes valueless again—unless it has worth as evidence of a past transaction. Information is an important part of us and what we do and, as knowledge, makes each of us unique. Information can destroy us or advance our intellect, be the cause of our winning or losing wars, and thrill us or bore us. It sustains us while we live and becomes the memory of us after we die. We must be good stewards of our information, respecting it, and above all, prudently protecting it and the rights of its subjects, as well as those who possess or own it.

To protect information, information processes, other people, and ourselves, we must know what types of losses can occur—even though we are unable to predict the size of losses. Identifying the losses requires that we know the vulnerabilities of the information, the processes associated with the information, and the stakeholders. For us to recognize the vulnerabilities, we must understand the nature of information that is owned and lost. Breaking down the characteristics of information into kinds, representations, forms, and media, and considering each separately provides us with methodical and comprehensive means of trying to achieve our goal. This approach shows that the nature of information and its protection are complex in both philosophical and practical terms, especially as we consider information in the context of the equally perplexing processes applied to it in cyberspace.

3

The Rise of Cybercrime

Cybercrime encompasses abuse (harm done *to* information, such as causing the loss of usefulness, integrity, and authenticity) and misuse (harm done *with* information, such as causing the loss of availability, possession, and confidentiality). Beyond the direct loss of information, however, abuse and misuse may result in losses of, or injury to, property, services, and people. Information security must protect against these concomitant losses as well as the direct losses. A criminal may need to cause only one type of loss to succeed in rendering information unavailable or unusable. Simultaneously defending against all potential losses is a formidable (but necessary) task, since we cannot predict which type of loss a perpetrator may cause.

Although an abuse or misuse of information is technically a crime only if it violates a criminal statute, I use the convention of calling all abuse and misuse crimes, except where I differentiate unethical conduct from criminal conduct, or abuse from misuse. I define a crime as any intentional misbehavior in which a victim suffers (or can potentially suffer) a loss, or in which a perpetrator reaps (or can potentially reap) an undeserved gain. In my definition, cybercrime encompasses any abuse or misuse of information that entails using a knowledge of information systems. Some business managers and others define cybercrime more narrowly, arguing that it encompasses only those crimes that require the use of computers or that could not be perpetrated without computers. Few, if any, crimes actually fall within this definition, because criminals can engage in almost all of the same types of fraud, larceny, or espionage with or without computers, although computers may facilitate the process.

Cybercrimes are essentially the same crimes that have occurred throughout history, but that are now committed in a new environment, with the new tools and targets of cyberspace. Cybercrime constitutes an increasing share of business crime, and also includes some so-called victimless crimes (e.g., prostitution, drug abuse, and suicide) and crimes against persons (e.g., bodily harm, kidnapping, and invasion of privacy). Many traditionalists argue that we need only reinterpret our current criminal statutes to protect against these crimes. Others, including those of us who are fighting the war on cybercrime, recognize a need for some new laws to achieve just and effective prosecution and raise awareness of the increased resources and skills needed to fight cybercrime in today's highly technical business environment.

The difference between an ordinary business crime and a cybercrime can be subtle. Valid statistics are difficult to produce because people have different concepts of what constitutes cybercrime and because the differences between business crime and cybercrime are fading as business increasingly relies on computers to process all types of information. When computers eventually encompass business processes entirely, cybercrime can go back to being called business crime—just plain embezzlement, fraud, piracy, larceny, and so forth—without regard to the roles played by computers or communication. For now, however, we need to distinguish between cybercrime and ordinary business crime as we attempt to learn more about appropriate security controls for cyberspace.

In this chapter, I offer an overview of cybercrime. In the next two chapters, I share information about some of the criminal methods and cases that I've encountered over the years, withholding victims' names and other identifying details to preserve confidentiality and avoid providing recipes for crime.

ABUSE AND MISUSE

Achieving information security requires understanding the nature of the abuse and misuse of intangible information and the tangible media in which it is stored. Accidental and intentionally harmful acts can be traced to the people who control, possess, or know information. Understanding the perpetrators is key to understanding their acts, a subject that I cover in some detail in Chapter 6. For now, however, the focus is on the abuses and misuses themselves.

Table 3.1 lists the many and varied terms that we use to describe information abuse and misuse.

Crimes often are combinations of the abuse and misuse descriptors listed in Table 3.1, and may involve direct and indirect misuse of information. For example, extortion and kidnapping involve ransom notes containing information that is misused to cause harm, but the information is not directly the subject of the crime as it is in an espionage case. If the ransom information is written by hand and sent through the postal service, the crime is an ordinary one. If the information is written and communicated electronically, it is a cybercrime. If extortion involves holding electronic information or an information processing system or service for ransom, it is a cybercrime. Similar arguments can be made for the other abuses and misuses in the list: Even murder and assaults have been planned or carried out using computers. In one case of criminal negligence, a computer-controlled robot stabbed a repairman to death after his associate failed to put the robot into a safe mode for maintenance purposes.

Distributing computer viruses and launching Trojan horse attacks may constitute trespass, destruction, fraud, violation of privacy, harassment, or other misuses and abuses of information. These techniques are all too common in today's business environment. Hackers and computer science students spew out thousands of different viruses, which victims

TABLE 3.1 Cybercrime Abuse and Misuse

General	*Property Acts*	*Economic Crimes*	*Physical Crimes*	*Personal Crimes*
Errors	Acts of nature	Fraud	Theft	Libel
Omissions	Disruption	Scam	Trespass	Drug trafficking and/
Negligence	Destruction	Embezzlement	Burglary	or possession
Recklessness		Bribery	Larceny	Pornography
Delinquency		Extortion	Smuggling	Harassment
Civil dispute		Racketeering	Plagiarism	Invasion of privacy
Conspiracy		Infringement	Piracy	Assault
		Forgery	Espionage	Sex attack
		Counterfeiting		Kidnapping
				Murder
				Suicide

inadvertently spread widely in cyberspace by sharing computer programs, sending and retrieving enclosed documents in e-mail or in diskettes, and visiting shady Web sites. Businesses whose employees' children play virus-infected games on their parents' computers at home are particularly vulnerable.

Much direct physical abuse in cyberspace involves computer destruction or larceny. As computers get smaller and more portable, they also become increasingly attractive targets of theft, and their fragility makes them vulnerable to damage—whether deliberate or accidental. While some criminals steal computers for the intrinsic value of the hardware and software, others profit from the information contained in the stolen computers. Such information is often more valuable than the hardware if the criminals know how to make use of it. They may, for example, use it for extortion, sell it to business competitors, or use it to extract credit card numbers and other personal identification information.

Levels of Abstraction

I describe abuse and misuse at three levels of abstraction, each more specific than the last. First is the question of ethics. At this level, we consider the motives and applicable ethical principles without regard to specific laws. Second is the question of crime. At this level, we consider the applicable statutes, common law, and civil actions. Third is the nature of the losses. At this level, we examine the loss of availability or utility, integrity or authenticity, and confidentiality or possession of information. We need to analyze the potential threats at each level of abstraction in order to identify material abuse or misuse, related vulnerabilities, and security safeguards that might be effective. Overlooking any of these aspects can result in incomplete or ineffective security.

For preventative security purposes, it is usually best to identify perpetrators' abuse and misuse of information at the loss level, because such abuse and misuse usually has the most direct correlation with the technical security controls needed to prevent the modification, use, copying, misrepresenting, observing, or taking of information. Preventing confidential information from being observed, for example, requires that its display on monitor screens be suppressed when the computers are not in use. Considering a perpetrator's attempt to engage in the unauthorized use or modification of information in computers leads logically to the implementation of good controls on password usage. Similarly, considering transaction fraud leads to controls that prevent fraudulent transactions, such as digital signatures or transaction-log records.

The Ethics, Crime, and Loss Considerations of a Software Theft

The following case illustrates the value of considering the abuse and misuse of information at three levels.

A small software company fired a programmer but neglected to cancel her authorization to access files on the company's computers. Following her termination, the programmer spent many hours downloading proprietary software from the company's computers over telephone lines into her home PC. Her intent, which she later admitted, was to use the software to start her own company. She had written and participated in developing much of the software and felt that she had some proprietary rights to it.

To protect the software at the ethics level, the stakeholders needed to consider the various parties' understandings about the proprietary rights to the software produced by the employees and possessed by the company. These rights should have been documented in employee contracts with informed consent clearly spelled out in written policies. The company may have also been negligent in tempting the perpetrator to act by failing to cancel her authority to use the computers.

At the crime level, the criminal justice agencies involved needed to consider the available evidence, the acts that were perpetrated, and the applicable statutes. The company needed to consider the validity and usefulness in court of any recorded evidence or lack thereof. They also had to decide whether to attempt to recover their loss via litigation and to weigh the legal consequences of their failure to revoke the perpetrator's authority.

At the loss level, the company needed to consider their administration of passwords and the methods that the perpetrator used to log on to their computers through their network and to download the software. The company also needed to consider how the events that occurred during those eighteen hours were monitored and recorded by their computer system. Such an assessment can help to identify operational and technical vulnerabilities and to improve the safeguards in the systems and communications.

Considering any of these types of abuses at the ethics and crime levels alone does not generally point the analyst toward all of the safeguards that would protect against them. But, understanding the motives of perpetrators at the ethics level can lead to the development of avoidance and deterrence safeguards. Understanding what acts constitute fraud, theft, conspiracy, or other crimes can lead to the use of legal safeguards. Criminal statutes act as deterrents, they help direct the resources and attention of law enforcers, and they serve to sanction, recover from, and correct losses.

Unfortunately, knowing what legal jurisdictions and categories a crime falls into is not as useful for security as it might be because the legal definitions of crime vary widely from one jurisdiction to the next. For example, computer larceny may mean either theft or burglary, which require different types of security controls. (Preventing theft requires protecting the information, while preventing burglary requires protecting both the information and the premises). There are at least fifty-four different federal and local computer crime laws in the United States alone, as well as a host of other statutes that may apply.

TRENDS OF BUSINESS CRIME

Business crimes always involve information. Increasingly, they involve computers as tools, symbols, and/or targets. Patterns are difficult to discern, however, because many crimes are not reported, or are reported inaccurately. Information owners and security practitioners generally learn about computer crimes when the media report the most widespread or intriguing examples, such as hacker or malicious virus attacks. However, many of the crimes that we hear about in this manner are the sensational, large-scale, or unusual cases, and we don't usually learn all of the relevant and correct details. Surveys of victims or potential victims of cybercrime are also often misleading because organizations tend to hide the extent and circumstances of their losses out of embarrassment and to keep the nature of their security secret. As a result, important cases with useful details are not made known to other potential victims except through the old boys' network of security and law-enforcement organizations, where specialists, even those from competing organizations, trust and talk to one another.

The lack of solid information can distort our view of the business crime problem. Experts predicate their perception of the problem on the crimes they themselves know about. Thus, even experienced information security specialists have differing views of the problem. There are some generalizations that most experts agree upon—and others that are hotly debated.

In general, it appears that the loss per case of business crime—including cybercrime—is increasing. However, the frequency of business crime, relative to the volume of transactions and the value of business information, seems to be decreasing. These trends are likely to become more pronounced as cybercrime constitutes an even larger share of business crime. I expect the number of cybercrimes to peak, then decrease within the next five to ten years—bringing the total number of business crimes down with it.

The rate of business crime will decrease as we use more, and more effective, controls to protect business computers and communications. Computer applications and transaction controls preclude much accidental and intentional misbehavior, and computers efficiently monitor and record the details of every transaction for automated analysis—a task too tedious to perform without computers. Such tools also make it easier for systems administrators to detect and resolve business anomalies. For example, administrators can immediately detect unauthorized duplicate payments to creditors and cancel them before the checks are cashed or credit is transferred.

In addition, the widespread use of cryptography will contribute to the decline in the rate of business crime. As a rapidly emerging standard of due care in information security, cryptography can dramatically decrease—or even eliminate—many types of information abuse, including computer-to-computer and user-to-user eavesdropping and misrepresentation in business transactions and agreements. The use of cryptography alone, however, will not stop crime. Systems must decrypt information into its vulnerable, plaintext forms for people to use, and people are the weakest link in an information security system. Thus, cryptography shifts the vulnerabilities, but does not eliminate the need for other types of controls.

To some extent, business crime will also diminish because computer controls make it more difficult for employees to engage in unauthorized business activities. Computer workstations impose a discipline on users that prevents them from engaging in many accidental or intentional acts that may cause losses. This marks a significant change from the days in which procedural controls consisted only of managers telling employees what they were, or were not, supposed to do. And, as computers become increasingly complex, fewer people have the necessary technical skills to successfully subvert an information system's functionality.

It would be a mistake to underestimate the ingenuity of future criminals. Any security advantage may be lost as a few technically competent criminals learn to package their crimes in computer programs and pass the automated crimes on for use by less-adept criminals. But although we can never make computers completely secure, we are steadily strengthening the technological barriers to reduce the number of experts who can break them down.

As the incidence of business crime diminishes, losses per case may escalate dramatically with very little—if any—additional effort on the part of the criminals. This is because of the increased size of business transactions and the greater availability of assets afforded by computers. The monetary size of a financial crime is determined only by the number of digits used and placement of the decimal point. The most recent major financial crimes, which entailed millions of dollars in losses, could not have taken place if the perpetrators had to rely on physical means to carry the money away. As we invoke more and more effective security controls, criminals are unlikely to risk detection for minimal gains; instead, they will focus their efforts on targets that are large enough to justify their risk. This could boost losses to new heights.

Losses involving computers tend to be far larger than those caused by equivalent crimes committed without computers. The £869 million ($1.4 billion) Barings Bank fraud is one of the most dramatic recent examples, but there are others as well, including a 1996 attempt in Russia to fraudulently transfer $10 million to several banks around the world, and the

How Much Money to Steal?

Financial criminals are no longer constrained by the weight of their booty: The amount they steal at any one time depends only on the number of digits and the placement of the decimal point—either of which involves any heavy lifting!

Criminals must ponder the question of how much money to steal. If they try to steal too much, they are more likely to be caught because the victims have no choice but to pursue them at any cost. Yet, if they take too little, they are not going to be able to hire good lawyers or flee the country. (Some of the dumb ones steal multiples of ten with lots of zeros, say $21,000,000, which make large amounts stand out like a sore thumb in a ledger for auditors to catch.)

The successful criminal knows the right amount to steal at any one time. Bob Courtney, an experienced computer security consultant, describes the case of a securities dealer who successfully stole several million dollars. The managers of his Wall Street firm, who were experts at managing money, were embarrassed. They invited the dealer to lunch and, over martinis, agreed to let him keep the money if he would promise to leave the country forever and never tell anyone what he had done.

$2 billion Equity Funding Insurance case. While these crimes were possible without computers, the losses would probably have been much smaller.

Hacker attacks do not usually involve large losses, except for the costs involved in restoring the availability, integrity, and authenticity of the information systems that were the targets of the attacks. These costs, however, can be significant. Similarly, potential losses from terrorist attacks on fragile strategic infrastructures, such as our communication, electric power, or transportation grids, are enormous. As the President's Commission on Critical Infrastructure Protection recently reported, a well-aimed,

The Biggest Computer Crimes

The largest (known) computer crime in the world occurred in Los Angeles in 1973, and resulted in the destruction of the Equity Funding Insurance Company, with losses of two billion dollars. The company's management tried to make Equity Funding the fastest growing and largest company in the insurance industry. Unfortunately, they attempted to gain that position by engaging in virtually every type of known business fraud. In the course of their downward spiral into crime, management created 64,000 fake people in their computer system and insured them with policies that they then sold to reinsurers. The government convicted twenty-two top executives, including two from the firm that audited the company, and sent them to prison. (For more details, see my book, *Crime by Computer*, published by Charles Scribner's Sons in 1976, and *The Equity Funding Papers*, written by Lee Seidler, Fred Andrews, and Marc Epstein, published by John Wiley & Sons in New York in 1977.)

A more recent case, and one which was widely reported by the media, was the 1995 collapse of the Barings Bank in London. The bank's trader in Singapore made some highly speculative investments through the Tokyo stock exchange. When the investments soured following the Kobe earthquake, he tried to hide the losses in error accounts in the bank's computers. The total loss was £869 million (for more details, see Stephan Fay's book, *The Collapse of Barings*, published by W. W. Norton in 1997).

The vulnerabilities and events were far more complex than described here, but the fundamental problem in both cases was a failure to segregate duties or to impose dual controls at the top management and audit levels and to apply them throughout the organization.

successful attack on one or more of these systems could put an entire
country out of commission.

THE ROLE OF COLLUSION IN BUSINESS CRIME

As many auditors know, one effective method of deterring business crime
is to make collusion necessary for successful perpetration. Collusion
increases the crime's complexity and the perpetrator's likelihood of being
caught. Collusion is often necessary in cybercrime because no one perpetrator normally possesses the required combination of skill, knowledge,
and authority. Once we effectively invoke the usual due-care management
and technical controls, business cybercrime is largely the province of
highly trusted employees who control the valuable information assets and
are constrained by few management controls. Such employees, especially
those who are unfamiliar with technical controls and processes, typically
need to cooperate with computer technologists to commit cybercrimes.
The technologist can—at least theoretically—subvert the technical controls
while the trusted business employee provides the necessary authorizations
to engage in fraudulent transactions. To guard against such collusion,
auditors and security experts need to urge management to strengthen the
human factors controls, such as segregating duties and requiring dual control in transactions. Computers are ideally suited for applying this kind of
control as well because they can automatically require identity authentication, require separate action for each transaction by two or more employees, review voluminous transaction logs, and identify anomalies.

Reports of collusion in cybercrime cases indicate a far higher frequency of collusion in large organizations than in small ones, but collusion
is a common occurrence in a wide variety of computer crimes. In one case,
the president of a retail business skimmed income to avoid taxes on $16
million by maintaining two completely different computer-based accounting systems. He needed assistance from the operations staff to maintain the
dual bookkeeping system, however, since he did not have the necessary
technical expertise. In another case, a funds transfer executive violated the
segregation of duties controls with assistance from an employee in a
remote branch who received the funds. Together, they managed to transfer
more than $50 million. The largest currency trading fraud in Europe
occurred when several traders, in cooperation with computer operations
staffers, hid their transactions within computer systems and electronic
media. Together, they caused more than $260 million in loss. And, the
Equity Funding Insurance fraud (see the previous sidebar, "The Biggest

> ## Collusion in a Funds Transfer Fraud
>
> In a European company, a funds-transfer clerk secretly observed his associate's private password as he typed it on the keyboard. The clerk, using his own and his associate's passwords, attempted to fraudulently transfer over $50 million to his accomplice's account in Lausanne. A bank clerk in Lausanne noticed the large transfer amount and called headquarters to confirm the transaction. The company easily caught the perpetrator and asked him why he had attempted the fraud. The perpetrator, a member of an extremist religious sect, claimed that God told him to do it. He is now serving a long prison sentence.
>
> The company added a number of security controls and practices, including strict segregation of duties to limit both voluntary and involuntary collusion, to restrict the observation of workstations, and to make such a crime more difficult to hide in the future. Collusion with God is another matter at the ethics level of crime.

Computer Crimes") required at least 22 co-conspirators, ranging from the company president to a member of the computer operations staff.

SMALL-BUSINESS CRIME IN CYBERSPACE

Business crime comes in many sizes, shapes, and forms—from a clerk stealing pencils to a CEO making off with millions. Small businesses and local government agencies may be among the most vulnerable to cybercrime. This may be the result of any or all of the following factors: an increasing reliance on computers, minimal security safeguards, the difficulties of segregating duties when there are few staff members, a tendency toward informal procedures, or a high degree of mutual trust among owners and employees. Small businesses often find it difficult to scale down the security recommendations that generally pertain to larger organizations with greater resources, security specialists, and ample budgets for protecting their information. In a small organization, for example, one individual is often responsible for operating the computer. That individual, who necessarily has complete knowledge about the computer and its contents, is generally in a position of total trust—which introduces the potential for crime if that individual is motivated to breach that trust.

A Small-Business Crime

Joe was the one and only computer programmer and operator in a small savings bank in California. Joe wore sandals and overalls and peered out of mounds of dirty hair, but he was a genius with the computer and could solve any problem—when he was not out surfing in the Pacific. Joe also had a few money problems. When his financial and creditor problems mounted, he decided to make a hit-and-run attack on the savings bank, with the collusion of his girlfriend.

He came in to work early one morning, ran the computer for the equivalent of an entire banking day in about twenty minutes, and engaged in only one transaction, moving $40,000 from a stranger's account into his girlfriend's account. He then removed the electronic and printed reports and audit log and turned the computer's clock back to the correct day. Unfortunately for him, the stranger inquired about her account before the girlfriend could withdraw the money, and Joe was caught.

Later, the president admitted that he should have suspected that something was amiss with his trusted hippie programmer. He saw Joe's new cars and the costly stereo equipment in Joe's expensive hillside pad, and observed behavior that was even stranger than usual, but did not want to disturb Joe, because he was so valuable and could do anything the bank needed if he was in the right mood.

There are many more Joes in small, cozy organizations stealing money, goods, and services. In fact, there may be more of them than there are dishonest button-down white-collar, computer-wielding clerks and executives in big organizations where segregation of duties and dual control are easier to achieve.

The Internet provides a whole range of new opportunities for crime against businesses. Criminals appreciate the anonymity afforded by computers, almost as much as they like the predictability of computers. Anonymity among those in collusion is very advantageous, because it allows the perpetrators to cooperate without requiring too much familiarity or trust. A host of well-known scams, such as repudiation of legitimate transactions, extortion, boiler-room investment and gambling fraud, credit card fraud, and pyramid schemes, are enjoying great popularity because of the Internet. The race between the criminals, with their new-found computer advantages, and the legitimate Web-site proprietors, with their authenticity controls and attempts to educate clientele in fraud resistance, is a close one.

THE RISE OF CYBERCRIMOIDS

I refer to the highly publicized incidents of supposed computer crime that are intensively covered by the news media as cybercrimoids. Press coverage of the Michelangelo virus in 1995 and 1996 was one example of a cybercrimoid. Journalists sometimes deliberately report such crimes as a coincident series of incidents—whether they result in significant losses or not—creating the appearance of an epidemic. Cybercrimoids began in the 1970s, and have included privacy invasions, attacks by high-energy radio frequency guns, commercial software piracy, and an endless series of computer viruses, as well as incidents with such labels as "salami round-down fraud" and "electronic letter bombing" (see Chapters 4 and 5). More recent crimoids include identity theft to loot victims' accounts and credit, and saturation of Internet gateway computers to deny use of commercial services. Some cybercrimoids have triggered some large losses and others—such as virus attacks and software piracy—persist, along with intense media coverage. And some publicized crimoids have apparently never actually occurred.

A journalist for the *London Times* fueled a recent cybercrimoid by reporting a series of extortion attempts that threatened London banks with the destruction of their computer systems. He described several other unrelated cases and depicted law enforcement agencies as gearing up for an extortion onslaught against banking. Eventually, *Der Spiegel* reported that the extortion attempts were a hoax perpetrated by one deranged person in Germany. In the meantime, a few individuals created great notoriety for the case and for themselves by perpetuating and expanding its significance.

Whole enterprises, as well as individuals within enterprises, can suffer from reports of highly publicized crimes that raise questions of security negligence. If, for example, a member of the board of directors of a large company read press coverage of either the Barings Bank fraud or the Equity Funding Insurance Company case, she might have been motivated to call the security manager of her company and demand more stringent security measures. This type of attention from top-level management is certainly good for the company if additional security measures are warranted, but if there are already sufficient security measures in place to protect from such catastrophes, the result may be a disgruntled security

> ## Important Controls Against Cybercrimoids
>
> A wide variety of safeguards are required to deal with new cyber-crimoids; the following list summarizes some guidelines for security managers to follow in preparing for future incidents:
>
> - Establish written policies and guidelines for revealing information about losses within and outside of your organization.
> - Organize emergency response multi-disciplinary teams of technical, legal, and public affairs specialists.
> - Automatically monitor computer usage, add timely detection, and encourage confidential reporting of unusual activities.
> - Search periodical news media and use news clipping services in a timely manner to find items of value for security purposes.
> - Cooperate with national and international organizations and government agencies to create trusted communication and cyberspace environments for business, and to encourage low-profile prosecution of criminals.

manager. If the security measures are not in place, the security manager may just be embarrassed by his failure to anticipate the need (or the executive's call). The high visibility of much-reported cybercrimoids raises awareness of the need to protect our valuable information resources, but security managers must learn to anticipate future crimoids whether real or hoaxes and be prepared to address them with intelligent planning and prudent controls to avoid negligence.

REPORTING CYBERCRIMES

The news media have been instrumental in alerting us to the need for information security, but they are also guilty of distorting the subject to some degree by focusing its coverage on the largest or most sensational types of cybercrimes. Unfortunately, some information security practitioners also contribute to the distortion. For example, the media—including the security trade media—have gradually changed the meaning of the word *hacker*. Many of the early hackers were law-abiding, ethical students with intense interest in computers (see Steven Levy's book, *Hackers* [Anchor/Doubleday, 1984], and Bruce Sterling's book, *The Hacker*

Crackdown [Bantam, 1996]). Today, the media (and some security experts) portray hackers as juvenile delinquents and other types of criminals—whether they are malicious or not. I distinguish between benign hackers and malicious hackers, the latter being those we fight against in information security.

The media has also created the perception that cybercrime is far more frequent, more high-tech, and more attributable to hackers than is probably the case. Many journalists portray any kind of attack on a computer—short of one involving a sledgehammer—as a virus attack perpetrated by a hacker. This perception may reflect a failure on the part of information security practitioners to clearly explain such incidents to the media. All too often, the practitioners use jargon that confuses outsiders, and they often use the jargon incorrectly—although only another technologist is likely to discern the inaccuracy. For example, a security practitioner may carelessly use the term *information integrity* when really meaning information authenticity. A journalist—especially one facing a deadline—is not likely to discern or question the difference in the concepts. And, sometimes, competent journalists write clear, accurate copy that is then massacred by editors who do not understand the technology but need to fit the article into a designated number of column inches. One writer, for example, complained that he hardly recognized one of his articles on cybercrime when it appeared in print.

Because the news media tend to emphasize computer involvement in coverage of all business crime, individuals in business and government assume that computers play a significant role in cases of information abuse or misuse. For example, even though the vast majority of the information that CIA spy Aldrich Ames turned over to the Soviets was in hardcopy format, the press branded his acts as computer crime because he entered some of the stolen information on his home computer and conveyed it to the Soviets on diskettes. In a similar vein, the FBI's current warning about foreign-sponsored economic espionage leads many people to conclude that the threat entails tapping into computers. According to the FBI, however, the primary threat is from bribery, deception, or hiring away key people; much of the information that is stolen is acquired from knowledgeable people rather than from computers. In general, overheard spoken information and stolen or forged information printed on paper probably far exceeds the amount of information stolen from or criminally modified in computers. (However, reported "low-tech" forms of crime seem to be diminishing as computers proliferate.)

Although failures in reporting are discouraging, the news media is effective in raising public awareness of security vulnerabilities and in

Glossary of Cybercrime Jargon

Software piracy.   Possessing or using software without the permission of the owner.

Trojan horse.   Software in which unauthorized computer instructions have been secretly inserted; or hardware in which unauthorized circuitry or mechanisms have been secretly inserted.

Virus.   Software that is made to secretly accompany or is secretly embedded in a computer program that replicates and inserts copies of itself into other software when executed in computers.

Hacker.   A computer enthusiast who is especially proficient; also, a person who experiments with or explores the contents of computers using unorthodox methods.

Malicious hacker.   A person who engages in hacking without authorization; or, a hacker who secretly distributes viruses to unsuspecting victims; or, a hacker who engages in software piracy; also a synonym for cracker.

Cybercrime.   A crime in which the perpetrator uses special knowledge of cyberspace.

Computer crime.   A crime in which the perpetrator uses special knowledge about computer technology.

motivating people to protect their information—at least when it is in computers. To convince readers that cybercrime is a big problem, a typical article begins with electrifying statistics on the numbers of crimes and amounts of losses, often attributing the statistics to a reputable source such as the FBI or a major accounting firm. Such an article then provides brief horror stories about current computer crimes, followed by quotes from information security experts detailing security products or practices that they use to prevent such crimes. Unfortunately, the crime statistics are nearly always erroneous and the experts' quotes reveal far too much detail about their organizations' security practices—thus compromising their employers' information and violating their own security rules.

In reality, we have no valid statistics on cybercrime frequency or size of loss. Even if there were valid statistics on cybercrime, beyond helping with actuarial insurance rate structures and legislation, they would be of little use to a particular organization for its own risk assessment. Each

Cyberspace Innumeracy

I receive frequent calls from journalists writing articles on cybercrime. The first question they usually ask is, "How much computer crime is there?" I tell them that I don't know, because not all such crimes are reported. If they persist, I suggest that *85.6* is a good number to use. There is a pause on the line, during which I hear the number being keyed into a computer. Then they ask, "85.6 what?" I respond "85.6 whatever you would like it to be. Use that number, and you will become an instant expert, settle any argument, and establish a fact." By the time these conversations are over, the journalists are crying, laughing, or calling me highly imaginative names (at which journalists excel).

I chose *85.6* as my experts' number after considerable research. I found that people are comfortable with the number, *85*. It is *most* on a scale of one hundred, a solid B average academic grade, and close to the familiar eighty-twenty rule of business. Appending the .6 added the appearance of precision and indicated that something significant must have been done to calculate the number. Adding a fourth digit would make it too ostentatious. Actually, my downfall was using .6. My friend, Juhani Saari sent me an e-mail from Finland, pointing out that 85.6 is the standard length of a credit card in millimeters—a real number! I have now changed the experts' number to a totally abstract 85.4. It is surprising and satisfying to see how far and wide my experts' numbers have traveled and have been used so successfully. When I say *most* during my lectures any place in the world, a listener will frequently correct me by saying it is 85.6 or 85.4.

Closer to home, an FBI agent was invited to speak on computer crime at my Rotary Club meeting in Palo Alto, California. He did not know much about the subject; so he must have quoted what he read in the last newspaper story about it, which stated an annual loss of $85.4 million. A newspaper reporter in the audience heard the speech and published the same number in his newspaper, and attributed the number to the FBI. This amount then became the number of choice around the world—directly attributable to the FBI.

Joking aside, our society is highly dependent upon numbers, yet we have little understanding of the meaning of numbers. The public will accept any statistic about crime or any number on any subject in print, and the more non-zero digits there are in the number, the more validity it conveys.

(continued)

> I make a hobby of tracking computer crime statistics to their sources to prove that they are nonsensical numbers. It is easy to do, especially in the case of such nonsense as "Only one in one hundred computer crimes is reported." How would anybody know what proportion is reported, if the number not reported is unknown? I have found loss figures ranging from $555 million (three digits of precision!) to $13 billion per year, and none of the sources can explain why their number differs from the rest. None report statistical error variances with their numbers. None has spent more than a few dollars conducting informal surveys using statistically invalid informal survey techniques. If you have not spent at least twenty thousand dollars on a survey, it is probably not worth anything. (Many victims refuse to admit their losses in survey questionnaires or publicly, and it is a violation of their security and an imprudent business practice to reveal the losses in response to unofficial inquiries.)

organization's circumstances differ significantly from the average incident represented in the statistics. Unfortunately, the limited surveys that are conducted on cybercrime are often conducted by individuals who are unfamiliar with cybercrime. Each survey respondent has a different definition of cybercrime and may be unaware of what actually happened, how it happened, or what the actual losses were. In addition, many victims do everything they can to avoid revealing their actual losses.

In all fairness, media coverage of cybercrime is improving as journalists become increasingly computer literate. Some of the better reporting comes from such journalists as John Markoff at the *New York Times,* Lou Dolinar at *USA Today,* Joshua Quittner at *Time,* and the freelancer Jonathon Littman.

DISTORTED PORTRAYALS OF CYBERCRIME IN THE ENTERTAINMENT WORLD

Movies, television programs, and novels often distort cybercrime. Some distortion is not deliberate but results from the failure of security experts to successfully communicate the concepts of computers and cybercrime to authors, screenwriters, and film directors. However, many of these individuals have a solid understanding of computers, but they know that human interest, not a computer, makes the best story. They often take literary license—anthropomorphizing the computers for entertainment because computers are actually boring, inanimate boxes, and even the computer displays leave a lot to be desired as entertainment. The role of computers in movies is to make noise, blink lights, display futuristic intelligent capabilities, and accentuate the human interest. Some of the classic films using computers include *Metropolis* by Fritz Lang, *Colossus: The Forbin Project*, and *WarGames*. More recent ones include *Sneakers, Hackers*, and *Jurassic Park*.

Deceptive Cyberfilm Techniques

We've all learned these basic tenets from the movies:

- Computer users, operators, and technicians always wear clean, white coats with badges and several pens in each pocket. They often carry clipboards and know instantly how to use anybody else's computer. Hackers, well . . . look like hackers and can do anything.
- All monitors display inch-high characters and three-dimensional, active animation with photorealistic graphics, and reflect themselves onto the faces and glasses of both heroes and villains.
- All computers interact with plain, free-form English. Typing "ALL OF THE SECRET FILES" on the keyboard gets you everything you want.
- Any encrypted data can be immediately decrypted while the ciphertext is being morphed into plaintext on the screen, and passwords can be guessed in a couple of obvious tries.
- Computers beep, fan motors hum, and tape reels spin, indicating intense electronic work underway, and nothing takes more than two seconds.
- All computer panels have hundreds of flashing lights and unlabeled buttons and switches, which produce bright flashes, puffs of smoke, showers of sparks, and explosive forces that blow people away, and the events propagate to cause destruction of hardware, entire rooms, buildings, and sometimes whole cities.
- Computers never have uninterruptable power supplies, backup, or disaster recovery plans.
- Eavesdropping on others' computers using directional radio antennas is always instantly successful.
- All electronically operated doors and gates, power plants, atomic reactors, and other computers around the world can be instantly connected to the villain's or hero's computer.

In *WarGames,* the Whopper computer had thousands of blinking lights that a woman in a white lab coat noted on a clipboard. She could not possibly have discerned anything useful from those lights in the limited amount of time available before the Whopper blew up in a cloud of smoke and flames when its "logic" was exercised too vigorously in playing games of tic-tac-toe. *Sneakers,* the second hacker movie by the writers and producers of *WarGames,* was a little more believable, but retained the blinking lights and wild screen displays that would drive a computer user crazy. These writers and producers are now making the third movie of a cybercrime trilogy, and they are finally using computers as tools to create the story. Perhaps it will be more accurate as a result.

The more recent movies *The Net* and *Hackers* are ho-hum routine computer stories for today's computer-jaded audiences. Advertisements for *Hackers* glorified young hackers who "rollerblade by day and battle against local law enforcement and the FBI on the Information Superhighway by night." The Web page that advertised the film encouraged everyone to "hack the planet," and solicited descriptions of hackers' "best hacks." At least, the Web page displayed this information before hackers attacked it and replaced the information with pornographic images.

The movie *Jurassic Park* actually has more to do with computer security—or lack thereof—than with ancient animals. By demonstrating incredibly poor information security, it could be used as an effective security training film on what not to do. It depicts at least a dozen serious breaches of information security practices—beginning with the remnants of food and drink left sitting on the computer. That the lone programmer who created the software single-handedly operates a computer as important as the one that controls the confinement of dangerous beasts is an absurd notion. The lack of an uninterruptable, independent power source for the system is equally idiotic. Unfortunately, such gross security violations still occur in the real world, although usually not all in the same organization.

Some recent novels about cybercrime include a good murder mystery, *Interrupt* by Toni Dwiggins, William Gibson's science fiction *Neuromancer,* and Tom Clancy's books about military heroes who can do no wrong. Screenwriters and novelists often exaggerate and distort computer capabilities to enhance the human drama; the events in actual cybercrimes are usually too outlandish and irrational to be believed in current fiction. But writers are improving the accuracy of their descriptions of computer technology with the help of outside experts and their own increasing experience with using computers.

CYBERCRIME LAW

As noted earlier, despite the media hype and high-tech labels, cybercrimes are basically nothing new under the law; they are the same types of crimes that have existed since our ancestors began trading goods and services. Although the tools and targets are certainly different, embezzlement still involves a breach of trust or fiduciary responsibility, and larceny still involves taking property that is owned by someone else with the intent of converting it to gain or depriving the owner of its use or possession.

While the Commercial Code adequately addresses all forms of business crime, the relevant statutes do not address a key difference between traditional business crime and cybercrime—treating information as intellectual property, and attaching all of the usual rights and privileges of property versus ethereal electronic information that we can't see or touch. This concept is critical in determining what crime (if any) has occurred, and when. For example, the major distinction between larceny and embezzlement lies in the issue of legal custody of the stolen article. In larceny, the thief never attains legal custody. In embezzlement, however, the thief is legally authorized by the owner to possess the article for some amount of time. The formulation of intent to steal the article may occur after it comes into the perpetrator's custody or concurrent with the initial possession. If the initial possession and intent to steal occur simultaneously, the crime is larceny. If the intent to steal occurs after the initial authorized possession, the crime is embezzlement. If the stolen article is information in the form of computer files, it is particularly difficult to establish possession and ownership, let alone the moment of intent to abuse or misuse. Similarly, embezzlement often involves forged documents and is addressed by forgery laws. Counterfeiting, in contrast to forgery, involves the production of a totally false document. In cyberspace, the law is concerned with what constitutes evidence of forged electronic documents and with the production of nearly perfect counterfeit documents by desktop graphics systems.

State legislatures began enacting computer crime laws in the 1970s. Nearly all states now have such laws, but the considerable differences among them make multi-jurisdiction cybercrime prosecution complex at best. The Federal Computer Fraud and Abuse Act (CFAA) of 1986 (18 U.S. Code, Section 1030) represents the government's attempt to deal with multi-jurisdiction cybercrime. Congress amended the legislation in 1994 to correct deficiencies that became apparent in the 1988 Internet Worm case (in which a student was successfully prosecuted under the CFAA for infecting more than 6,000 computers on the Internet) and the proliferation of computer viruses. Under the current version, now called the National Infrastructure Protection Act of 1996, it is an offense to merely "cause the transmission of a computer program, command, code, or any information, knowingly and as a result of such conduct, intentionally causing damage to a computer." While the wording is ungrammatical and awkward, damage to a computer is liberally interpreted to include affecting the informational content of a computer in a harmful manner as well. The CFAA defines a computer as "an electronic, magnetic, optical, electrochemical, or other high speed data processing device performing logical, arithmetic or storage functions, and includes any data storage facility or communications facility directly related to . . . such device." The only devices specifically excluded in the statute's definition of computers are "automated typewriters or typesetters and portable hand-held calculators."

The evolution of the CFAA's definition of computers is both humorous and revealing. An early draft defined a computer as an "electronic device." When I challenged legislators to specifically include other types of computers, including magnetic, optical, chemical, biological, mechanical, hydraulic, and pneumatic types, they added these descriptors to the bill, excluding—at the last moment—automatic typewriters (whatever they may be), portable hand-held calculators, and typesetters. Unfortunately, the description does not fully recognize ongoing changes in computer and communication technology. It doesn't, for example, differentiate between a single computer and two or more computers that communicate over a network, and doesn't deal with devices with embedded computer processor chips, such as small calculators, cash registers, telephones, and gasoline pumps. These omissions sometimes provide openings for defense attorneys to argue the relevance of the law to their clients' crimes.

The general understanding of information security, based on the CIA foundation, also poses some additional problems for cybercrime prosecution. This definition limits the interpretation of damage to information to impairing its integrity or availability. Thus, a perpetrator may harm the authenticity or utility of information without penalty, because integrity does not mean validity, and availability does not mean usefulness. Some jurisdictions are dealing with the need for better definitions. California, for example, has amended its computer crime statute several times to make it applicable to current technology.

The current U.S. Sentencing Guidelines for judges, the Commercial Code, and evidentiary laws are still adequate to prosecute many cybercrimes. New laws in the works cover everything from cyberspace commerce to the export of cryptography products. In addition to their role in bringing criminals to justice, some criminal statutes have a potential deterrence value and are crucial for ensuring that law enforcement agencies receive adequate budgets and resources to enforce them.

There are two basic rules that law enforcement organizations should follow in investigating and prosecuting cybercrimes: Try to investigate and prosecute a case by assuming that no computer was involved, and, if you cannot avoid the role of the computer to make the case, get an expert on that particular computer to assist with the investigation and prosecution.

THE FUTURE OF CYBERCRIME

I can make a few predictions about the future of cybercrime and its effect on our use of information:

- The future will bring new cybercrimes that we have not anticipated. Information security practitioners need to be perpetually alert to recognize them. My more detailed and complete foundation and lists of abuses and misuses described in Chapter 10 may be of help in analyzing them and devising new security safeguards to prevent them.
- We won't see an end to new cybercrimoids with cute names any time in the near future. Because they gain, and hold, the public's attention, the media are likely to continue emphasizing this type of computer crime. The press would probably not have given so much attention to computer viruses if they were called *harmful replicating codes.*
- A stream of new technologies will be the targets of criminals using ingenious new techniques that system designers naively, or in their haste, ignore. For example, *push* and *agent* technologies, in which unattended software works to find and deliver previously specified types of information and services, are ripe as subjects and objects of subversion and as tools for crime. Other new technology examples include speech recognition products, authentication of user identity services (certificate authorities), three-dimensional displays for applications like spreadsheet computing, and commercial use of the Internet. Embedded systems in smart homes, toys, appliances, clothing, sports equipment (such as skis and golf clubs), and vehicles are also attractive for exploitation and candidates as subjects of new cybercrimoids.

The prospects from the criminal's point of view must be mouth-watering.

C H A P T E R 4

Computer Abuse and Misuse

We need to know as much as possible about abuse and misuse of computers to effectively protect our information. Knowledge of vulnerabilities and controls alone is not sufficient. This chapter describes ten insidious types of crimes that are associated with computers in the roles of subjects, objects, tools, and symbols, and suggests some means for preventing such attacks.

As I mentioned in Chapter 1, computers are the subjects of crime in computer virus distribution, Trojan horse attacks, logic bomb use, and *data diddling*—my term for putting false data into computers. Computers can also be the targets of crimes, as in theft of them, or serve as the tools for committing crime, as in counterfeiting and forging. In some cases, computers play an indirect role in crime, as when used as a symbol for deception, such as in falsely advertising the use of a computer or to facilitate computer virus hoaxes. This chapter also discusses software piracy and the issues associated with privacy violation, espionage, and information warfare. (I've saved the discussion of computer crimes associated with computer networks for the following chapter.)

Access versus Use

Access is an unfortunate term applied to computers that causes considerable confusion, especially with regard to criminal law. We understand what it means to access or approach and enter a physical location, but entering a computer is downright impossible. We approach a computer at the moment that we initiate an electrical signal in a circuit, such as flipping an on-off switch or depressing a key on a keyboard. If electrical power is present, the computer reacts to the electrical signal by immediately executing a program—often the boot program. In reality, we have approached and *used* the computer, and would do well to say so using the correct terms—approach (or enter information) and use.

Similarly, we should abandon our use of the term *access* with regard to information and networks. We locate information and/or open information files. When we use a network, we send or receive messages, or monitor information that passes through the network. In both cases, *use* is a more precise—and more accurate—descriptor of our actions than *access*.

COMPUTER VIRUSES AND RELATED CRIMES

The news and entertainment media have perverted the use of the word *virus* to a point that it is confusing for even the most knowledgeable computer users. Any program or code that does harm is correctly referred to as malicious, but it is not a virus if it does not have the means to propagate or replicate itself. Viruses actually convert computer programs into a form of Trojan horse computer programs, and are closely related to logic bombs, but there are some differences between these types of crime tools, which I will describe in the following pages. The one thing that these crimes—along with trapdoor attacks, spoofing, and data diddling—have in common is that the computer is the *subject* of the crime.

Computer Viruses

A computer virus is actually a specific type of malicious code that replicates itself and inserts copies or new versions of itself in other programs when it is executed with the infected program. Inserting itself usually means that it replaces an instruction in the target program with an instruction to transfer control to the virus, which is stored elsewhere in the memory. Whenever the program transfer instruction is executed, it dutifully transfers control to the virus program, which then executes the replaced instruction and performs its dirty work of inserting itself in other programs. The virus program then transfers control back to the infected program where it left off, leaving no other trace of any change. In a slightly more sophisticated virus scheme, the virus may append code to the target computer's operating system that puts a modified virus code into other programs.

The dirty work performed by the virus payload may be as simple as letting the user know it is present, or something as insidious as destroying the entire contents of the computer memory. We generally consider computer viruses to be parasitic because they do not usually kill the host programs and permit them to function normally after infecting others. However, some viruses do carry harmful payloads that attack the host system; they may destroy or change data files or do other kinds of damage.

There are presently more than 10,000 identified viruses that affect the PC and Apple operating systems. In addition, a few viruses affect other operating systems such as UNIX. There are, however, no known viruses that attack the large-scale mainframe computer operating systems. This is probably because the virus makers have easy access to the desktop and laptop computing environments, and because of the proliferation and casual exchange of software for these environments.

Computer viruses reached crimoid status in 1987 when *Newsday* published an article by Lou Dolinar that described three viruses that had

The Killer Computer

The media typically label any malicious software meant to attack a computer as a virus. The Fox Network's X-Files TV episode titled "The Killer Computer" provides a good example of the misuse of the term virus. This episode tells the story of a computer that takes on a mind and will of its own, kills a few people, and challenges its creator to stop it. The creator, a crazy computer genius, then writes a program, which the characters in the story refer to as a virus, to destroy the killer computer. In reality, that program is not a virus; it is simply a set of computer instructions intended to stop the killer computer. (In a somewhat predictable ending, the killer computer starts coming back to life as the curtain closes.)

appeared within a two-month period. A number of software companies responded to the apparent epidemic, introducing virus protection products. These companies were accused (undeservedly, in my view) of stimulating the virus writers to engage in a one-upmanship game of virus and antivirus escalation and competition. The one-upmanship among malicious virus writers continues today with the emergence of macro, encrypted, and polymorphic viruses. In addition, program tools for writing viruses are available on the Internet to help unskilled malefactors develop new viruses.

Although viruses cannot be activated in data files because data files are not executed as programs, viruses can be activated through execution of imbedded or attached macro programs that accompany data file documents. When a user executes a word processor program (e.g., Microsoft Word) to open a file for viewing, the embedded or attached macro programs are automatically executed to format the data contents. Macros can be infected with *macro viruses* that also execute when the user opens a file. This type of virus (most notably, *Microsoft Word Concept, Impostor,* and *Wazzu*) is becoming increasingly common. The bizarre *Maddog* virus, for example, changes the letter *a* to *e* throughout infected documents that happen to be in use at 8 PM on any day.

An *encrypted virus* is one that can encrypt and decrypt itself. The encrypted part hides the virus function and the secret key it uses. When the virus infects a program, the decryption part, which is not encrypted, decrypts the encrypted part using the key it was last given and executes the virus payload. After doing its dirty work, the encryption part re-encrypts the virus function—using a new secret key each time—and passes it, along with the key, to the encrypted part for the next decryption. This technique hides the body of the virus and makes it appear different in each reincarnation. Only the decryption part remains the same. The objective of the encrypted virus writer is to leave as little code as possible that can be recognized as part of a virus (called the virus signature). Fortunately, good antivirus software can usually recognize this type of signature, even though it may be only ten or fifteen bytes long.

A *polymorphic virus* is slightly more sophisticated than an encrypted virus. It creates a new decryption part to perform the decryption, and uses a different set of instructions each time it is replicated. Antivirus forces have created a new weapon to use against polymorphic viruses. The *Generic Decryption Scanner* has three parts: a computer software emulator (virtual computer) that acts like a real computer within the computer; a virus signature scanner that looks for clues to infected programs; and an emulator controller. The controller executes the program suspected of being infected, along with the virus if there is one, in the computer emulator. It looks for telltale signs of infection during execution. The host computer cannot be damaged because the virus is executed in the self-contained virtual computer environment.

Limited Prosecution of Virus Writers

One of the few prosecutions for malicious hacking took place in England in 1995 and ended with a guilty plea. The case—the first of its kind in British legal history since passage of the Computer Misuse Act in 1990—followed an investigation by Scotland Yard. The perpetrator, known as the Black Baron, was a twenty-six-year-old unemployed computer programmer. He pled guilty to hacking into business computers and planting the computer viruses known as SMEG/Pathogen and SMEG/Queeg.

Eleven charges, including one for inciting others to plant the virus encryption kernel in new viruses, stemmed from his activities during a period between October 1993 and April 1994. The viruses gained the attention of anti-virus developers around the world when they were distributed through the Internet and freely circulated in the computer underground. The Baron even distributed a sample virus through virus exchange underground bulletin board systems. According to British authorities, tracing the viruses and repairing the damage that they caused cost "well in excess of half a million pounds."

According to newspaper reports, in 1993, another English virus writer, the president of ARCV (Association of Really Cruel Viruses), was arrested in connection with telephone fraud charges. A year earlier, the Australian news media identified a student at the University of Queensland who was allegedly responsible for writing and releasing the Dudley and NoFrills computer viruses. At various times since then, these viruses infected SunCorp, a large Australian insurance firm; Australian Telecom; and the Australian Taxation Office, which is similar to the IRS in the United States. In America, a teenager is reported by a newspaper to have admitted writing a number of viruses that victims unknowingly spread widely throughout cyberspace. His Satan Bug crashed U.S. Secret Service networks in 1993. Since then, another of his creations known as *Natas* ("Satan" spelled backwards) became one of the most common computer viruses in the Americas. To date, none of these latter virus writers has been prosecuted, as far as I know.

For more information about the ongoing war between virus writers and virus protection techniques, refer to the January 1997 article by Carey Nachenberg in the *ACM Communications Journal.*

MALICIOUS HACKERS

The people who create and release viruses are malicious hackers. We don't know a lot about these hackers because, with some exceptions (see the related sidebar), remarkably few have been publicly identified or prosecuted.

VIRUS HOAXES

The Internet is continually flooded with information about computer viruses and Trojan horse attacks. Computer virus hoaxes are deceptively interspersed among notices of real viruses. While these hoaxes do not infect systems, they can be time consuming and costly. In 1996, a bulletin from the U.S. Department of Energy Computer Incident Advisory Capability (CIAC) (http://ciac.llnl.gov, tel. 921-422-8193) identified several Internet hoaxes, provided a history of hoaxes, and explained how to identify a hoax. CIAC is now spending more time debunking hoaxes than handling real virus incidents—issuing advisories to address warnings that appear on the Internet.

Understandable (if unnecessary) paranoia fuels the virus hoaxes that continue to flood the Internet. For example, the *Good Times* virus hoax started in 1994 and is still circulating through the Internet today. Instead of spreading from one computer to another by itself, Good Times relies on word of mouth to pass it along.

Successful virus hoaxes incorporate two key ingredients: technical-sounding language and credibility by association. If a warning uses the proper technical jargon, many individuals—including technical experts—tend to believe it is real. For example, the Good Times hoax report says that "if the program is not stopped, the computer's processor will be placed in an nth-complexity, infinite, binary loop which can severely damage the processor." Although this sounds convincing when you first read it, a little research reveals that there is no such thing as an nth-complexity infinite binary loop, and that processors are designed to execute loops of program instructions forever without damage.

Credibility by association refers to the individual or group that initiates the warning. If the janitor at a large technological organization sends a warning to someone outside of that organization, people on the outside

The Really Nasty Virus Hoax

According to D. Ferbrache in his book, *Pathology of Computer Viruses* (© 1992 Springer-Verlag, quoted by permission), one of the first known computer virus hoaxes took place in October 1988. The hoax, known as the 2400-baud modem virus, was introduced in a memo from computer user Mike RoChenle and billed as "probably the world's worst computer virus yet."

RoChenle went on to describe his "discovery" of the virus during a late night bulletin board session in which he was attempting to download files. Instead of a normal download operation, he claimed to have stumbled into a virus that corrupted his computer's hard disk drive, distributing itself on the modem subcarrier present in all 2400 baud (and higher) modems. According to RoChenle, the modem, once infected, transmitted the virus to other modems that used a subcarrier. The virus then attached itself to all binary incoming data and infected the host computer's hard disk. Although it was possible to eradicate the virus from the modem by resetting all of the virus registers by hand, there was no known method of preventing the virus from spreading. Because 1200 baud modems were immune to the virus, bulletin board users were advised to drop down to 1200 to avoid the virus.

The bogus virus description spawned a humorous alert by Robert Morris III. According to Morris, a new virus was on the loose, entering computers via the power line to change the serial port pinouts and reverse the direction in which disks spin. Morris credited his imaginary virus with infecting more than 300,000 systems in Murphy, West Dakota in only 12 minutes.

Morris then issued the following tongue-in-cheek guidelines to avoid spreading the virus:

1. Don't use the powerline.
2. Don't use batteries either, since there are rumors that this virus has invaded most major battery plants and is infecting the positive poles of the batteries. (You might try hooking up just the negative pole.)
3. Don't upload or download files.
4. Don't store files on floppy disks or hard disks.
5. Don't read messages. Not even this one!
6. Don't use serial ports, modems, or phone lines.
7. Don't use keyboards, screens, or printers.

(continued)

> **8.** Don't use switches, CPUs, memories, microprocessors, or main-frames.
>
> **9.** Don't use electric lights, electric or gas heat or air-conditioning, running water, writing, fire, clothing, or the wheel.

tend to believe it is real. The prestige of the company backs the warning, making it appear authentic—even if the individual sending it doesn't know anything at all about computer viruses.

According to CIAC, there are several methods to identify virus hoaxes. You should be suspicious of a hoax if a virus warning advises you to pass the information along to your friends. Similarly, a warning that claims to be from the Federal Communications Commission (FCC) should raise a red flag. According to the FCC, it has not disseminated warnings on viruses (and never will); such warnings are not a part of its responsibility.

CIAC recommends against circulating virus warnings without first checking with an authoritative source such as an information security manager, an antivirus vendor, the computer science department of a local university, or a computer incident advisory team. These authorities usually have current information about known viruses and warnings. You can also call or check the Web site of the company that produces the product that is supposed to fight the virus. For example, checking the PKWARE Web site for the current releases of PKZip would stop the circulation of the warning about PKZ300, since there is no released version 3 of PKZip. Another useful Web site is the Computer Virus Myths home page (www.kumite.com/myths/), which contains descriptions of known hoaxes.

Real warnings about viruses and related security problems are issued by a number of response teams including the CIAC, and are digitally signed by the sending team using PGP cryptography. If you download a warning from a team's Web site or validate the PGP signature, you can usually be assured that the warning is real. Warnings without the name of the person sending the original notice or warnings with names, addresses, and phone numbers that do not actually exist are probably hoaxes.

Upon receiving a warning, you should examine its PGP signature to be sure that it is from a real response team or antivirus organization. To do this, you will need a copy of the PGP software and the public signature of the team that sent the message. The CIAC signature is available from the CIAC Web server. If there is no PGP signature, check to see if the warning includes the name of the person submitting the original warning. If possible, contact that person to verify that he or she actually wrote the warning. If there is any question as to the validity of the warning, send it to the experts and let them validate and distribute it. When in doubt, do not release a virus warning to others.

Trojan Horse Attacks

Trojan horse attacks are accomplished by secretly inserting malicious computer instructions into other people's programs. Computer viruses spread to other programs and computers (when users innocently pass infected programs to one another) using the Trojan horse technique. When the victims execute their programs—now Trojan horse programs—the malicious instructions execute as well.

The secretly inserted code in a Trojan horse program is considered a virus if it perpetuates itself in other programs, but otherwise, it does its dirty work from within the program in which it is hidden. The code can engage in any malicious act within the privileges of the host program, or break out to operate with any other program or by itself. Criminals use Trojan horse attacks to commit fraud, embezzlement, theft of services, sabotage, and espionage.

Unfortunately, the Internet facilitates Trojan horse attacks to some extent. Some Web sites insert a "magic cookie" into the *cookies* file of a user's computer when the user visits the site. The cookies file, which retains information about the user and browsing preferences, can be useful for both the Web site proprietor and the user, but it can also be a Trojan horse to introduce malicious code that can harm the computer or invade the user's privacy. It is important to remember that when you visit a Web site, it is also visiting your computer. For that reason, it's a good idea to avoid questionable sites, just as you would avoid going into sleazy-looking commercial establishments, and delete cookie files before Web sites use them to cause you harm.

Although hardware Trojan horses are quite rare, they too can pose a danger to computer security. *Chipping,* the term used to describe the process of creating a hardware Trojan horse, involves inserting secret circuits directly onto microchips during the design and manufacturing phases. Kevin Mitnick, the malicious hacker I introduced in an earlier chapter, was attempting to remotely insert data into a chip design specification file in a Motorola computer before he was arrested on other charges. Although chip manufacturers occasionally find logic flaws in their chip products, the flaws are (as far as I know) the result of errors rather than purposeful attacks and therefore do not qualify as Trojan horses.

Bomb Attacks

A *logic bomb* is computer instruction coding in a program that triggers the execution of a malicious act if and when certain criteria are met. Any change in value or state in a computer can trigger a logic bomb. For example, a specified time in a computer's time-of-day or day-of-year clock may trigger a time bomb. One programmer inserted code in his employer's computer and programmed it to trigger—and wipe out the company's entire personnel file—if his name was ever removed from the file.

Trapdoor Abuses

Computer programs are labyrinths of computer instructions, with multiple branches and entry points, as well as loops of instructions to be executed repeatedly, the last instruction transferring control back to the first one. An instruction may act on data, such as adding to a sum, or may transfer to another portion of the program, or to another program entirely, to execute instructions in sequence there. Programs are organized in groups of subprograms—self-contained objects that incorporate their own instructions and data as well as standard entry and exit points for the first and last instructions to be executed.

Security requires that programmers adhere strictly to the client's specifications when constructing programs and subprograms, but specifications are sometimes ambiguous and can be interpreted differently by different programmers. Programs are exceedingly complex at the level of the individual instructions, presenting the opportunity to cover a multitude of sins. For example, good practice requires that when program X calls upon the use of program Y, X provides only the data necessary for Y to do its job. The programming effort to gather all of the data together to pass them on to Y can be tedious; so a sloppy, simpler method is to make data available to Y by having X indicate to Y where the data may be found. Therefore, Y may access a larger array of data to pick out the data it needs. This violates the principle of least privilege by giving a program more data than it needs, and weakens the security in a system of programs. System designers should construct programs that function together in a computer to be suspicious of one another. This practice can significantly minimize the damage that a rogue program can do.

Programmers construct programs like large, complex buildings. They often insert temporary instructions that serve as scaffolding to support some unfinished parts of the program while they work on other parts. The temporary instructions are useful for representing unfinished portions of the program while testing the parts that are complete—allowing programmers to temporarily execute one part of the program at a time, with intermediate printouts to check partial results. Programmers are supposed to remove the so-called scaffolding if it is not part of the program specifications, but sometimes they retain the dummy instructions to serve as place marks for future changes or corrections to the program.

Trapdoors are sequences of instructions retained in programs, or purposely introduced into programs, for both good and malicious reasons. They may be redundant or unused transfer of control paths, dummy instructions, extraneous tasks, and entry or exit points that are not necessary. Malicious programmers take advantage of these trapdoors to engage in abuse. For example, in one case, when a programmer put the letter *E* in a numeric data input field from the keyboard, he programmed the payroll program to obtain its next stream of instructions from a data file. The programmer who included this trapdoor intended to use it to help debug the program at later times without having to change the program instructions. All he had to do was input a new data file with the instructions included in it and enter an *E*. A user of the program discovered the trapdoor and started using it, introducing a data file that caused the program to provide him with overtime hours that he was not entitled to every time he entered *E*.

The buffer overflow trapdoor is a particularly insidious programming error that criminals may exploit for their own purposes. A buffer is a location in memory that a program allocates for temporary data storage. If the program stores data in a buffer that exceeds the buffer size, the data overflows and overwrites whatever is stored in the adjacent area. Almost anything can occur then, depending on what the adjacent area contains. If it is program code, the computer executes the data as computer instructions. If it is not program code, the computer is likely to produce incorrect results. Every program should be sufficiently robust to provide buffer overflow detection, even though programmers dislike the extra efforts required to provide such protection. Without it, a criminal can input extra data to execute as program code or to replace correct data. If a program has overflow detection, the criminal has to subvert the detection code before modifying or supplementing the data. The most recently updated versions of commercial software are generally the safest because software vendors soon discover failures to detect buffer overflows and quickly correct them. In the past, early versions of UNIX and Microsoft's Windows NT operating systems have been particularly poor in detecting buffer overflow failures.

Asynchronous Attacks

Computer operating systems often perform tasks in an order different from that in which they are requested so as to take advantage of limited resources. TCP/IP networks (including the Internet) transmit packets of information that arrive at their destinations in different sequences than the order in which they are sent. This introduces the chance for flawed functionality, such as permitting programs to make undesirable changes between the time the information is validated and the time it is used. For example, an operating system queues printer jobs and may select the next job out of sequence if the printer is already set to handle that type of job. Ingenious criminals can use this asynchronous characteristic to exchange one print job under one user's name with the print job for another user. Security controls are bypassed by attacking information after the controls were applied (i.e., when the job is queued) but before the information is used (i.e., prior to printing). We refer to this type of attack as a time-of-check-to-time-of-use (TOCTTOU) attack. Unfortunately, such attacks are difficult to prevent unless we place execution of controls close in sequence to the use of the information and apply task sequencing that cannot be modified (such as by using cryptography).

Software Flaws

Software flaws are common, but some provide greater opportunities for abuse than others. Sometimes they even trip up the criminals, as was the case in a 1988 Internet worm case in which a computer science student was convicted of a federal computer crime. The student's flawed Trojan horse program, which he sent out over the Internet, went wild and propagated from computer to computer until more than 6,000 computers were saturated with copies of the program and had to be shut down. In this case the student exploited a vulnerability in a popular UNIX e-mail freeware product called *Sendmail*. The original program designer purposely incorporated the vulnerability in Sendmail as a convenience for programmers who maintained the software and updated the code. (Sendmail is still in use throughout the Internet, and many users probably have never updated it to remove this vulnerability.)

Criminals can—and do—exploit even the simplest flaws, such as a failure to limit the amount of data that can be placed in a fixed-length data field. No vendor or product is immune to such flaws, as illustrated by a problem in the HP-UX PASSWD buffer overrun. Due to insufficient bounds checking on password inputs in HP-UX system versions 9.x and 10.x, users could overwrite the buffer of the PASSWD(1) program while it is executing. By supplying a carefully designed password extension to the PASSWD(1) program, intruders could force PASSWD(1) to execute arbitrary commands. The extended password included the commands that were placed beyond the queuing space bounds into the program code, where they would have been executed. Since the PASSWD(1) program had privileged Setuid root status (allowing it to do anything), it might have allowed intruders to run arbitrary commands with root privileges. The vendor of this system cannot be considered negligent in this case, because the vulnerability exceeds human capacities to develop perfect computer systems. Nearly all vendors have had similar experiences.

The Therac-25 Accidents

Abuse can derive from pure negligence as well as from intentional acts. The best documented incident of negligence, that of the Therac-25 radiation therapy system, is described in an article ("An Investigation of the Therac-25 Accidents") by Nancy G. Leveson and Clark S. Turner that appeared in the July 1993 edition of *IEEE Software*. Therac-25 is a computer-based electron accelerator radiation therapy system that was implicated in six incidents from June 1985 to January 1987, including three deaths directly attributed to radiation overdoses.

The Therac-25 designers and manufacturer incorporated three flaws in the system: (1) enabling the operator to edit the command line in the control computer to change the state of the machine so that the machine began to deliver radiation before the changes in the command had taken place; (2) an ability to bypass safety checks when a program counter reached zero; and (3) removal of certain hardware safety interlocks leaving it to easily changeable software to perform those interlocks. The third, ultimately fatal, flaw allowed high dosage X-rays to directly enter patients' bodies. The high dosage was only supposed to take place when a target was in the line of fire to produce a safe electron beam for delivery to the patient.

The Therac-25 accidents demonstrate how system failures can be directly attributable to failures during the system development phase. The developers did not correctly anticipate and validate the ways in which the systems would be used. They failed to understand the users of the systems, and did not constrain them to safe procedures. In this case, the incidents were unintentional, but a criminal could have exploited the same flaws to intentionally harm—or kill—patients.

DATA DIDDLING

I use the term *data diddling* to describe the act of intentionally entering false information into computers, or intentionally modifying data in computers for some illicit purpose. Data diddling is probably the most prevalent type of computer crime; it requires no knowledge of computer programming and only limited knowledge of how the computer applications work. Unfortunately, the people who are authorized to enter data into computers do a great deal of serious crime. Over the years, such individuals have used data diddling to accomplish an impressive array of crimes, including accounts payable and receivable fraud, bank fraud, sabotage, inventory theft, and payroll fraud.

Data diddling generally destroys the authenticity of the information entered into computers. For example, a data entry clerk who was the girlfriend of the president of a motorcycle club in Sacramento, California changed the ownership of registered cars in the Department of Motor Vehicles computer to the names of car thieves. Car theft victims were unpleasantly surprised when they reported the thefts and discovered that there was no record of their ownership. The clerk changed the ownership records back to show the rightful owners after the thieves had time to resell the cars as their own. She was selling this service for one hundred dollars a pop until she was caught on camera after a thief spilled the beans and an undercover cop paid her for a sting theft.

SUPERZAPPING

Superzapping involves the use of utility programs to modify information in computers. It avoids or circumvents the approved application programs that process the information, and leaves no trail of evidence. The term for this method derives from Superzap, the well-known utility program used by computer operators and system programs to make changes directly to the memory system of mainframe computers.

Utilities are dangerous, albeit valuable tools, that should be used with care. In one case, a computer operations supervisor at a bank in New Jersey used a utility program to increase the balances of several friends' accounts. The friends withdrew the money as it arrived, and the supervisor destroyed the withdrawal slips. His plan was to stop the thefts before the end of the current audit period to avoid detection. His friends, however, were too greedy to stop and forced him to proceed further. When the auditors found the logged fraudulent transactions in the branch computer system (which the supervisor did not know about), they investigated to see who had the ability to cause the discrepancies. The supervisor was the only one to fit the bill.

Many information security managers recognize the vulnerabilities of utility programs and take care to carefully control and monitor their use.

COMPUTER LARCENY

Computer larceny involves the theft and burglary of desktop and laptop computers, as well as computer components. Such thefts have reached epidemic proportions in recent years and are continuing to increase, threatening to exceed the high frequency of IBM Selectric typewriter thefts during the 1970s. The gray market for stolen computers has now surpassed that of the stolen car market, and the situation is likely to continue to increase at an ever-accelerating rate as the miniaturization and portability of computers progresses. Insurance industry analysts estimate the current annual cost to U.S. business at more than $8 billion, and that figure covers only the value of the hardware, not the software or stored information, or business lost during recovery. One large bank is reporting the average loss of one PC per day worldwide. Burglaries seem to happen in local epidemics. For example, PCs worth several million dollars were stolen from Philadelphia suburban office complexes and industrial parks in only a few months in 1996.

Although the information stored in the stolen computers is often far more valuable than the hardware itself, many thieves do not yet realize this. When they do, of course, they have to figure out how to gain from the situation. Some, although relatively few, thieves are already taking advantage of the value of the computer content, using the information for extortion, espionage, fraud, or resale.

Stopping computer larceny requires applying the same types of security processes that we use to protect very small, high-value items, such as jewelry. Attaching bulky steel cables and padlocks to miniature computers (as we do to secure bicycles to telephone poles) is contrary to the trends of miniaturization and portability. Commercial services, such as the Stolen Computer Registry in Tivoli, New York (www.nacomex.com/stolen) and Comtrace Online Monitoring service (www.comtrace.com), are already registering the serial numbers of computers and computer parts to facilitate identification and recovery. Intel Corporation and other computer chip makers began to laser-etch serial numbers onto their products in 1995 in an effort to combat the problem of chip theft. (Computer chips are worth far more than their weight and volume in platinum, a fact that is well know by some burglary gangs.)

EXTORTION AND SABOTAGE

Employees, ex-employees, vendors, customers, and contractors are among the likely sources of extortion and sabotage attempts against software and data in computers. In two highly publicized cases of disputes over completion of, and payment for, software development, frustrated contractors secretly inserted logic bombs in software. The logic bombs were designed to destroy data or stop processing operations if the customers did not comply with demands for the completion of contracted payments.

Downsizing organizations during periods of economic recession can cause widespread discontent among employees, potentially increasing the frequency of extortion and sabotage incidents. Fragile electronic systems are subject to many kinds of physical attacks, ranging from sophisticated high-energy radio frequency guns (no use has been verified) to simple, but very effective, baseball bats, guns, gasoline, and explosives. Disgruntled users can saturate systems by exceeding limits of anticipated workloads. We can avoid most of these types of attacks by increasing our controls over physical access to systems, separating often unstable development systems from production systems, analyzing audit logs and following up on the information, and practicing humane staff reduction procedures.

INFORMATION ANARCHY USING ENCRYPTION

Information anarchy occurs when those who are not ultimately accountable for information encrypt it and have exclusive control of the keys. This danger is increasing in business and government organizations that fail to control employees' use of cryptography. Employees' use of strong cryptography without overriding independent key management and decryption capabilities can destroy the value of information and cause serious damage to the business or to the security of the organization.

Information encryption using secret keys is the most powerful security ever invented. Unfortunately, however, nearly anyone can misuse this type of control and cause great loss. Computer users can easily encrypt information with readily available software, hardware, and keys so that they are the only ones who can decrypt it. If an encryption process fails, or a user loses an encryption key, or does not cooperate with the owner of the information for any reason, the encrypted information may be lost entirely. Information that we must retain for long periods, such as audit logs and archival records, may be lost after being encrypted if the keys and/or the hardware and software needed to decrypt it become obsolete and plaintext copies are no longer available.

In many companies, employees accumulate privileges to use information as they move from one job assignment or position to the next. Managers assign information and systems use privileges, but sometimes fail to remove those privileges—even when the employee no longer works for the organization. An individual can capture information by encrypting it, then do anything at all with it—entirely free of constraints or observation. For example, an employee could safely encrypt trade secrets and transmit them from work facilities with impunity. Although the employee could use other methods to achieve the same results, such as downloading the information to diskettes and physically carrying them to other systems, none of the alternative methods offers the same ease, assured total control, and finality as encryption.

As organizations accumulate huge stores of information, they are forced into a position of greater trust as increasingly empowered employees seek to use and share that information. The military principle of need-to-know is often at odds with the need to share and disseminate information in the business world. And, sharing usually predominates—especially in organizations that apply the knowledge management strategies of modern business. But where do we draw the line on sharing information? Businesses are well advised to take periodic inventories of their information systems and review employees' rights to use that information, revoking and reissuing information access privileges to suit current personnel assignments and business needs.

Anyone can achieve absolute communications privacy by using strong cryptography that is impervious to cryptanalysis, even by government efforts. If individuals can communicate the information they control with absolute secrecy, they can violate their employer's and others' privacy with impunity by stealing, selling, or using their victims' information without detection. Absolute secrecy in communications allows small groups of geographically independent extremists, pornographers, and other criminals to advance their causes without fear of detection or prosecution.

DESKTOP FORGERY AND COUNTERFEITING

Loss estimates from desktop forgery and counterfeiting are enormous, stimulating an already growing concern for this misuse of computers. Cybercriminals can now forge business documents and create counterfeit ones at very low cost and with reasonable quality. Paper documents such as checks, entertainment and transportation tickets, and stocks are easy prey. The counterfeiters don't need anything more than relatively low-cost computers with graphics software, scanners for document digitizing, appropriate paper stock, and high-quality color printers. Counterfeiting and forgery are popular pastimes on many college campuses as students counterfeit sports and entertainment tickets and forge grades.

There are many opportunities to counterfeit or forge documents; and if criminals do encounter problems, they merely steal the necessary equipment to make new and better originals. In 1996, for example, after Florida purchased special computers to make driver's licenses that are virtually impossible to counterfeit, thieves broke into five driver's license offices and stole the computers and supplies that they needed to print counterfeit licenses.

Successful prosecutions for this type of computer crime are fairly commonplace because law enforcement agencies and courts are familiar with forgery and counterfeiting—regardless of how the documents are actually generated. The infamous malicious hacker, Cap'n Crunch, and several of his associates were convicted of counterfeiting San Francisco Bay Area Rapid Transit tickets in 1992. A Canadian criminal was convicted in 1988 of using a color copier to produce $24,000 in counterfeit $50 and $100 bills. One gang created phony checks printed with the name of a bank in Maine and the MICR code of a bank in Florida. The checks bounced back and forth between the two banks, each one alternately visually and automatically sorting the checks and incorrectly forwarding for payment to the other bank. The scheme came to an end when an alert bank clerk finally noticed that the name of the location of the bank was misspelled on the checks. This stopped the fraud, but not before the poor-spelling swindlers got away with a considerable amount of money.

Electronic document interchange (EDI) offers one natural solution to the problems of desktop forgery and counterfeiting, as do depository trust services, ticketless travel, and electronic money. These services eliminate the paper documents that can so easily be counterfeited and forged. But, because the use of paper is strongly embedded in our culture, many businesses are experimenting with the use of special inks, security threads in paper, secure document readers, high-quality etched and holographic images, substrate printing (watermarks), and microprinting. They are also training and motivating document handlers to be alert to counterfeit documents.

SOFTWARE PIRACY

The term *piracy* is much too glamorous for the harmful acts it represents. Copying and using commercial software that somebody else has purchased is common theft, and those who do it are thieves.

The practice that led to software piracy began back in the 1960s when computer programs were considered free-for-the-asking rather than commercial products. That was when the idea of the *SHARE Users Group* of IBM computer owners got started to share software and programming experience among many diverse companies. Programs that required hundreds of thousands of dollars of programmer time to develop were freely exchanged by companies such as North American Rockwell, AT&T, Chase Manhattan Bank, General Electric, General Motors, and my employer at the time, General Dynamics. The programmers who wrote the programs assumed that they owned them, and carried them from one job to the next. IBM gave away their software as part of their computer sales, and software development was considered a cost of doing business.

In those mainframe days when computers occupied entire rooms, the software actually cost more than the hardware. Companies seldom budgeted enough to produce software in accordance with sound engineering principles; development was left in the hands of programmers with little or no engineering training. Eventually, however, computer users began to realize the value of their programs and discovered that they could withhold useful programs from general distribution and barter them for other useful programs. The barter system soon gave way to direct sales. The software market became a reality by the end of the 1960s when management finally acknowledged that software was a valuable commodity. IBM and other vendors unbundled the software from the sale of computer hardware and sold it separately. The commercial software industry reached new heights with the advent of desktop computers in the 1970s, spawning a $75 billion market.

Unfortunately, however, at least from a commercial perspective, software buyers could easily copy the programs they purchased and then give or sell them to other users. Many people, especially programmers, never fully abandoned the concept of free software and carried their practice of sharing to commercial software products, and the software industry nearly floundered in its infancy. Today, it is still limping along because of unauthorized copying and distribution. Each copy of a commercial program that is pirated takes money away from software development efforts—slowing the creation of software required to match the rapid advances in computer hardware capabilities. Each time we purchase a commercial software product, some portion of the purchase price compensates, in part, for the hundreds or thousands of thieves who make and use illegal copies.

According to Carol Bartz, the president and chairman of Autodesk, Inc. (www.autodesk.com), software firms lose 20 percent of industry sales from piracy. The Software Publishers Association (SPA) (www.spa.org), which represents 1,300 software firms, and the Business Software Alliance (BSA) (www.iis.com/clients/portfolio/bsa.html) claim that the industry lost $13 billion in 1995 and in excess of $11 billion in 1996. Although losses are decreasing in the United States—where illegal copies account for 25 to 50 percent of the software in use—they are increasing elsewhere in the world. The SPA calculates software loss statistics for business users in countries outside of the United States by comparing the volume of a country's computer hardware imports to its software imports, focusing on 27 popular business applications. Although the resulting statistics are rough guesses, there is no doubt that the losses due to piracy are significant.

As an example of the impact of piracy, to paraphrase Bartz's comments, software firms are reluctant to pursue the educational market for fear that once they sell a few copies to schools, millions more will be illegally copied in the name of educating children. Schools have traditionally been one of the greatest sources of piracy, with teachers setting bad examples for their students by stealing software "for a good cause." School administrators and local governments share the blame for software piracy in schools by failing to budget appropriately for software purchases. Some software firms are now offering low-cost product licenses to schools in an effort to provide the necessary software and reduce piracy.

Other small software companies have just given up trying to control piracy and offer their products as shareware. They make the products freely available through the Internet and ask users for voluntary payments. In some cases, companies give their software away in hopes of selling upgrades. This strategy can be effective in capturing a market and has worked well in a number of instances (e.g., Netscape). Still other companies believe that piracy actually helps their marketing efforts by providing free advertising and helping to build a market. To some extent, however, shareware and free software practices weaken the distinctions between paid-for and free software and confuse the whole notion of commercial software.

According to Bartz, individuals who buy a few copies of a program and then make copies for their business associates are responsible for much of the piracy. Volume, assembly-line counterfeiters do not pose nearly as big a problem. For many firms, the Internet is viewed as the Home Shoplifting Network. Many hackers routinely collect illegal software just to have complete collections from each vendor—much like collecting baseball cards. Bartz estimated that AutoCAD had 90 percent of the computer-aided design (CAD) market in China, yet her company's sales there were negligible.

Technological solutions, such as using cryptography and embedded secret switches to restrict program use to the purchaser, have largely failed. Some software companies insert suicide switches in their programs that cause the software to stop working, or to cause damage, if the user fails to enter a code that must be purchased periodically from the vendor. This technique has resulted in civil suit damages against some imprudent vendors, as well as criminal prosecution for selling dangerous products. The technique doesn't win any points in a highly competitive industry either; other vendors are willing to sell programs without Mickey Mouse protective devices.

Software companies are now trying to encourage users to buy legitimate copies by including a range of features such as free or low-cost upgrades and good user support. They also offer site licensing with large discounts for unlimited copying and use of copies within organizations. The civil litigation efforts pushed by the SPA and BSA—bringing suits against companies that violate purchase contract agreements—are having some success. Many companies settle suits out of court to avoid the embarrassment of having their employees publicly identified as thieves. The associations also sponsor telephone hot lines (the SPA's hot line number is 1-800-388-7478) that make it easy for individuals to blow the whistle on their employers or associates for pirating software.

The FBI and other law enforcers are attempting to stamp out software piracy. The FBI Computer Crime Squad, which is based in San Francisco, teamed with Microsoft, Adobe, and Autodesk in an eight-month sting operation in 1996. Dozens of agents simultaneously raided homes and offices, confiscated computers, and shut down nationwide piracy rings in seven U.S. cities. Piracy rings operate underground through difficult-to-join BBSs and Internet chat boards through which their participants exchange and sell stolen software.

Intellectual property rights—and our society's view of such rights— are the underlying issues in software piracy. We cannot resolve the problem until we effect a change in moral social norms and piracy becomes unacceptable in respectable society worldwide. When other countries realize that unauthorized copying and use is damaging their own fragile software industries, their view of piracy may change. The demise of the free-software society of the 1960s and the arrival of individuals who realize that the successful, profitable sale of computers and software is essential to their future careers and personal success may do the trick.

PERCEIVED LOSS OF PRIVACY IN CYBERSPACE

Privacy is a poorly understood concept. Many people who should know better use *privacy* incorrectly as a synonym for confidentiality and sometimes even for information security. Privacy is a human right to limit the distribution of personal information and to control information about oneself. It is strongly implicit as a civil right in the U.S. Constitution and the Bill of Rights, and is an explicit civil right in several U.S. state constitutions and the constitutions of several other countries and the European Union. Privacy extends to a person's "personal space" as well. We consider intruding upon one's thoughts, computer, or office without due cause to be a violation of privacy. Merely gaining use of another person's computer without permission, even without observing or modifying anything, is a violation of that person's privacy.

Unlike the news media and many civil libertarians, I believe that the use of computers has resulted in a significant increase in privacy rather than a loss of privacy. We have more privacy today than we have had at any time in history, and our potential for privacy is still increasing—especially as the kind of information we consider private diminishes. Certainly, using computers offers a greater potential for privacy than printing our personal information on paper and storing it in manila folders and file cabinets where it is accessible to many people.

Concern for privacy today is rooted in the large-scale actions of governments, institutions, and businesses possessing and using (but not necessarily *knowing*) personal information about their citizens, customers, and employees. Individuals who believe that they have been subjected to an invasion of privacy can call on a veritable army of civil rights advocates for support. The news media regularly expose real and potential violations of privacy. All types of organizations around the world are under great pressure to protect privacy. Any institution or organization that violates— or even appears to violate—personal privacy faces prompt and vigorous redress by the news media, the ACLU, privacy advocates such as Robert Ellis Smith (publisher of the *Privacy Journal*, 5101719@mcimail.com), and a variety of anti-harassment organizations. Depending on the severity of the violation, the perpetrator may also face legal action in one or more courts. Virtually anyone has access to low-cost, effective redress, even if it consists of seeking assistance from the local media or consumer protection services.

Information security is essential in protecting personal privacy. In addition to protecting the confidentiality of information, we are concerned with the possession, accuracy, completeness, and validity of our personal information. And, of course, we are also concerned about the way in which such information is used, and the purpose for which it is used. We need to apply the six elements of security that I introduced in Chapter 2—availability, utility, integrity, authenticity, confidentiality, and possession—to address these concerns. Avoiding the use of a person's information to his or her detriment is not sufficient. To truly protect personal information such as that in a personnel file, we need to apply a combination of controls—using cryptography to protect its confidentiality; restricting users' rights to view, change, or use it; making backup or duplicate copies to ensure availability; and using transaction log checks to protect its validity and completeness.

Privacy violations occur when people see others' personal information whether the violators use the information or not. Computers are now doing many of the tasks that people used to do, and we've become accustomed to revealing personal information to computers rather than to people. In some companies, for example, employees can update their own personnel files through their PCs, inserting changes directly into the record without revealing potentially embarrassing details to another employee. This type of capability increases our perception of personal privacy, but leaves some questions unanswered. Is privacy violated when our personal information is stored in a computer that is not under our control? Is privacy violated when the computer uses it? Even if no one else knows the information?

There are four circumstances of loss of privacy to consider: (1) another person knows our information, (2) another person knows and acts upon the information, (3) a computer not under our control contains our information, and (4) the computer acts upon the information, but does not disclose it to anyone. For example, if you enter your own personal information into a computer and the computer subsequently uses the information to unfairly deny you use of your ATM card, has your privacy been violated? I would suggest that even though no other person has seen your information, the bank that owns and controls the computer has violated your privacy, but legally the jury is still out on this technicality.

Privacy protection is not just an issue in the United States. A 1995 directive from the European Union (EU) requires member nations, and many countries that do business with member nations, to establish privacy protection commissions and to comply with an elaborate set of privacy regulations. A number of countries, including Sweden, the United Kingdom, Germany, France, and Canada, have already established such commissions. To date, the United States has not complied with the directive, and faces sanctions from the EU.

The costs involved in establishing and maintaining privacy commissions and for registering and controlling personal information files are enormous and, in my view, unjustified. In reality, personal privacy can be accomplished most effectively on a smaller scale, employing targeted controls. Vertical legislation in the United States (e.g., the Fair Credit Reporting Act and Computer Fraud and Abuse Act) is effectively controlling large-scale alleged violations in the specific industries and organizations where personal privacy is a major issue (e.g., credit-reporting services, health care industry, and insurance companies). This type of targeted approach, combined with business and societal pressures to comply with the privacy guidelines published by the Organization for Economic Cooperation and Development (OECD) (www.oecd.org), is likely to be more effective in the long term than the mandated registration compliance procedures advocated by the EU.

The Netherlands, like the United States, is taking a moderate approach to privacy legislation. Between 1990 and 1995, more than 50,000 personal data files were registered through voluntary self-regulation with guidance from privacy codes of ethics in Holland. If self-regulation lags, however, the law authorizes the government to issue specific privacy regulations by decree. So far, it has not used this authority, which speaks well for the success of this approach.

The concept of what information should remain private changes continually. Today, there is less confidential information and thus less need for confidentiality than ever before in our history. People openly reveal personal information that would have been considered private only a few years ago. They willingly disclose medical problems, sexual experiences, religious beliefs, marital relations, and financial conditions on television talk shows, in bars, on airplanes, and in the company of strangers. The only information left to protect is the most sensitive, which requires both a thorough understanding of the nature of the information and strong measures, such as cryptography, to protect it. In applying security, we must first ask if it is necessary, then we need to determine what types of protection are required. Ensuring the possession and authenticity of such information may be far more important than its confidentiality.

INTERNATIONAL COMMERCIAL ESPIONAGE

Spying is as old as the beginnings of history. Moses and Joshua both employed spies, and Sun Tzu, the great Chinese general, wrote about the importance of spies in warfare in 400 BC. More recently espionage has played major roles in the twentieth-century wars. Today, the level of espionage activity is increasing, although the focus has changed from warfare to commercial enterprise. According to law enforcement agencies, many governments are blatantly spying on businesses based in other countries for the benefit of their own indigenous commerce (e.g., French government espionage activities against IBM and Hughes Aircraft). However, because most surveys of espionage activities include the huge, relatively open business of pirating software and recorded entertainment, the extent of secretive espionage activities such as stealing business plans and research data is difficult to determine. Even when such trade secret crime culminates in litigation, the settlements are often kept secret.

In 1996 the American Society of Industrial Security (ASIS) (www.asisonline.org) surveyed U.S. companies' industrial security managers. Although the survey failed to define clearly what constitutes a U.S. company or whether reported illegalities were based on U.S. laws or those of the other countries, the results are interesting. The survey ranked countries that have illegally acquired U.S. intellectual property by number of reported incidents in which citizens of the identified country were the perpetrators. The countries ranked from most to least frequently engaged in commercial espionage were: People's Republic of China, Canada, France, India, Japan, Germany, South Korea, Commonwealth of Independent States, Taiwan, United Kingdom, Israel, Mexico, Pakistan, Singapore, and Hong Kong. The list seems to roughly follow the same order as the size of country and extent of software piracy. Notice that the United States is not included in the list, which leads us to question the objectivity of the survey and leaves the most interesting question unanswered, of how often U.S. intelligence agencies, companies, and citizens engage in commercial espionage against non-U.S. companies.

Espionage is the murkiest type of crime and the one that we know the least about. In many cases, a business that possesses stolen information will contact the victimized company and quietly negotiate a means for

Cyberespionage

Cyberespionage is the term that has been coined to describe the use of computers and networks to obtain secret information. Although cyberespionage is closely linked to business espionage, the two are not synonymous because many incidents of business espionage do not involve computers or networks.

I receive occasional calls for help from victims of suspected espionage. The victims of these alleged crimes always focus on information in computers as the likely source of loss, especially if a competitor has gained some otherwise inexplicable advantage. When I ask how a competitor might obtain valuable business or product information, the victim almost always blames a hacker for attacking files in the computer system. But, when I inquire about the existence and location of printed documentation or diskettes containing backup programs and files, many alleged victims admit that such documents and copies do exist, often lying about in unlocked offices.

If thieves—competitors or otherwise—can obtain valuable information by picking it up and carrying it away from an unoccupied office or unguarded trashcan, why would they go to the trouble, and incur the potential exposure, of hacking into a computer system that has—at least theoretically—some degree of security? I always suggest that victims of business espionage first look into the simple explanations for information loss before they investigate the high-tech possibilities. Their investigation is likely to expose some very real, and potentially dangerous, vulnerabilities that can be remedied with relatively simple, nontechnical solutions such as locking doors and file cabinets and teaching people to be circumspect about revealing information. Stealing information from a computer system is usually a last-ditch effort that criminals adopt only when all other avenues appear blocked.

returning the information and sanctioning the perpetrator. According to the *Wall Street Journal* (www.wsj.com), this type of settlement is fairly routine in the oil industry. Media reports on business espionage are understandably scarce; businesses are reluctant to admit either committing espionage or being victimized by it. According to FBI Director Louis Freeh in his report to Congress, the Bureau investigated more than 800 cases of business espionage in 1996, twice the number of cases reported in the two previous years. Some of the nontraditional espionage methods revealed in the FBI report included the following, many of which do not directly involve the use of computers or wiretaps:

- Asking someone who has the information to reveal it, sometimes (but not always) in exchange for compensation
- Exploiting joint ventures and joint research, or directly purchasing parts or all of other companies
- Manipulating employees based on cultural, personal, or ethnic commonalities and vulnerabilities
- Marketing survey ploys for gathering competitive intelligence and offering alleged employment opportunities as a guise to solicit information from applicants eager to share their knowledge
- Intelligence gathering in public exhibitions, conferences, travel conveyances and terminals, clubs and bars, and restaurants
- Purchasing "information" services from individuals, including some information brokers who make espionage a business, and illegally obtained information their primary product
- Hosting visits from foreigners who act beyond the stated purpose of their visits

---

Visitor Alert

Although most visits by foreign businessmen are entirely legitimate and beneficial for both the host business and the visitors, security-conscious businesses are usually wary of visits and enforce some stringent regulations regarding visitor access to sensitive areas and information.

I once sponsored a Japanese banking group that was studying U.S. bank security systems. I arranged for them to visit the computer center of a large local bank. The bank, happy to display its systems and facilities to the distinguished group, opened its double mantrap security doors, and allowed the group to tour the computer room. Some members of the group took photos of everything they saw, including the S.W.I.F.T. funds transfer activity with screens full of active information. The visitors' study of security methods revealed some gaps that the bank had obviously never considered.

There is also an urban legend about some foreign visitors to U.S. manufacturing plants who coated the soles of their shoes with adhesive to pick up fragments of materials used in the manufacturing processes. While this story probably has no basis in fact, it does raise some interesting possibilities for covert espionage.

Confusion Abounds

The wording of the Economic Espionage Act illustrates the confusion that can result from a failure to recognize the difference between confidentiality and possession of information. Keeping information secure from theft is not the same as keeping information secret. What about the theft of encrypted information in which no secret is lost, only possession? The use of the words *secrets* and *espionage* make it clear that only knowledge is covered. The words from the act "to keep the information secret" and "the information derives economic value, actual or potential, by virtue of not being generally known" make it additionally clear that only secrecy of knowledge is at stake, not possession of data which is not knowledge. A computer program, for example, might not derive economic value by virtue of not being generally known. It derives value by virtue of not being in others' possession for use. Therefore, a computer program may not qualify as a trade secret under the statute unless knowing how it works is at issue.

Theft of information would be covered by larceny laws if the information is a commercial product or used in automatic systems as an intangible commodity. But, would the theft of a commercial computer program be covered by the espionage law or by the larceny laws? Strictly considered, we do not value software for the secrets it contains but for its possession to buy, sell, and use.

The new legislation also raises some difficult questions for employers and employees. Management must now rewrite employee confidentiality agreements to distinguish between "trade secrets," data not meant to be knowledge, and other proprietary, confidential information. Failure to distinguish among these elements could weaken the claim that information is a trade secret. How can employees know, before experiencing federal prosecution, whether the employer's claim that information is a trade secret is sustainable? The sponsors of the act argue that no prosecution should be brought when the employees merely take with them the accumulated knowledge and experience acquired during their employment.

Some governments even recruit malicious hackers to help them conduct business espionage. One leader of a hacker group in Germany told me that foreign government representatives approached members of his group to recruit them for espionage activities. According to Dr. Clifford Stoll in his book, *The Cuckoo's Egg,* the German hackers caught in attacks against U.S. government systems were actively conveying information to Russian agents. Malicious hackers and professional espionage agents are also teaming with informants inside target companies to obtain the information that they want.

The Economic Espionage Act

Until President Clinton signed the Economic Espionage Act of 1996, the U.S. government did not have a federal trade secret theft statute. The federal statute now supplements state trade secret laws by dealing with thefts by foreign governments and business organizations that are owned or managed by foreign governments, and thefts of information related to, or included in, a product that is sold in interstate or foreign commerce. The Act defines a trade secret to be financial, business, scientific, technical, economic, or engineering information, whether tangible or intangible and regardless of how it is stored. In addition, it specifies that the owner must take "reasonable measures" to keep the information secret, and requires the information to derive economic value (actual or potential) by virtue of not being generally known. Because the statute requires no specific security of the information, we must apply the standards of due care. Experience with state prosecutions of trade secret theft cases will probably provide guidance concerning the somewhat vague wording of the federal legislation.

Penalties under the Economic Espionage Act are up to $500,000 and 15 years in prison (10 years if a foreign government interest is not involved). The Act also gives the government the right to seize any proceeds from the sale of trade secrets or property obtained as a result of wrongdoing. Federal prosecutors are authorized to file civil proceedings for injunctions to prevent violation of the Act. Realistically, a $500,000 fine may be an insignificant penalty for stealing trade secrets potentially worth millions or billions of dollars. The legislation may require some fine-tuning before it can truly be effective in discouraging international business espionage.

INFORMATION WARFARE

Cybercrime is also raising international concerns in the arena of information warfare. The U.S. Department of Defense Science Board issued a chilling report in January 1997 that stressed the need for extraordinary effort because "current practices and assumptions are ingredients in a recipe for a national security disaster." It goes on to warn of a possible "electronic Pearl Harbor," predicting the attacks on U.S. information systems by terrorist groups, organized criminals, and foreign espionage agencies are likely to be widespread by the year 2005. The report, which was prepared by a task force of computer and information systems experts from the military, industrial, and academic sectors, recommends $3 billion of additional spending during the next five years to improve the security of the nation's telecommunications and computing infrastructure, and calls for the appointment of an "information-warfare" czar in the Defense Department. The *Wall Street Journal* called the study and report "a manifesto for warfare in the information age," a sentiment that was echoed by the President's Commission on Critical Infrastructure Protection in October 1997.

According to the report, the U.S. military is highly vulnerable to abuse of its 2.1 million computers and 10,000 local-area networks. It criticizes current Pentagon efforts as inadequate and urges the military to begin using a five-level warning system under which, as attacks are detected, information systems of the national security establishment would first be closely monitored and ultimately disconnected from outside information systems. Moreover, it reports that the U.S. telecommunications, electric power, banking, and transportation industries are vulnerable to attack by anyone seeking to confront the United States without confronting its military forces. "We have built our economy and our military on a technology foundation that we do not control and, at least at the fine detail level, we do not understand."

The report also calls for spending $580 million in the coming years on research and development, mainly in the private sector, in an effort to develop new software and hardware to provide security, including a system to automatically trace hacker attacks back to their origins. Defense Department systems, it said, should carry warnings to make clear the Department's "presumption that intruders have hostile intent and warn that the Department will take the appropriate response."

SUMMARY OF COMPUTER ABUSE AND MISUSE

Even after we gain an understanding of the various ways in which computers can be abused and misused to commit crimes, we don't necessarily have a clear grasp of the elements of an information security system that can effectively deal with the many and varied threats posed by abuse and misuse. Table 4.1, which compares misuse techniques with normal computer use, is based on research that I conducted at SRI International with Dr. Peter G. Neumann and Tom Lunzer on behalf of the U.S. Department of Justice. (For more details on this research and the resulting model, see *A Summary of Computer Misuse Techniques*, Twelfth National Computer Security Conference, Baltimore, 1989.)

The Misuse and Abuse model presents misuse and abuse techniques in the column on the far left (Misuse Techniques), and gives a few examples of each technique. The techniques are arranged in a descending hierarchy, listing those that are external to the computer at the top of the

TABLE 4.1   Model of Computer Misuse and Abuse

Misuse Techniques	*Computer Role*	*Normal Use*

External misuse
  Shoulder surf
  Misrepresent
  Scavenge
	Object	Approach

Hardware misuse
  Eavesdrop
  Physical attack
	Object	Power up

Masquerade
  User ID impersonation
  Spoof
	Symbol	Logon

Program attacks
  Trojan, virus attack
  Bomb attack
	Subject	Use applications

Controls bypass
  Trapdoor attack
  Violate authority
	Subject	System use

Active misuse
  Deny service
  False data entry
	Subject	Active use

Passive misuse
  Browse
  Observe
	Object	Active use

Failure to perform Omit duties	Subject	Perform
Indirect misuse Use in a crime	Tool	Proper use

model and moving downward to represent techniques that are internal to the computer and finally, those that reside within computer applications. For example, normal use consists of using a computer after approaching, starting, and logging on. Misuse means, for example, after a physical attack with the computer as the object, spoofing, with the computer as a symbol for a deception. To engage in program attacks using the computer as a tool is the next logical alternative. The final techniques (i.e., at the bottom of the model) represent indirect misuse, those that cause harm by inaction when actions are required. The column in the middle of the model (Computer Role) refers to the four roles that computers can play in cybercrime (as I described in Chapter 2). Lastly, the model indicates the computer's normal use, for comparison with the misuse, in the column on the far right.

5

Network Abuse and Misuse

Network abuse and misuse is essentially the same as computer abuse and misuse, except that it involves two or more computers linked to communicate. It also results in the same types of crimes as computer abuse and misuse: fraud, larceny, sabotage, and espionage. But the new technologies of our electronic age, especially the Internet, amplify and automate the effects of network abuse and misuse, enabling criminals to increase both the frequency and scope of their crimes—often with no more effort than traditional methods and with less likelihood of being caught. Networks permit criminals to put some distance between themselves and the scenes of their crimes, and make it possible to prey on hundreds or thousands of victims at a time. Credit card thieves, for example, can now steal and resell hundreds of thousands of card numbers in a single day using the Internet. In the past—before the advent of the Internet and computer-savvy thieves—the same type of criminal would be satisfied with stealing and selling ten or twelve cards in a day.

The multiple entry and exit routes inherent to networks significantly increase the vulnerabilities of computers to abuse and misuse. Dial-up communications exist between any two computers equipped with modems and connected to a telephone service. Once a computer is connected to a telephone service, callers around the world can—at least theoretically—use it. Local, metropolitan, and wide-area networks, which are all becoming increasingly common in our business and personal lives, are vulnerable to a variety of abuse and misuse techniques through the computers that serve as switches and hosts.

I'll begin this chapter by describing the network crimes perpetrated through the Internet, including methods used by Web site impostors, pornography peddlers, and stalkers, as well as "spammers" and "flooders." I'll then describe more general types of crimes that are based directly or indirectly on network use. These include personal identity theft, e-mail spoofing (impersonation), LANarchy (loss of control over LANs), and banking and business fraud. The chapter ends with a detailed description of automated crimes, which I introduced in Chapter 1.

INTERNET CRIME

The Internet is a non-secure network with more than one hundred million users around the world. One of the Internet's greatest strengths—its open anonymous nature—is also its greatest weakness, making it ripe for abuse and attracting attention from an array of unsavory individuals and advocacy groups including terrorists, neo-Nazis, pornographers, and pedophiles. Fraudsters of every stripe engage in securities boiler room operations, illegal gambling, Ponzi pyramid schemes, credit card fraud, and a variety of other illicit activities. In addition, legitimate businesses that send hundreds of thousands of unsolicited messages and advertisements over the Internet harm its effectiveness by saturating vital nodes and threatening to shut down some parts of the network. The Internet is many things to many people. Many of us seldom consider its darker side and potential for misuse, but we're all vulnerable to such misuse in one or more ways.

Web Site Authenticity Attacks

Web site authenticity attacks are remarkably common, and equal-opportunity, occurrences. The U.S. Department of Justice, the CIA, the Air Force, and the U.K. Labour Party have all been subjected to Web site attacks. In some cases, the damage is relatively minor—inserting graffiti or pornographic images into the pages or altering the text to deliver threats or taunts. But, even these relatively harmless acts erode the trust in the authenticity of Web sites and introduce the prospect for more harmful types of attacks.

While Web site developers and managers are accustomed to deleting the obvious results of an attack—erasing the juvenile messages and graffiti—they are often unprepared for dealing with more subtle types of attacks on the authenticity of information on their Web sites. A criminal can attack the authenticity of Web site information, for example, by modifying a price list or inserting advertisements for products or services that the business does not offer. Even if a business is not legally committed to sell products at the altered prices listed on the Web site (and this is still an open question), it is certainly open to criticism from existing or prospective customers.

Although there are many reasonable methods for protecting the authenticity and integrity of Web site information, many Web site providers ignore them until it is too late. Even after a Web site attack, most site owners fail to practice reasonable site security on a continuing basis—leaving the door open for criminals to sharpen their skills and exercise their imaginations in new, and increasingly harmful, Web site attacks. Methods for attacking and for preventing attacks on computers that operate Web sites to destroy their authenticity are described in the remainder of this chapter.

The Dirty War of Pornography and Cyberstalking

The Internet offers the most efficient means for distributing pornography since video stores and long overcoats with big pockets were invented. In a blatant misuse of network technology, the Internet is being flooded with an unprecedented level of pornographic text and video. Child pornography is the most insidious form of this blight.

A trade journal reported that a not-so-helpful individual advocates a somewhat dubious means for reducing the victimization of children in child pornography. He suggests using synthetic, computer-generated images of children in sexual graphical fantasies, taking advantage of computer animators' ability to make virtual people look real. A new type of pornography—without real actors and models—would flood the Internet, depicting the ultimate in Barbie and Ken orgies.

Law enforcement sting operations provide an effective means of exposing and prosecuting illegal Internet distribution of pornography because of the easy impersonation the Internet affords.

Internet stalking was introduced to the public in 1994 in an episode of CBS's *Eye to Eye* newsmagazine and a move called *Cyberstalker*. In both, real and fictitious "stalkers" used the Internet to threaten others with violence and death. Since that time, there have been numerous incidents of "cyberstalking," and some attempts to deal with the problem. The Internet Content Coalition (www.netcontent.org), for example, managed to convince the U.S. Parole Commission (www.usdoj.gov/uspc) to deny Internet and computer entry to certain high-risk parolees. But, despite the growing list of stalking incidents, there have been few practical suggestions for eliminating this type of Internet use.

Because cyberstalking is a worldwide problem, massive international cooperation is required to resolve it, and, despite some suggestions for high-technology solutions, only a radical change in moral values is likely to reduce it. In the meantime, the methods that law enforcement agencies are currently using with some success to lure child pornographers into legal entrapment offer some hope for apprehending stalkers. Ultimately, however, we will need to create and enforce new laws to deal with stalking on an international level—laws that preserve basic civil rights while still ensuring some level of decency in Internet use. Ubiquitous employment of cryptography to preserve the authenticity and integrity of information on the Internet, with international trusted third-party administration of keys, may provide another solution, but it also threatens to constrict the open and anonymous nature of the Internet.

IP Spoofing

Spoofing is generally defined as any type of deceptive impersonation using computers. Internet spoofing consists of sending messages with disguised return addresses through networks to make it difficult, or impossible, to trace the original source. IP spoofing changes the Internet Protocol (IP) source address to accomplish the same goal.

Internet criminals often need anonymity in their attacks on victims' computers to avoid apprehension. If you send an extortion letter through the U.S. mail, it is not wise to include a return address that could lead law enforcement agencies back to you. The Internet, however, has a built-in system for incorporating return addresses on all data packets. Criminals must circumvent this system by changing the IP address of each data packet that they send through the Internet in order to avoid detection and capture for their misdeeds. IP spoofing, which substitutes a legitimate IP address for that of the criminal's computer, provides this means.

IP spoofing is a form of misrepresentation. Criminals use this technique to avoid leaving a "trail" back to their computers and, sometimes, to lay a false trail to deceive their victims. If criminals use the forged IP address of a computer that they can monitor, they can also gain insights into how the victims respond to attacks.

Fortunately, changes in Internet communication protocols and the use of third-party authentication signatures are gradually making IP spoofing more difficult to accomplish. For more information about this technique, see the trade journal, *Network Security* (May 1996, Elsevier Publishing), article "Internet Holes, Part 9: IP Address Forgery and How to Eliminate It" by Dr. Fred Cohen. Also see *Dirty Tricks at War*, by James F. Dunnigan and Albert A. Nofi (Morrow and Co., 1995).

Web Spoofing

Web spoofing is a relatively new crime method that is more dangerous, and more difficult to detect, than IP spoofing. Although no successful Web spoofing attacks have yet been reported, the technique has been widely discussed in hacker magazines and bulletin board services and should be considered a very real threat in the near future. Web spoofing takes advantage of a vulnerability in the World Wide Web that allows any computer connected to the Internet to insert itself between another Internet user's computer browser and the Web. In that intervening position, the computer can be made to act like a provider of a Web site and can observe, steal, and alter any information passing between the unfortunate Web-browsing victim and the Web. The vulnerability extends to Web browsers currently in use, including some of the most popular Web browsers. Web spoofing is effective even if the connection to a Web site is apparently secure.

To initiate a Web spoofing attack, a criminal needs to gain control of a widely visited Web site, then alter it to act as an intermediary site. This alteration requires significant skill in Web-related programming. Alternatively, a Web spoofer could attempt to break in to well-known Web servers and install spoofing software there.

Users need not erroneously type a site name (as in the sidebar example) to be caught in a spurious Web environment, only visit a site that a perpetrator has compromised, then follow one of the altered links on the compromised Web page to the perpetrator's Web site. This allows users to visit any other Web sites, but inserts the spoofing Web server in the middle, where it is able to capture (and mediate) the user's Web communications. The only way for a user to safely leave this compromised Web page is to

A Web Spoofing Example

Ric Steinberger at SRI Consulting offers the following description of a Web spoofing attack, which involves establishing a malicious Web server, then deceiving Web users into entering a Web site using the malicious Web server as an intermediary.

When Web browser users visit a Web site, they usually type something similar to the following Web site address: *www.company.com*.

It is easy, however, to make a mistake and accidentally type *www.c0mpany.com*, using a zero instead of "o".

If *c0mpany.com* actually exists, a perpetrator can set up his Web site to mimic the real www.company.com site. And, he can keep this bogus site inserted between unsuspecting browser users and the "genuine" sites that they visit. If a user requests a secure Web connection, the perpetrator's Web site can set one up—but between the user site and the desired genuine site that the user wishes to visit. If Web users have their browsers configured to trust certificate authorities (which is often the default state for browsers), establishing what they perceive as a "secure" Web connection does not defeat the spoofing Web server.

directly type in a known, safe Web site address using an *Open Location* button, or to use a bookmark that points to a safe Web site address.

Web spoofing is possible because of the ways in which Web servers interpret Web site addresses. Browser users can "chain" together Web site addresses to allow them to visit the sites represented by the last "link" in the chain. For example, if a browser user (unknowingly) sent the Web site address *www.evil.com/http://www.company.com* by selecting a hot link that pointed there, the Web server would conduct him to *www.company.com*, but would relay communications through *www.evil.com*. (Note that many Web servers will return an error message to the user upon receiving such a Web site address; only servers that are configured to disassemble the chained Web site address and process it will respond without error.)

Web spoofers can make it very difficult for victims to discover the deception by using JavaScript programs to display spurious location and status information on the browser, hiding the presence of the intermediate Web server. The only sure way for a user to detect the presence of an attacking Web server is to view either the HTML source or JavaScript program document information. Because Web spoofing is so difficult to detect, criminals can use this technique to steal or alter a victim's confidential information, with little danger of detection for several days or weeks—if ever.

Web users should adhere to the following recommendations to protect themselves from Web spoofing:

- Ensure that the browser's location line stays visible, and verify that it refers to an acceptable location.
- Exit from a browser when it is no longer needed and restart it as necessary. This reduces the possibility of spending significant amounts of time in a spurious Web environment.
- Configure Web browsers to trust only well-known certificate authorities (e.g., RSA Data Security (www.rsa.com), VeriSign (www.verisign.com)).
- Use bookmarks to visit locations where secure data transactions are involved.
- Periodically review entries in bookmark files to ensure that they do not refer to intermediate Web sites.
- Java, JavaScript, and ActiveX can facilitate spoofing. Enable them only as necessary, such as when visiting known safe locations (e.g., your corporate intranet).

Refer to the following resources for additional information on Web spoofing:

- *Internet Security for Business* by Terry Bernstein, Amish Bhimini, Eugene Schultz, and Carol Siegel (John Wiley, 1996)
- *Managing Internet Information Services* by Cricket Liu, *et al.* (O'Reilly & Associates, 1994)
- *Practical Unix & Internet Security* by Simson Garfinkel and Gene Spafford (O'Reilly & Associates, 2nd Edition, 1996)

Spamming, Flooding, Pinging, and Denying Service

Spamming is the term used to describe the technique of flooding computers with multitudes of e-mail messages or sending large numbers of unwanted messages to many Internet users. Although these are two of the more extreme (and obnoxious) forms of spamming, there are others—and new ones emerging every day. Spamming, which began in 1996 when a law firm sent e-mail advertisements to thousands of Internet sites, is worse than junk mail, because victims pay for the connect time and resources to receive it and lose use of their Internet connection while being bombarded.

Flooding and *pinging* (also known as *echo spamming*) are attacks on Internet service providers. They fill the providers' queues and/or saturate their communication ports, to deny service to their customers. Although voice communication systems are vulnerable to similar problems with flooding (as when a radio station announces that listeners must immediately call a telephone number to win a prize), telephone companies have learned to handle the problem by accepting only a portion of incoming calls when traffic increases suddenly or dramatically. Internet designers did not, however, recognize the need for this selective process until it was too late. Information systems vendors are now attempting to develop products to deal with these types of problems, using solutions similar to those that the telephone companies have used successfully for many years.

SYN DENIAL OF SERVICE FLOODING ATTACK

The SYN Denial of Service flooding technique attacks the Internet IP protocol's three-way initialization handshake procedure. Normally when an attacker, using an Internet browser, tries to attach to another computer, the browser computer's IP protocol stack program sends a synchronization packet called *SYN*, which contains the IP address of the browsing computer. The receiving computer responds to receiving that address by sending a synchronization acknowledgment packet called *SYN-ACK;* it then holds a reserved memory space and pointer called a *Session Open* while waiting for the browser to respond with a confirming ACK packet. When this happens, the session is disconnected, and real communications begin.

In a SYN flood attack, the perpetrator sends SYNs to the victim computer, using bogus IP return addresses. The victim computer replies by sending SYN-ACKs and stores copies of them in a queue. The SYN-ACKs wander aimlessly and disappear because they contain a bogus IP address that is not the address of any computer. The potential for abuse arises at the point where the victim computer has sent an acknowledgment (SYN-ACK) back to a presumably legitimate address, but has not yet received the ACK message. The victim's queue waits for matching ACKs until the process exceeds a time limit (typically 90 seconds). Because the victim computer can open only a limited number of sessions, and the attacker continues to send bogus SYNs, the victim computer runs out of memory space for connections and is effectively shut down.

A computer under attack may appear to be running normally in most respects—servicing outgoing connections and logged-in users as usual. The attack becomes apparent, however, when someone attempts to make an incoming connection, trying, for example, to reach a Web site.

Depending on the rate of attacks, the victim computer may either react sluggishly or not at all to incoming connection requests. SYN flooding attacks are said to deny service to the victim's users because the technique degrades the victim computer's ability to give service to legitimate connection requests.

Security experts have been aware of this type of attack for years but chose not to disclose it to the general public for fear of increasing the incidence of such attacks. In 1996, the Panix Company had the dubious distinction of becoming the first publicly acknowledged victim of SYN flooding. The company was out of business for about a week, under continuous attack—presumably by a perpetrator using a low-speed computer modem. Since that time, dozens of shorter attacks have been reported, including a 40-hour attack on the WebCom World Wide Web Service.

SNIFFER ATTACKS

Sniffers are computer programs that act covertly to search individual packets of data as they pass through packet-switching networks like the Internet. Malicious hackers use sniffers to capture information that they can use to subvert a victim's computer for illicit purposes.

In a sniffer attack, information destined for an Internet host computer node flows through many, occasionally hostile, computer nodes in its journey through the massive network. Sniffers can operate as secret components in authorized nodes, as phantom (i.e., invisible) nodes connected to the network, or as Trojan horses buried in other software. They search each packet of data passing by for desirable information to capture, such as user passwords from the initial packets of a logon process in some other node. Most security experts agree that the Internet is currently suffering from an epidemic of sniffer attacks in which tens of thousands of passwords have been stolen. In the future, criminals may extend the capabilities of sniffers to perpetrate more, and more harmful, acts such as automated crime.

Passive Hacking

Powerful new Web browsers that execute Java applets and ActiveX program code allow hackers intent on attacking to sit back and wait for victims to come to their Web sites. (*Web* takes on a new, ominous meaning here.) Anytime you visit a Web site, the visit can have disastrous results. A hacker's Web site may, for example, send you an unwanted gift of applets to execute in your private PC domain; such "gifts" can even pass through seemingly secure firewalls. At one time, if you were using the Netscape mail client with the Shockwave plug-in, an applet might have been able to obtain your mail and send information about your internal network such as your network address, host computer name, logon user ID, and encrypted password back to the hacker's Web site for use in future attacks. The hacker's Web site may even entice you into creating your own user ID and password to gain further services from the site, causing you to inadvertently provide the hacker with a user ID and password that you use for other services and resulting in the classic identity theft described in the next section. The foreign applet may simply cause your PC to crash but remain as an unwelcome guest that sends you back to the hacker site when you reboot to pick up another copy of the applet that crashes your system again. An applet could also set your browser to act as a surrogate for the hacker Web site and destroy other Web sites when you visit them.

The obvious way to prevent these problems is to avoid visiting untrusted Web sites. If you venture into dangerous turf, at least be sure to disable Java and ActiveX in your browser while you are doing it. If your organization has a firewall, it should be set up to block Java applets and other dangerous types of files as well as to block your entry to known dangerous Web sites. The best general advice is to be as careful out on the Web as you would be on unfamiliar city streets.

Identity Theft

Identity theft refers to a criminal's illegal use of someone else's identity to take advantage of the victim's credit or reputation. It offers a very good reason to be concerned with the confidentiality of personal information. Identity theft may begin with stealing a wallet or purse, rifling a U.S. mailbox, dumpster diving for financial statements in the trash, or eavesdropping on the Internet. An identity thief can use such innocuous information as name, address, and social security number to begin an identity theft. Even a personal telephone calling card number or junk mail advertising for a new credit card can give this type of criminal an opening to begin plying his craft. And, although identity theft is nothing new in the world of crime, the Internet has vastly increased the ability of thieves to gather personal information about a victim and to duplicate and disseminate it in a wide range of criminal pursuits.

Identity theft can rob a victim of tangible assets by draining bank accounts or maxing-out a credit card, as well as of intangible assets such as reputation. Along the way, the thief may commit fraud against others using the victim's identity and totally decimate a good credit rating that took years to establish. The thief may even change the victim's mailing address to his own to receive bills and overdue notices that would notify the victim that something is amiss. A woman in California eventually enjoyed the satisfaction of knowing that the culprit who stole her identity was convicted of the crime. Unfortunately, however, she missed attending the sentencing because the court sent the scheduling notice to the culprit's address in her name.

In many cases, financial institutions will compensate their customers who are victimized by identity theft for their monetary losses. There is no compensation, however, for the time that can be lost proving the situation or restoring a reputation, or for the stress that a victim is likely to go through in trying to destroy all aspects of the duplicate identify. A provision in California's identity theft statute recognizes the problems with reestablishing identity, permitting victims to promptly obtain a police report of the crime, which they can use to repair credit ratings and correct records.

Legislators and various law enforcement organizations, including local police fraud units, the U.S. Secret Service, postal inspectors, and the FBI, are actively addressing identity theft. Credit reporting services are also attempting to control the use of personal credit information to eliminate its fraudulent use. Until the various organizations manage to plug the most obvious leaks, however, it is advisable to carefully guard the confidentiality of identity information and financial transaction records, and to periodically check credit rating information to ensure that nothing untoward is taking place.

E-MAIL SPOOFING

E-mail spoofing is the term applied to the counterfeiting and forging of e-mail messages, but the euphemism doesn't fully convey the insidious nature of the crime. According to information security managers, e-mail spoofing—sending e-mail messages in the names of others—is a growing epidemic on the Internet. Although a considerable amount of e-mail spoofing is harmless—perpetrated by jokesters strictly for amusement—some is serious misbehavior.

The sheer size and anonymity of cyberspace demand the information passing through the Internet be subjected to both authentication and accountability controls. The most effective way to invoke these controls is through the use of independent trusted third parties called *certificate authorities* (CAs), which provide digital signatures and encrypted communication of electronic authentication certificates. CAs authenticate the

A Case of E-mail Forgery

A famous case of e-mail forgery occurred in California in 1996. The spurned girlfriend of the CEO of a large software firm won a wrongful termination suit against the company and collected a $100,000 settlement. Until she was fired, the girlfriend was an executive assistant to a vice president in the company. Among other things, she was responsible for changing her supervisor's passwords, providing him with new codes, and managing his e-mail account. A key piece of evidence in the termination suit was a copy of an e-mail message that her supervisor, the vice president, allegedly sent to the CEO that said, "I have terminated Adelyn per your request." The CEO denied that he had fired the woman because she refused to have sex with him, maintaining that the e-mail message was a spoof.

In 1997, the company challenged the veracity of the e-mail message. The district attorney subsequently indicted and tried the jilted girlfriend for felony computer network intrusion, creating false documents, and perjury in a superior court. The company found computer audit records showing that someone had logged on from a remote address and switched back and forth between the vice president's and another employee's e-mail accounts on the day and time that the questionable e-mail message was sent. The vice president proved that he was driving his car and talking on his cellular phone at the time the e-mail message was sent. Even though investigators were unable to retrieve the last numbers dialed from the woman's home computer, she was convicted and sentenced to one year in prison and fined $100,000.

identities of users by exchanging personal information known only to the communicating parties. CAs log messages for later audit, and they use investigative software to trace the source of messages. In addition, they initiate criminal and civil litigation for wrongdoing.

CAs are not foolproof, however. If a criminal has the means to enter a legitimate user's workstation and sufficient knowledge to use the appropriate passwords, he can bypass the authentication procedure and successfully impersonate the user. Solving this problem requires security for authentication of users independent of workstations in the form of portable identity verification devices (tokens) and PIN numbers. This control authenticates a person by what she knows (i.e., the PIN) and what she possesses (i.e., the token).

LANarchy

LANarchy is a breakdown of information security due to a failure to document the presence and connections of equipment within an organization that uses multiple local- and wide-area networks (LANs and WANs). If the information security department and auditors are unaware of the existence of systems and their network connections, their security may be faulty at best, and nonexistent at worst. Criminals can insert phantom nodes (i.e., computers or workstations) into the networks without the owners' knowledge, and can establish secret connections that create unauthorized tunnels for communication. Tunneling can be used to create covert channels for information using embedded protocols and encryption. Large business and government organizations may lose control of their computing and communications equipment and network connections during mergers and acquisitions as well as in the course of normal evolution.

Accurate inventories of computer and communications equipment and network connections are a major part of the solution to LANarchy. Organizations need to apply security standards to managing network configurations, controlling new installations and continually auditing existing facilities. An organization should be able, at any time, to detect and identify all equipment connected to its networks. There are a number of tools available to help accomplish this, such as Fluke Communication's *LANMeter* (www.fluke.com) network diagnostic tool. In addition, organizations should ban the indiscriminate installation of modems, provide controlled modem pools, and require that outside communications go through secure gateways with automatic callback or secure logon and logoff protocols.

Electronic Banking and Electronic Data Interchange (EDI) Fraud

Internet banking and electronic data interchange (EDI) offer new opportunities for some types of fraud, such as money laundering by substituting electronic documents for paper ones. Although there are not yet any documented cases of EDI fraud, there are a growing number of cases in which EDI fraud is suspected of playing a role.

Business transactions are largely based on trust. We trust that participants are who they say they are, and that they will do, or have done, what they claim, for example as indicated by the transactions documented in their credit histories or the employment positions that are listed in their resumes. Such trust is far more difficult to accomplish at the speeds, distances, and anonymity of the Internet. Criminals understand this fact and exploit it effectively. For example, they impersonate the officials of successful companies by obtaining their bank account numbers, tax ID numbers, and so forth. They can retrieve much of this information by identity theft from credit histories stolen or obtained legitimately from credit reporting services, published business records, and by deception. Then they use the information to assume the identity of the officials and obtain credit secured by the value of the officials' companies.

The Salami Fraud

Salami fraud, which refers to the technique of taking small slices to deceptively acquire the whole salami, is another flamboyant financial crimoid that is effectively automated by cyberspace. In one example of salami fraud, an enterprising programmer in a bank was assigned to write a program to refund excessive interest collections from Visa cardholders. The program, which was written and tested by only the one programmer, did exactly as required with one important exception: It reduced the refunds to randomly selected cardholders by twenty-five cents each, and accumulated the rake-offs in the programmer's own Visa account. The cardholders did not know exactly what they were supposed to receive and, therefore, could not detect any discrepancy. After an alert bank auditor finally noticed the programmer's upscaled life style, a court successfully convicted him for bank fraud.

The salami fraud technique pays off only when it is automated and only when there are a sufficient number of victims to draw from. Its success relies on the victims not noticing small individual losses. Perpetrators of this technique must have extensive programming expertise and the ability to enter and use automated financial systems. For these reasons, the salami technique is not widely used—or at least, not widely reported. It may actually take place quite frequently and successfully, with the victims blissfully unaware of their losses.

One of the oldest urban legends among auditors and accountants is the salami round-down technique that I described in my earlier book, *Crime by Computer* (Charles Scribner's Sons, 1976). Although no one has actually ever perpetrated this crime (as far as I know), it has been reported many times in the media. The small amounts of money taken in this classic technique are the accumulated fractions of pennies left over from calculating account balances. The computer rounds the balance to the nearest penny to fit into the account balance field. For example, when 0.14

Collusion in a Big Bank Fraud

On February 5, 1995, Reuters News Service reported, "BANK WORK-ERS STEAL 1,630 MILLION YEN, CLEANUP ON A MAJOR BANK CRIME." According to the story, three conspirators used a personal computer money transfer system at a Tokyo bank to successfully trans-fer 140 million yen to an account in another bank using a settlement system operated by personal computers, then withdraw the money on the same day. The following day, the thieves sent a total of 1,490 million yen in three unauthorized transfers from the accounts of various com-panies with the same intent. This time, however, the bank stopped them before the completion of the theft.

One of the people involved in the thefts was an employee of the Tokyo bank's systems department. Another was an employee of a soft-ware house who had worked for the bank under contract as an on-site system development engineer. The third was the president of the soft-ware house, allegedly associated with Japanese organized crime activi-ties. The crime was apparently motivated in part by debts owed to organized crime groups.

The SRI-Tokyo staff discovered that the thieves used a "one-time" transfer application that was intended for occasional funds transfers. This type of funds transfer service requires four passwords: one for the company that wishes to transfer the money; one which is assigned by the bank for the intended recipient of the money; one for the fund's transfer service; and one that is defined for each transfer transaction. According to newspaper accounts, the first three passwords are stored on the host computer in the bank in encrypted form. The staff of the systems department is able to obtain those passwords, but only with "the top manager's approval." The bank confirms the transfer by letter to the customer who initiated it on the following day, whether the trans-fer occurred or not.

This crime is probably attributable to a combination of security lapses including a failure to segregate responsibilities, a failure to prop-erly monitor contract employees, and a failure to strictly maintain pass-word security. Overall, it raises questions about the security of electronic funds transfer. But, it also indicates that some level of secu-rity was effective because the greedy thieves were caught before they could complete their second attempt.

Salami Fraud in a Bank

Some time ago, I received a telephone call from a bank customer who is also a computer programmer. He suspected, from reviewing his bank statements, that he was the victim of a salami fraud. The statements showed a shortage of a few cents several times each year.

Although most of the staff at the bank denied knowing what a salami fraud was, I finally reached the chief information officer (CIO), who admitted that the bank had received several complaints about small discrepancies in customers' accounts and that they had "a problem with some programmers." The customers were readily compensated for their losses, but the bank refused to do anything further about the problem. According to the CIO, the cost of an investigation would be too great compared to the small compensation payments to customers, which amounted to a few hundred dollars. I suggested that he should at least watch for excessive living styles and personal problems among his programming staff, but, as far as I know, that's as far as the bank was willing to go to control the situation.

percent is multiplied by a balance of $4302.27, the result is $6.023178. When that is rounded down to $6.02, there is a remainder of $0.003178 that could be summed with hundreds of other round-down remainders until a penny is accumulated and credited to a perpetrator's account. While this is obviously a very slow way to steal any significant amount, there is no apparent loss and the account balance totals are correct, since money is not removed from the accounts, only rearranged a bit. It would be difficult for anyone to discover that the fraud was happening, even if there was some suspicion. (Actually, there is a standard banking algorithm for distributing both round-downs and round-ups in a set of interest-bearing accounts. The distribution of the accumulated roundings among the accounts ultimately compensates each account holder fairly.)

Protection from Financial Internet Fraud

Protecting financial transactions from fraud requires the application of age-old transaction security techniques—specifically, segregation of duties and accountability. In addition, electronic transactions require a means to authenticate users. This is usually accomplished through the use of digital signatures and/or document encryption. The U.S. Bar Association has now accepted the concept of legal digital signatures, but there is still some doubt about the circumstances that constitute a proper signature in contractual commitments and the demonstration of legally "sufficient" security. Utah has made digital signatures legally binding under some circumstances.

Law enforcement agencies, especially the FBI and Secret Service, and regulatory agencies such as the U.S. Controller of the Currency and their counterparts in other countries are gearing up for the onslaught of automated financial crime. As the network equivalents of financial fraud emerge, we are starting to see an array of problems, including, but not limited to:

- Funds transfer fraud
- Money laundering
- Bust-outs (bankruptcy of fraudulent companies)
- Credit card fraud
- Ponzi pyramid schemes
- Recovery fee frauds
- Tax and customer duty frauds
- Antitrust violations

The problems are compounded by the wide range of legislation in various national and international jurisdictions affected by Internet financial fraud and by limitations on eavesdropping practices occasioned by increasing use of strong cryptography. For example, some banks advocate adopting Federal legislation to bar non-banks from issuing electronic money, and are negotiating agreements with the Internet service providers (ISPs) to share the liabilities inherent in international electronic money transactions.

AUTOMATED CRIME

The concept of automated crime began with hacker tools and security testing software, such as "sniffers," which malicious hackers currently use to capture information to subvert victims' computers for illicit purposes. In the future, however, computer-savvy criminals could enhance the functions of sniffers and similar malicious hacker tools to commit totally automated crimes. With the appropriate tools and an understanding of the vulnerabilities inherent in a victim's computer system, a criminal could gain root authority in the computer, perpetrate criminal acts, convert those acts to criminal gains, and conclude by totally deleting any evidence of the crime.

There is no shortage of tools for malicious hackers, or of sources for those tools. In addition to the numerous hacker bulletin boards and magazines, a number of legitimate sources offer utility programs that can be used in malicious hacker attacks; many of these program tools are available free of charge. For example, the ComSec Ltd. company (www.comsecltd.com) which serves more than 2,000 computer security specialists worldwide, offers *Setspass*, which can be used to change supervisory passwords if an attacker is physically able to enter a LAN system server. Another service offers *Getser*, which gathers the serial numbers of servers currently logged on to a network. *Tempsup* creates temporary supervisor-equivalent user IDs; *Xsend* can cause a denial of service attack by saturating users with broadcast messages; *Hack.exe* makes it possible to masquerade as any logged-on user, and *Netcrack* performs an alphanumeric password search if a system allows unlimited logon attempts. Legitimate security specialists use the latter tool to test their employers' systems for weak passwords.

Unlike traditional criminals who have no opportunity to test their crimes before executing them, the creator of an automated crime has the luxury of being able to test and enhance it and obtain the assistance of other experts until it operates flawlessly in a variety of circumstances. Because automated crimes take place in the totally predictable world of computer systems, they can execute any number of times under exactly the same circumstances—and render exactly the same results. Or, the creator can tweak the automated crime to fit a particular set of circumstances, much like we create application scripts to fit specific computing requirements.

Anatomy of an Automated Crime

A fully automated crime would involve the following six steps, all carried out by a program or a suite of programs executed automatically in sequence, without human intervention.

1. Scanning or searching to find computers containing the desired assets to attack
2. Finding the vulnerability in the selected system(s) in preparation for the attack
3. Using that vulnerability to gain entry, resources, and authority
4. Engaging in an abusive or criminal activity
5. Converting that activity to some form of gain for the perpetrator and/or loss to the victim

   6. Eliminating evidence to avoid discovery of the perpetrator and the
   criminal activity

   The perpetrator could use a computer program such as *SATAN*
(Security Administrators' Tool for Analyzing Networks) to accomplish the
first two steps. This program, which is available through the Internet as
freeware, was released in April 1995. It is designed to scan computers,
probe for vulnerabilities, and report security weaknesses in network computers that run the UNIX operating system. SATAN probes for 15 well-
known vulnerabilities that may exist in UNIX systems, and reports the
information back through the Internet to the SATAN operator. Because the
source code is readily available, a competent programmer could easily
modify it to extend SATAN's capabilities to probe for new vulnerabilities
and to take advantage of the vulnerabilities that are discovered rather than
reporting them.
   Since SATAN can automatically probe many computers in a network
without interruption, it could provide sufficient information to select an
appropriate target computer. The current version of SATAN explores the
security aspects of a targeted computer system—or literally hundreds of
targeted computer systems to make decisions regarding vulnerabilities to
pursue. An enhancement, a "break-in" scanning level, would extend this
capability in future versions—further accomplishing steps 3 and 4 of an
automated crime.
   A security probe in SATAN contacts the target host system using a
TCP/IP-based protocol, such as simple mail transport protocol (smtp), file
transfer protocol (ftp), or remote procedure call (rpc). The target system,
mistakenly identifying the SATAN probe as one from a trusted computer,
responds by returning whatever data suits the service requests. (The criminal may need to use another technique, such as IP spoofing, to accomplish
this type of impersonation.)
   The program can accomplish step 4 in an automated crime in any
number of ways to engage in many types of crime such as fraud, theft,
espionage, or sabotage. A single automated crime may perform multiple
crimes. A logic bomb that executes on a privileged basis when specific conditions are met within the target system is probably the most likely technique for "delivering" the crimes.
   Step 5 of the automated crime is conversion to criminal gain. Gain,
however, may be merely the satisfaction of successfully sabotaging the target computer, with no removal or conversion of information. In a financial
system fraud, conversion to criminal gain could involve establishing a line
of credit, while in a banking system fraud it could involve transferring

funds from one bank's computer to the perpetrator's account in another bank's computer. We may consider the conversion—and this step—to be complete when the funds are transferred and credited to the account in the other bank system. If, however, the transferring bank detects that the transfer is fraudulent and reverses the transaction before the funds are safely "delivered" to the criminal's account, there is no conversion to gain. Considering the many banking regulations in place, criminals using the automated crime program may find that it is necessary to remove stolen funds as cash in order to achieve irreversible gains.

Step 6, the final step in an automated crime, may be unnecessary if the crime is a hit-and-run situation in which the criminal does not care whether his actions are discovered. If, however, the crime is to remain covert and the perpetrator is to remain anonymous, the last act of the program is to eliminate any evidence that would lead to detection and identification. It may also eliminate evidence that would be useful in a subsequent prosecution. Eliminating all evidence of the crime is likely to be a formidable task, especially in a network situation where multiple copies of transaction records and logs are likely to exist. The automated crime designer needs to consider—and deal with—the possibilities of backups, shadow copies, audit logs, residual data in computer buffers, discarded printer paper, printer memories, and data remaining in unas-signed disk sectors. The crime program can, however, deal with these items individually, eliminating the most obvious first, then moving on to the less obvious and more difficult items. The designer could, for example, program the automated crime to anticipate and avoid specific criminal laws, rules of evidence, and legal precedence.

Article 1030§(a), (5) of the Computer Fraud and Abuse Act of 1996 states: "Whoever knowingly causes the transmission of a program, infor-mation, code, or command, and as a result of such conduct, intentionally causes damage without authorization, to a protected computer, shall be punished. . . ." This may be construed as criminalizing the transmission of an automated crime, but only if the perpetrator (not necessarily the author) uses it in a specific crime against a specific victim. Creating and distributing automated crimes, and even cautiously advertising them, is probably not a crime under this statute.

CONCLUSIONS

It is clear that new technology spawns new ways to engage in many types of crimes. Criminals develop new types of attacks even before the new information systems or networks are available to the general public. Unfortunately, designers of new products and services don't seem to anticipate this, and often fail to include sufficient protection mechanisms in their first releases. After they get burned a couple of times, they retrofit security into the products, usually at far greater cost and with less effectiveness than if they had designed adequate security into the products in the first place. The cellular telephone industry provides a good example of this type of security lapse. Despite warnings of weak security standards, during the early 1970s cell phone manufacturers released models with embedded computer chips that could easily be compromised and cloned. After billions of dollars of fraud, the designers frantically attempted to make the phones secure, but were interrupted by the introduction of digital cellular telephones. Manufacturers then installed halfhearted cryptography in the new digital products and watched the hackers create software tools to break their security as well. The designers continue trying to develop unbeatable cell phones.

An information security products industry is gradually developing as computer and network vendors fail to deal effectively with network crime. Security should have been embedded in computer and network products in the first place, then integrated to work with the security features of the products with which they interface. Instead, users have had to buy firewall systems, cryptography and user authentication products, computer entry control software, and physical possession protection devices separately, then try to integrate them all with systems products. It is clear from looking at product comparison articles in industry trade journals that security continues to have low priority among computer and network vendors. The articles compare price, performance, and other features, but rarely—if ever—mention security. This, of course, is not the vendors' or trade journalists' fault alone. The fault ultimately lies as well with the purchasers who do not demand, and are often unwilling to pay for, adequate security.

6

Cyberspace Abusers and Misusers

We can learn more about computer and network abuse and misuse from the actual abusers and misusers than we can from information security experts. The abusers are, after all, the people whose misbehavior we need to stop. I have spent a significant portion of my career chasing after these individuals and interviewing them to identify their capabilities and motives. I believe that the knowledge that I've gained through this experience is valuable for implementing security safeguards to protect information from the many, very real threats to it. Much of my experience, however, conflicts with the "traditional" views of security experts. For example, popular knowledge holds that the perpetrators of computer crime are "high-tech" insiders motivated by opportunity and greed. My direct experience and contact with perpetrators indicates otherwise.

This chapter describes the computer criminals that I have interviewed over the years—embezzlers, thieves, and terrorists—and explores both their crimes and their motivations. In the next chapter, I discuss hackers and malicious hackers, who typically perpetrate a different type of crime, for different reasons, and require different safeguards to keep them away from your valuable information.

CHARACTERIZING THE PERPETRATORS
OF CYBERCRIME

People who intentionally abuse and misuse information cover the spectrum of criminals. Although it is impossible to characterize these criminals in a single profile, there are some interesting and useful criminal phenomena that we need to know to be effective in protecting information. Several of these characteristics differentiate cybercriminals from white-collar criminals. I refer to these as SKRAM—the criminal's skills, knowledge, resources, authority, and motives.

Skills

Skills already possessed or acquired (the *S* in SKRAM) vary significantly in three major areas: formal learning, experience with information systems, and social interaction with people. Although social skills may be of minimal importance in committing crimes against computers, such skills are clearly desirable for manipulating and/or deceiving gullible people, steps that are often essential for gathering the necessary technical knowledge to execute a crime or for converting crime to gain. Criminals that can combine interpersonal skills with strong information processing skills are in a good position to use computers to take advantage of people, if they so choose. Some of the most successful computer criminals are the ones with the best social skills, not necessarily the greatest formal education or the strongest computer skills.

Some of the criminals that I have interviewed have learning disabilities. They are unable to function in formal classroom education, which affects their interpersonal skills. They are limited to learning from hands-on experience, making computers a good source of learning and offering them an area in which they can excel. Computer application skills often come naturally to otherwise disfunctional people, or they easily and enthusiastically acquire them.

Knowledge

Knowledge (the *K* in SKRAM) is another obvious necessity for crime. I divide criminals into three classes: those who create the tools for crime; those who have the necessary skills and knowledge and who plan and carry out crimes; and those who use others' knowledge and follow scripts to act out crimes. Packaging crime scripts for others to use in the computers of victims make it possible for perpetrators to engage in crimes without having a high degree of knowledge. In some cases, acquiring the knowledge or tools for crime is as simple as downloading the scripts (algorithms) and program tools from Internet Web sites or bulletin boards, or copying them from hacker magazines such as *Phrack* or *2600*.

If criminals don't have a thorough understanding of the environments and circumstances of their crimes, they are likely to fail or be caught. Criminals greatly fear the unknown and unpredictable aspects of their crimes that might lead to their failure and identification. For this reason, they usually know more about the crime scene than anyone else in the world, making them formidable adversaries for victims and security practitioners. Unlike the criminals who have the luxury of studying the pertinent crime environment and carefully planning their attack, security practitioners must typically learn all aspects of the environment quickly, gathering the details about many potential vulnerabilities and plugging the gaps in a comparatively short amount of time before criminals can attack them.

Perpetrators who do not possess sufficient knowledge to begin their crimes must obtain it before moving forward. They do this by studying available sources, practicing deception where necessary, and—if all else fails—stealing it. Hackers, such as Dark Dante, engage in outright burglary to gain the necessary knowledge of the target environment. Although lock picking is a popular subject among burglars, deception to obtain keys through social engineering is the preferable means of obtaining knowledge. Criminals can also often practice their crimes on systems identical to the real targets.

Resources

Resources (the *R* of SKRAM) represent the means to engage in the abuse and misuse of information. In most cases, the resources are relatively basic and easy to obtain. We can never assume that criminals can't attack valuable information because they do not have the necessary money, or the wherewithal to acquire them. In most cases, criminals are remarkably skilled at borrowing or stealing what they need, or in using innovative means of attack that minimize the resources they need. Information may, however, be more secure in an uncommon type of system and media simply because fewer people have the necessary resources to obtain or manipulate the data. And, utilities and other tools are generally more difficult to obtain for the less popular operating systems and applications than they are for the common ones such as Microsoft's Windows and Intuit's Quicken.

Authority

Authority (the *A* of SKRAM) refers to the assigned use rights or privileges that a criminal has, or needs to acquire, in order to perpetrate crime. Criminals gain the necessary authority to abuse or misuse computer information files by having a user ID and password (or password token), along with the open, read, write, control, append, and delete privileges that enable them to manipulate the files. Authority may consist of the right to use specific computer applications, to perform certain transactions, or to enter rooms or buildings where information is stored or used. Owners, custodians, managers, and administrators (such as Web site managers) grant various kinds of authority to others by both formal and informal agreements. In addition, criminals often obtain authority through theft of identity. The ultimate level of authority, and one that is ideal from a criminal's perspective, is called root access, superuser, or systems administrator, depending on the type of computer in use. This level generally provides all of the possible rights to use and manipulate information files, as well as to assign or change other users' levels of authority.

Motives

Motives (the M of SKRAM) are often difficult to understand and thwart. Perhaps that explains why they are also generally the most overlooked aspect of information security. Psychologists and criminologists warn that it is nearly impossible to create a taxonomy of motives because any such taxonomy would be too complex and change continually. In the remainder of the chapter, however, I attempt to describe some of the motives that I have encountered in my interviews with computer criminals and explain how their crimes might have been avoided had their motives been better understood.

MOTIVES AND THE CYBERCRIMINAL

Although there is no way to describe a "typical" cybercriminal, my interviews over the years have revealed a number of common traits among these individuals. They are, for example, typically white-collar criminals who engage in fraudulent business practices associated with their otherwise legitimate occupations, e.g., a broker engaged in the sale of phony stocks. In psychological terms, they can be said to exhibit the differential association syndrome. They also frequently tend to anthropomorphize the computers that they attack, yet they assume that attacking a computer does no harm to people. Many cybercriminals exhibit the Robin Hood syndrome, rationalizing that they are taking from victims who—in their view—can afford it. And they may attempt to achieve a commendable goal at the expense of harming others. The following paragraphs describe these traits in more detail and explain some criminals' motives for their crimes.

The Differential Association Syndrome

The differential association syndrome describes the situation in which people engage in certain crimes because it deviates from accepted practice among their peers or associates, at least initially, in only small ways. For example, an embezzler may start by taking small things like paper clips, pencils, and paper to use at home. This isn't viewed as a crime because, after all, "everyone does it." But the little thefts escalate into bigger and bigger thefts until, at the peak of her career, the embezzler may take thousands of dollars from the company accounts.

This syndrome applies to the theft of computer services as well as financial gain. Employees often use business computers for personal purposes. Again, the excuse is that "everyone does it." Two programmers who were convicted of stealing computer services from their employer—for running a side business rescoring sheet music—fell into this trap. They told me that many fellow employees were using the computer for their own purposes, running the department football pool, recording bowling scores, and printing graphical images of naked ladies. They believed that they were doing only what others were doing, and that it was a common and accepted practice. Of course, it was hard for them to justify using three-fourths of the mainframe computer's memory as their business grew, and they were surprised to find themselves in federal prison for their misdeeds.

What Criminals Fear

Unpredictable environments and circumstances are often the cybercriminal's greatest fear. Unpredictability increases the potential for getting identified and caught in some unanticipated way, with all of the attendant shame and loss of standing in the eyes of friends, family, and associates. (Professional criminals, in contrast, often take pride in their criminality and find esteem in their criminal culture. This is only one way in which "typical" cybercriminals differ from professional criminals.)

Most criminals have a healthy fear of being caught. Some few, however, view apprehension as a solution to their heavyweight personal problems. The New York bank embezzler from a few years ago told me, as we sat chatting in his prison cell at Riker's Island, that getting caught was the best thing to have happen to him. He was trying to support a wife and two daughters on a teller's salary and driving a taxi at night. Incarceration solved his problems of gambling debts owed to the Mafia loan sharks, who stayed away from him because of the notoriety he received and his sudden loss of income. Imprisonment took him away from his usual habitats and helped cure his addiction to gambling. It also ended his constant fear of discovery by bank auditors of his million-dollar embezzlement scheme.

As our electronic environments grow increasingly complex, predictability is key to successful crime. The New York bank embezzler had predicated his successful three-year crime on predictability. He knew exactly how the systems worked; the auditors always gave him two weeks' notice of their arrival, and went through the same routine step-by-step each time. People are the chief unpredictable factors in crime—people who may detect wrongdoing and stop it, or join in to share the proceeds. People, unlike computers, are irrational; people never do exactly the same thing in the same way—even given the same set of circumstances and the same input each time. In contrast, computers always perform exactly the same way given the same input. Making computers unpredictable would, therefore, make them less attractive as environments for crime and lead to more powerful safeguards.

Complexity is also a deterrent to crime. Individuals who resort to crime as a solution to their problems generally seek the easiest, most familiar way to accomplish their goals, usually often avoiding the complexities inherent in using computers unless there are no other options. For these individuals, attacking computers is the last resort; they simply cannot figure out any other way to commit the crime. Their reluctance to use the computer is often well-founded. If it is difficult for software developers to legitimately produce bug-free programs under the best circumstances, imagine how difficult it is for criminals to accomplish the same task under covert conditions. If a perpetrator makes just one error in the program for his crime, and it doesn't execute flawlessly the first time it is used, he is likely to be caught. Alternatively, of course, if the program does operate as planned and the crime is successful, there is a

If At First You Succeed . . .

Strictly speaking, this case may not be classified as cybercrime, but it is instructive nonetheless. A smart criminal replaced the blank deposit slips on the customer service counters in a Washington, D.C. bank with ones MICR-encoded with his account number. When customers filled the slips out, the computer dutifully deposited the money into the perpetrator's account. He went into the bank a few days later claiming that he was moving to another state and needed $250,000 in cash but would leave the remaining $40,000 there. The bank teller, very trustful of a customer who leaves a big chunk of cash behind, complied with his request for cash.

The fraud was successfully repeated in Chicago, Los Angeles, and New York before the American Bankers Association distributed a warning to banks to remove blank deposit slips from countertops.

strong temptation—given the predictable nature of computers—to repeat the attack.

The Personification of Computers

Computers are ideal targets of crime in some ways; they do not scream or fight back when abused or misused. Many cybercriminals would be horrified if they were forced to physically confront their victims or to witness the anguish caused by their actions. Most of the cybercriminals I have encountered could not engage in a person-to-person crime if their lives depended on it. They could not look victims in the eye and rob or attack them, but have no problem attacking or robbing a computer because a computer does not look back or exhibit anguish. Cybercriminals often distinguish between the unacceptable practice of doing harm to people and the impersonal acts of doing harm to or through computers. Yet, many receive a measure of satisfaction in their crimes by personifying the computers that they attack, viewing them as adversaries and deriving some enjoyment from ripping them off.

On the other hand, if witnessing the human victim's anguish is part of the cybercriminal's motivation in committing a crime—such as sabotaging a computer system for revenge—the computer makes a very unsatisfactory victim. Computer virus writers, for example, can only imagine the torments of their victims.

Criminal Motivations

Many people assume that the opportunity to engage in abuse or misuse of information is a strong temptation to engage in crime. If that were true—if opportunity were a prime motivator of crime—we would have had to give up using computers a long time ago. Instead, information specialists and computer users are honest and ethical the vast majority of the time—despite their constant exposure to valuable information. In most cases, the computer technologists are so dedicated to the challenge of making computers work correctly that the thought of abusing or misusing them never enters their consciousness. Violations of trust are remarkably rare, at least based on my 45 years of experience in the computer industry, among system programmers and analysts.

Clearly, the motives of criminals are complex. In many cases, even the criminals don't fully understand their motivations and often change their stories during the life cycle of the crime—expressing one motive when they are initially apprehended, another at arraignment, and still others at trial or during subsequent parole hearings. I have interviewed some criminals at all of these stages, and their expressed demeanor, motives, and attitudes change considerably over time. (I find that the best time to interview criminals to learn about their crimes is while they're still in prison. They are often bored and remorseful and willing to assist me to help others from getting into the same serious trouble they're experiencing. For more details on this, see my earlier books, *Crime by Computer* and *Fighting Computer Crime*, published by Charles Scribner's Sons in 1976 and 1983.)

Despite the common view that greed usually motivates individuals to commit business crime, I have found that most cybercriminals are attempting to solve intense personal problems. At the time that a criminal perpetrates the crime, he is indeed attempting to achieve some type of gain. Law enforcement agencies and the news media usually interpret this as greed or a desire for high living, but my interviews with criminals indicate that intense need, rather than greed, causes them to commit crimes. The problems that they're attempting to resolve run the usual gamut of human difficulties—problems with a marriage or love relationship, failure to progress as fast as others in a career path, a need for money to settle outstanding debts, feeding addictions, and so on. Overall, the cybercriminal perceives himself as a problem solver rather than a criminal.

THE ROBIN HOOD SYNDROME

In cybercrime, the Robin Hood syndrome refers to stealing from the rich and keeping the booty—a significant variation on the old story. The victims of cybercrime are often organizations that—at least in the criminal's mind—can afford to suffer a relatively small loss to help solve the criminal's intense personal problems. In some cases the criminal also rationalizes that the organization (often his employer) has contributed to his predicament and has a responsibility to participate in the solution. For example, the chief accountant for a fruit and vegetable packing company concluded that his Mafia-connected managers were getting rich at his expense. So he embezzled his share from the company—approximately $1 million over a three-year period.

THE HIGHER ETHIC MOTIVE

The higher ethic motivation stems from a conflict of choices confronting the criminal. For example, the criminal's revulsion at stealing money from a bank may be overcome by a greater concern for financial deficiencies in caring for an invalid child or wife. In such cases, it is relatively easy to rationalize that the good to be done compensates for the harm that may be done. The higher ethic may also play a role in the Robin Hood syndrome.

Collusion

One fact of business life that works against computer crime is that the technically skilled individuals capable of creating or modifying programs for illicit purposes are usually not directly associated with the activities involved in converting criminal activity to gain. And, the individuals that are associated with conversion-to-gain activities do not usually have sufficient technical knowledge to modify computer operations for their criminal purposes. In other words, successful computer crime often requires at least two individuals from opposite sides of the computer screen—the technically skilled programmer, analyst, or operator and an individual with knowledge about the organization's operations. Segregation of duties, an important security control, is intended to prevent this type of collusion. To be truly effective, however, the segregation must be extended to segregate the systems as well as the users. This is why many security-conscious organizations maintain separate systems for test and development and for production.

Crossover individuals, those employees who work on one side of the screen (e.g., as programmers or operators) and then switch over to work on the other side (e.g., as users), are potentially dangerous because they can bring both expertise and opportunity to the crime. Again, the threat can be minimized by segregating systems and responsibilities so that individuals can use only the system and files required by their specific job assignments.

Many information security specialists differentiate threats from "insiders" (employees in an organization) and "outsiders" (individuals such as hackers who attack from outside of the organization). This is a false—and potentially dangerous—distinction. Threats are based on SKRAM—knowing who has the elements to perpetrate a crime. An outsider may have more SKRAM than an insider and, therefore, pose a greater threat to the organization. And, the distinction between inside and outside is blurring quickly in these times of downsizing, contract employees, and freelancers. An insider can quickly become an outsider, yet still retain the necessary SKRAM to commit crimes against the organization. In some cases, insiders cooperate with outsiders to commit crime.

SEVEN KINDS OF CYBERCRIMINALS

My study of cybercriminals reveals seven significant profiles. Unfortunately, however, no criminal fits exclusively in any one profile. Instead, the profiles overlap one another in fuzzy relationships.

Pranksters.   These individuals perpetrate tricks on others. They generally do not intend any particular or long-lasting harm. Juvenile exuberance prevails.

Hackers.   These individuals explore others' computer systems for education, out of curiosity, to achieve idealized social justice, or to compete with their peers. They may be attempting to gain the use of a more powerful computer, gain respect from fellow hackers, build a reputation, or gain acceptance as an expert without formal education. I'll discuss hackers and their particular motivations in more detail in the next chapter.

Malicious hackers.   Sometimes called crackers, these individuals are intent on causing loss (in contrast to achieving illegal gain) to satisfy some antisocial motives. Many computer virus creators and distributors fall into this category. Because malicious hackers differ greatly from other types of criminals, I describe them in a separate chapter to give them the attention they so richly deserve.

Personal problem solvers.   By far the most common kind of criminal encountered during my studies, these individuals often cause serious loss in their pursuit of a solution to their own personal problems. They may turn to crime after conventional problem-solving methods fail, or they may see crime as a quick and easy way to solve their problems. Several have told me that they believed that solving their problems justified breaking the law. Others felt that the law was unjust or did not apply to them. Still others asserted that they planned to return what they had taken when their own situation improved. They generally believed that the victim was rich enough to afford the loss and would not miss what was taken or used. Or they were trying to cause the least grief for the least number of people as in the higher ethic rationalization.

Career criminals. These individuals earn part or all of their income from crime, although they do not necessarily engage in crime as a full-time occupation. Some have a job, earn a little and steal a little, then move on to another job to repeat the process. In some cases they conspire with others or work within organized gangs such as the Mafia or Yakuza in Japan. The greatest organized crime threat comes from groups in Russia, Italy, and Asia. The FBI reported in 1995 that there were more than 30 Russian gangs operating in the United States. According to the FBI, many of these unsavory alliances use advanced information technology and encrypted communications to elude capture.

Extreme advocates. Better known as terrorists, these individuals and groups have strong social, political, and/or religious views and are intent on changing conditions by engaging in crime. Their crimes usually involve violence against people or property and are calculated to achieve a high level of publicity to bring attention to the terrorists' causes. To date, terrorists have rarely engaged in cybercrime, although the Red Brigades in Europe came close by destroying more than 60 computer centers during the 1980s. Terrorist groups, especially the highly organized ones sponsored by rogue countries such as Libya and Iran, are likely to turn their attention to our fragile information, utility, and transportation infrastructures when their current methods lose their impact. Such groups could plan an attack on a worldwide basis, using cryptography to communicate, then carry out their acts through the Internet.

Malcontents, addicts, and irrational and incompetent people.
These individuals run the gamut from the mentally ill to those addicted to drugs, alcohol, competition, or attention from others, to the criminally negligent. In general, they are the most

difficult to describe and the most difficult to protect against. We have no way of determining who is sufficiently irrational to trigger an attack against an organization or individual because of a perceived affront. We also have no way of predicting negligence. Criminal negligence is common in the abuse and misuse of computers. Programmers in New Zealand, for example, were convicted of criminal negligence when they failed in their duty to inform the captain of an airliner that they had reprogrammed his navigation system. He flew the plane into a mountain in Antarctica that, according to his navigation computer, was not supposed to be there, killing 80 tourists.

In attempting to protect information resources, we need to be prepared for the unexpected. We can't limit safeguards to only one type of problem or one attacker profile. Instead, we need to institute a program of broad-based protection against a vast array of potential threats. All too often, information owners and security managers react only to the latest publicized type of threat, inadvertently opening the door to another type of loss. While we need to be concerned with copycat crimes, we also have to constantly guard against the unknown and unexpected. And, we need to be constantly vigilant. There are no seasons for security breaches and no types or locations of businesses or organizations that are immune to abuse and misuse of information.

THE CYBERCRIME RATIONALIZATION

Criminals often need to rationalize their misbehavior. These people are not all bad. They love and are loved, have friends, have loving families, do good deeds (often to compensate for their bad ones), have pets that love them, engage in many honest activities, and have all of the other saint and sinner qualities that make them human. In many cases, criminals deny—to themselves and anyone else—that what they do is really a crime. After all, in many cases it just involves manipulating transitory electronic pulses. For example, the bank embezzler in Minneapolis didn't modify his bank balance. That would have been a crime. He merely modified the computer program so that it ignored his bank account overdraft for a while. According to him, no money was actually stolen and no one was losing anything—as long as he replenished his account before anyone noticed.

International intellectual property pirates often rationalize their espionage and theft by claiming that it is okay to break the laws of foreign

What Some Cybercriminals Have Told Me

- I was only trying to make the managers of my company aware of the vulnerabilities of their computer systems.
- I knew that if I did not destroy our competitor's computer center, I would be laid off from my computer operator job, and the affair that I was having with the president's wife would end. After all, he supplied the gasoline.
- I knew that the executives in the company were engaged in a massive fraud. I was the computer administrator and could see it happening. But they were treating the rest of the staff and me so well with high pay and freedom to go to conferences and seminars that I was as dedicated to the success of the business as they were.
- If the authorities had only let us continue what we were doing for a short time, we could have solved our problems and saved the company, shareholders, and insurance customers from economic ruin.
- The bank desperately needed my information security consulting services but did not realize it. I was going to demonstrate how easy it was to engage in the first step in a funds transfer fraud and show them the results so that they'd hire me to help. The first step was so easy that I decided to try the next step to see if it could be done as well, and the bank would be even more impressed. Nobody noticed what I had done. The next step was so easy as well, that I decided to see how far I could go. I never thought that I could succeed in doing the entire crime. I planned to return the money that I stole and appear as a hero.
- I was going to engage in a Trojan horse attack against their computer systems. Then I realized how difficult and dangerous that would be. Instead, I just called the funds transfer room from a pay phone, impersonated an international vice president, and told them where to transfer the money.
- How could the prosecutor and the judge think this was such a terrible crime? I only changed two instructions in the computer program. [The credit union was out of business for two weeks while they tried to find the reason that their computer would not process accounts correctly.]
- I was going to stop transferring the money to my friends' accounts for them to withdraw before the end of the month when I expected

(continued)

> that the shortages would surely be noticed, but my friends liked
> getting the money so much that they got greedy and forced me to
> continue. If I had stopped soon enough, the bank would not have
> been able to determine where the money had gone. My friends did
> not understand the bank's practices, and they would have killed me
> if I did not continue.

countries as long as they do not break the laws of their own country.
Besides, they feel that they are justified because other countries are so rich
and theirs is so poor. When it comes to rationalization, however, convicted
security people take the cake. Two of the information security specialists
who were convicted of crimes told me that they were merely trying to
carry out their objectives of protecting information owners.

I've heard a lot of rationalization from criminals over the years,
some of it remarkably convincing. I sometimes wonder if there is the
slightest chance that I might have done the same thing under the same
adverse circumstances. The accompanying sidebar summarizes some of
my favorite rationalizations, gathered during interviews with unsuccessful
cybercriminals.

SOCIAL ENGINEERING AND GULLIBILITY

My studies of computer crime lead me to believe that gullible people represent one of the greatest vulnerabilities in information security. The hacker
community uses the term *social engineering* to describe the deception of
people through various techniques in order to obtain critical information
necessary to perpetrate attacks on systems, but social engineering may
simply involve inducing someone to reveal confidential information.
People may reveal sensitive information voluntarily (e.g., when they
answer a survey questionnaire, present a lecture, or publish an article) or
involuntarily when deceived by an adept hacker or criminal.

Social Engineering Techniques

I compiled the following list of social engineering methods from my investigations of computer crime cases and interviews with criminals and victims.

Baiting. The perpetrator's communication includes expected jargon and sufficient facts to imply that the perpetrator has the authenticity, authority, and right to know the information being sought: "He already knows so much that providing a little more should be okay."

Name-dropping. An effective means of obtaining desired information, this technique involves identifying key individuals—by name and telephone number—within the target organization and/or using those names familiarly in communication with others in the organization. Telephone operators answering calls coming into some large organizations often reveal a considerable amount of information when exposed to a good name-dropper. Similarly, asking for an individual by title generally leads to a series of secretaries, each one of whom contributes organizational and name information along the way. Using the names of well-known individuals as supposed friends is also a common practice, since attempting to verify the acquaintance is difficult because well-known people are difficult to contact, and secretaries protect them from such inquiries.

Bulletin-board reading. Many organizations' bulletin boards are located in public areas, and many other bulletin boards are available to individuals who have gained entry to facilities as legitimate visitors or as impostors posing as authorized persons. Bulletin boards are often filled with personal information about employees, employee activities, and relatively sensitive business information, such as computer equipment available, meeting announcements, reports on meetings, and copies of official business documents. Electronic bulletin boards on the Internet are common sources of useful information for social engineering, and pirate hacker boards explicitly serve this purpose.

Reading initial logon screens. Detailed system descriptions and logon protocol instructions as well as help desk telephone numbers and system availability hours often appear on screens that are displayed before entry of user IDs, secret passwords, and acceptance of logon.

Mixing fact and fiction. Fictitious information is often made highly believable when it is mixed with factual information that the victim already knows. The fictional information can then be used for baiting and establishing authority.

Exaggerating and lying.   Exaggerating and lying are common practices among malicious hackers and are often communicated through electronic bulletin boards or conveyed to journalists. Exaggeration and lying can elicit a wide range of responsive information useful for social engineering.

Asserting authority (pulling rank).   Claiming to have the authority to request or order others to provide information and engage in transactions is a common means of committing fraudulent activities.

Impersonating real or fictitious individuals.   Impersonating or masquerading as individuals that have the authority to receive information is another social engineering method. Obtaining the information for the impersonation from one person for use in deceiving another person is a common ploy.

Intimidating, threatening, and shocking.   Intimidating victims with harsh or intense language and urgent messages is a way to coerce them into revealing sensitive information. Threatening to perform acts that are physically, organizationally, or mentally harmful in order to create fear is another way to obtain information.

Scorning, browbeating, belittling, aggravating, and exhausting.   These are negative ways to force people to reveal information. Being bothersome and persistent may wear people down so much that they provide information simply to stop the harassment. Implying that the victim is less than adequately informed on a subject is a way to deceive the victim into providing the information to prove his or her worth or value.

Praising, sympathizing, flattering, or aggrandizing.   These are positive ways to coerce people into giving information by flattering them and creating an enthusiasm to supply information.

Persistently calling false alarms.   This method consists of attacking safeguards until the victim becomes frustrated enough to disable the safeguard or control in order to gain relief. The victim thereby becomes vulnerable to providing information.

Engaging in conspiracy.   In the pigeon-drop fraud, two or more people conspire to deceive a victim, in some cases adopting separate roles to cause the victim to trust one of the people and oppose the other. Having more than one person engage in social engineering adds a higher degree of intimidation or authenticity in a deception.

Learning from Loss Experience

The following examples demonstrate how social engineering techniques have been used to commit—or further the commission of—computer crime. (I'll discuss solutions to social engineering techniques in Chapter 14.)

- A telephone company thief dialed the voice telephone number of a company computer operator late one night explaining that the telephone line he was using to reach the computer was not working properly. He asked the computer operator to tell him the telephone number of another port into the computer. The computer operator indicated that he was not supposed to reveal such information over the telephone. The thief insisted, and acted desperate and angry. He explained that the need for entry was urgent and threatened the operator with the loss of his job. He claimed to be an important user who could have the operator fired if he did not comply. The computer operator finally relented and gave the thief the needed number.

- The same thief demonstrated another technique for Dan Rather of CBS Television News. The thief called a service representative at a New York bank, posing as another service representative. By convincingly using jargon typical of the position, he managed to increase the credit limit on Dan Rather's bank account. The thief had learned the jargon and terminology through previous casual conversations with service representatives in which he had posed as a customer.

  This case illustrates how easily some service people can be intimidated and deceived into revealing valuable information or taking action, especially when their supervisors are not immediately available to give guidance. Intimidation can be effective when the criminal impersonates an individual that the service representative is trained to serve and does not want to offend.

- An oil company engaged a consultant to conduct an intrusion test of its computers. The consultant called a service station near the oil company's main computer center and asked to be connected to the computer center help desk. The service station attendant informed the consultant that he had called the wrong number and had reached a service station. He said that the main computer center was nearby, however, and gave the consultant the unlisted telephone number of the help desk.

(continued)

Using social engineering against victims who are associated either formally or informally with people having the target information is a common means of penetrating an information source. Perpetrators may have to make several telephone calls to various people to identify a source. In this case, the service station happened to be a customer of the oil company's computer center and therefore had the local telephone help number.

- A U.S. brokerage firm brought suit against a proxy solicitation service, charging that their employees stole secret information by impersonating brokerage executives over the telephone. The scheme, which was reported in the *Wall Street Journal,* was alleged to have occurred over three to four years and involved at least twelve employees who misappropriated confidential, proprietary, and nonpublic information. Callers are alleged to have duped lower-level employees in the order department into giving out information about trades in Xerox Corporation and Pinelands Incorporated stock. In one incident, the caller identified himself as an individual on the alleged victim's trading desk. When pressed by the victim for further identification, the caller insisted that he was the named individual from "Trading, second floor" and gave a nonexistent victim telephone extension. The investment business is based on mutual trust and involves a high volume of often rapid, informal telephone communication—making violations of trust relatively easy. Social engineering in this context is usually discovered after the fact, by evidence of unusual trading activity rather than by any formal means of identification and authentication of callers.

- A gang of seven individuals, including two funds-transfer employees in a large bank, attempted to transfer $70 million to two banks in Europe. The employees were aware that voice telephone funds-transfer orders were recorded on magnetic tape. Using tapes of the voices of funds-transfer professionals at three large customer corporations of the bank, the other five conspirators practiced impersonating the voices so that they would be accepted on the magnetic tape. Unfortunately for the perpetrators, they attempted to transfer too much money at one time, and the accounts of the three customer corporations were overdrawn. The three customers noticed this and immediately informed the bank, which stopped the funds transfer before the conspirators could complete the fraud. A court convicted all seven perpetrators of serious crimes.

In this case, the ongoing recording of important business messages was an important control. The recording significantly complicated the fraud, even though it may not have been material in discovering the crime.

- A highly intelligent thirty-one-year-old criminal convicted of perpetrating federal crimes in his acquisition of over $200,000 in a long series of attacks involving several banks, large corporations, and a check-cashing company, described a variety of social engineering techniques that he claimed were instrumental to his success. According to the miscreant, at least two-thirds of his social engineering acts were successful.

  He admitted using telephone calls and e-mail intrusions to penetrate very large companies, and relied on the impersonal relationships of employees to elicit information. In a typical attack, he called an employee or a manager in a large company, impersonated an e-mail administrator in the company, and informed the user that the secrecy of his e-mail user ID and password had been compromised and that his password must be changed immediately. The impostor then urged the victim to reveal the current password so that he could issue a new one. When he had obtained the user ID and password, the impostor logged onto the victim's account, read and analyzed the victim's stored mail, and sent messages to other employees in the victim's name to learn more about the business associates and functions of the employee. He then sent messages in the name of the victim to other employees, asking them to take specific actions, such as authorizing the issuance of checks to accomplish his frauds. If his victim was a manager, the perpetrator would send messages to the manager's employees demanding that they perform critical duties. He often conducted the e-mail sessions during the lunch hour, when the victim was unlikely to be using his e-mail service. He explained that using the e-mail service before or after working hours (in the morning and evening) looked suspicious.

  From this case, we learn the relative ease with which criminals can conduct social engineering, the vulnerabilities of e-mail, the extent of the gullibility of employees and managers (especially in large corporations), and the times of day that are propitious for attacks. The criminal's understanding that certain times of day were not suitable for his activities is typical of the lessons learned through experience. *(continued)*

■ An accused mass murderer and computer technologist admitted spying on a woman programmer with whom he was infatuated. He snooped through the young woman's calendar and internal company mailbox, cruised past her automobile to observe its contents, took down license plate numbers of suspected boyfriends, and watched her apartment at night to see whether she was entertaining. Because he had previously worked in military intelligence, he believed that he was part of an elite society, entitled to collect information about others. He said, "I feel I can, in essence, get away with things that normal people can not get away with . . . people who do not have security clearances." He went on to say, "I saw no difference between the government's ability to spy on people and my ability to do the same thing as long as I did not harm anybody."

This sad case shows that a broad spectrum of individuals are capable of engaging in social engineering, ranging from those playing innocent pranks to severely deranged mass murderers.

Displaying artifacts.   Showing that one possesses a badge, uniform, clipboard, computer listing, laptop computer, or any of a variety of official-looking or intimidating artifacts (including physically threatening devices such as guns) is one way to convince a victim of the authority and need-to-know status of a deceiver.

Enticing and sexually attracting.   An attractive individual is often effective in obtaining cooperation and information. In fact, voice and appearance can be used in a number of ways to disarm or identify with a victim to make the victim feel comfortable or agreeable to provide assistance and information.

Eliciting loyalty.   Siding with the victim in a dispute or joining together in a cause can form a bond that can be used to disarm an individual.

Intelligence gathering.   Information can be gathered by observation, such as analyzing traffic of people or communications. A great deal of sensitive information can be easily gathered by sending questionnaires to companies. Organizations should be wary of questionnaires that ask prying questions and/or do not offer confidentiality for respondents.

A Summary of Protective Techniques

If we know what motivates criminals, we may become more effective in our security efforts. The following list describes the various motivational strategies, along with the steps that we can take to implement security controls selections.

Personal problem solving. Helping employees to solve their problems legitimately by offering confidential advisory services is an enlightened management concept.

The higher ethic. We can stifle doing good by doing bad by providing codes of good conduct and ethics training.

Differential association. Reduce the "everybody is doing it" excuse by maintaining guides of good practice in the office environment and setting good examples in management behavior. We can blunt the stealing from the rich by placing value even on low-cost items and explaining the consequences if everybody pilfered.

Robin Hood syndrome. Management has an obligation to point out the consequences of loss to information owners and emphasize individual trust and responsibility in training and in training manuals, as well as to set good examples.

Pay back stolen value. Point out the difficulty of repaying or restoring unethical gains, and offer means of loaning money.

Personifying computers. Program computers to confront users with warning banners on their screens explaining the consequences of misbehavior that harms real people.

Predictability. Vary, hide, and delay some business decisions. This helps to keep even trusted people a little off balance.

Copycat victimization. Be aware of current loss experience suffered by others.

Social engineering. Remember that criminals often require knowledge about an organization, its environment, and its information infrastructure. Be wary of providing too much unnecessary detail to anyone, for any purpose. Avoid gullibility.

Finally, know thy enemies and understand their motives. It's better to defend against intrusion than to try to pick up the pieces after a successful attack against valuable information resources.

7

The Disastrous Hacker Culture

A lot has been written about hackers since 1971 when I first documented the menace that some of these individuals and groups can represent. In reality, hackers—and hacking—have also changed considerably in that time. The original hacker ethic of pushing technology to its extreme without causing harm to others has been subverted by a new wave of malicious hackers. These individuals have extended the ethic to include self-serving motives, primarily those of gaining notoriety, career, and wealth through uninhibited hacking. This infuriates the older, more idealistic generation of hackers, and also poses a great threat to society, which is being forced to impose ever more rigorous controls to safeguard its valuable resources.

Although hacking is not a new threat to information security, it is constantly evolving. Hackers continually grow more sophisticated in their methods for penetrating sensitive information systems. And, they use the Internet to communicate their techniques and tools to one another around the world, sharing new ideas and methods for subverting security controls, subverting systems, and stealing or sabotaging information. Business and government organizations are faced with the specter of technically sophisticated 12-year-old hackers competing to outdo one another, often without realizing—or caring—about the underlying damage they may cause with their computer exploitations.

In this chapter, I again call on my years of experience in dealing with hackers of all persuasions to provide insights that should help organizations defend against the very real threat of hacker attacks. We all need to understand, however, that the hacker problem will continue to plague us until, or unless, we manage to reduce the attraction it holds for the talented young. To some extent, we may accomplish this by imposing harsher penalties against malicious hackers when they are caught and convicted, and by using stronger controls such as cryptography to safeguard valuable information. But we also need to consider positive, constructive methods for directing youngsters into mainstream computer technology before they are trapped in the dead-end hacker culture.

WHAT IS HACKING?

To some extent, the definition of hacking depends on who you ask. Generally speaking, a "hack" used to be a quick fix or clever solution to a restriction. A hack was an ingenious, but temporary, fix or "make-do" rather than an attack on a system. Tricking a dumb machine into performing an unintended task was the predominant characteristic of a hack. Even a simple trick like sticking cellophane over pre-recorded tapes to reuse them as "blank" tapes can be described as a hack. Back in the 1960s, malicious hacking started with compromising telephone systems and stealing telephone services but soon spread to computers.

When we extend the term to the individuals who practice the art of hacking, however, the definitions become murkier. The Random House Second Edition of Webster's Dictionary (Ballantine Books, 1996) defines hacker as "a computer enthusiast who is especially proficient" or "a computer user who attempts to gain unauthorized access to computer systems." *Webster's II New Riverside University Dictionary*, which was cited in a 1990 legal decision against the Legion of Doom hacker group, defines a hacker as "one who gains unauthorized, usually non-fraudulent access (use) and those (sic) who enjoy investigating computer operating systems."

Bruce Sterling, author of *The Hacker Crackdown*, takes a rather positive view of the activity, explaining that the term *hack* "can signify the freewheeling intellectual exploration of the highest and deepest potential of computer systems. Hacking can describe the determination to make use of computers and information as free and open as possible, and can involve

Cap'n Crunch, Hero of the Phone Phreaks

Cap'n Crunch claims to be the inventor of the Blue box that generates the 2600-hertz tone that is used to subvert telephone call accounting systems (note that several others have made the same claim). Phone phreaks now command an arsenal of such boxes, designated by a spectrum of colors that range from Beige and Chartreuse to Neon and Paisley. Each of these boxes carries out specific hacking tasks. The versatile Pearl box, for example, can produce tones in the range from 1 to 9999 hertz, including 2600, 1633, 1336, and other crucial tones.

Since I wrote the definitive biography of the notorious hacker called Cap'n Crunch in a chapter of my book *Crime by Computer* in 1976, I have followed his career for more than twenty years. I met him again several years ago at the preview of the movie *Sneakers* in San Francisco. Hackers from the whole Bay Area were invited. Crunch was highly visible at the preview, as were references to him in the movie we were watching (much improved in accuracy than the earlier movie *WarGames* by the same writers and producers). He reminded me (as he always does when we meet) of his vulnerability while in prison to coercion by other prisoners who have tried to get him to reveal hacker and phone phreak secrets. (On one occasion, Mafia prisoners broke his back in a Pennsylvania prison when they discovered that he was giving them incorrect information. My plea to the judge to get him out of there worked.)

At the movie preview, Crunch mentioned his trips to Russia and the Ukraine in 1988—the then Soviet government treated him quite royally, with a complimentary car and a chauffeur. Ironically, Cap'n Crunch continued to complain about other hackers who electronically attack him and try to lure him into criminal conspiracies again.

---

the heartfelt conviction that beauty can be found in computers, that the fine aesthetic in a perfect program can liberate the mind and spirit." Sterling also tells about malicious hackers who, in his terms, are scofflaws who break into computers without permission. "They have a hatred of authority and do not regard the current rules of electronic behavior as respectable efforts to preserve law and order. Police, businessmen, politicians, and journalists are stupid people."

The *New Hacker's Dictionary* (written by hackers) offers six definitions for hacking and hacker:

- A person who enjoys exploring the details of programmable systems and how to stretch their capabilities, as opposed to many users, who prefer to learn only the minimum necessary
- One who programs enthusiastically (even obsessively)
- A person good at programming quickly
- An expert in a particular language or operating system, i.e., a UNIX hacker
- One who enjoys the intellectual challenge of overcoming or circumventing limitations
- A malicious meddler who tries to discover sensitive information by poking around

It also presents two basic principles hackers live by:

1. The belief that information sharing is a powerful positive good and that it is an ethical duty of hackers to share their expertise by writing free software and facilitating access to information and to computing resources wherever possible.
2. The belief that system cracking for fun and exploitation is ethically OK as long as the cracker commits no theft, vandalism, or breach of confidentiality.

Unfortunately, both of these principles express an idealism that is most remarkable for its self-serving irresponsibility and lack of respect for the computer privacy of people and organizations.

Much of the discrepancy in the various definitions lies with the difference between benign and malicious hackers. I define a benign hacker as anyone who is a proficient computer hobbyist, with a zeal for exploring computers and pushing them to their limits. The benign hacker may know how to cause unauthorized execution of a program in a computer but does not do so. A malicious hacker, on the other hand, is someone who routinely executes programs in other people's computers without their express or implied permission. Malicious hackers frequently engage in criminal acts while exploring others' computers, and violate the privacy of computer users and owners. They may also engage in software piracy, in spreading computer viruses, and in fraud, burglary, and theft.

In reality, there is great need to differentiate between benign and malicious hacking. Malicious hacking *always* does some type of damage; at the very least, it violates someone's privacy and uses someone's property without permission. This is true even if the hacker does not intend any harm or doesn't realize that a victim would view his actions to be malicious. (In fact, it is true even if the victim never knows that an attack occurred.) For example, some years ago, a notorious hacker was accused of hacking a computer that he presumably didn't know was used to automatically monitor heart patients. Those patients could have suffered simply because computer resources were unavailable for monitoring (such process control computers, in general, are very sensitive to extraneous interruption). And, because computer users feel a very real need to protect themselves from hackers, and recover the integrity and authenticity of their systems after attacks, they are forced to spend considerable amounts of money on specialized programs, technical staffs, and devices to safeguard their property. This expenditure further adds to the losses attributable to hacking. In the absence of the hacker menace, they would normally need no more than a reasonably good password entry control and a no trespassing warning screen banner (the equivalent of a sturdy lock and door) to meet a standard of due care.

Read More about It

For more information on hacking and infamous hackers, I suggest any or all of the following texts:

- *Hackers,* by Steven Levy (Anchor/Doubleday, 1984)
- *Cyberpunks: Outlaws and Hackers on the Computer Frontier,* by Katie Hafner and John Markoff (Hyperion, 1986)
- *The Cuckoo's Egg,* by Clifford Stoll (Doubleday, 1989)
- *The Hacker Crackdown: Law and Disorder on the Electronic Frontier,* by Bruce Sterling (Bantam, 1992)
- *Approaching Zero: Data Crime and the Underworld,* by Bryan Clough and Paul Mungo (Viking, 1994)
- *Masters of Deception,* a hackers' gangland book by Michelle Slatalla and Joshua Quittner (Harper Collins, 1995)
- *Takedown,* by Tsutomu Shimomura and John Markoff (Hyperion, 1996)
- *The Fugitive Game* and *the Watchman,* by Jonathon Littman (Little, Brown, 1996 and 1997)

It is interesting to note that some of these books so infuriated the hacker community that the authors suffered retribution in the form of damaged credit histories and stolen credit card numbers.

Masters of Deception

The authors of *Masters of Deception,* a nontechnical but revealing book, are journalists, and Mr. Quittner joined the *New York Times* and then Time Magazine as a computer technology reporter. The authors received guidance from Bruce Sterling (author of *The Hacker Crackdown*) and John Perry Barlow and Mike Godwin of *Electronic Frontier Foundation* fame, which gives the book a certain amount of civil libertarian persuasion.

The book reports in a highly factual and descriptive storytelling style about the formation and battles of two groups, Masters of Deception (MOD) in Queens, New York and Legion of Doom (LOD) in Texas. (Hackers hate to be called members of gangs; they refer to themselves as members of groups, which is more descriptive, since they are usually very loosely organized.) The book neither condemns nor praises the young hackers of the MOD and LOD groups and hacking in general. (The star of the MOD group, who is not really its leader, is the infamous and celebrated Phiber Optik, a convicted felon.)

A good deal of the book is taken up with the electronic warfare between MOD and LOD (whose leader, Erik Bloodax, served a stint as the moderator of Phrack, a hacker electronic bulletin board). The victim companies of the attacks are mercilessly portrayed as bumbling in their security efforts and receive little sympathy for the technical difficulties of fending off hoards of juvenile hackers who have seemingly unlimited time to beat down their systems. The hackers, in their usual irrational reasoning, claimed to believe that they were doing a public service by exposing the companies' vulnerabilities.

This book is important and valuable for information security specialists, because it provides significant insights into the culture and nature of the hacker community, important for dealing with any kind of hacker attacks. *Masters of Deception* demonstrates again the importance of defending our computer systems starting with resistance to social engineering, which is often the beginning of many hacker attacks to gain needed technical information.

WHO IS A HACKER?

In 1996, SRI International completed a study of more than 80 hackers and their associates in the United States and Europe. During the interviews, it became clear that the once honorable pursuit of hacking (as described by Levy in his 1984 book) had largely disappeared. In today's hacker culture, malicious hackers regularly engage in fabrications, exaggeration, thievery, and fantasy. They delight in presenting themselves to the media and general public as idealistic do-gooders, champions of the underdog, the "little guys" working against big computer vendors and doing good deeds along the way. Juvenile hackers often fantasize their roles as Clark Kents who become the Supermen of cyberspace. Unfortunately, their public persona is far from the truth.

Although malicious hackers range in age from preteen to senior citizens, they are characterized by an immature excessively idealistic attitude. Regardless of age, they act like irresponsible kids playing cops and robbers in a fantasy world that can suddenly turn real when they are caught. Even the youngest malicious hackers, however, quickly become "street smart" with advice and guidance from older hackers posted on outlaw bulletin board systems and Internet hacker chat boards, and in hacker magazines.

Hackers require varying degrees of explicit knowledge about the technical and operational aspects of the systems they attack. They generally obtain this information from other hackers, moles, or potential victims, or by studying available or stolen materials. The most common methods of obtaining information about a specific system targeted for attack is through social engineering or from informants. The hacker culture is a meritocracy, in which individuals rise in status according to the amount of knowledge and tools they possess. Social engineering skills (i.e., the ability to collect information through deception) are extremely valuable for gathering the information that hackers need to conduct successful attacks. Many of the most effective malicious hackers are, therefore, the ones who excel at social engineering.

A few malicious hackers have managed to turn their lives around and obtain responsible positions in information technology. These individuals have done so, however, only by totally rejecting the hacker culture and its values. For the most part, these are intelligent, talented individuals who could have achieved successful careers early in life. Instead, they wasted a significant portion of their lives, then spent more years making up for that waste. Malicious hacking is truly a dead-end pursuit for most who enter into it.

My studies indicate that hackers fear incarceration more than anything else. Hacker activity seems to dwindle immediately following well-publicized arrests and/or convictions. Hackers are well aware that their illegal activities are vulnerable to scrutiny by law enforcement agencies such as the police, FBI, and Secret Service—after all, who knows better

The Musical Master Spy

Recent studies of actual hacker crimes reveal that there are many misconceptions about hackers. In one instance, members of the U.S. military, testifying before the U.S. Armed Services Committee in Congress in 1994, described a "master spy" that posed a major threat to U.S. security. The military chiefs feared that an East European spy ring had successfully hacked into American Air Defense systems and learned some of its most well-guarded intelligence secrets. A 13-month investigation however, revealed that a 16-year-old British music student was responsible for the break-ins. The culprit, known as the Datastream Cowboy, had downloaded dozens of military files, including details of ballistic missile research and development, and had used a company's network in California for more than 200 logged security breaches—all using a $1,200 computer and modem. He was tried and convicted in 1997, and fined $1,915 by a London court. After his conviction, the media offered the musical hacker considerable sums for the book and film rights to his story, but he declined, preferring to continue his musical studies and concentrate on winning a place in a leading London orchestra.

than a hacker how easy it is to monitor someone else's computer? This knowledge should lead us to step up our surveillance activities of known hacker groups and increase the use of sting operations to legally entrap hackers. We then need to engage in vigorous prosecutions and publicize examples of lengthy prison sentences meted out to hackers.

HOW MUCH HACKING IS THERE?

There are no valid statistics to determine how much hacking really occurs, and there never will be because we can't quantify what we do not know. That is, there is no way to estimate the total number of hacker events that could lead to valid, representative samples for the surveys. Many victims who could respond to surveys do everything they can to avoid mentioning their embarrassing experience, and the real malicious hackers are not talking either—only the hacker wannabes, who are prone to exaggerating their partly fictitious exploits. Theoretical tests for detecting hacker attacks suggest that many go unnoticed, and there is no generally agreed upon definition of a hacker attack. Finally, qualified researchers have never found sufficient funding to do valid surveys and test their success.

In May 1996, the head of the GAO testified at a U.S. Senate hearing that hackers were attempting to break in to military computers approximately 250,000 times each year. He estimated that 65 percent of the attacks are successful, and only four percent of these are detected. In considering this testimony, it is important to understand that one hacker can make any number of automated attacks against one or more computers in only one session of computer use, accounting for hundreds of thousands of attacks in just a few seconds. How would the GAO know that only four percent are detected (or that 96 percent are undetected)? They would have to know the total number of attacks, which no one knows. (Penetration testing of systems is not a valid source of statistics about real attacks.)

HOW A HACKER HACKS

I am often asked how an unauthorized person (i.e., a malicious hacker) can cause one or more computer programs to perform unwanted activities (i.e., hack) in somebody else's computer. There are several obvious ways. One is for the malicious hacker to physically intrude onto the premises containing the computer and impersonate its owner. Such impersonation may be easy if the owner has not protected the computer by requiring a secret password to start its operation and initiate its operating system. Even if a password is required, the hacker may be able to guess it (using a password cracking tool that tests many passwords), find it written somewhere, observe it during use (i.e., shoulder surf), or deceive the owner into revealing it. If all else fails and the hacker can't start the computer without a password, he can reinstall the operating system. This makes the hack a little more difficult and time-consuming, but not impossible.

Another, indirect way to gain control is for the malicious hacker to deceive the legitimate user into entering and executing a Trojan horse program in the computer. A Trojan horse program contains computer instructions—unknown to the user—that perform the hacker's attack. Alternatively, the hacker may take advantage of a known vulnerability of a computer operating system such as UNIX or Microsoft Windows. This is usually the most technical method and requires detailed knowledge of the operating system (unless a prepackaged search tool such as SATAN is used).

A Hypothetical Attack

Any computer is vulnerable to attack, even if it is protected with effective password entry control. In this example, I'll illustrate how a hacker can exploit a known vulnerability in an early UNIX operating system. We have no way of knowing how many hackers took advantage of this vulnerability (which was discovered by security people), but we do know that the vulnerability existed for at least 10 years (and may still exist in some systems). Some variations of this vulnerability have appeared in a number of other operating systems as well.

The UNIX logon record contains four contiguous fields for storing four fixed-length words as follows:

USER ID	PASSWORD	CRYPT MASTER	CRYPT PASSWORD

- The first field, *USER ID*, is where UNIX stores the user's identification after the user enters it from the keyboard at logon. It is usually the nonsecret name of an authorized user already registered in the computer's list of user IDs.
- UNIX uses the second field, *PASSWORD*, to store the user's six-character password when the user enters it.
- UNIX uses the third field, *CRYPT MASTER*, to store the user's password in encrypted form, obtained from a stored list. This list, the access control list, contains the authorized user IDs and a master encrypted password associated with each ID, described, in part, as follows:

USER ID #1   CRYPT MASTER PASSWORD #1
USER ID #2   CRYPT MASTER PASSWORD #2
.   .   .
USER ID #N   CRYPT MASTER PASSWORD #N

- UNIX uses the fourth field, *CRYPT PASSWORD*, to store the password that was stored briefly in the PASSWORD field, after UNIX encrypts it. UNIX uses a generally available program called *CRYPT* to perform one-way cryptography. (It is called one-way cryptography because nobody can reasonably decrypt the scrambling without first knowing the crypto key, in this case the password, and text to be scrambled. Obviously, if one knew the key, decryption would be unnecessary.)

The UNIX operating system accepts a user logon in the following way: When you log on and type your user ID, UNIX places that information in the USER ID field of the logon record. UNIX then uses that information to look up and obtain a copy of the matching encrypted password from among the user IDs and master encrypted passwords stored in the access control list. UNIX stores a copy of this master encrypted password in the CRYPT MASTER field of the logon record.

When you type your secret password, UNIX stores it in the PASSWORD field of the logon record. UNIX now has the input needed from you and from the access control list in the first three fields of the logon record. UNIX then encrypts the password received from you (stored in the PASSWORD field) and places the result in the CRYPT PASSWORD field in the logon record. UNIX immediately erases the PASSWORD field in the logon record to minimize the time that the password is present in the computer in clear text form, where a malicious hacker might capture it. (It doesn't matter if a hacker captures an encrypted, well-chosen, password, because it can not be decrypted.)

Finally, UNIX compares the encrypted password (derived from the password received from you) in the CRYPT PASSWORD field of the logon record to the encrypted master password in the CRYPT MASTER field (copied from the access control list). If they are equal, then you have entered the correct password and are accepted by UNIX as the user you claim to be.

This very secure process requires a field-length limit control for each field of the logon record. If a word has too many characters to fit in a field, it is rejected. The programmer who programmed the UNIX operating system, however, made a fatal mistake that violates good operating system specifications. The second field of the logon record, PASSWORD, was designed to hold the six-character password entered from the keyboard, but had no field-length limit check. If a user entered a password with more than six characters, the excess characters were stored in the next field of the logon record, replacing any characters stored there.

A malicious hacker could exploit this vulnerability by obtaining the valid user ID of an authorized user, then creating a password using any six characters and encrypting it using CRYPT (which is available in any UNIX system). The hacker would then type in the user ID to logon to the system. UNIX would use it to look up the same user ID and the correct matching master encrypted password in the access control list data file, and store a copy of that master encrypted password in the CRYPT MASTER field of the logon record. The hacker would then type in twelve characters—the six password characters he created followed by the six characters of the encrypted form of the password. Because there was no field limit control, the first six characters enter the PASSWORD field of the logon record and the second six characters overwrite and replace the six characters of the master encrypted password in the CRYPT MASTER field of the logon record. UNIX dutifully encrypts the password received from the hacker in the PASSWORD field of the logon record, stores it in the CRYPT PASS-WORD field, and then compares it with the contents of the CRYPT MAS-TER field, which is now the hacker's encrypted version of his own password that he created. Because the fields match, UNIX accepts the malicious hacker as the valid user whose ID the hacker is using. Mission accomplished.

There is no way for UNIX operators or users to know that an impostor is using the system unless the real user attempts to logon with the same user ID at the same time. If the system control is set to prohibit multiple logons by the same user, one of the users—either the impostor or the valid user—would fail to achieve a logon. If that happened, and if the legitimate user reported it, the attack might be detected.

UNDERSTANDING THE HACKER CULTURE

If we are to stop young people from entering the malicious hacker culture, we must understand what it is, how it works, and how it attracts them. While it is certainly true that there is no such thing as a "typical" hacker profile, I have found some common characteristics among the malicious hackers that I've interviewed. In general, the culture is populated with young males, ranging from about 12 to 24 years old, with a few older participants. The few females in the culture are highly recognized and notable exceptions, such as Susan Thunder, Kyrie, and Charlotte Boregard.

The hacker culture encompasses a wide variety of individuals, ranging from children engaged in playing pranks on one another, to deeply studious people attempting to learn the wonders of information technology by trial and error; from hardened criminals to, explorers and to thinkers, from juvenile delinquents to terrorists. Hackers come from all economic and social strata—from the very poor to the very rich and from the best and worst of families—with representatives from all ethnic and racial backgrounds. Unfortunately, the culture seems to attract more than its share of inveterate liars, exaggerators, thieves, impractical idealists, anarchists, sexual deviants, and mentally ill individuals. These unsavory elements dangerously rub shoulders (figuratively) with the well-balanced, generally responsible, clean-living kids who begin hacking simply for entertainment or from peer pressure. Some hackers delight in deviating from acceptable practices of behavior, while others conform strictly to societal norms—at least when they are away from their computer keyboards. Many would never consider committing crime "in person" but have no hesitation (let alone remorse) about using computers to lie or steal.

Hackers almost always use pseudonyms—called handles—to hide their real identities. They choose names from science fiction or television—most of them quite bizarre—to support their fantasies. Many hackers are independent in nature; they deplore being members of clubs or organized, managed groups. However, many do seek anarchistic associations with other hackers in loosely structured groups such as the Legion of Doom and Masters of Deceit. Such groups are totally fluid, with frequent comings and goings, and remarkably little long-term loyalty. Some encourage face-to-face meetings, such as at the monthly meetings of *2600* magazine readers, which are held in 20 U.S. cities at 5:00 PM on the first Friday of each month (in the telephone lobby of Citicorp Tower in New York City and in a shopping mall at the Pentagon in the Washington, D.C. area).

Hacker Revenge

When I irritated several hackers on a chat room board some years ago, they posted my home telephone number on several hacker BBSs. One of them used simple social engineering to add a call-forwarding feature to my home telephone service, then convinced a telephone company sales representative to call-forward my incoming calls to an 800 number answered by a men's hair restoration company. (I happen to be extremely follicle impaired.) Because of the prank, callers were unable to complete calls to my home, a fact that caused my family considerable anguish due to a serious medical emergency at my home on that day.

These meeting are entirely without order or agenda and generally resemble cocktail parties except for the clothes worn, the content of the chitchat, and the drinks and hors d'oeuvres served. Other groups consist of people who have never met, never intend to meet, and can identify one another only by their hacker handles. Competition and deceit flourish in this type of anonymous relationship. (Threats of death, bodily harm, and extortion occur in this culture as well, but they never have been carried out to my knowledge.)

Many hackers attempt to justify their activities by claiming that they are protecting society from the vulnerabilities of insecure computers and communications facilities. They claim that many companies and government agencies have inadequate security, and see it as their hacker duty to identify and publish these weaknesses to warn the public, which might otherwise be harmed by the security flaws. Their attacks and writings are meant to coerce "the establishment" into corrective action, and to force the errant organizations to apologize for the harm done to society. They generally express great disdain for the telephone companies, Microsoft, and other big businesses and government—a theme that is echoed endlessly on the hacker bulletin boards and in *2600* magazine articles.

Hackers are often guilty of other crimes in addition to using others' computers without authorization. They are, for example, usually the creators and disseminators of computer viruses, and may engage in burglaries to steal technical manuals and equipment in their quest for knowledge about information and communications technology. Many hackers are also engaged in software piracy.

Some parents of hackers ignore their nefarious activities, while others actually encourage them. More commonly, however, the hackers' parents are blissfully unaware of what their children are doing. They indulge them with costly equipment and the freedom to do whatever they wish. A few older people in the hacker culture act as "Fagins," luring young people into malicious hacking. Some hackers are anarchists and civil libertarians hiding behind their civil rights, some are skinhead Nazis or extreme right-wingers, and still others are merely older people possibly with career problems who amuse themselves by engaging directly or vicariously in malicious hacking activities. A few malicious hackers have engaged in other types of criminal activities—either independent of their hacking activities or associated with it. And, because the culture is largely anonymous and populated primarily by young people, it is an easy target for pedophiles, as some recent prosecutions have indicated. The only common factor among hackers is the use of personal computers and modems connecting them.

Hacker Sympathizers

Some individuals don't view hacking, or hackers, as a major problem. These sympathizers encompass a wide variety of individuals—all with their own rationales and motivations—but they represent an important aspect of the hacker culture, since they encourage young people to embark on the dead-end journey into malicious hacking or to continue on the path once they've started. I have extensively interviewed some of these dissidents and find them to be ominous.

Many hacker sympathizers believe that hacking is a problem only to the individuals or organizations that do not provide sufficient safeguards. In their view, victims of hacker attacks share some or all of the blame for such attacks because they fail to provide effective safeguards. So, penalties against the hackers should be mitigated by the degree to which the computer owner/user did or did not provide effective protection. Of course, this view assumes that controls are always available and practical to prevent such attacks, and that is not the case. An attack by a sufficiently resolute hacker will *always* succeed, given enough time. Effective information security requires constant vigilance on the part of the owners and users to drive hackers to easier targets. While a hacker can be singleminded in his pursuit and choose his time of attack, a victim must defend from any adversary, in all ways, and at all times—all while maintaining productive use of the information systems.

Most hacker sympathizers do agree that "real crimes" should be prosecuted, but their definition of "real crime" is often tainted by their own prejudices against the establishment. To many hacker sympathizers, some crimes against telephone companies, credit reporting services, and giant corporations—especially those viewed as unfriendly to the environment—are justifiable. They rationalize that such organizations "deserve it for the harm they cause to society." They defend hacker attacks as "protests" or civil rights exercises. They seem to accept a hacker's violation of the privacy of computer owners while strongly supporting the right to privacy otherwise. These arguments, which are often widely reported by the media, deliver a mixed message to impressionable young hackers: Hacking is okay, except when you cause harm, but causing harm is okay as long as you harm someone or something that causes harm to our society. It's little wonder that some young hackers are surprised when they end up facing criminal charges for their actions.

In reality, there is no justification for hacking in others' computers. We own our computers and (with exceptions) do not make all of their services freely available to others. Our right to privacy should not depend on how much or how little security we apply. Outside of a few cases in which security may be required by law, or by regulations such as in banking, the amount of security that we choose to apply is strictly a business decision. If a business chooses to rely on the deterrent value of criminal law, rather than applying strong security constraints to its computer systems and networks, it does not share any responsibility for a hacker attack against that system unless blatant vulnerabilities constitute a danger to others.

Failed Rehabilitation by a Hacker Sympathizer

I met Dark Dante when he was 18 years old. A friend of mine, a reformed hacker, brought him to my office at SRI International for a chat. I was doing research on computer crime on a grant from the U.S. Department of Justice at the time and was interviewing hackers.

Dark Dante and a hacker friend were competing to see who could take over control of the UCLA mainframe computer from the other, much to the consternation of the Computer Services department. The skinny, nervous kid sitting in my office did not look like much of a threat to anyone, but when he entered cyberspace, his handle took on ominous dimensions. He became Dark Dante with a very modest weapon, a little Radio Shack TRS-80 computer in his bedroom. (Jonathan Littman reveals the full story of Dark Dante in his excellent book, *The Watchman* [Little, Brown, 1997].)

Unbeknownst to me, my friend convinced SRI to hire Dark Dante as a computer operator in order to rehabilitate him. Dark Dante quickly worked his way up to systems programmer and gained a high government secrecy clearance, but he could not resist the challenge of hacking. One thing led to another, and he began breaking in to Pacific Telephone Company facilities—high-tech *Mission Impossible* style—and stealing computer and telephone equipment and documents. He was also monitoring FBI and Soviet Consulate private communications, infiltrating federal investigations of mobsters and former Philippine President Ferdinand Marcos, and stealing data files from government computers. (He is quoted in newspapers: "I like something challenging. . . . To be physically inside an office, finding the flaws in the system and what works, was intellectually challenging. It proved irresistible. It was not for ego or money. It was fun. And at the time, it seemed pretty harmless.")

Dark Dante and his pal were caught when a storage rental company manager broke into his locker after he failed to pay the rent and discovered the stolen equipment. Dark Dante was indicted on serious charges, including espionage. He skipped out on bail and was a fugitive for several years until he got into trouble again in a radio station contest scam. He had rigged the local telephone system in Los Angeles to make himself the ninth caller in a call-in contest and won $30,000, a Porsche automobile, and a free Hawaiian vacation. While one of the co-conspirators was on bail for another computer crime, he helped the FBI to trap Dark Dante. The FBI rented him an apartment with computers, phone lines, and pagers. Among other things, he helped seize Dark Dante's computer, resulting in evidence used to convict him, and helped gather evidence against the other conspirator, who was ultimately prosecuted and convicted.

Dark Dante spent five years in jail as a fugitive awaiting trial, and has probably served the longest incarceration of any hacker. He ultimately pled guilty to charges of computer fraud, mail fraud, intercepting wire and electronic communications, money laundering, and removing property to prevent seizure. As of this writing, he is trying to get a probation restriction lifted that prohibits him from using a computer for three years. It is ironic that the misguided help of do-gooders contributed to setting this hacker on the path to becoming a fugitive from the FBI.

In my view, the media has been partially responsible for the general public's past lenient view of malicious hacking. Here are two examples of how they (the media) sometimes mislead the public about hackers and their activities:

- They typically quote maximum penalties faced by hackers, stating the sum of all of the possible penalties for all of the charges as if they were to be served sequentially. Although quoting these maximum penalties is correct in showing the total exposures, convictions are seldom achieved on all charges, maximum penalties are rarely applied, and penalties are nearly always applied concurrently rather than sequentially. Add to that the fact that hackers typically serve less than one half of their prison sentences, and the reports are clearly misleading.

- They report that hackers obtain "free" telephone time or computer services, neglecting to mention the actual dollar value of the time or services stolen by the hackers. Using the term "free" implies that the services are available free of charge, and creates a prejudiced view of the crime. After all, how serious can it be to take something that is "free"?

HACKING AS A CRIME

Unauthorized use of others' computers, information, and networks is a crime in most legal jurisdictions in the Western world. The greatest losses from hacking are usually the costs of the victim's staff to repair the damage done to computer-stored information and to restore the integrity and authenticity of computer and communication systems. Restoring the confidence of staff and customers, improving security, increased insurance premiums, and staff time to assist in investigations also add to the cost of an attack. Hacking becomes big-time crime usually when hackers advance to sabotage, larceny, espionage, credit card theft, and fraud after gaining control of victims' computers or when they are recruited by serious criminals to advise and assist them. But this escalation has occurred relatively rarely so far as we know.

Laws against computer crime vary widely among state and federal jurisdictions, complicating enforcement and conviction. In New York, for example, Penal Law #156 requires that computer owners post warnings against trespass. If there is no warning banner on the logon screen warning intruders to "keep out," prosecutors may have difficulty winning a conviction for illegal computer entry. Texas computer crime law requires that "adequate security" be in place before any unauthorized computer use can be prosecuted. Other laws against malicious hacking, such as the British Computer Misuse Act and the U.S. Computer Fraud and Abuse Act, link the degree of penalty for the crime to its technical sophistication—attaching minimal penalties for unauthorized computer use and maximum penalties for unauthorized modification or destruction of information in a computer. In my view, these laws are badly formulated; the legislators do not understand that merely using a computer can do massive damage in some cases (e.g., when it is a process control computer in which time of response is critical) or that unauthorized modification or destruction of information—even on a massive scale—may result in minimal harm (e.g., when a copy is preserved for recovery or the information can be easily recreated). The invasion of privacy alone should be sufficient to apply significant penalties to unauthorized use, even if the hacker does not intentionally perform any harmful actions.

Law enforcers have made arrests at gunpoint in a few instances of vigorously investigated suspected computer hacker crimes. Civil rights activists complain when the police burst through doors with guns drawn to conduct searches of hackers' homes. However, they ignore the targeted hackers' public postings about the terrible things including murder and other hideous harm that they will do, or would like to do, to any officer investigating them. They have the right to protect themselves in the face of such threats, even though the threats may be juvenile braggadocio. There is no dispute that the U.S. Constitution First, Fourth, and Fifth Amendment protection of free speech and from unreasonable search and seizure should be afforded to hackers as well as drug dealers. However, computer technologists and enthusiasts do not have some special privilege to abuse these rights and to be protected in special ways from the generally accepted practices of law enforcement officers and the judicial process.

Rules of evidence generally require that law enforcement agencies retrieve information from computers under highly controlled conditions to ensure its integrity and authenticity and to avoid collection of irrelevant information. All too often, officers are bewildered by a hacker's sophisticated computer environment and are unable to extract the pertinent evidence from the jerry-rigged system. Some hackers even insert logic bombs into their computers to destroy evidence if police or parents use normal procedures to view information. Efforts are currently underway in many jurisdictions to restate evidence rules, produce new guidelines, provide additional training for officers, and generally make computer searches more reasonable. These improvements should ultimately solve the problems of excess on both sides.

Understandably, there is considerable controversy over penalties for hackers once they are caught and convicted. Except in extreme cases, judges rarely incarcerate malicious hackers for a first offense, particularly those who did not attempt to gain from their crimes. But it is sometimes difficult to tell what is a first offense. When juvenile hackers are tried in Juvenile Court, their cases are handled confidentially and the records sealed. So, law enforcement agencies have no way of differentiating first-time adult offenders from long-term juvenile offenders. Keeping the crimes confidential also loses much of the deterrent effect that publicizing the arrests and convictions could have on offenders. Unfortunately, when hackers are incarcerated they often become tutors for other prisoners, either voluntarily or under coercion. In effect, the prisons become gradu-

Catching an International Hacker

As far as I know, the first federal case in which investigators used a security computer program tool to help catch a malicious hacker occurred in March 1996. The investigators used a commercial computer program called iWatch (the first letter stands for *intruder*) that they ran on a government computer at Harvard University. The iWatch program captures network data that flow between computers so that they can be saved and analyzed. The software watches for hacker signature activity and presents just those portions to the user, much as during a telephone wiretap the human monitor is supposed to hang up unless the call is related to the case under investigation. Because the search was conducted by iWatch, human eyes never saw the communications of the legitimate users, and their privacy was not violated. In this case the FBI viewed passwords that the hacker was using.

The program searched the Internet for the targeted criminal among 16,000 university computer users. The FBI programmed iWatch to identify various handles used by the hacker, as well as his computer use habits, sites that were attacked, and accounts that were hit. The hacker called himself Griton (Spanish for "screamer"). Once the FBI knew the passwords and login names that the hacker was using, the data were again scanned, and whenever these words were found, the software presented the words plus eighty characters around them so that investigators could see the words in context. iWatch was left to work undisturbed through November and December in 1995 until investigators narrowed the thousands of possibilities to one unauthorized hacker. The FBI identified his real name and location while he was using a Harvard computer as a staging point to illegally enter numerous other Internet sites, including computers operated by the U.S. Navy, NASA, and Caltech's Jet Propulsion Laboratory from his home in Buenos Aries. Argentine police raided his home in December 1995; the 21-year-old hacker was charged with possession of unauthorized devices (illegal use of passwords) under the Computer Fraud and Abuse Act (18USC 1029), unlawful interception of electronic communications under Title 18 USC 2511, and destructive activity in connection with computers under Title 18 U.S.C. 1030. He remained free, because the U.S. charges against him are not among those designated under the current U.S.-Argentine extradition treaty. He finally agreed to extradition to stand trial in the U.S., possibly because the U.S. justice system is kinder than the Argentine system. He pled guilty and was sentenced to three years' probation and a $5000 fine.

ate schools for crime, and hackers are often more dangerous in prison than outside. There is little doubt, however, that significant prison sentences can have important deterrent value; juvenile hackers are shocked to find that their peccadilloes are serious enough to deserve incarceration. Society, with its increasing dependence on information technology, needs to make it clear that violating the confidentiality of other people's computers and information is a serious offense.

First offenders do, however, generally deserve a chance to extricate themselves from the hacker culture. One of the most effective punishments for juvenile hackers is to deprive them of the use of computers. In April 1996, an enlightened St. Louis magistrate placed a 19-year-old alleged hacker under house arrest while he faced computer fraud charges. The man was prohibited from using modems, computers, or computer parts, and further ordered to not even discuss computers during his house arrest. While the last stipulation may have been impossible to enforce, the order was intended to remove the man—at least temporarily—from the hacker culture.

Computer viruses, those annoying and sometimes costly bugs that we have all become accustomed to dealing with in one way or another, are generally written and distributed by hackers (by definition). But, because these hackers are difficult to identify in the huge, anonymous maze of cyberspace, they are rarely apprehended or prosecuted. One exception occurred in Britain in 1995 when the infamous Black Baron pleaded guilty to 11 charges related to writing and distributing computer viruses costing victims "well in excess of half a million pounds," and was sentenced to prison. Strangely enough, the few of those who are caught are often identified because of their desire for celebrity status; they freely admit responsibility for their viruses in the underground hacker network and have been known to grant interviews with the media. (Unfortunately, the publicity of the Black Baron case brought attention to his viruses that encouraged other hackers to further distribute his viruses around the world!)

CONFERENCES WHERE HACKERS GATHER TOGETHER

Hackers love meetings and conferences. They are opportunities to brag about their exploits, get a look at their distant electronic buddies and enemies, identify and schmooze with law enforcers who also attend, and further develop their reputations. (They can also be an occasion to get drunk, space out on drugs, and trash the hotels in which they meet.) They might even learn a little to increase their hacking skills and knowledge. (I continue to be amazed that parents let their teenagers go off to Las Vegas or to Almere in the Netherlands by themselves.)

The four big periodical conferences are the Hack-Tic conferences held every four years at various campgrounds in the Netherlands, the annual 2600 conferences in New York City, annual DefCon meetings in Las Vegas, and the Hacker Conferences held each year at Lake Tahoe in California. Other smaller conferences such as SummerCon in Atlanta and HoHoCon held in Texas (near Christmas time) are held as well. The California hacker conferences are meetings for the original generation of hackers who seem to worry mostly about protecting their products from piracy and do not include the malicious hacking content of the others. The 2600 conferences seem to consist mostly of diatribes against the telephone companies and big business. The DefCon conferences are somewhat more sinister, yet they have some aspects in common with mainstream security conferences—show up, and well-known companies are there to recruit new employees. DefCon V at the Aladdin Hotel in Las Vegas in 1997, where one thousand hackers showed up, included such activities as contests to identify the undercover law enforcement people who attended. Speakers reported very little that is of any importance or any new hacking methods or system vulnerabilities, and they exaggerated many of the claims of hacking achievements. (Really malicious hackers are not going to reveal their most powerful methods and current illegal activities publicly.)

The Hack-Tic conferences in the Netherlands are in a different league than the DefCons. The Galactic Hacking Party (GHP) was held in 1989, followed by the Hacking at the End of the Universe (HEU) conference in 1993 and the Hacking in Progress (HIP) conference in 1997. The latter was a reported $180 thousand affair with a 1,000 seat circus tent, 250 computer work areas, 800 kilowatts of power, ten megabits per second fiber wiring, twelve pay telephones (that were promptly compromised), and a gravestone for Bill Gates. Over fifteen hundred people and their computers attended the HIP, mostly from the Netherlands and Germany, with a smattering of people from the United Kingdom, Belgium, and the United States. The attendees were wary about sharing information and probably overestimated the importance of what they each knew. Speakers failed to reveal much of immediate use for hacking, and strangely, they made no mention of firewalls.

The main topics of the previous HEU meeting were social engineering, lock picking, and trashing. The 1997 HIP topics covered technology and politics, including attacks on the Electronic Data Systems Corporation (for controlling too much personal information) and Microsoft, Internet vulnerabilities, and DES and PGP cryptography cracking. The Chaos Computer Club from Hamburg, Germany described its attacks on ActiveX and Java programming languages and Microsoft Internet Explorer. It seemed everybody was there to protect society from presumed exploitation by the military-commercial establishment.

THE NEW GENERATION OF HACKERS

My two-year recent study of hacker threats against the public switched telephone systems in Europe and America indicates that the latest generation of hackers is hacking for financial gain, in addition to traditional objectives. The two most prominent means of accomplishing this are through call-sell telephone fraud and commercial software and computer game piracy, all of which are on the rise. In addition, these hackers are using paid informants within target organizations along with social engineering to gather the necessary knowledge for their initial attacks.

Hackers as Security Experts

Despite some media predictions, there is little prospect for easing tensions between information security managers, who are the defenders of information and computers, and the malicious hackers, who are the violators. In an article in the MIT *Technology Review,* "Hackers Taking a Byte out of Computer Crime," Wade Roush says that "as members of tiger teams . . . and developers of password or encryption systems, ex-hackers are often better grounded in real-world challenges of keeping information secure than the information security profession." This ignores the issue of trust and business sensitivity needed in the work, and the fact that keeping information secure is mostly a matter of good management and motivation of computer users, not just secure technology. And hackers have little, if any, management and business experience. Their knowledge is largely restricted to the computer operating systems that they have hacked.

Why would information security managers hire malicious hackers—practicing or "reformed"—to engage in real, live tiger team attacks against their systems? These hackers have lied, cheated, and stolen—and they have treated other computer users with disdain. Based on my experience, many reformed hackers may still possess the hacker mindset and may continue

A New Generation Hacker

I sat in the spartan lobby of the Hamburg, Germany Holiday Inn nervously awaiting the arrival of a hacker whom I planned to interview for an extensive research project on the dangers to the United States of hacking public switched telephone systems. A writer for a German magazine had arranged the contact. Just as I was beginning to doubt that he would show up, a huge, cherubic youth walked in and introduced himself. The 18-year-old hacker was dressed entirely in black with a Minnesota Vikings cap stuck backwards on his oversized head.

After I gained his trust, he told me his real name and a bit about his family and background. He made a living from selling cheap PCs and modems stuffed with special programs, developed by his "research department" that made his products into telephone connectors allowing telephone calls to be placed anytime and anyplace without charge. He had a great market among Turkish guest workers in Germany, who used the products to make calls to their families in Turkey, as well as sales to lawyers and other professionals. The only problem was that he had to supply the PCs with new numbers when the American telephone companies that his customers were defrauding in the calls they were making changed their security codes. The numbers were easy enough to obtain from his spy who worked for an American telephone company, but finding his customers to update their systems was a big job.

This youthful hacker got a lot of help from his group of hackers, who were organized into research, development, marketing, accounting, and sales departments. They were spread around the world in Finland, Denmark, Italy, and elsewhere. He advertised successfully without cost by being a magazine and TV celebrity. He was the frequent subject of media attention, demonstrating his products and services. The German police largely ignored him, since he concentrated on defrauding telephone companies in other countries and took great pains to hide his compromising of the Deutschebundespost telephone services. But he monitored the secure police telephones anyway, just to keep track of them with the assistance of a mole who worked for the police.

To get him to tell me his secrets, I had to pay for him to travel with me all the way to my next field research stop in Amsterdam, where he immediately turned tail and headed back to Hamburg when the Dutch hackers I was interviewing threatened him. The travel was not without incident. Besides the expense of obtaining two airline seats for him (he did not fit in one seat), during a stopover in Düsseldorf I had to get him a hotel room at the Marriott. Like a huge bat, he sleeps during daylight and is busy hacking all night. We attracted great attention walking to dinner in the hot Düsseldorf summer evening, him in his black attire with a bandana over his face, cowboy style (he wanted to travel incognito) and me in my business suit.

Over dinner (consisting of four Coca Colas) he told me some of his amazing feats. He claims that he can shut down all of Manhattan by interfering with the online computer-controlled air conditioning systems in the buildings there. He claimed to have caused the collapse of a European business in Florida by creating huge phone bills for them. Mostly, he surprised me with his descriptions of the changes in the new generation of hackers—particularly, of hackers who have given up the old hacker ethic and now hack for profit, and of the new hacker practice of using moles in companies targeted for attack. (The moles are usually the hackers' friends or old school chums who "went straight" and got real jobs.)

He calls me in California periodically asking for help—for example, to get a hacker friend sprung from jail in the United States, which I describe in the next sidebar, "The Maximillian Hacker Case." Each call begins with some strange beeps, clicks, and whistles. He wanted to make enough money selling his illicit products to go straight and open a computer store in Hamburg. However, these days he claims to be a successful computer consultant specializing in security—much to my chagrin.

to consort with other malicious hackers, who may coerce or influence them.

Responsible information security managers are well advised to avoid cooperation with malicious hackers—even so-called reformed ones. There are plenty of well-educated, experienced computer experts who have proven themselves by their academic and work achievements in the types of technical environments being tested. Dan White, national director of information security at Ernst & Young, (www.eyi.com), was quoted in *Information Week Magazine* (March 13, 1995, page 13): "The risks involved with hiring a hacker are simply too great. There's no assurance that a hacker will leave systems well enough alone after his work is done."

Phiber Optik is one of the most belligerent hackers that I know and have interviewed. This 25-year-old New Yorker spent nearly a year in jail in 1995 for breaking into telephone systems as part of the Masters of

The Maximilian Hacker Case

On November 14, 1994 I received a call from my hacker contact in Hamburg asking me to give advice to his friend Max (Maximilian, associated with the Paradox hacker group), who was in federal prison in Virginia awaiting sentencing for a felony crime.

The news media reported that the U.S. Secret Service had arrested Max on September 29, 1994 upon his arrival at Dulles airport as the leader of an international ring of criminals selling telephone calling card numbers. The charges claimed that he and his group stole forty thousand numbers that accounted for one and a half million dollars in long distance calls. The Secret Service lured him to the United States, with the help of one of his associates who worked for Cleartel Communications in Washington, D.C. (Starting back in 1992, his associates in the United States gathered the calling card numbers and then sent them by e-mail to a hacker in London, who forwarded them to Max in Spain.)

I agreed to talk to Max, and he called me collect on November 17 from prison, where he was awaiting sentencing after pleading guilty. He said he was facing ten years in prison, but he thought that could possibly be reduced to six years. His plan was to try to get it reduced to three years of house incarceration by cooperating with the telephone company victims of his crime, with my assistance. (He boasted that he could teach security vulnerabilities. When I suggested that he stop associating with malicious hackers, he responded that he needed to stay in touch with them to get more information that would be valuable for the telephone companies.)

His attorney in Washington, D.C. told me that he had already set up meetings with two telephone companies so that Max could reveal his knowledge. I gave him Jim Christy's name at Project Slammer, part of Air Force Investigations (Jim now works for SAIC).

For me, the case was concluded when I read in the February 2, 1995 *Washington Post* that Max was sentenced to five years and restitution of one million dollars by Judge Cacheris in the U.S. District Court in Alexandria, Virginia.

Deception (MOD) group. Today, while still on probation, he calls himself a computer security consultant. His attitude and experience got him into serious trouble again when an Internet service provider (ISP) retained his services through an accounting company to test their computer servers. He made a serious error, according to a *Wall Street Journal* article by Jared Sandberg (July 10, 1997), when he sent a control message to the system to download the password file by e-mail to his computer. Because of misconfigured software, the ISP broadcast the control message on the Internet to servers throughout the world, and each one dutifully downloaded its password file to his computer. The hacker's computer was inundated with files of passwords, including one from the Australian Navy. A vice president of the ISP firm said, "We trusted an expert. . . . It's a gut feeling." He learned the hard way that hackers are only experts at hacking, not as computer security consultants who understand their accountability to protect systems.

In a similar alleged incident reported in a newspaper, three hackers in Houston, all former members of the Legion of Doom, formed an information security consulting company to provide penetration testing for business clients. They needed to learn how to become information security consultants and devised a scheme, using their considerable social engineering skills, to accomplish this. They masqueraded as the Landmark Graphics Corporation, an actual large Houston software publisher, and requested proposals by telephone from a number of information security consulting firms to conduct a security review. Their purpose was to rapidly collect materials on information security consulting methods, prices, skills, and knowledge needed. At least six consulting firms and individuals sent detailed proposals to the home address of two of the three hackers. In the telephone calls requesting proposals, the hackers indicated that they were preparing to conduct a security audit at Landmark and needed information to sell the idea to upper management. When asked to give a callback telephone number, the hackers used a telephone company test number that was continuously busy. Their scam was discovered when Landmark began receiving inquiries about preparing the proposals.

One thing we learn from this incident is that information security consultants can be as gullible as anybody. But the case points up the extent to which businesses conduct transactions and satisfy requests on the basis of telephone calls and, increasingly, by fax and e-mail communications. The consultants should have asked for a request for a proposal on the company's letterhead, and should have asked the hackers to provide information about the information security staffing and structure in Landmark, which would have further confirmed their identity. The consultants could also have easily checked the hackers' story by calling the Landmark Company directly, or looked up the name of the company's industrial security manager in the ASIS or ISSA professional membership directories and contacted him or her directly.

I find that many hackers are very narrow in their knowledge, having acquired it from reading current product manuals and by trial and error. Give me a technologist who has studied Knuth's *Theory of Programming*. There are plenty of them around; we do not have to do our hiring in the back alleys of cyberspace. I tell hackers that if they want to succeed in life, they should go back to school, receive a degree, earn a living working in technology, and prove their trustworthiness and expertise in positive ways. Then they could become successful consultants with proven track records in the working environments in which they have experience.

This admonition is equally applied to business managers who might be tempted to retain hackers. They have a responsibility to their organizations and to legitimate consultants to avoid the implied support of the hacker culture.

How to Treat Our Hacker Adversaries

In addition to implementing and advising on security controls and practices, information security experts must attempt to reduce the number of malicious hackers and their opportunities to do harm.

Unsavory Practices to Avoid

There are several practices that information owners and protectors should avoid, because these practices can erode the trust among us that is necessary in the battle against malicious hackers. These practices include:

- Use of excessively realistic social engineering testing against people
- Providing public platforms and support for unsavory persons such as malicious hackers and their associates and supporters
- Associating with such persons on a peer basis and/or supporting their agendas, publishing, and promotional materials
- Hiring hackers who represent themselves as security consultants

But there are members of the information security industry who disagree. For example, an information security conference provided a public platform for a convicted computer criminal, a hacker magazine publisher, and a former malicious hacker intent on becoming an information security consultant. The conference, which billed the session's panel as "the first information warriors," gave the unsavory trio the opportunity to espouse their causes, objectives, and beliefs to the attendees. The director of the organization that sponsored the conference—and the panel—indicated that the session had been requested by members of the U.S. military who wanted an opportunity to see and hear their adversaries in person.

In another similar situation, a well-known information security consultant made a presentation at a hacker's meeting, instructing the hackers on electromagnetic eavesdropping and techniques for using (and defending against) high-energy radio frequency signals. He justified his presentation on the basis that he received valuable feedback from the hackers who attended, believing that knowing the hacker techniques and motives enabled him to better defend against their attacks.

While it is certainly important for security specialists to attend conferences and to gather as much first-hand information about their adversaries as possible, they should do so unobtrusively, and without openly encouraging the hackers in their current activities or in their ambitions to become information security specialists themselves. In the same vein, the computer trade media should refrain from reporting on hacker meetings in the same way that they report legitimate computer technology conferences. Such coverage merely legitimizes these meetings and their participants.

Ethics of Information Security Product Vendors

Most information security product vendors conduct extensive tests on a new product before releasing it to market. But the tests are designed to demonstrate that the product meets its specifications—that it does what it is supposed to do. The tests don't attempt to determine what else the product can do, or may fail to do, under attack from imaginative, experienced hackers. To overcome this weakness in the usual testing procedure, a few security product companies are publicly challenging hackers to try to break or otherwise defeat their products and offering a reward to those who can do so. "Challenge-based" testing may be helpful for improving the product, but offering the safeguards for hackers to attack in the name of valid testing sends the wrong message. These companies could achieve their goal more effectively by using students in university computer science departments to do the testing.

Superficially, the results of hacker-based challenge testing seem to be useful. If the challenge motivates a wide range of realistic attempts to defeat a security product and the product withstands the challenge, that product must indeed be effective. Nevertheless, the numerous concerns associated with involving hackers in product testing clearly outweigh any benefits. Consider the following points:

- Product testing based on challenges to hackers is typically neither reproducible nor objective. Empirical testing requires carefully controlled and monitored testing conditions. Hacker-based product testing essentially opens Pandora's box and allows anyone to attempt to gain unauthorized access. In addition, the objectivity of such tests is questionable because the vendor (rather than independent third parties) typically decides whether anyone has succeeded in attacking the system(s) being tested.
- The mission of information security practitioners as well as vendors of security products should be to protect information by discouraging perpetrators. Hacker-based tests, in contrast, encourage intrusion into systems and reward anyone who succeeds.
- Bona fide malicious hackers are unlikely go to the trouble of perpetrating direct attacks on security products. Rather, they would engage in social engineering to defeat the product by seeking operational and management weaknesses, find weak implementations, and probe for alternate routes ("leakage") around a security product in the system.
- Vendors that draw hackers' attention to a product and tempt them to attack it will increase the hackers' knowledge about it and draw their attention to the product at customer sites as well. Such a situation could actually increase attacks against customers who purchase the product.

In short, security product testing based on challenges to hackers is neither effective nor safe. Any assurance of product security that it provides is questionable, and it may actually increase security dangers for customers using the product. Most importantly, however, responsible people in our field should not encourage the adversaries we fight by associating with and encouraging them in the name of testing security product effectiveness.

High Trust for Information Security Specialists and Vendors

Information security specialists and vendors must work with the sensitive information possessed by their customer organizations because it is their job to help protect it. In addition, information about the security being employed is also of the highest sensitivity. This requires a higher level of trust than for other types of consultants and vendors. Holding the specialists and vendors and their staffs to a higher trust requires that they have impeccable records, and be free of any arrests or convictions for crimes that could be associated with their work. Preserving both the image and substance of trustfulness requires that those in the practice of information security be above reproach.

8

The Artisans of Information Security

If you were to ask an information security specialist to explain the essence of his job, he is likely to tell you that it is to apply safeguards to protect information systems and networks. "From what?" you may ask, and he will answer, "from unauthorized access." If you suggest that his job might be a little different, like defending his organization from an adversary who is intent on abuse or misuse of the organization's information and systems, he would be likely to agree, "Oh yes. That too." A little more wheedling will elicit the response that he is protecting the confidentiality of information from disclosure, its integrity from modification, and the availability of systems. If you suggest that this does not seem to cover stealing, observing, misrepresenting, or using information, he is likely to insist that confidentiality, integrity, and availability (CIA) cover those acts too (in spite of what dictionaries say).

Current information security art deals primarily with computers and networks, rather than with information or with abusers and misusers of information. Information security trade journals, for example, rarely carry articles dealing with criminal forensics, embezzlement, transaction controls, or segregation of duties, and it is rarer still to find articles that relate to information activities outside of computer or network operating systems.

For the most part, information security practitioners defend computers and networks from hacker attacks, but not from malicious hackers. They are familiar with hacking as a game of technical one-upsmanship. However, in the competition between them, hackers engage in social engineering against the security specialists, but many of the security specialists do not know how to effectively use social engineering against the hackers—or are not interested in using this technique. Information security specialists are largely unaware of the **SKRAM** of the malicious hackers, embezzlers, con artists, and extortionists that compete against them because they are likely to come from different work experience backgrounds.

Information security practitioners are generally computer scientists and engineers who specialize in computer and communications security. As such, they focus on protecting computer operating system software from intrusion, while many malicious hackers and other computer criminals focus on abusing and misusing information any way they can. For example, when a typical information security practitioner interviews an information owner to discover vulnerabilities that should be controlled, she often begins by asking what is the most important system to protect. It would not occur to most practitioners to begin by asking who the information owner's potential adversaries are or how they might want to harm the organization. In contrast, many computer criminals typically have an application systems background and are likely to be familiar with one or more aspects of information management such as spreadsheets, double-entry bookkeeping, inventory control, or transaction processing—aspects that the security specialist usually has little or no knowledge about. These differences produce a huge mismatch between information security practitioners and their antagonists.

Protecting the computer systems and networks certainly plays a major role in ensuring the security of information resources in those systems, but it represents only one facet of the total challenge facing information security practitioners. To fully protect information resources, security practitioners need to expand their attention to the full spectrum of potential loss and the people who cause the loss. You must know and understand your adversaries to prevail against them. Security is not a game; it is a war and there are no fair-play rules.

OCCUPATIONAL ORGANIZATION

Information security has not yet attained professional status, but it is a recognized folk art—occupying that vast, undefinable position between science and craft. Its practitioners (or artisans) engage in various types of work. Many work for organizations that want to protect their information and are large enough to hire specialists to help them achieve this. (I use the word "help" in this context because the primary responsibility for security always lies with the information owners. Information security practitioners support the owners by implementing, advising, or administering security.) Other information security practitioners work as consultants. They typically work for consulting and systems development and integration contracting firms (like SRI Consulting) or for the major accounting firms. Some are independent consultants.

In large organizations, information security practitioners typically report to the Information Technology unit or, less commonly, to general management along with the Industrial Security, Human Resources, Legal, and Public Affairs departments. The certification process for information security practitioners is administered by the International Information Security Certification Consortium. Certification indicates that a practitioner has passed a comprehensive exam dealing with computer and network security and is familiar with the usual security foundation: CIA.

Like any other occupation, information security has a mix of superstars, chiefs, journeymen, and neophytes. The superstars are generally consultants who seek business using high visibility through speaking engagements, trade press articles, and media quotes. The chiefs are the managers of information security departments in large companies. They usually have journeyman computer technology backgrounds, but a few have broadened their roles in their organizations by learning to protect all types of information—at all stages in its life cycle. Journeymen are typically computer or network specialists or technical writers who install, monitor, administer, and advise on controls and write security guidelines and standards to instruct information owners.

At typical information security conferences, at least half of the attendees are neophytes in the field. This indicates that the folk art of information security is expanding and that a significant proportion of the practitioners are relatively new to the field. Most conferences also attract a few academics who specialize in information security, and a small but growing number of computer science graduate students who are specializing in security despite the lack of formal academic degrees in the field.

Most research on information security is conducted by the U.S. Department of Defense and the military establishment in the United States and other computer-intensive countries. This explains why so much of the information that is released about security is skewed toward security-conscious organizations such as the military and must be recast to fit the applications (and personnel) of most commercial and other government organizations.

Integrity and Trust

In addition to all of the usual job requirements for a high-level position in the IT department, information security specialists must have a high level of integrity and strong ethical values. This is because their role requires them to assist the organization in protecting its most valuable information assets, including information about the security system itself. Good judgment is also extremely important, since the security practitioner is likely to be called upon to advise others in handling sensitive information.

In the future, as we move toward an increasingly global economy, information security practitioners are likely to experience conflicting loyalties between their employers and their countries. In a worst-case scenario, for example, a U.S. citizen employed as an information security manager by a French-owned company operating in South Africa could discover that the U.S. government is conducting espionage against the South African

---

Questionable Practices?

I was called as an expert witness in a civil suit brought by a former information security manager who was suing his employer for wrongful termination.

The company had fired the manager for removing a computer program from company premises. The ex-security manager believed that the company was making illegal use of the purchased software package by extensively modifying it. Company management would not listen to his arguments, and failed to inform the security manager that they had negotiated the practice with the software provider and had the legal right to modify the program. In frustration, the security manager took the program from the premises to show it to some attorneys to gather support for his argument. Removing it from company premises was an alleged violation of his own security regulations and resulted in his termination. The ex-security manager did win the suit, but received only a token settlement from the jury.

Clearly, both parties had some fault in this case, but did the security manager violate good conduct when he removed the program from the premises? Or just display a lapse in judgment?

division of his French employer. Where should the practitioner's loyalties lie in this type of situation?

Information Security Conferences and Associations

There are nine major information security conferences each year, along with numerous other regional and specialized gatherings for information security practitioners. The major conferences are:

National Information Systems Security Conferences. Held in Baltimore or the Washington, DC area every October, these conferences are jointly sponsored by the U.S. National Security Agency (NSA) National Computer Security Center, and the National Institute of Standards and Technology (NIST) Computer Systems Laboratory. These conferences, which have been held for the past twenty years, are generally recognized as the premier technology conferences. They are well attended with more than 1500 attendees and attract a large proportion of government workers and contractors.

Computer Security Institute Conferences. Sponsored by the Computer Security Institute (which is part of the Freeman Publishing Company), these conferences began in 1974 and are the longest-running commercial information security conferences. They are held in large cities around the United States, and generally attract a large attendance of more than 1500 people and feature the largest exhibits of vendor products. Although the information that is presented in these conferences is somewhat repetitive each year, they are extremely valuable for neophyte and experienced practitioners.

MIS Training Institute Conferences. Sponsored and run by the MIS Training Institute, these conferences cater primarily to computer (EDP) auditors. They have existed for about twenty years and present content similar to that of the CSI conferences, but are on a smaller scale.

Information Systems Security Association Conferences. These are smaller conferences sponsored and run by the ISSA, which is the only U.S. national member-owned association of information security practitioners. They are similar in format and style to the CSI conferences, but again, on a smaller scale and run on a volunteer basis.

Computers, Freedom, and Privacy Conferences.   Sponsored jointly by the IEEE Computer Society, the Association for Computer Machinery (ACM), and local organizations such as law schools, these conferences deal primarily with the social and political implications of computing. These conferences attract a significant number of civil libertarians, privacy advocates, mature hackers, journalists, and members of the Electronic Frontier Foundation, which fights for civil rights and attempts to limit excessive powers of the criminal justice agencies. Eight such conferences have been held to date.

IEEE Computer Security Conferences.   These are small, limited-attendance conferences sponsored by the Institute of Electrical and Electronic Engineers Computer Society, always held in Oakland, CA, at which elite information security researchers and academics present highly technical papers.

Computer Security Applications Conferences.   Sponsored by the Aerospace Computer Security Association, these small annual conferences have been held since 1984.

Compsec Conferences.   Sponsored by the Elsevier Advanced Technology Publishing Company, these are the premier European information security conferences. They have been held in London each year since 1984, and have a format similar to the CSI conferences but on a smaller scale. Many of the speakers are from the United States, and British companies that market mostly U.S. security products dominate the vendor exhibits.

National (now International) Computer Security Association Conferences.   These conferences are sponsored by the International Computer Security Association, a relatively new information security company that started as an anti-virus service vendor. The conferences are now associated with a security product certification service and have expanded beyond anti-virus remedies into general information security.

In addition, there are several annual conferences that focus on specific aspects of security, such as the RSA Cryptography conferences in San Francisco, the Computer Security Institute's Netsec conferences, and computer vendor conferences. The International Federation of Information Processing (IFIP) Technical Committee Eleven (TC-11) sponsors a prestigious and mostly academic international conference every three years in various parts of the world. A number of other conferences and organizations concerned—at least to some extent—with information security have disappeared in the past ten years, but there are numerous practitioners who offer independent seminars for business and governmental organizations around the world. Many of these seminars are under the auspices of the major security and audit companies, including the MIS Training Institute and the Computer Security Institute.

Information security started as a new subject in sessions at the semi-annual American Federation of Information Processing Associations (AFIPS) conferences beginning in 1967 until the organization disbanded in the 1980s. From 1975 to 1985, Jerry Lobel, now an independent consultant, ran a popular series of conferences sponsored by the Honeywell Corporation, his employer at the time in Phoenix, Arizona. The conferences had an attendance of about two hundred pioneers in the art.

The information security seminar business is important because of the lack of academic programs. Ken Cutler provides many seminars for the MIS Training Institute, and John O'Leary, Dr. Eugene Schultz, and others provide seminars for the Computer Security Institute. Bill Hancock in Texas, Jerry FitzGerald and Charles Cresson Wood in California, and Martin Smith in London provide seminars independently and for local organizations throughout the world.

Information security practitioners tend to be active in a number of organizations, including the Computer Security Institute, the International Computer Security Association, and the Information Systems Security Association. Of these, only the latter is an independent, voluntary organization of information security specialists; the others are larger, profit-oriented businesses. Along with these security-specific organizations, several computer technology groups, including the Association for Computing Machinery, the IEEE, the British Computer Society (BSI), the International Federation of Information Processing Society (IFIP), and the Data Processing Management Association (DPMA), have special interest groups that focus on information security. In Europe, and in the United Kingdom in particular, the U.K. Department of Trade and Industry (DTI), the European Computer Manufacturers' Association, the Information Security Business Advisory Group, and the European Commission DG XIII actively participate in various facets of the information security art. *All* of the organizations and groups mentioned thus far, however, focus on the technological aspects of security rather than the larger goal of protecting information from computer crime losses.

A relatively new organization founded in 1989, the Association of Certified Fraud Examiners (headquartered in Austin, Texas) is attempting to bridge the gap that exists between traditional fraud examiners and those concerned with a wider view of information security—those focusing on computer and network security, cybercrime, and the protection of tangible assets. This Association (www.cfenet.com) claims to have more than 20,000 members worldwide, drawn from backgrounds including criminal justice, forensic accounting and auditing, law, and information security. It is currently developing a certification program and sponsors regional conferences that instruct attendees on, among other topics, techniques to assess fraud risks, planning investigations using available resources, how to investigate using computer tools, and how to recognize asset misappropriation schemes.

Organizations and conferences are particularly important for information security practitioners because of the lack of academic programs specializing in security. These groups and gatherings represent the practitioners' primary means of meeting face-to-face and exchanging information on the latest techniques for recognizing and dealing with information security breaches.

THE ROLE OF CRIMINAL JUSTICE IN INFORMATION SECURITY

The criminal justice agencies are beginning to focus on cybercrime and, as a result, are gradually catching up to the cybercriminals. The FBI maintains the National Infrastructure Protection Center (NIPC) with computer crime investigation units in Washington, DC, New York, and San Francisco. A special division, the Computer Crime and Intellectual Property Section of the Department of Justice, targets cybercriminals, and the U.S. Attorney's office has established a network of prosecutors who are specially trained to serve as computer and telecommunications coordinators. These prosecutors, who serve as the "resident experts" on computer crime, are a far cry from the U.S. attorneys in the 1980s who largely ignored the issue of computer crime, claiming that it did not require any special treatment. The U.S. Secret Service in the Department of the Treasury also plays an important role in computer crime investigations and arrests, especially in dealing with domestic malicious hackers. The Computer Fraud Squad in Scotland Yard and the Royal Canadian Mounted Police Computer Crime Unit are equally advanced in dealing with computer crime. U.S. Federal authorities are, however, restricted by laws that leave juvenile crimes in the realm of state prosecution. The Feds must rely on local law enforcement organizations to make arrests and prosecute.

Law enforcement organizations have stumbled a number of times in dealing with electronic evidence in computer crime investigations. The challenge is to gather the original form of data pertinent to the investigation from computers and on computer media using carefully worded search warrants and protecting the chain of evidence to use in court. There is a very real danger of violating the suspects' privacy and business by including non-pertinent data in the evidence gathering process. And, in a few cases, considerable harm has resulted from the denial of use of equipment and data seized from suspects and their employers.

I remember one unfortunate incident ten years ago when federal agents in Las Vegas raided a business that they suspected of illegal activity. They had a search warrant, and took a local computer science student with them to help retrieve information from the company's computer system that reputedly contained much of the evidence in the case. In those days, law enforcement officers knew little about computer systems in general, and even less about the offbeat system the company was using. The student wasn't too familiar with the computer system either; he accidentally erased the entire contents of the computer, destroying the evidence along with the company's only set of records—and effectively ending the business operation. Neither the company nor the government had any interest in pursuing justice any further. Fortunately, situations like this are now quite rare, probably since law enforcement personnel have considerably more experience with computer operations and use special software to selectively collect relevant evidence.

To be efficient in detecting and prosecuting cybercrimes of all types, law enforcement agencies need to train officers to be proficient across a broad spectrum of information systems environments. The ideal computer crime investigator in criminal justice needs to have a multidisciplinary background in computer technology and information systems applications. And, the expert needs to be able to call upon other specialists for support. Many law enforcement organizations are working toward this goal by providing more and better training for all officers involved with investigating and prosecuting computer crimes. The Treasury Department at Glencoe, Georgia and the FBI Academy in Quantico, Virginia have the largest training programs.

A MULTIDISCIPLINARY APPROACH TO INFORMATION SECURITY

A multidisciplinary background, with experience in computer technology as well as a variety of information management applications, is equally important for information security practitioners outside of the criminal justice community. In some respects, my own background and experience mirror that of the information security folk art, progressing through the early days of computer security and learning much through trial and error and from other practitioners feeling their way through the maze. Although we encountered computer security problems back in the 1950s when I began working as a computer programmer for General Dynamics, we didn't call them by that name—or recognize the potential for loss that they introduced.

Notable Associates

Throughout my career, I have had the pleasure of associating with some of the most intelligent and creative people imaginable. Fortunately, most of these individuals were involved in protecting information.

I met Wallace Bruschweiler during the 1970s shortly after I had embarked on my career in information security. An industrial security consultant who founded his own company—Data Security Holding, Inc.—in the Netherlands in 1972, Wallace knows many of the top management people and police chiefs in many countries around the world and is fluent in most of their languages. He sponsored seminars on computer crime and security that I taught throughout Europe. I didn't know what a secure computer center was until I helped Wallace design them to withstand bombs, rockets, Uzi bullets, and fiery propaganda brochures scattered about by the Red Brigade terrorists. Wallace taught me valuable lessons in physical security as well as computer security techniques designed to withstand the wrath of terrorists.

Individuals deeply committed to advancing the cause of computer security during the 1970s included Willis Ware, Peter Neumann, James Anderson, Steve Lipner, Carl Levitt, Steve Walker, Roger Schell, and Robert Morris. All were associated with, or supported by, the U.S. military establishment—largely because that was the only organization actively engaged in large-scale researching of computer security. (The military dominance is also one reason that business information security is shortchanged today.) Bill Murray, Bob Courtney, and Harry DeMaio (of Deloitte & Touche and formerly, IBM) were among the pioneers who led the way in business information security in the early years.

Bob Courtney, the first information security manager in IBM in the early 1970s, wrote the first corporate information security policy and was an originator of confidentiality, integrity, and availability as the elements of information security. He was also an early proponent of risk assessment, and

A Career in Information Security

I began my career in 1954 after receiving a Master of Arts degree in mathematics from the University of California in Berkeley. (There were no computer science degrees in those days, or classes in computer technology or security. Applied mathematics was as close as academics came to dealing with computer technology.)

I spent those early days programming a Univac 1103 mainframe computer for General Dynamics in San Diego. My fellow programmers and I were delighted to realize that our immediate management had no idea of what we coded into our computer programs. They had neither the time nor the ability to read code and merely checked the results. My boss insisted that we make our programs check-sum themselves each time they ran. (This meant that we had to code a loader program to add up all of the coded instructions and program data as if they were a column of numbers, then print them along with the number we had originally derived when the program was initially completed and placed into use. This was to prove that nothing in the program had changed.) It was a good practice and most of us recognized that it should be done, although no input error had ever been found. We often played a shortcut hack out of sheer orneriness—coding the loader program to print a random number twice and skip the check-summing entirely.

I learned some other joys of hacking in those early days also, sitting at that huge console with arrays of colored blinking lights that looked like a Christmas tree in full electronic bloom. My associates and I relieved the pressures of our tedious work by occasionally perpetrating supposedly harmless hacks on one another and on management. The only real security problems we faced—aside from the 1955 earthquake and frequent equipment fires—were caused by unhappy or burnt-out programmers sabotaging their code or just walking away from it (which was much the same as sabotaging it, since there were no programming documentation standards in place in those days). There were few if any repercussions for such activities, though, since management did not consider software to be a valuable commodity. Software piracy or theft had no meaning.

I started thinking in terms of computer security in 1967 when, as the proprietor of a computational service bureau, I faced the problem of a computer programmer using our company computers to run his own competitive service. I began clipping trade press articles about programmers in other states and other companies performing similar—and

(continued)

more serious—acts using others' computer equipment and/or information. As chairman of the Professional Standards and practices Committee for the ACM, I led the effort to write the first computer ethics guidebook in the late 1960s.

When I moved on to become director of computer services for SRI International in 1969, the computer system I was responsible for was housed in a steel tank to protect it from Soviet spies. Some criminologists at SRI engaged in a research project for the U.S. National Science Foundation (NSF) were intrigued by my collection of computer crime articles. As a result of their interest and funding by the NSF, I spent the next six years of my career along with Susan Nycum, Director of Computing at Stanford University, chasing computer criminals. The studies attracted a great deal of media attention and my colleagues and I appeared on a number of television news magazines and wrote books and reports introducing the general public to the dangers of computer crime.

My research studies continued, with funding from the U.S. Department of Justice Bureau of Justice Statistics, through three periods of serious recession in the United States. (It is interesting to note—but hardly surprising—that information security suffers greatly during periods of business recession because its funding is discretionary in many organizations and often considered non-critical—at least in comparison with other business functions.)

During the 1970s, I had the opportunity to work closely with New Scotland Yard and to train its first computer crime detective superintendent. Although we talked boldly about computer crime in the United States during those days, and the news media gave significant attention to it throughout the world, officialdom and business management ignored the growing problem. However, this changed during the 1980s when management could no longer ignore the growing problem—and the need for protection grew.

In 1986, I started a new, security service at SRI, the International Information Integrity Institute (I-4), with the help of my associate Dr. Bruce Baker and SRI management. I-4, now led by James Anderson and Susan Swope at SRI Consulting, continues to support the information security programs of 75 of the largest international corporations. It competes with the European Security Forum, which was modeled on I-4 and is owned by its members.

In my career I have always looked for ways to provide security using the least constraining solutions available. For example, I enjoy being able to tell a large company to let each division decide for itself the required length of its passwords rather than having one standard for the company. I encouraged them to reduce their five-level information classification scheme to a simplified two-level scheme that employees would be more likely to support, and I once told a department store chain that had a system that was out of control to surround its computer programmer office complex with perimeter security but not constrain the programmers within while they tried to resolve the most serious systems crisis.

takes a loss experience approach to security. Bob is also the only security specialist I know who was shot in the line of duty. He claims it happened when he was investigating a computer crime for a bank. He called the bank executives into a conference room (Agatha Christie style) to announce which of them was the culprit. When he identified the embezzler, the individual yelled, "You son of a bitch," pulled a gun from his briefcase, and shot Bob. As luck would have it, the bullet lodged in Bob's address book in his coat pocket, seriously bruising his hip, but providing him with a great story for his colorful and amusing security conference presentations.

Dr. Peter Neumann is an eminent security researcher who served as my mentor at SRI. Peter holds doctorate degrees in physics and mathematics and was a Fulbright Scholar. He began programming in 1953 and joined SRI in 1971, where he still serves as Principle Scientist in the Computer Systems Laboratory. He is representative of the U.S. government's approach to information security although he works in the private sector as well; he frequently briefs the NSA and serves on many prestigious government panels and commissions. He is also the originator and moderator of the ACM-sponsored Risks Forum on the Internet, which is the basis of his book *Computer Related Risks* (ACM Press, Addison-Wesley, 1995). Peter's fundamental thesis is that you cannot have a secure computer application without a truly secure operating system. He is still searching for such an operating system—much like Diogenes with a strong light.

Bill Murray became a friendly competitor in our business information security one-upmanship club when, after replacing Bob Courtney at IBM, he became a consultant for Deloitte and Touche. When we all appeared at the same conferences we frequently engaged in a friendly but contentious peer rivalry. Bill is a very effective business management consultant with a sound technical understanding. He has been an intense critic of the U.S. government security policies and, in particular, of the

National Security Agency and FBI. He is an inspiring and passionate speaker and writer, and is an extremely popular presenter on the information security speaking circuit. John O'Mara, a fire extinguisher salesman early in his career, was another important pioneer in business information security—despite the fact that he never claimed to be an information security expert. John was, however, a talented organizer and impresario of the annual Computer Security Institute Conferences. John is now a venture capitalist in New England after selling the Computer Security Institute to Freeman Publishing in San Francisco.

Dr. Willis Ware of the Rand Corporation is generally regarded as the senior statesman and scientist of information security. From the beginning of the folk art, Willis has been a persistent, thoughtful, and demanding leader, especially within U.S. government agencies and organizations. He is notable for his insatiable curiosity and understanding the "big picture." Willis consistently worked for more rational U.S. government policy and legislation concerning privacy, the secrecy of the NSA, cryptography, and computer security. The Secretary of Commerce appointed him to be the chairman of the Computer Systems Security and Privacy Advisory Board, which was established as part of the Computer Security Act of 1987 to deal with all of those issues. Willis is a fellow of the National Academy of Engineering, the IEEE, the National Research Council, the ACM, and the American Association for the Advancement of Science, among many other prestigious appointments.

Willis's speeches are aimed at the general policy level, but always include practical advice about the things that we should be doing on a day-to-day basis. His orientation is U.S. national interests, with a strong military focus, but he is a very effective senior statesman for information security worldwide.

Notable information security practitioners in the world of academics with whom I am associated include scientist Eugene (Spaf) Spafford at Purdue; Dorothy Denning of Georgetown, an incredibly intelligent supporter of difficult causes; Karl Levitt at U.C. Davis; Klaus Brunnstein of Hamburg, Germany; the late Professor Emeritus Harold Joseph Highland at the State University of New York; and my old friend Lance Hoffman at George Washington University. In England, the prestigious London School of Economics has an active information security research center headed by Professor James Backhouse. Professor Fred Piper heads the information security department at the Royal Holloway College of the University of London in Surrey. Professor D. Ulrich Sieber in Germany, Dr. Matti Tenhunen in Finland, and Judge Stein Schjolberg are the academic experts on computer crime in Europe.

This list would not be complete without a mention of my long-time associate Susan Nycum, who worked with me for about twenty years, beginning with our research into computer criminals in the early 1970s. Susan, who is now partner-in-charge of the Baker & McKenzie law firm in Palo Alto and a fellow of the ACM, is a wonderfully intelligent lady and a good sport for letting me drag her through the New York subways and prisons chasing computer criminals to interview. She now deals with software piracy, among other legal issues, for Silicon Valley firms.

It is frustrating to end these profiles without describing the many other important people and their interesting lives. I am thinking of Juhani Saari in Finland; Alan Brill at Kroll Associates; Fred Cohen of computer virus fame at Sandia Labs; Dr. Mich Kabay, a social psychologist in Canada; consultant Lynn McNulty, former burden carrier at NIST; consultant Jim Settle, formerly the computer crime guru at the FBI; competing consultants Bob Campbell and Bob Abbott; Marr Haack, my contact in the insurance industry; Bill Cook in Chicago and Mark Rasch at SAIC in Virginia, former computer crime prosecutors along with Stewart A. Baker, former NSA legal council and now at Steptoe & Johnson LLP, my contacts in the legal profession; entrepreneur Will Ozier, who runs the Generally Accepted Systems Security Principles (GAASP) committee; Peter Sommer, who wrote the Hackers' Handbook in London under a pen name; Professor Henry Beker, who is the consummate security entrepreneur President of Zergo Consultants; David Hind, who was the first Scotland yard computer crime detective; Ken Wong, a top consultant in London; and Donald Davies, cryptographer extraordinaire. Add to this list my associates at SRI Consulting, including Dr. Bruce Baker, with whom I started the I-4 service; Dr. Douglas Webb, Ed Blackwell, and Ken Lindup, with whom I have performed security reviews for 20 years; Charles Cressen Wood; and our research fellow Stein Schjolberg, who is a judge in the judiciary in Norway. Finally, I include all of my unnamed clients, including the I-4 club of top information security managers from some of the largest multinational corporations in the world, most of whom I had the pleasure of introducing to the inner sanctum of information security.

ADVANCING THE STRATEGIC VALUES OF INFORMATION SECURITY IN BUSINESS

Information security managers in large business organizations need to clearly communicate their objectives to top management and make a concerted effort to enlist management support for their information security policies. To do this effectively, security practitioners need to establish their own credibility and advance the strategic value of information security within the organization. I developed the following list of prerequisites through years of discussion with, and observation of, executives in a wide range of business endeavors. I'll summarize them here, then discuss them in more detail in the following pages.

- Learn the business first, including its goals, culture, key managers, history, and competitive universe.
- Identify the ways that security is already valued and the ways in which management views security.
- Aim to have the fewest security constraints possible while providing sufficient protection for information resources, rather than implementing the most security controls that can be tolerated.
- Establish security control standards from which to deviate in controlled ways to meet business needs.
- Recommend voluntary, confrontational security controls as well as preventive ones.
- Recognize that the amount of confidential information and the time needed to maintain that confidentiality are shrinking, while the importance of preserving the ownership and possession of information is increasing.
- Simplify the information classification controls to meet business needs.
- Heed the security imperative: Business has no patience for excessive, impractical security advice.

Learn the Business

An information security manager must understand the needs and goals of the business in order to provide sound advice on matters of profit, productivity, and growth as they relate to protecting sensitive information. She should first seek approval for her efforts from security oversight management (e.g., the Chief Information Officer) and the information security management committee, if one exists. These individuals should be aware of, and actively support, the business mission relative to information security.

The security manager should also make it a point to know other managers in the organization, particularly the managers of business units that are most critical to the organization's mission, to become visible, and to become familiar with their practices and cultures. David Packard, the founder of Hewlett-Packard, refers to this technique as "management by walking around," and it is sound business policy for information security managers.

The need to understand business culture may best be explained through example. A centrally controlled international company that provides human resource services to employees around the world must meet the stringent requirements of privacy laws in the countries where its employees live. It uses a central human resources system to serve all employees and achieve a uniformity of controls. The central system is, however, intractable and highly constrained. An international company that is organized as a loosely bundled collection of many national companies can maintain separate human resource systems for each company and country, adhering to the privacy laws of the individual countries only. An information security manager must understand the underlying reasons for security constraints, as well as the advantages and disadvantages of various business structures and their impact on security requirements.

Identify the Ways That Security Is of Value

Decentralizing computing resources (in the form of client-server computing) has generally resulted in more responsive and innovative information services at the departmental level, as well as the use of localized security controls. Security can often be better suited strategically to local applications. In some situations, security may be relaxed at the local level—a condition that is impossible when security is implemented on a corporate-wide basis, and must meet the high-water mark.

An observant security manager should recognize the security and vulnerability aspects of significant business actions. Organizations often achieve information security as the result of a business technique implemented for some other reason. Just-in-time secret decision making, which shortens the time that information is kept secret, is one example of this, since it changes the confidentiality needs of the business. Other examples include the practices of allowing employees to directly update their personnel records on-line and adjusting employee compensation at the local level to avoid communicating sensitive salary information. Also, companies can program computers to make simple decisions automatically so that fewer people need to know the information used in the decision-making process. Although these practices offer distinct enhancements to information security, they are not recognized as such in security literature. They do, however, involve avoiding vulnerabilities by removing assets away from potential threats—or removing potential threats away from assets. If, for example, you do not create an extra copy of information, it is not exposed to threats (since it doesn't exist), while the value and (hopefully) security of the original increases. A security expert may only recognize the security advantage of not having an additional copy, but a business person is likely to realize the strategic value of the information for her company.

Aim at Having the Fewest Constraints Possible

Business managers are generally pleased to have security managers take an interest in their business unit's needs and culture—as long as that interest does not result in security constraints that threaten business requirements. They welcome advice and support from outside experts as long as the objective of the advice is to enhance the business unit's goals rather than adding security constraints to achieve maximum protection. After all, business involves taking risks to make money, and it is sometimes prudent to suffer information loss in return for lower costs and/or greater flexibility. Security practitioners need to recommend prudent levels of security that do not interfere with, or degrade, business activities. Less security may be advisable even if it increases vulnerabilities, if it frees employees to spend more time enhancing business rather than being constrained by security. The security advisor should be flexible and willing to assist in both increasing and reducing security, as long as he carefully explains due care implications to avoid negligence.

Information security managers need to be innovative when working with business managers. Security that is transparent and least constraining to information owners, users, and custodians and service providers is likely to be more effective in the long run than dogmatic policies that force individuals to make end runs around the controls requirements. For example, it may be perfectly reasonable to eliminate the use of computer logon tokens and revert to permanent passwords, which can be written and safely stored in billfolds. This level of security is likely to be effective as long as the users are sufficiently knowledgeable and motivated to create good passwords and protect them as they do their own money. Similarly, a manager could adapt regular credit cards rather than "smart cards" as tokens for entry controls. Users already possess credit cards and need not add more plastic to their bulging wallets.

Some practitioners may interpret ideas for reducing security as heresy. But these concepts are consistent with the knowledge management theory of business. They emphasize the need for flexibility and the willingness to tolerate increased security controls in some situations in exchange for decreased security in others in order to meet business requirements. The objective of information security is to balance the value of the freedom of information with the possibly greater value of security constraints to enhance products and services. In other words, security is not intended solely to reduce loss; it is also intended to enhance the productivity, profitability, and growth potential of the business.

Establish Flexible Security Standards

Because businesses are likely to encounter situations in which it is practical to delay or avoid implementing normal security controls, information security managers need to think of security standards as baseline requirements from which there will be some deviation, rather than as absolute requirements. Any deviation from the baseline should be controlled and documented, but not require a lengthy, painful approval process. Alternatively, a business may choose to provide control objectives in discretionary guidelines instead of mandatory standards, or leave it up to the information owners themselves to achieve the effects of security controls.

Recommend Voluntary Security Controls

Information security managers need to consider recommending voluntary, confrontational security controls (e.g., warning signs) as well as preventative ones. One human resources director that I encountered in my strategic value of security study found that confrontational security with voluntary compliance was superior to preventative security controls in some business venues. This means that we need to trust people to carry out security in their own way, given proper instruction; we need to confront these individuals only if they violate basic requirements or repeat their offenses. This approach requires a security orientation that emphasizes avoidance, deterrence, detection, recovery, and reward in addition to prevention.

The willingness to be voluntarily constrained for security purposes is an important concept in business security. The practice is to ask whether the user is cleared to act on or to receive specific information rather than denying or restricting use based on pre-approved access control lists. Voluntary compliance transfers the responsibility for security to the individual users and relies on trust and examination of audit logs (after the fact) to detect unauthorized acts and determine the level of compliance.

Recognize Changes in the Nature
of Information Protection

Information security managers need to recognize that the amount of confidential information that requires protection is diminishing, as is the length of time for which it needs protection. At the same time, the importance of protecting information possession—including ownership and use—is increasing. One reason for these changes is that more information is being used automatically, with no need for human knowledge of it. Consequently, we may need a finer-grained differentiation of information confidentiality and possession and a shift in emphasis of security and policy from one to the other.

Many business people admit that it is increasingly difficult to keep business secrets. They generally believe that the knowledge management theory of business, with its emphasis on openness, results in less information that is confidential. This is especially true of financial information. Information is moving too fast, through too many channels, and is stored in too many places, in too many forms, to keep it secret for very long. It makes good business sense for organizations to assume that information about sensitive business transactions is (or soon will be) known by parties who can perpetrate harm, and focus on appropriate actions to avoid such harm rather than trying to keep the information secret. The best confidentiality security may be the "Silicon Valley security control" that relies on the rapid obsolescence of information to avoid the need for security. By the time your adversaries get the information, it is too late to be of use to them, or harm to you.

The half-life of information secrecy is diminishing rapidly because of the increasing ease with which people who change employment positions and loyalties may copy, observe, and convey information. Intense media coverage, cultural openness, the portability of computers, and the ubiquity of networks also contribute to the trend. To counter this trend, information security practitioners need to advise on business strategies that recognize the lack of secrecy. We can do this, for example, by making several alternative plans and maintaining unpredictability among the alternatives until the last possible moment. One public affairs executive that I know just assumes the worst-case situation, that information automatically becomes public as soon as it enters his company's computer system. Information managers need to recognize and understand such points of view for what they are: defensive strategies that help to deal with the realities of business information rather than a lack of confidence in security controls.

Information possession is a totally different type of security matter; it may have absolutely nothing to do with confidentiality. However, information owners may need to prove that they have rightful (or original) owner-ship of their proprietary information if possession is lost. If thieves steal intellectual property, or make copies of it, without ever knowing its con-tents, no violation of confidentiality occurs. Commercial software piracy is a good example of this type of loss, since the content of the programs is not normally confidential. As intellectual property such as computer pro-grams, databases, and e-mail play an increasingly strategic role in busi-ness, so too does their possession. Information security managers should work closely with the organization's legal department to ensure that staff members understand the benefits and limitations of protecting informa-tion possession. This is particularly important in information technology environments.

Simplify Information Classification Controls

In my experience, classifying information in business into several levels to protect its confidentiality seldom works well. Classification is a military concept that requires significant expenditure of resources as well as an employee clearance scheme, in order to be effective. Many organizations attempt to implement this type of control without creating appropriate employee clearances or assigning employees to administer it. In addition, employees often find that classifying information into multiple, standard levels of sensitivity is a difficult, subjective, and time-consuming process. And, for the most part, such classification focuses solely on confidentiality rather than also considering the equally or more important need to protect the information's integrity, authenticity, possession, and availability.

Security advisors should work closely with business unit managers to find ways of simplifying and improving information classification schemes. One possible scheme is to use a two-level arrangement: a public level for which controls are discretionary and a classified level at which some controls are mandatory. It may even be possible to eliminate infor-mation classification altogether, assuming that all business information is sensitive and needs to be appropriately protected. In some cases, it may be prudent to eliminate confidentiality protection for some types of informa-tion, and train employees to treat sensitive information as if their competi-tors already know it.

Heed the Security Imperative

Joan Reynolds, a respected information security officer retired from her tenure at Chemical Bank in New York City, gave me a profound insight into the relationship between information security and business units. I call this the Information Security Imperative: *Business has no patience for excessive, impractical security advice.* Joan reminded me that an information security manager gets only one chance to perform a security service for a business manager. If the advice is wrong or does not work, the business manager will eagerly tell his colleagues that he tried to make security work, but failed; therefore, he is not obligated to follow future security advice of the information security manager. That business unit manager is unlikely to ever call up the information security manager, and the business unit will never benefit again from security advice—no matter how good it may be.

As information security practitioners, we need to change this imperative attitude. The motives and desire for prudent security must come from the business managers, not the security advisors. For example, a Web site marketing manager that I interviewed in my study now seems to understand that security is his responsibility because it is his group that is developing the Web site. Our role, as security advisors, is to assist in this challenge. Business managers need to understand that information security exists to further the business mission, not merely to protect information from loss. Information security practitioners need to determine how few security constraints are necessary, rather than how much security is achievable and can be tolerated. And, the security controls that are implemented need to be as transparent and unobtrusive as practical.

$\mathcal{9}$

The Current Foundation for Information Security

We need a new model to replace the current inarticulate, incomplete, and incorrect descriptions of information security. The current models limit the scope of information security mostly to computer technology and ignore the sources of the problems that information security addresses. They also employ incorrect meanings for the words they use and do not include some of the important types of loss such as stealing copies of information and misrepresenting information. The current models also hold information security practitioners accountable for the protection of information. This is incorrect; information owners are primarily responsible for protecting their information. Information security practitioners merely assist them in that effort.

In this chapter, I first summarize the current state of information security, which is based on models from a number of authoritative sources. Then, I explain two of these models in detail, along with a framework for information security. The models, in order of their appearance here, are: the *Generally Accepted System Security Principles* (*GASSP*) model, which was created by an independent group of information security practitioners, and the *Code of Practice* model, published by the British Standards

Institute, and the *Control Objectives for Information and Related Technology* (CobiT)—which was created in 1995 by the Information Systems Audit and Control Foundation. Finally, I quote an informal and intuitive set of definitions by an eminent computer scientist, and end by showing how our errors in defining information security are creeping into criminal laws. In the next chapter, I propose a new framework for information security.

THE CURRENT FRAMEWORK MODEL

In Chapter 1, I referred to the limitations of using confidentiality, integrity, and availability (CIA) as the sole elements in the information security foundation. Recognizing these limitations, the U.S. Department of Defense (DoD) added two additional elements: authenticity of people and nonrepudiation. As used here, repudiation is a form of misrepresentation by rejecting information that is actually valid. For example, fraudsters can deny making computer transactions that they actually have made, thus repudiating them. It is particularly important because users of the Internet can take advantage of its anonymous nature to engage in deception. But, while the U.S. DoD added repudiation to the CIA list, it does not accommodate other equally important aspects of misrepresentation. For example, individuals can claim that they have made transactions which, in fact, they did not make. This misrepresentation, the inverse of repudiation, is just as insidious and is also not covered by CIA.

If the DoD had added loss of authenticity of information to the framework, they could have included all aspects of misrepresentation. They did not do this, however, because they did not want to create confusion between authenticity of computer users, which is the current understanding of authenticity, with authenticity of information. This is a shortsighted approach in that it concentrates on the technical controls of authenticating people rather than considering many other criminal acts that adversaries can perpetrate. There is no reason why authenticity can not apply to both people and information, just as integrity applies to both people and information.

Besides having significant gaps, CIA is actually backwards for the purposes of business information security. This is because of the foundation's military roots and emphasis on confidentiality. In business, the first priority of security is to assure availability; if we do not have information available, its integrity and confidentiality are of no concern. Integrity is the second priority in business security; if information is not complete and readable, there is little need for us to keep it confidential. In general, confidentiality is the least significant element in business information security. For business security purposes, then, the foundation should be expressed as AIC rather than CIA.

The current body of literature on information security, which is based on CIA, is often incorrect and dangerously incomplete. Although our adversaries are using the same documentation—and some may be led astray by its shortcomings—smart criminals are likely to identify the weaknesses and conclude that we are overlooking many viable vulnerabilities and threats. While the security experts are busy defending CIA, the criminals can take advantage of the failings to engage in a variety of crimes.

Unfortunately, the elements of the foundation are not the only areas of weakness in the current model. Our current policies, standards, surveys, and assessment methods are also inadequate for describing information security and losses. They, like the foundation, are incomplete and do not use terminology correctly or consistently, which makes it difficult—if not downright impossible—to conduct effective assessments, identify controls, or establish priorities for information security. Most security experts focus on four universal losses caused by human misuse and abuse of information: destruction, disclosure, use, and modification. This produces a somewhat awkward, but all too accurate, acronym: DDUM. Even when some experts replace "destruction" with "denial of use," the list is both incomplete and redundant. DDUM is grossly deficient. It does not include misrepresenting, withholding, locating, repudiating, or observing information. It also overlooks failure to provide information, replace it, or delay or prolong its use. Also, there is no inclusion of stealing a copy of information (although taking all copies constitutes loss of availability, which is covered). Disclosure, the first D in DDUM, refers only to what possessors of information may do to cause a loss, not necessarily what an adversary does when he observes it.

Although DDUM is incomplete—and has been ever since security staffs wrote these four words in the first information security policies back in the early 1970s—it is commonly touted by security experts. At this point, I suspect that some agree that we now know much more about losses and should have a broader scope for information security.

The current model's use of only three functions to protect information—prevention, detection, and recovery—is clearly inadequate when we consider the need to avoid, deter, mitigate, and so forth. Finally, the model's emphasis on performing risk assessments to achieve the security objective of reducing risk is also deficient because it does not deal with the objective of meeting a security standard of due care. (I address this problem and its solution extensively in Chapters 11 and 12.)

GENERALLY ACCEPTED SYSTEM SECURITY PRINCIPLES

The current state of information security as a folk art is best described in a draft of the Generally Accepted System Security Principles (GASSP), which was created by an independent committee, under the dedicated direction of Will Ozier. Will wrote a description of it that was published in the fall 1997 edition of the Computer Security Institute's *Computer Security Journal*. The committee derived its nine pervasive principles from the nine principles stated in the 1992 document *Guidelines for the Security of Information Systems*, which a task group under the auspices of the Organization for Economic Cooperation and Development (OECD, www.oecd.org) developed. The nine pervasive principles in the GASSP cover accountability, awareness, ethical respect for the rights of others, the need for all viewpoints, proportionality of security application, controls that must work together and in timely fashion, periodic assessment, and security that works for the good and rights of affected parties.

The GASSP document provides evidence of how incomplete, incorrect, and inarticulate the information security folk art actually is today and has been during the past few years while the committee was writing the document. The document is superb in representing the general practice; its faithful depiction reveals the terrible state of the general practice. While it claims to be useful for legal, social, and other related areas of information security, the GASSP document is written primarily by and for computer security technologists and reflects the inward-focusing and self-serving nature of the folk art, as well as its equally deficient OECD source.

If an information owner were to use this document (along with a good dictionary) to discover what information systems security should achieve, she would find that GASSP addresses only the modification, denial of use, and disclosure of knowledge. The document does not address the concept of information that is not knowledge, and does not explain who would or could cause these losses. In addition, the objectives of security stated in the document do not include protection of its usefulness, validity, or possession. For example, there is no provision for preserving information in the right language (usefulness), or for ensuring that it represents the desired facts and reality (validity), or that copies have not been stolen or pirated. The unfortunate information owner may conclude that systems security as defined in GASSP does not protect information from very much.

The information owner may wonder about some of the definitions in the GASSP document when she compares them to the dictionary meanings. She will find that the GASSP document largely ignores dictionary meanings because the authors chose to use the commonly used "coded" meanings of CIA/DDUM in the folk art, meanings that often differ from common English-language definitions.

GASSP also overlooks important security safeguards. It identifies only prevention, mitigation, and transfer, ignoring avoidance of loss, deterring abusers and misusers, sanctions against those who cause a loss, recovery, and correction of failed security after recovery. Security must certainly include the means to avoid threats and vulnerabilities, such as eliminating unnecessary copies of information that might otherwise require protection. What good is security if it does not try to deter abusers before they start? Or security that lacks penalties to bring abusers to justice? Finally, it is a poor practice that does not recover from and correct a security problem to prevent it from happening again. These measures are missing from the GASSP draft as well.

The GASSP document does address the very important elements of information security education, awareness, and training measures to inform computer users about the principles and practices that support information protection, but it says nothing about the need to motivate people to apply that education or awareness. What good are education, awareness, and training if people are not motivated to use the security practices they learn about to protect their information? Without positive motivation, security training may instruct users how to effectively avoid, compromise, or ignore security. This is human nature; we all dislike the constraints imposed by security in the performance of our jobs. The situation will not change unless we provide positive motivation to help users realize the inherent rewards of information security and reward them for practicing good security.

GASSP's failure to address information that is not knowledge is a serious flaw in the document—and in the security model itself. Unfortunately, it is also a concept that is not recognized by many security practitioners. Most of us own lots of valuable information that is not knowledge, including object computer programs, intermediate results of calculations, constants, engineering or scientific tables, detailed accounting data, and so forth. This information may or may not be stored in our computers. Because the GASSP document defines *information system* to include manual systems, its principles should address business, scientific, engineering, or artistic information in desks and filing cabinets, printed on paper, or spoken. But, it is clearly oriented toward computer systems and the information that resides in them. While this accurately reflects the nature of the information security folk art today, it is not sufficient.

GASSP recognizes the dangers of threats in stating its nine principles, but does not recognize the sources of threats or the vulnerabilities that attract threats. Even more disturbing, however, the document fails to recognize the fundamental purpose of information systems security: *protecting information from abusers and misusers*. Again, this is an accurate depiction of current limited thinking in information systems security.

GASSP never actually admits (or advises its readers) that there are adversaries who pose threats to information. This may explain why the document overlooks the issues of deterrence and sanctions. After all, deterrence and sanctions act on abusers and misusers, not on threats. This again is not a failure on the part of the GASSP authors; it is a reflection of the current state of information security, which is primarily directed by computer security technologists who fix vulnerabilities and install controls in computers and networks to protect against disembodied threats such as disclosure, unauthorized use, denial of use, and modification rather than against the people who perform these acts. The computer technology experts concentrate on technological security controls rather than addressing the human frailties that lead to misuse and abuse, elements that they are not well equipped to deal with.

Current information security, as it is accurately depicted in the GASSP document, starts and ends with the tidy, limited array of technical threats. It mostly ignores security as it relates to the nasty, confrontational problem of stopping people from misbehaving and harming other people and institutions through attacks on information. Although one of the GASSP principles addresses ethics, it deals only with respecting the rights of others in the security process—not with the concept that security is supposed to protect against our adversaries' unethical acts. The subject of unethical acts is addressed in information crime laws, which are listed as a source for the GASSP document, but criminal law is largely ignored by the document, and by the information security folk art.

The folk art of information security is self-serving in that it largely ignores the responsibility of information owners to protect their own and others' information. This deficiency is clearly evident in the GASSP document, which states that "the principles incorporate the consensus, at a particular time, as to the principles, standards, conventions, and mechanisms that information security practitioners should employ, that information processing products should provide, and that information owners should acknowledge to ensure the security of information and information systems." This definition confuses the roles of accountability, as does the art itself. When an information owner reads this definition, she is likely to interpret it as meaning that information security practitioners, along with computer security controls, will protect her information. She has no responsibility for security, or protecting information other than acknowledging the principles, standards, conventions and mechanisms. The only fortunate feature of this quoted sentence is that the information security specialist is accurately called a practitioner, which is consistent with the folk art status of his specialty.

The proportionality principle states that "information security controls should be proportionate to the risks of modification, denial of use, or disclosure of information." This too perpetuates the myth of the value of risk assessment—a value that has never been clearly demonstrated. It also ignores the predominant practice of selecting controls based on due care and availability. However, the GASSP Committee offers an example which states that some organizations do base security implementations on "a prudent assessment of 'due care' (such as the use of reasonable safeguards based on the practices of similar organizations), resource limitations, and priorities." This clearly violates the stated principle of proportionality (and is the only concession that the GASSP Committee made to my remonstrations). Technologists continue to falsely believe that selection of safeguards can be based on a "scientific" cost/benefit risk analysis which calculates the probability and size of future losses and compares the results to the cost of reducing them by measured amounts.

Although it may seem that the GASSP Committee failed in its duty to recognize some important issues, losses, controls, and principles, this is not necessarily the case. The committee was faithful to its plan of documenting only the current general practice of information security and the associated body of knowledge, at least in computer systems security. Thus, it is the folk art that is at fault, not those who describe and document it. The failure began with the military and early security technologists who focused attention on the security of computer systems (as implied by the titles of the GASSP and OECD guidelines). These technologists still dominate the information security folk art today and still lack a basic understanding of how to protect information from abuses and misuses. This is especially disturbing when you consider that laws are being made and people convicted and sent to prison based on this unscientific folk art.

THE BRITISH CODE OF PRACTICE

The U.K. Department of Trade and Industry (DTI) has served the information security field well for many years. It is similar to the U.S. Department of Commerce National Institute of Standards and Technology (NIST) except that it is devoted to commerce, while NIST primarily serves the computer security needs of government as dictated by the Computer Security Act of 1987. (Although NIST claims that what it does for government also applies to business, that is not true in the broader security context of protecting business information, because the goals and possession of information are different.)

The DTI organized a committee of information security specialists—ten British and European based companies, the British Computer Society, and several government agencies—to write a guide to information security controls called *The Code of Practice* (PD 0003). It was based partly on the Shell UK Company's internal information security standards. These standards were based on the proprietary SRI International I-4 baseline controls that I developed in the early 1980s. The second version of PD 0003 was adopted by the British Standards Institute (BSI) as the work of the BSI Section, BSFD/12 Information Security Management, and is published as BSI BS 7799: 1995 *Code of Practice for Information Security Management.*

The *1995 Code of Practice* is one of the best guides in the field; experienced security specialists often recommend that organizations use it to develop their internal security standards. It is also an example of the works that perpetuate the obsolete concepts of confidentiality, integrity, and availability, while overlooking possession, authenticity, and utility. Despite its title, the document does not have statutory force, although it does carry the authority of the BSI. And, because it was written primarily by computer security technologists who are not particularly careful users of the English language, it is not clear or consistent in some areas. It incorrectly defines integrity to include accuracy and implies that computer software is not information. Further, it does not address the major threats to information, such as theft of copies or misrepresentation. This is not the fault of the task force that assembled it, however. They followed the generally accepted practices in this inarticulate folk art, just as the GASSP committee did.

The code defines the CIA elements as:

Confidentiality.   Protecting sensitive information from unauthorized disclosure or intelligible interception.

Integrity.   Safeguarding the accuracy and completeness of information and computer software.

Availability.   Ensuring that information and vital services are available to users when required.

It is satisfying to see that the definition of confidentiality includes "intelligible interception" as a threat, along with disclosure. This recognizes unauthorized observation of sensitive knowledge as a threat, and counts it as a violation of confidentiality. Unfortunately, this recognition is not carried forward to the only control identified in the document that deals explicitly with confidentiality. Section 4.1.3 states that users should sign a confidentiality (nondisclosure) agreement, but says nothing about forbidding unauthorized users from intercepting (observing) information.

The code circularly defines *availability* as available. The code incorrectly defines the word *audit* by not distinguishing an audit from a review of any system of controls. In business, *audit* is used to mean compliance and verification of a business system. We should reserve the word to refer to the act performed by professional auditors, and reserve *review* as the act performed by an information security specialist or information owner.

Another problem in the code is that the section on network access control does not mention cryptography. The code briefly discusses cryptography, but only in a section on developing and maintaining application systems, as a means of protecting highly sensitive data. As is typical in many writings about cryptography, it confuses knowing information with possessing it, an important distinction for security. Section 8.2.3 explains that secret keys are to be *known* only to authorized users. This section demonstrates how poorly we sometimes articulate information security. A reader can easily assume from this description that users know cryptographic keys. In practice, however, users never know their keys, since keys typically range from 40 to 2,000 symbols in length. They are calculated and used automatically by computers as "noledge" (see Chapter 3). Because people engaged in the use of cryptography possess and use their keys (rather than knowing them), security is concerned with preserving the exclusive *possession* of keys. Cryptography has a negative reputation because many people believe that it involves the odious tasks of creating, memorizing, and using long strings of meaningless symbols. Competent cryptography and key management vendors design their products to be used in ways that are totally transparent to users, since they know that the weakest aspect of cryptography is the users' direct involvement.

In summary, the code is incomplete in dangerous ways, incorrect in some important points, and unfortunately follows the deficient traditions of many other information security documents. Yet it is still one of the best guides available for meeting a standard of due care, and I recommend it (with obvious caveats) as the best that we have produced to date. The DTI and the task group are currently revising the code, but it will probably continue to reflect the present folk art body of knowledge.

COBIT: CONTROL OBJECTIVES FOR INFORMATION AND RELATED TECHNOLOGY FRAMEWORK

The Control Objectives for Information and Related Technology (CobiT) framework is another valuable source of control objectives for achieving a standard of due care in information security. It was developed by a group of European chapters of the Information Systems Audit and Control Association, primarily for use by auditors. CobiT, which was published in December 1995, is available from the sponsor, the Information Systems Audit and Control Foundation, in Rolling Meadows, IL (research@ isaca.org).

The CobiT framework is briefly stated as follows: "The control of IT (information technology) processes that satisfy business requirements is enabled by control statements considering control practices." The framework provides more than 300 detailed control objectives and categorizes them into three dimensions, namely:

- IT domains—planning and organization, acquisition and implementation, delivery and support, and monitoring
- Information criteria—effectiveness, efficiency, confidentiality, integrity, availability, compliance, and reliability
- The IT resources that are managed—people, applications, technology, facilities, and data

CobiT's working definitions of confidentiality, integrity, and availability as elements of its information criteria are as follows:

Confidentiality. Concerns the protection of sensitive information from unauthorized disclosure.

Integrity. Relates to the accuracy and completeness of information as well as to its validity in accordance with business values and expectations.

Availability. Relates to information being available when required by the business process, now and in the future. It also concerns the safeguarding of necessary resources and associated capabilities.

Unfortunately, these definitions are confused and generally incorrect, much like other definitions that we find in the current information security folk art.

CONFLICTING DEFINITIONS: MESSAGE CONFIDENTIALITY, INTEGRITY, AND AUTHENTICITY

In a presentation to a group of information security specialists, a cryptography expert from Bellcore (now part of SAIC) described security requirements that can be satisfied by the use of cryptography and digital signatures. He placed message authenticity, integrity, and confidentiality in this category. In his description, authenticity referred to the process of ensuring that messages come from the correct senders and arrive at the correct receivers; integrity meant that the same message arrives as was sent; and confidentiality meant that the message is not disclosed during transmission. In the context of his presentation, then, authenticity concerns the identity of people, integrity concerns changing information during transmission, and confidentiality concerns exposing information to disclosure.

When this same expert later broached the subject of nonrepudiation, which he did not include in his description of authenticity, integrity, and confidentiality, he defined it as ensuring that the sender of a message could not successfully claim that he did not send it. The expert did not address the possibility that a person could falsely misrepresent that he sent it.

What is wrong with these word uses? Nothing is wrong in the context of his audience of information security specialists. They knew exactly what he meant at the level of abstraction he was using. The terms were meant to describe the benefits of using cryptography and digital signatures, and he succeeded admirably in that goal. The trouble is that he used incorrect meanings for the terms and did not differentiate confidentiality from possession—not mentioning that it is possible to steal information without violating its confidentiality. For example, if a thief steals the ciphertext but not the key to decipher it, the information remains confidential, but exclusive possession of a form of the information is lost.

The Orange Book

The Orange Book (U.S. DoD Standard 5200.28-STD, *Trusted Computer System Evaluation Criteria,* December 1985) is one of the most renowned publications on computer security, and has had a profound influence in encouraging computer manufacturers to include security in their products for many years. It was published by the U.S. National Security

Incorrect Definitions

There are a number of element definitions that the U.S. Defense Information Systems Agency (DISA) accepts, but which I think are incorrect and/or incomplete. The following are the official definitions from the International Standards Organization (ISO/IEC 7498-2: *Information Technology—Open Systems Interconnection—Basic Reference Model—Part 2: Security Architecture*) with my comments appended for each:

Identification and Authentication. "Establishing and confirming who or what you are. The 'who' may be a user, an application, a system, or data."

These are control objectives, not basic elements that define information security.

Access control. "Authorizing the 'who' to use specific rights or permissions."

This too is a safeguard objective, not a basic element that defines information security.

Data integrity. "Ensuring that information has not been modified, added, or deleted during its storage or transit."

This is not a definition; it is a means of achieving integrity. However, the definition implied here is excellent if the scope is data in computer and communication systems. There is also some inconsistency in referring to "data" in the name and "information" in the definition.

Data confidentiality. "Ensuring that information is protected and not disclosed to unauthorized parties."

Protection covers all of the aspects of security and is meaningless here. Disclosure is correct, but the more important threat of unauthorized observation is missing.

Data availability. "Ensuring that information is present, accessible, and fit for use."

"Availability" means that data should be present or accessible. Being fit for use concerns its utility, not its availability. That is why utility must be an element along with availability.

Auditability. "Ensuring the existence of adequate audit trails that provide records of activity."

> Auditability is a control objective, not a basic element that defines information security.
>
> **Nonrepudiation.** "Ensuring that parties in a transaction cannot deny that the transaction took place."
>
> This is not general enough, since repudiation is only one of many ways that information may be misrepresented, and misrepresentation of information is not covered by any of the other elements in these definitions. This is one reason why authenticity of information must be added to the list of elements defining information security. Authenticity addresses all of the forms of misrepresentation, not just authenticity of people (as in the first item) and nonrepudiation. Finally, repudiation is not limited to transactions; any information can be repudiated.
>
> The definitions were likely written by technologists without the benefit of advice from experts in articulating definitions such as lawyers.

Agency's National Computer Security Center, which is notable, among other things, for having at one time had a staff of more than 400 military computer security technologists. The strong military influence may explain why the book does not bother to define confidentiality, even though confidentiality is one of its major topics—along with computer entry, computer integrity, and computer authenticity. *The Orange Book* does not distinguish between confidentiality and possession, and fails to discuss the integrity and authenticity of information or computer applications.

The definition of data integrity presented in *The Orange Book* glossary is so far from correct that it's impossible to criticize constructively. It's just plain wrong!

Data integrity. The state that exists when computerized data is the same as that in the source documents and has not been exposed to accidental or malicious alteration or destruction.

What happens if the data are computed and there are no source documents?

NEUMANN'S VIEW OF INFORMATION SECURITY TERMS

In his book *Computer-Related Risks* (ACM Press, Addison-Wesley, 1995; parts reprinted by permission of the ACM and the author), Dr. Peter Neumann takes a broad view of the requirements for making information systems dependable and trustworthy. His book represents an accurate depiction of the current information security folk art from the information systems technologist's perspective. He states that this broad view requires "closely related security, integrity, and reliability of systems." According to Neumann, "Any or all of these concepts may be constituent requirements on a particular application, and the failure to maintain any one of them may compromise the ability to maintain the others. Consequently we do not seek sharp distinctions among these terms [security, integrity, and reliability of systems]; we prefer to use them more or less intuitively."

Let us look at how he defines the common terms of the art, keeping in mind that he is referring to security of information systems not information alone. His definition of security of computer systems is that "it implies freedom from danger, or, more specifically, freedom from undesirable events such as malicious and accidental misuse. Security is also a measure of how well a system resists penetrations by outsiders and misuse by insiders."

He defines computer system integrity separately from security, stating in his book that integrity "implies that certain desirable conditions are maintained over time. For example, system integrity relates to the extent to which hardware and software have not been altered inappropriately." In contrast, he states that "data integrity relates to data items being as they should be [this is Bob Courtney's definition from his pioneer days at IBM]. Integrity of people relates to individuals behaving in an appropriate manner. Integrity encompasses avoidance of both accidental and intentional corruption."

According to Neumann, security and integrity (along with reliability) inevitably overlap. Because the concepts are inherently interrelated, we must necessarily consider them together. Furthermore, he explicitly says, "there is never an absolute sense in which a system is secure or reliable." He refers back to these definitions later in the book, stating, "The informal definition of security given [previously] implies freedom from undesirable events, including malicious and accidental misuse. . . . In this natural usage, security would be an all-inclusive term spanning many computer-system risks."

Neumann uses the following definitions of computer security terms in his book:

> Confidentiality (or secrecy) means that information is protected from unintended disclosure. Computer-system mechanisms and policies attempt to enforce secrecy—for example, to protect individual rights of privacy or national defense. The system does not accidentally divulge information, and is resistant to attempts to gain the location of such information. *[page 96]*

> Integrity means literally that a resource is maintained in an unimpaired condition, or that there is a firm adherence to a specification (such as requirements or a code of values). In the computer sense, system integrity means that a system and its system data are maintained in a (sufficiently) correct and consistent condition, whereas (user) data integrity means that (user) data entities are so maintained. In this sense, the danger of losing integrity is clearly a security concern. Integrity could be related to unintended disclosure (in that non-release is a property to be maintained), but is generally viewed more as being protection against unintended modification. From the inside of a system, integrity involves ensuring internal consistency. From an overall perspective, integrity also includes external consistency; that is, the internals of the system accurately reflect the outside world. Related to external consistency are notions such as the legality of what is done within the system and the compatibility with external standards. Integrity in the larger sense also involves human judgments. *[page 97]*

> Availability means that systems, data, and other resources are usable when needed. . . . *[page 97]*

> Timeliness is relevant, particularly in real-time systems that must satisfy certain urgency requirements. . . . It is thus a special and somewhat more stringent case of availability. *[page 97]*

As he says, there is considerable overlap; the definitions are intuitive and do not make sharp distinctions between the terms. This reflects the general thinking of the U.S. government, a world in which he plays a significant role, and a world in which computer operating system security dominates the security art. But Neumann's terms sometimes apply to both the computer systems and the information they contain, and at other times apply to either the computer systems or the information.

I suspect that Neumann's caveats about sharp distinctions and intuitive meanings are ways of telling us that he realizes his definitions may not adhere strictly to generally-accepted meanings and that he is reflecting the growth of the coded meanings of the terms in the computer technology art. For example, I know from conversations with him that he prefers to reserve *authenticity* to apply to the identity of system users rather than to information, to avoid confusion—even though he readily applies *integrity* to systems, data, and people. Therefore, he includes authenticity of data and systems intuitively in the meaning of *integrity*.

Neumann uses the common folk art definition of confidentiality with one important addition: He adds that confidentiality means that the system is resistant to attempts to gain the location of accidentally divulged information. This comes close to adding *observation* to *disclosure*. His definition seems to be strictly from the perspective of what computer-system mechanisms and policies attempt to enforce, which may be adequate for his purposes.

Neumann's definition of confidentiality omits protection from theft by a perpetrator of a copy of information for which he may be authorized only to modify or use. I conclude that given his definitions, stealing and only using information (e.g., software piracy) do not fall within his concept of computer security (except, of course, for his caveat of claiming informality and intuitiveness for his definitions). Disclosure (making known or divulging) does not include taking information without knowing its content, as I have stated previously. His addition of *resistance to attempts to gain access to information* at the end of the definition of confidentiality still does not address the resistance to action of a person locating and taking possession of the information without violating its confidentiality. However, this may be unfair nitpicking, given the informal and intuitive nature of his definitions.

In conclusion, I believe that Neumann's informal and intuitive definitions cover many of my elements of computer security—but not in particularly obvious ways. In addition, his willingness to make do with intuitiveness and a lack of sharp distinctions may contribute to a failure by information owners and policy makers (who may not know the coded meanings of the CIA terms in the art) to recognize specific important ways that losses may occur. While the lack of sharp distinctions may be acceptable for technological safeguards inside computers and operating systems, such distinctions are necessary in the broader scope of information abuse and misuse. They provide insights that information owners need in order to deal effectively with abuse and misuse.

IMPLICATIONS OF THE CONFUSION SURROUNDING SECURITY TERMINOLOGY

Our imprecise use of security terminology has some serious implications. The terminology in the Health Insurance Portability and Accountability Act of 1996 (PL 104-191), which President Clinton signed into law in August 1996, is just one example. The purpose of Subtitle F of the act is to improve "the efficiency and effectiveness of the healthcare system by encouraging the development of a health information system through the establishment of standards and requirements for the electronic transmission of certain health information." The act calls for standards to protect the "privacy" of personal health information. (The word "privacy" is used incorrectly here. Privacy refers to a human and constitutional right or freedom. It refers to people and not to information. The word meant here is *confidentiality*, which we apply to information, to protect the privacy of people.)

Under the act, any person or organization that maintains or transmits health information

> shall maintain reasonable and appropriate administrative, technical, and physical safeguards that will ensure the integrity and confidentiality of the information; protect against any reasonably anticipated threat or hazard to security and integrity of the information; unauthorized uses or disclosures of the information; and ensure compliance by the officers and employees with safeguards.

It is clear that the security terminology in this very long sentence is confused, as usual. But it is doubly serious here, because it has become a part of law. Ensuring "integrity and confidentiality" alone would not protect against allowing or creating invalid information, or stealing of information. The statement should include authenticity and possession. The second mistake involves separating integrity from security, which raises questions about the meaning of security. After all, what is security if it does not encompass integrity? Further, "unauthorized uses or disclosures," as threats to be prevented, implies protection of confidentiality, which is an element of security, but it omits stealing unless stealing results in unauthorized uses. If disclosure is to be explicitly identified, then the threat of observation is a serious omission.

To be fair, these errors are not repeated in the Penalties section, where the act states, "A person who knowingly violates the confidentiality of a unique health identifier, or obtains individually identifiable health information, or discloses such information to another person, can be fined up to $50,000. . . ." By including both the violation of confidentiality and the obtaining of information, the act includes observation as well as disclosure and violation of possession. This is typical of several laws that are deficient and sloppy in describing security, but complete in describing the unlawful acts that are covered. Such writing is probably the result of lawyers who draft legislation relying on the sloppy wording by information security specialists for the former, and on their own profession of law for describing acts correctly to be penalized for the latter.

CONCLUSION

My displeasure and frustration with the current state of the information security folk art is obvious. The current security framework of the CIA/DDUM model, as illustrated in the GASSP document and other publications, is clearly inadequate. The model that I suggest in the next chapter is significantly more valid and complete. I believe that we should universally adopt this new model in our security research and analysis, as well as in our policies and other writings. However, we must recognize that we need to modify the model over time to reflect continual changes in information security. In any case, we should not be satisfied with the current model, which is limited and obsolete.

10

A New Framework for Information Security

Our new information security framework must express, in practical language, the means for information owners to protect their information from their adversaries. Then, and only then, will we have the valid basis for the pervasive principles that the GASSP Committee is trying to achieve.

In this chapter, I present a comprehensive new information security framework which I believe resolves the problems of the existing models. Then I demonstrate the need for six security elements: availability and utility, integrity and authenticity, and confidentiality and possession, to replace the CIA foundation in the new security framework and use the new framework to present a list of potential information losses. I also present the new models in another form, the Threats, Assets, Vulnerabilities model, and include detailed descriptors for each topic in the model. At the end of the chapter, I present the Clark-Wilson Integrity model, which is particularly important for business transaction systems. These models support the new security framework, demonstrating their contribution to advance information security from its current technological stage as a folk art to become the basis for an engineering and business art in cyberspace.

PROPOSAL FOR A NEW INFORMATION SECURITY FRAMEWORK

The new security framework model incorporates six essential parts: (1) the foundation elements or characteristics of information to be preserved, (2) the sources of loss of these characteristics, (3) the losses, (4) the safeguard functions to protect information from the losses, (5) the methods of safeguard selection, and (6) the objectives to be achieved by information security.

This model is based on my goal of meeting the owners' needs to preserve the desired *security elements* of their information from intentional and accidental *acts* of abusers and misusers (and from physical forces) that would cause *losses*. This is to be done by applying *safeguards and practices* that are selected by *standards of due care* and from special needs to achieve desired *objectives*. Figure 10.1 presents this model in diagrammatic format, followed by detailed descriptions of each part.

SIX ESSENTIAL FOUNDATION ELEMENTS

I can demonstrate that at least six foundation elements in the proposed framework model are essential to information security. If any one of them is omitted, information security is deficient in protecting information owners. I use six scenarios of information losses, all derived from real cases, to

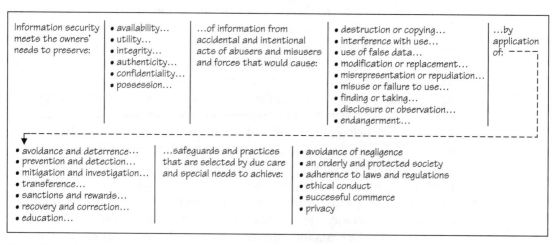

FIGURE 10.1   Proposed information security model.

demonstrate my contention. Then I show how each scenario violates one, and only one, element of information security. Thus, if we omit the element from information security, we must also remove the scenario from the concerns of information security, but I think we can all agree that these scenarios all fall well within the range of the abuse and misuse that we need to protect against.

Loss Scenario 1: Availability

A rejected contract programmer, intent on sabotage, removed the name of a data file from the file directories in a credit union's computer. Users of the computer and the data file no longer had the file available to them because the computer operating system recognizes the existence of information available for users only if it is named in the file directories. The credit union was shut down for two weeks while another programmer was brought in to find and correct the problem so that the file would be available. The perpetrator was eventually convicted of computer crime.

The other elements of information security—utility, integrity, authenticity, confidentiality, and possession—do not address this loss, and their state does not change in the scenario. The owner of the computer (the credit union) retained possession of the data file. Only the availability of the information was lost, but it is a loss that clearly should have been prevented by information security. Thus, the preservation of availability must be accepted as a purpose of information security.

It is true that good security practice might have prevented the disgruntled programmer from having use of the credit union application system, and his work could have been monitored more carefully. The credit union should not have been dependent on the technical capabilities and knowledge of only one person, and should have employed several controls to preserve or restore the availability of data files in the computer, such as maintaining a backup directory with erased file names and pointers. The loss might have been prevented, or minimized, through good backup practices, good usage controls for computers and specific data files, use of more than one name to identify and find a file, and the availability of utility programs to search for files by content or to mirror file storage.

The severity of availability loss can vary considerably. A perpetrator may destroy copies of a data file in a manner that eliminates any chance of recovery. In other situations, the data file may be partially usable, with recovery possible for a moderate cost, or the user may have inconvenient or delayed use of the file for some period of time, followed by complete recovery.

Loss Scenario 2: Utility

In this case, an employee routinely encrypted the only copy of valuable information stored in his organization's computer, then accidentally erased the encryption key. The usefulness of the information was lost and could be restored only through successful cryptanalysis.

Although this scenario can be described as a loss of availability or authenticity of the encryption key, the loss focuses on the usefulness of the information rather than on the key, since the only purpose of the key was to facilitate encryption. The information in this scenario is available, but in a form that is not useful. Its integrity, authenticity, and possession are unaffected, and its confidentiality is greatly improved.

To preserve utility of information in this case, I suggest that management require mandatory backup copies of all critical information, and control the use of powerful protective mechanisms such as cryptography. Management should require security walk-through tests during application development to limit unresponsive forms of information. It should minimize the adverse effects of security on information use, and control the types of activities that enable unauthorized persons to reduce the usefulness of information.

The loss of utility can vary in severity. The worst-case scenario would be the total loss of usefulness of the information with no possibility of recovery. Less severe cases may range from a partially useful state with the potential for full restoration of usefulness at moderate cost.

Loss Scenario 3: Integrity

In this scenario, a software distributor purchased a copy (on diskette) of a program for a computer game from an obscure publisher. The distributor made copies of the diskette and removed the name of the publisher from the diskette copies. Then, without informing the publisher or paying any royalties, he sold the diskette copies in a foreign country. Unfortunately, the success of the program sales was not deterred by the lack of an identified publisher on the diskette or in the product promotional materials.

Because the diskette copies of the game did not identify the publisher who created the program, the copies lacked integrity. (The meaning of *integrity* is a state of completeness, wholeness, and soundness.) However, the copies did not lack authenticity, since they contained the genuine game program and only lacked the identity of the publisher, which was not necessary for the successful use of the product. Information utility was maintained, and confidentiality and availability were not at issue. Possession was also not at issue, since the distributor bought the original diskette. But copyright protection was violated as a consequence of the loss of integrity and unauthorized copying of the otherwise authentic program.

Several controls can be applied to prevent the loss of integrity of information, including using and checking sequence numbers and checksums or hash totals to ensure completeness and wholeness for a series of items; performing manual and automatic text checks for required presence of records, subprograms, paragraphs, or titles; and testing to detect violations of specified controls.

The severity of information integrity loss also varies. Significant parts of the information can be missing or misordered (but still available), with no potential for recovery. Or, missing or misordered information can be restored, with delay and at moderate cost. In least severe cases, an owner can recover small amounts of misordered or mislocated information in a timely manner for use at low cost.

Loss Scenario 4: Authenticity

In a slight variation on the preceding scenario, another software distributor obtained the program (on diskette) for a computer game from an obscure publisher. The distributor changed the name of the publisher on the disk and in title screens to that of a well-known publisher, then made copies of the diskette. Without informing either publisher, he then proceeded to distribute the diskette copies in a foreign country. In this case, the identity of a popular publisher on the diskettes and in the promotional materials significantly added to the success of the product sales.

Because the distributor misrepresented the publisher of the game, the program did not conform to reality: It was not an authentic game from the well-known publisher. Availability and utility are not at issue in this case. The game had integrity because it identified a publisher and was complete and sound. (Certainly, the distributor lacked personal integrity because his acts did not conform to ethical practice, but that is not the subject of the scenario.) The actual publisher did not lose possession of the game, even though copies were deceptively represented as having come from a different publisher. And, while the distributor undoubtedly tried to keep his actions secret from both publishers, confidentiality of the content of the game was not at issue.

What if someone misrepresents your information by claiming that it is his? Violation of CIA does not include this act. Remember the stockbroker in Florida (in Chapter 1) who cheated his investors in a Ponzi scheme.

He stole $50 million by claiming that he used a super-secret computer program on his giant computer to make profits of 60 percent per day by arbitrage (a stock trading method in which the investor takes advantage of the small differences in prices of the same stock in different markets). He showed investors the mainframe computer at a Wall Street brokerage firm and falsely claimed that it and the information stored therein were his, thereby lending validity to his business.

This stockbroker's scheme was a computer crime if there ever was one. But the CIA foundation does not address it as such because its definition of integrity does not include misrepresentation of information. (Remember that integrity means only that information is whole or complete; it does not address the validity of information.) Obviously, confidentiality and availability do not cover misrepresentation either. The best way to extend CIA to include misrepresentation is to use the more general term *authenticity*. We can then assign the correct English meaning to integrity: wholeness, completeness, and good condition. Peter Neumann and Bob Courtney are correct when they say that information with integrity means that the information is what you expect it to be. This does not, however, necessarily mean that the information is valid. *Authenticity* is the word that means conformance to reality.

A number of controls can be applied to ensure authenticity of information. These include confirming transactions, names, deliveries, and addresses; validating products; checking for out-of-range or incorrect information; and using digital signatures to authenticate documents.

The severity of authenticity loss can take several forms, including lack of conformance to reality with no recovery possible; moderately false or deceptive information with delayed recovery at moderate cost; or factually correct information with only annoying discrepancies. If the CIA foundation included authenticity, with misrepresentation of information as an associated threat, Kevin Mitnick would probably have faced a far more difficult challenge in perpetrating his crimes. Computer vendors might have understood the need to prove computer operating system updates genuine to avoid misrepresentation with fakes before their customers ingested them into their computers.

Loss Scenario 5: Confidentiality

A thief deceptively obtained technical information from a bank's technical maintenance staff. He used a stolen key to open the maintenance door of an automated teller machine (ATM), and secretly inserted a radio transmitter that he purchased from a Radio Shack store. The radio received signals from the touch-screen display in the ATM that customers use to enter their PINs and receive account balance information. The radio device broadcast the information to the thief's radio receiver in his nearby car, which recorded the PINs and account balances on tape in a modified VCR. The thief used the information to loot the customers' accounts from other ATMs. The police and FBI caught the thief after elaborate detective and surveillance efforts. He is now serving a 10-year sentence in federal prison.

The thief violated the secrecy of the customers' PINs and account balances, and he violated their privacy. Availability, utility, integrity, and authenticity were unaffected in this violation of confidentiality. The customers' and the bank's exclusive possession of the PINs and account balances information was lost, but not possession per se because they still held and owned the information. Therefore, this was primarily a case of lost confidentiality.

According to most security experts, confidentiality deals with disclosure, but confidentiality can also be lost by observation, whether that observation is voluntary or involuntary, and whether the information is disclosed or not disclosed. For example, if I leave sensitive information displayed on my unattended computer monitor screen, I have disclosed it and it may or may not lose its confidentiality. If I turn the monitor off, leaving a blank screen, I have not disclosed sensitive information, but if somebody turns the monitor on and reads its contents without my permission, then I have lost confidentiality by observation. We must prevent both disclosure and observation to protect confidentiality.

Controls to maintain confidentiality include using cryptography, training employees to resist deceptive social engineering attacks intended to obtain their technical knowledge, and controlling the use of computers and computer devices. Security also requires ensuring that resources for protection not exceed the value of what may be lost, especially with low incidence. For example, protecting against radio frequency emanations in ATMs (as in this scenario) is probably not advisable considering the cost of shielding and the paucity of such high-tech attacks.

The severity of loss of confidentiality can vary. The worst-case scenario loss is when a party with the intent and ability to cause harm observes a victim's sensitive information. In this case, unrecoverable damage may result. But information may also be known to several moderately harmful parties, with a moderate loss effect, or be known to one harmless, unauthorized party with short-term recoverable effect.

Loss Scenario 6: Possession

A gang of burglars aided by a disgruntled, recently fired operations supervisor broke into a computer center and stole tapes and disks containing the company's master files. They also raided the backup facility and stole all backup copies of the files. They then held the materials for ransom in an extortion attempt against the company. The burglary resulted in the company losing possession of all copies of the master files, as well as the media on which they were stored. The company was unable to continue business operations. The police eventually captured the extortionists with help from the company during the ransom payment, and they recovered the stolen materials. The burglars were convicted and served long prison sentences.

Loss of possession occurred in this case. The perpetrators delayed availability, but the company could have retrieved the files at any time by paying the ransom. Alternatively, the company could have re-created the master files from paper documents, but at great cost. Utility, integrity, and authenticity were not issues in this situation. Confidentiality was not violated because the burglars had no reason to read or disclose the files. Loss of ownership and permanent loss of possession would have been accomplished if the perpetrators had never returned the materials or if the company had stopped trying to recover them.

The security model must include protection of possession of information to prevent theft. Confidentiality, by definition, deals only with what people possess and know, not what they possess without knowing. Our increasing use of computers magnifies this difference; huge amounts of information are possessed for automated use and not necessarily held confidentially for only specified people to know. Computer object programs are perfect examples of information we do not know but possess by selling, buying, bartering, giving, receiving, and trading until we ultimately control, transport, and use them. We have incorrectly defined confidentiality if we include the protective efforts for possession.

We protect the possession of information by preventing people from unauthorized taking, taking copies, and holding or controlling it—whether or not confidentiality is involved. The loss of possession of information also includes the loss of control of it and may allow the new possessor to violate its confidentiality at will. Thus, loss of confidentiality may accompany loss of possession. But, we must treat confidentiality and possession separately to determine what actions criminals might take and what controls we need to apply to prevent their actions. Otherwise, we may overlook a particular threat or an effective control. The failure to anticipate a threat is one of the greatest dangers we face in security.

The controls that can protect the possession of information include using copyright laws, implementing physical and logical usage limitation methods, preserving and examining computer audit logs for evidence of stealing, inventorying tangible and intangible assets, using distinctive colors and labels on media containers, and assigning ownership to enforce accountability of organizational information assets.

The severity of loss of possession varies with the nature of the offense. In a worst-case scenario, a criminal may take information, as well as all copies of it, and there may be no means of recovery—either from the perpetrator or from other sources such as paper documentation. In a less harmful scenario, a criminal might take information for some period of time but leave some opportunity for recovery at a moderate cost. In the least harmful situation, an owner could possess only one copy of information, leaving open the possibility of recovery from other sources (e.g., backup files) within a reasonable period of time.

Conclusions about the Six Elements

We need to understand some important differences between integrity and authenticity. For one, integrity deals with the intrinsic condition of information, while authenticity deals with the extrinsic value or meaning relative to external sources. Integrity does not deal with the meaning of the information with respect to external sources, that is, whether the information is timely and not obsolete. Authenticity, in contrast, concerns the question of whether information is genuine and, for example, not out of date with respect to external sources. A user who enters false information into a computer has possibly violated authenticity, but as long as the information remains unchanged, it has integrity. An information security technologist who designs security into computer operating systems is concerned only with information integrity because she can not know if any user is entering false information. In this case, the security technologist's job is to ensure that both true and false information remains whole and complete. The information owner, with guidance from his information security advisor, has the responsibility of ensuring that the information conforms to reality, that is, that it has authenticity.

Some of the types of loss that information security must address require the use of all six elements of preservation to determine the appropriate security to apply, depending on the information kind, representation, form, and/or media. Each of the six elements can be violated independently of the others, with one important exception: A violation of confidentiality always results in loss of exclusive possession, at the least. Loss of possession, however—even exclusive possession—does not necessarily result in loss of confidentiality.

Other than that exception, the six elements are unique and independent, and often require different security controls. Maintaining the availability of information does not necessarily maintain its utility; it may be available but useless for its intended purpose, and vice versa. Maintaining the integrity of information does not necessarily mean that the information is valid, only that it remains the same or, at least, whole and complete. Information can be invalid and, therefore, without authenticity, yet it may be present and identical to the original version and, thus, have integrity. Finally, who is allowed to view and know information and who possesses it are often two very different matters.

Unfortunately, the written information security policies of many organizations do not acknowledge the need to address many kinds of information loss. This is because their policies are limited to achieving CIA. To completely define information security, the policies must address all six elements that I've presented. Moreover, to adequately eliminate (or at least reduce) security threats, all six elements need to be considered to ensure that nothing is overlooked in applying appropriate controls. These elements are also useful for identifying and anticipating the types of abusive actions that adversaries may take—before such actions are undertaken.

For simplification and ease of reference, we can pair the six elements into three double elements, which you should be using to identify threats and select proper controls, and associate them with synonyms to facilitate recall and understanding (on the right):

availability and utility	(usability and usefulness)
integrity and authenticity	(completeness and validity)
confidentiality and possession	(secrecy and control)

Availability and utility fit together as the first double element. Controls common to these elements include secure location, appropriate form for secure use, and usability of backup copies. Integrity and authenticity also fit together; one is concerned with internal structure and the other with conformance to external facts or reality. Controls for both include double entry, reasonableness checks, use of sequence numbers and checksums or hash totals, and comparison testing. Control of change applies to both as well. Finally, confidentiality and possession also go together because, as I discussed previously in this section, they are interrelated. Commonly applied controls for both include copyright protection, cryptography, digital signatures, escrow, and secure storage.

The order of the elements here is logical, since availability and utility are necessary for integrity and authenticity to have value, and these first four elements are necessary for confidentiality and possession to have material meaning.

We lose credibility and confuse information owners if we do not use words precisely and consistently. When defined correctly, the six words

---

What the Dictionaries Say about the Words We Use

The following definitions of security and the elements are relevant abstractions from *Webster's Third New International Dictionary* and *Webster's Collegiate Dictionary, Tenth Edition.*

Security.   Freedom from danger, fear, anxiety, care, uncertainty, doubt; basis for confidence; measures taken to ensure against surprise attack, espionage, observation, sabotage; resistance of a cryptogram to cryptanalysis usually measured by the time and effort needed to solve it.

Availability.   Present or ready for immediate use.

Utility.   Useful, fitness for some purpose.

Integrity.   Unimpaired or unmarred condition; soundness; entire correspondence with an original condition; adherence to a code of moral, artistic or other values; the quality or state of being complete or undivided; material wholeness.

Authenticity.   Quality of being authoritative, valid, true, real, genuine, worthy of acceptance or belief by reason of conformity to fact and reality.

Confidentiality.   Quality or state of being private or secret; known only to a limited few, containing information whose unauthorized disclosure could be prejudicial to the national interest.

Possession.   Act or condition of having or taking into one's control or holding at one's disposal; actual physical control of property by one who holds for himself, as distinguished from custody; something owned or controlled.

are independent (with the exception that information possession is always violated when confidentiality is violated). They are also consistent, comprehensive, and complete. In other words, the six elements themselves possess integrity and authenticity, and therefore they have great utility. This does not mean that we will not find new elements or replace some of them as our insights develop and technology advances. (I first presented this demonstration of the need for the six elements in 1991 at the fourteenth NSA/NIST National Computer Security Conference in Baltimore.)

My definitions of the six elements are considerably shorter and simpler than the dictionary definitions, but appropriate for information security.

Availability.   Usability of information for a purpose.

Utility.   Usefulness of information for a purpose.

Integrity.   Completeness, wholeness, and readability of information and quality being unchanged from a previous state.

Authenticity.   Validity, conformance, and genuineness of information.

Confidentiality.   Limited observation and disclosure of knowledge.

Possession.   The holding, control, and ability to use information.

COMPREHENSIVE LIST OF INFORMATION LOSSES

The threats that cause losses come from people who engage in unauthorized and harmful acts against information such as embezzlers, fraudsters, thieves, saboteurs, and hackers. They engage in using, taking, misrepresenting, observing, and every other conceivable form of human misbehavior. Natural physical forces such as air and earth movements, heat and cold, electromagnetic energy, living organisms, gravity and projectiles, and water and gases also are threats to information.

Extensive lists of losses often include fraud, theft, sabotage, and espionage along with disclosure, usage, repudiation, and copying. The first four losses in this list are criminal justice terms at a different level of abstraction than the latter four and are not well suited for most security purposes, since they require an understanding of criminal law, which many information owners and security specialists lack. For example, fraud includes theft only if it is performed using deception, and larceny includes burglary and theft from a victim's premises. What constitutes "premises" in an electronic network environment?

Many important types of information loss, such as false data entry, failure to perform, replacement, deception, misrepresentation, prolongation of use, delay of use, and even the obvious taking of information, are frequently omitted from lists of losses. Each of these losses may require different prevention and detection controls, a fact that we can easily overlook if our list of potential losses is incomplete—even though the losses we typically omit are among the most common reported in actual loss experience. The people who cause unusual losses are often aware that information owners have not provided adequate security. It is, therefore, essential to include all types of potential losses in our lists, especially when unique safeguards are applicable. Otherwise, we are in danger of being negligent, and those to whom we are accountable will view information security as incomplete and/or poorly conceived when a loss does occur.

"The Complete List of Potential Information Losses" sidebar presents a comprehensive, non-legalistic list of potential losses to information that I compiled from my 28 years in computer crime and security research. I have simplified it to a single level of abstraction to facilitate understanding by information owners and to enable them to select effective controls. The list makes no distinction among the causes of the losses; as such, it applies equally well to accidental and intentional acts. Cause is largely irrelevant at this level of security analysis, as is the underlying intent or lack thereof. (Identifying cause is important at another level of security analysis. We need to determine the sources and motivation of threats in order to identify appropriate avoidance, deterrence, and recovery controls.) In addition, the list makes no distinction between electronic and physical causes of loss, or between spoken, printed, or electronically recorded information.

The loss pairs (e.g., availability and utility, etc.) correspond to the six elements of information security that I outlined previously. Some types of loss in one element grouping may have a related effect in another grouping as well. For example, if no other copies of information exist, destroying the information (under *availability*) may also cause loss of possession, and taking (under *possession*) may cause loss of availability. Yet, loss of possession and loss of availability are quite different, and may require different controls. I have simply placed losses in the most obvious categories, the places where a loss prevention analyst is likely to look first.

Here is an abbreviated version of the complete loss list for convenient use in the information security model:

Destroy

Interfere with use

Use false data

Modify or replace

Misrepresent or repudiate

The Complete List of
Potential Information Losses

Availability and Utility Losses

Destroy, damage, or contaminate

Deny, prolong, accelerate, or delay use or acquisition

Move or misplace

Convert or obscure

Integrity and Authenticity Losses

Insert, use, or produce false or unacceptable data

Modify, replace, remove, append, aggregate, separate, or reorder

Misrepresent

Repudiate (reject as untrue)

Misuse or fail to use as required

Confidentiality and Possession Losses

Locate

Disclose

Observe or monitor and acquire

Copy

Take or control

Claim ownership or custodianship

Infer

Exposure to All of the Other Losses

Endanger by exposing to any of the other losses

Failure to engage in or allow any of the other losses to occur when
instructed to do so

Misuse or fail to use

Locate

Disclose

Observe

Copy

Take

Endanger

Users may be unfamiliar with some of the words in the lists of losses, at least in the context of security. For example, *repudiate* is a word that we seldom hear or use outside of the legal or security context. I have previously identified it. According to dictionaries, it means to refuse to accept acts or information as true, just, or of rightful authority or obligation. Information security technologists became interested in repudiation when the Massachusetts Institute of Technology developed a secure network operating system for its internal use. They named the system *Kerberos*, taking the name of the three-headed temple dog of Greek mythology. Kerberos provides a means of forming secure links and paths between users and the computers serving them. Unfortunately, however, in early versions it allowed users to falsely deny using the links. This did not present any particular problems in the academic environment, but it did make Kerberos inadequate for business, even though its other security aspects were attractive. As the use of Kerberos spread into business, repudiation became an issue, and nonrepudiation controls became important.

Repudiation is an important issue in electronic data interchange (EDI) and Internet commerce, which require digital signatures, time stamps, and other authentication controls. I could, for example, falsely claim that I never ordered merchandise and that the order form or electronically transmitted ordering information that the merchant possesses is false. Repudiation is also a growing problem because of the difficulty of proving the authorship and/or source of electronic missives. And, the inverse of repudiate—claiming that an act that did not happen actually did happen, or claiming that false information is true—is also important to security, although it is often overlooked. Repudiation and its inverse are both types of misrepresentation, but I include both *repudiate* and *misrepresent* on the list because they often require different types of controls.

Other words in the list of losses may seem somewhat obscure. For example, we seldom think of prolonging or delaying use as a loss of availability or a denial of use, yet they are losses that are often inflicted by computer virus attacks.

I use the word *locate* in this list rather than *access* because, as I explained in Chapter 1, access can be confusing with regard to information security. Although it is commonly used in computer terminology, its use frequently causes confusion, as it did in the 1988 Internet worm trial and in computer crime laws. For example, access may mean just knocking on a door or opening the door, but not going in. How far "into" a computer must you go to "access" it? A perpetrator can cause a loss simply by locating information, because the owner may not want to divulge his possession of such information. In this case, no access is involved. For these reasons, I prefer to use *entry, intrusion,* and *usage*—as well as *locate*—when I'm referring to a computer as the object of the action.

I have a similar problem with the use of the word *disclosure.* Disclose is a verb that means to divulge, reveal, make known, or report knowledge to others. We can disclose knowledge by:

- Broadcasting
- Speaking
- Displaying
- Showing
- Leaving it in the presence and view of another person
- Leaving it in possible view where another person is likely to be
- Handing or sending it to another person

Disclosure is what an owner or potential victim might inadvertently or intentionally do, not what a perpetrator does, unless it is the second act after stealing, such as selling stolen intellectual property to another person. Disclosure can be an abuse if a person authorized to know information discloses it to an unauthorized person, or if an unauthorized person discloses knowledge to another person without permission. In any case, confidentiality is lost or is potentially lost, and the person disclosing the information may be accused of negligence, violation of privacy, conspiracy, or espionage.

Loss of confidentiality can also occur by observation of knowledge, whether the victim or owner disclosed it, resisted disclosure, or did nothing to protect or disclose it. Observing is an abuse of listening, stealing a copy and viewing or listening to it, spying by eavesdropping or shoulder surfing (looking over another person's shoulder or overhearing), or tactile feeling, as in the case of reading Braille. We should think about loss of confidentiality as a loss caused by inadvertent disclosure by the victim and observation by the perpetrator. Disclosure and observation of information that is not knowledge converts it into knowledge if cognition takes place. Disclosure always results in loss of confidentiality by putting information into a state where there is no longer any secrecy, but observation results in loss of confidentiality only if cognition takes place.

Loss of possession of information (including knowledge) is the loss from the unintended or regretful giving or taking of information. At a higher level of crime description, we call it larceny (theft or burglary) or some kind of fraud. Possession seems to be most closely associated with confidentiality. I've placed the two together in the list because they share the common losses of taking and copying (loss of exclusive possession). I could have used *ownership* of information, since it is a synonym for possession, but *ownership* is not as broad, because somebody may rightly or wrongly possess information that is rightfully owned by another. The concepts of owner or possessor of information, along with user and provider or custodian of information, are important distinctions in security for assigning accountability for the security of assets. This provides another reason for including possession in the list.

The category *endangerment* is quite different from, but applies to, the other losses. It means that a person has been remiss (and possibly negligent) by not applying sufficient protection to information, such as leaving sensitive or valuable documents in an unlocked office or open trash bin. Leaving a computer unnecessarily connected to the Internet is another example. Endangerment of information may lead to charges of negligence or criminal negligence and civil liability suits that may be more costly than direct loss incidents. My baseline security methodology, which is described in Chapter 12, invokes a standard of due care to deal with this exposure.

The last loss in the list—failure to engage in or allow to occur any of the other losses when instructed to do so—may seem odd at first glance. It means that an information owner may require an act resulting in any of the losses to be carried out. Or the owner may wish that a loss be allowed to occur, or information be put into danger of loss. There are occasions when information should be put in harm's way for testing purposes or to accomplish a greater good. For example, computer programmers and auditors often create information files that are purposely invalid for use as input to a computer to make sure that the controls are working correctly to detect or mitigate a loss. A programmer bent on crime may remove an invalidity in a test input file to avoid testing a control that he has neutralized or avoided implementing for his nefarious purposes. The list would surely be incomplete without this type of loss, yet I have never seen it included or discussed in any other information security source.

I describe the losses in the list at the appropriate level for deriving and identifying appropriate security controls. At the next lower level of abstraction (e.g., read, write, and execute), the losses would not be so obvious and would not necessarily suggest important controls. At the level that I choose, there is no attempt to differentiate losses that make no change to information from those that do, since these differences are not important for identifying directly applicable controls or for performing threat analyses. For example, a loss from modification changes the information, while a loss from observation does not, but encryption is likely to be employed as a powerful primary control against both losses.

Examples of Loss and Suggested Controls

The following examples illustrate the relationships between losses and controls in threat analysis. Sets of loss types are followed by examples of the losses and applicable controls.

Destroy, damage, or contaminate. Perpetrators or harmful forces can damage, destroy, or contaminate information by electronically erasing it, writing other data over it, applying high-energy radio waves to damage delicate electronic circuits, or physically damaging the media (e.g., paper or disk) containing it.

Controls include disaster prevention safeguards such as locked facilities, safe storage of backup copies, and write-usage authorization requirements.

Deny, prolong, or delay use or acquisition. Perpetrators can make information unavailable by hiding it or denying its use through encryption and not revealing the means to restore it, or keeping critical processing units busy with other work. Such actions would not necessarily destroy the information. Similarly, a perpetrator may prolong its use by making program changes that slow the processing in a computer or slow the display of the information on a screen. Such actions might cause unacceptable timing for effective use of the information. Information acquisition may be delayed by requiring too many passwords to retrieve it or by slowing retrieval. These actions can make the information obsolete by the time it becomes available.

Controls include making multiple copies available from different sources, preventing overload of processing by selective allowance of input, or preventing the activation of harmful mechanisms such as computer viruses by using antiviral utilities.

Enter, use, or produce false data.   Data diddling, my term for false data entry and use, is a common form of computer crime, accounting for much of the financial and inventory fraud. Losses may be either intentional, such as those resulting from the use of Trojan horses (including computer viruses), or unintentional, such as those from input errors.

Most internal controls such as range checks, audit trails, separation of duties, duplicate data entry detection, program proving, and hash totals for data items to protect against these threats.

Modify, replace, or reorder.   These losses result from actions that are often intelligent changes rather than damage or destruction. *Reordering*, which is actually a form of modification, is included separately because it may require specific controls that could otherwise be overlooked. Similarly, *replace* is included because you might not otherwise include the idea of replacing an entire data file when considering modification. Any of these actions can produce a loss inherent in the threats of entering and modifying information, but including all of them covers modifying data both before entry and after entry, since each requires different controls.

Cryptography, digital signatures, usage authorization, and message sequencing are examples of controls to protect against these losses, as are detection controls to identify anomalies.

Misrepresent.   The claim that information is something different than it really is or has a different meaning than intended arises in counterfeiting, forgery, fraud, impersonation (of authorized users), and many other deceptive activities. Hackers use misrepresentation in social engineering to deceive people into revealing information needed to attack systems. Misrepresenting old data as new information is another threat of this type.

Controls include user and document authentication methods such as passwords and digital signatures, and data validity tests. Making trusted people more resistant to deception by reminders and training is another control.

Repudiate.   This type of loss, in which perpetrators generally deny having made transactions, is prevalent in electronic data interchange (EDI) and Internet commerce. Oliver North's denials of the content of his e-mail messages is a notable example of repudiation, but as I mentioned earlier, the inverse of repudiation also represents a potential loss.

We can control repudiation most effectively through the use of digital signatures and public key cryptography. Trusted third parties, such as certificate authorities with secure computer servers, provide the independence of notary publics to resist denial of truthful information as long as they can be held liable for their failures.

Misuse or Fail to Use as Required.   Misuse of information is clearly a part of many information losses. Misuse by failure to perform duties such as updating files or backing up information is not so obvious and needs explicit identification. Implicit misuse by conforming exactly to inadequate or incorrect instructions is a sure way to sabotage systems.

Information usage control and internal application controls that constrain the modification and/or use of trusted software help to avoid these problems. Keeping secure logs of routine activities can help catch operational vulnerabilities.

Locate.   Unauthorized use of someone's computer or data network to locate and identify information is a crime under most computer crime statutes—even if there is no overt intention to cause harm. Such usage is a violation of privacy, and trespass to engage in such usage is a crime under other laws.

Logon and usage controls are a major feature in many operating systems, such as Microsoft Windows NT and some versions of UNIX, as well as in add-on utilities such as *RACF* and *ACF2* for large IBM computers and *Watchdog* and *DACS* security products for PCs.

Disclose.   Revealing information to people not authorized to know it is the subject of business, personal, and government secrecy. Disclosure may be verbal, by mail, or by transferring messages and/or files electronically or on disks or tape. Disclosure can result in loss of privacy and trade secrets.

The military has advanced protection of information confidentiality to an elaborate art form. One comprehensive example is the *TCSEC Orange Book Evaluation Criteria* sponsored by the U.S. NSA.

Observe or monitor.   Observation is the inverse of disclosure. Workstation display screens, communication lines, and monitoring devices (e.g., recorders and audit logs) are common targets of observation and monitoring. Observation of output from printers is another possible source, as is shoulder surfing—the technique of watching screens of other computer users.

Physical entry protection for input and output devices represents the major control to prevent this type of loss. Preventing wiretapping and eavesdropping is also important.

Copy.   Copy machines and the software *copy* command are the major sources of unauthorized copying. Copying is used to violate exclusive possession and/or privacy. Copying can destroy authenticity, as when used to counterfeit money or other business instruments.

Location and use controls are effective against copying, as are unique markings such as those used on U.S. currency and watermarks on paper.

Take.   Transferring data files in computers or networks constitutes taking. So does taking small computers and diskettes or documents for the value of the information stored in them. Perpetrators can easily take copies of information without depriving the owner of possession or confidentiality.

A wide range of physical and logical location controls apply to these losses; most are based on common sense and a reasonable level of due care.

Endanger.   Putting information into locations and/or conditions in which others may cause loss in any of the previously described ways clearly endangers the information, and the perpetrator may be accused of negligence, at the least.

Physical and logical means of preventing information from being placed in danger are important. Training people to be careful, and holding them accountable for protecting information, are also important.

Physical Information and Systems Losses

Information can also suffer from physical losses such as those caused by floods, earthquakes, radiation, and fires. Although these losses may not directly affect information, they do damage or destroy the media and/or environment that contains the information. Water, for example, can destroy printed pages and damage magnetic disks; shaking or radio frequency radiation can short-out electronic circuits, and fires can destroy all types of media. Overall, there are seven natural ways that physical loss may occur by application of: extreme temperature, gases, liquids, living organisms, projectiles, movements, and energy anomalies. Each way, of course, comes from specific sources of loss (e.g., smoke or water). And, the various ways can be broken down further to identify the underlying cause of the source of loss. For example, the liquid that destroys information may be water flowing from a plumbing break above the computer workstation, caused in turn by freezing weather. Following are the seven major sources of physical loss with examples of each:

Extreme temperature.   Heat, cold

Examples: sunlight, fire, freezing and hot weather

Gases.   War gases, commercial vapors, humid or dry air, suspended particles

Examples: Sarin nerve gas, PCP from exploding transformers, air-conditioning failures, smoke and smog, cleaning fluid and fuel vapors, paper particles from printers

Liquids.   Water, chemicals

Examples: floods, plumbing failures, precipitation, fuel leaks, spilled drinks, acid and base chemicals used for cleaning, computer printer fluids

Living organisms.   Viruses, bacteria, people, animals, insects

Examples: sickness of key workers, molds, contamination from skin oils and hair, contamination and electrical shorting from defecation and release of body fluids, consumption of information media such as paper or of cable insulation, shorting of microcircuits from cobwebs

Projectiles.   Tangible objects in motion, powered objects

Examples: meteorites, falling objects, cars and trucks, bullets and rockets, explosions, wind

Movement.   Collapse, shearing, shaking, vibration, liquefaction, flows, waves, separation, slide

Examples: dropping or shaking fragile equipment, earthquakes, earth slides, lava flows, sea waves, adhesive failures

Energy anomalies.   Electric surge or failure, magnetism, static electricity, aging circuitry; radiation: sound, light, radio, microwave, electromagnetic, atomic

Examples: electric utility failures, proximity of magnets and electromagnets, carpet static, decomposition of circuit materials, decomposition of paper and magnetic disks, EMP from nuclear explosions, lasers, loudspeakers, high-energy radio frequency (HERF) guns, radar systems, cosmic radiation, explosions

Although falling meteorites clearly pose little danger to computers, it is nonetheless important to include all such unlikely events in a thorough analysis of potential threats. In general, you should include every possible loss in your threat analysis. Then consider it carefully; if it is too unlikely, document the consideration and discard the item. It is better to have thought of a source of loss and to discard it, than to have overlooked an important one. Invariably, when you present your threat analysis to others, someone will try to surprise you with another source of loss that you have overlooked.

Insensitive practitioners have ingrained inadequate loss lists in the body of knowledge from the very inception of information security. Proposing a major change at this late date is a bold action that may take significant time to accomplish. However, we must not perpetuate our past inadequacies by using the currently accepted DDUM as a complete list of losses. We must not underrate or simplify the complexity of our subject at the expense of misleading information owners. Our adversaries are always looking for weaknesses in information security, but our strength lies in anticipating sources of threats and having plans in place to prevent the losses that they may cause.

It is impossible to collect a truly complete list of the sources of information losses that can be caused by the intentional or accidental acts of people. We really have no idea what people may do—now or in the future. We base our lists on experience, but until we can conceive of a loss, or a threat actually surfaces or occurs, we can not include it on the list. And, not knowing the threat means that we can not devise a plan to protect against it. This is one of the reasons that information security is still a folk art rather than a science.

The Challenge of Complete Lists

I believe that my lists of physical sources of loss and information losses are complete, but I am always interested in expanding them to include new sources of loss that I may have overlooked.

While I was lecturing in Australia, for example, a delegate suggested that I had omitted an important category. His computer center had experienced an invasion of field mice with a taste for electrical insulation. The intruders proceeded to chew through the computer cables, ruining them. Consequently, I had to add rodents to my list of sources. I then heard about an incident in San Francisco in which the entire evening shift of computer operations workers ate together in the company cafeteria to celebrate a birthday. Then they all contracted food poisoning, leaving their company without sufficient operations staff for two weeks. I combined the results of these two events into a category called Living Organisms.

At another conference, an individual suggested that I add aging of circuits to the Energy Anomaly category in my growing list.

THE FUNCTIONS OF INFORMATION SECURITY

The model for information security that I've proposed includes eleven security functions instead of the three (prevention, detection, and recovery) included in previous models. These functions, which I cover in detail in Chapter 12, describe the activities that information security practitioners and information owners engage in to protect information, as well as the objectives of the security controls that they use. Every control serves one or more of these functions.

Although some security specialists add other functions to the list, such as quality assurance and reliability, I consider these to be outside of the scope of information security; there are other specialized fields that deal with them. Reliability is difficult to relate to security except to say that perpetrators can destroy the reliability of information and systems, which is a violation of security. Thus, security must preserve a state of reliability, but not improve it. Security must protect the auditability of information and systems as well. The reverse is also true, namely, that security itself must be reliable and auditable. Peter Neumann is right about the overlap of security and reliability. I believe that my security definitions include the destruction of the reliability and auditability of information at a different level of abstraction. For example, reliability is reduced when the authenticity of information is reduced by changing it from correct representation of fact.

Similarly, I do not include such functions as auditing, authentication of users, and verification in my lists, since I consider these to be control objectives to achieve the eleven functions of information security. Auditing, for example, achieves the detection of deficiencies and anomalies in systems.

There is a definite logic to the order in which I present the eleven functions in my list. A methodical information security practitioner is likely to apply the functions in this order when resolving a security vulnerability.

1. First, the practitioner must determine if a security problem can be avoided altogether.
2. If the problem can not be avoided, the practitioner needs to try to deter potential abusers or forces from misbehaving.
3. If the threat can not be avoided or deterred, the practitioner attempts to detect its activation.
4. If detection is not assured, then the practitioner tries to prevent the attack from occurring.
5. If prevention fails and an attack occurs, then the practitioner needs to stop it or minimize its harmful effects through mitigation.
6. The practitioner needs to determine if another individual or department might be more effective at resolving the situation resulting from the attack, or if another party (such as an insurer) might be held accountable for the cost of the loss.
7. After a loss occurs, the practitioner needs to search for the individual(s) or force that caused or contributed to the incident, as well as any parties that played a role in it—positively or negatively
8. When identified, all parties should be sanctioned or rewarded as appropriate.
9. After an incident is concluded, the victim needs to recover or assist with recovery.
10. The stakeholders should take corrective actions to prevent the same type of incident from occurring again.
11. Finally, the stakeholders must learn from the experience in order to advance their knowledge of information security and teach it to others.

THREATS				ASSETS	VULNERABILITIES		
OFFENDERS	ABUSE/ MISUSE	METHODS	LOSSES	ASSETS LOST	CONTROL OBJECTIVES	CONTROLS (types)	CONTROL GUIDES
Have/Acquire Skills • Learning • Technology • People **Knowledge** • Direct • Indirect **Resources** • Computer services • Transport • Financial **Authority** • Employment • Contract • Ownership • Possession • Custodian • Right • Other **Motives** • No intent • Negligence • Errors and omissions **Intentional** • Problem solving • Gain higher ethic **Extreme Advocacy** • Social • Political • Religious	• Errors • Omissions • Negligence • Recklessness • Delinquency • Civil disputes • Conspiracy • Natural disruption • Destruction • Theft • Privacy • Trespass • Burglary • Larceny • Forgery • Counterfeiting • Smuggling • Fraud • Scam • Embezzlement • Bribery • Extortion • Racketeering • Infringement • Plagiarism • Piracy • Espionage • Antitrust • Contract • Securities • Employment • Kickbacks • Laundering • Libel • Drugs • Pornography • Harassment • Assault • Sex attack • Kidnapping • Murder • Suicide	**External** • Heat/cold • Gases/air • Water • Chemical • Bacteria • Viruses • People • Animals • Insects • Collision • Collapse • Shear • Shake • Vibrate • Liquefy • Flows • Waves • Separate • Slides • Electric • Magnets • Aging • Radiate • Sound • Light • Radio • Atomic **Masquerade** • Impersonate • Spoof **Program** • Trojan • Virus • Bomb • Bypass • Trapdoor **Authority** • Violation **Active** • Deny service • False data entry **Passive** • Browse • Observe **Failure** • Omit duty **Indirect** • Crime use	**Availability & Utility** • Destroy • Damage • Contaminate • Deny • Prolong • Accelerate • Delay • Move • Misplace • Convert • Obscure **Integrity & Authenticity** • Insert • Use • Produce • Modify • Replace • Remove • Append • Reorder • Misrepresent • Repudiate • Fail to use **Confidential & Possession** • Locate • Disclose • Observe • Monitor • Acquire • Copy • Take control • Own • Infer • Expose to loss • Endanger • Fail instruction	**Information** • Spoken • Printed • Magnetic • Electronic • Optical • Radio • Biological **Computer** **Commlines** **Networks** **Facilities** **Buildings** **Transport** **People**	• Avoidance • Deterrence • Prevention • Detection • Mitigation • Sanction • Transfer • Investigate • Recovery • Correction	• Organization • Physical • Development • Automation • Operation • Voice • Network • Access • Training • Motivation • Management • Applications • Printing • Audit • Disaster recovery	• Cost effective • Due care • Complete • Consistent • Performance • Sustain • Automatic • Tolerated • Consequences • Override • Failsafe • Default • Instrument • Auditable • Non-repudiate • Secrecy • Universal • Independent • Unpredictable • Tamperproof • Compartment • Depth • Isolate • Least • Accountability • Trust • Multifunction • Deception • Positional • Transparent

FIGURE 10.2 Threats, Assets, Vulnerabilities model.

254

Selecting Safeguards Using a Standard of Due Care

Information security practitioners usually refer to the process of selecting safeguards as risk assessment, risk analysis, or risk management. As I indicated in Chapter 1, selecting safeguards based on risk calculations is a fruitless and expensive process. While many security experts and associations advocate using risk assessment methods, many organizations ultimately find that using a standard of due care is far superior and more practical. One sad experience of using risk assessment is often sufficient to convince information security departments and corporate management of its limitations.

The standard of due care approach is simple and obvious; it is the default process that I recommend, and that is commonly used today instead of more elaborate "scientific" approaches. The standard of due care approach is recognized and accepted by many legal documents and organizations and is documented in numerous business guides. The 1996 U.S. federal statute on protecting trade secrets (18 USC § 1831), for example, states in (3)(a) that the owner of information must take "reasonable measures to keep such information secret" for it to be defined as a trade secret. (Refer to Chapter 12 for complete information on using a standard of due care.)

THREATS, ASSETS, VULNERABILITIES MODEL

Pulling all of the aspects of losses together in one place is a useful way to analyze the threats and vulnerabilities in real crimes, and to create effective scenarios to test real information systems and organizations. The model illustrated in Figure 10.2 is designed to help you do this. You can outline a scenario or analyze a real case by circling and connecting the appropriate descriptors in each column of the model.

In this version of the model, the Controls column lists only the subject headings of control types; a completed model would contain hundreds of controls. If you are using the model to conduct a review, I suggest that you convert the Vulnerabilities section of the model to Recommended Controls. This model is probably incomplete; Dr. Fred Cohen at Sandia Laboratory in Livermore, CA (www.sandia.gov) is currently attempting to create a more comprehensive version. (Subsequent chapters will deal with any descriptors that I haven't yet addressed, and Chapter 13 focuses on the control guides listed in the last column of the model.)

CLARK-WILSON INTEGRITY MODEL: A FRAMEWORK FOR BUSINESS APPLICATIONS SECURITY

The greatest losses occur at the convergence of valuable assets and trusted people who can easily attack them and convert such efforts to gain. These losses occur in business applications where customers and employees are using computers to conduct transactions to further commerce in business, and services in government and other institutions. Applications include sales transactions, bookkeeping, inventory management, customer services, accounts payable and receivable, payroll, personnel, and much more. Because these types of applications are the focus of much business crime, they should be the primary focus of information security.

Unfortunately, however, the computer systems technologists that dominate information security have little interest in, or knowledge of, business applications. So, by default, application systems owners, designers, programmers, users, and auditors are left "minding the store" for application security. These individuals are seldom expert in information security, and their positions typically involve other responsibilities and objectives. In addition, these individuals are likely perpetrators of applications-based crimes.

While auditors are likely to understand business controls—since their job is to ensure compliance with the application specifications and the effectiveness of accounting controls—their work often begins after applications are in operation. And, they typically do not have the time or charter to be directly involved in developing application requirements or specifications or to assist in their design or programming. Auditors must also take care to maintain their vaunted independence (their valuable contribution to security) and should not help to develop systems that they may subsequently audit.

Using the Clark-Wilson Integrity (CWI) model promises to be a useful step in developing a seamless security continuum that encompasses computer operating systems, application systems, and the people who use the applications. It was developed in 1988 by former school chums David Clark, a professor of computer science at MIT, and David Wilson, an accounting executive at Ernst and Whitney (its name at that time). This partnership mirrors the type of cooperation that is necessary to develop a seamless security continuum—one in which application security experts work together with all of the various technological and accounting experts. Although the CWI model is still relatively obscure and incomplete, its greatest value is formula-like expression of traditional accounting controls (e.g., segregation of duties, transaction authorization, logging, and verification) and well-formed transaction requirements that are amenable to double entry, no erasure, and balanced bookkeeping controls. The model's use of formulas and system architecture appeals to technologists, while its expository language appeals to application specialists such as accountants and auditors. Figure 10.3 illustrates the CWI model. For more information about it, refer to Clark and Wilson's own description of it in "A Comparison of Commercial and Military Computer Security Policies," in the April 1987 *Proceedings of the IEEE Symposium on Security and Privacy* (©1987 IEEE, paraphrased here by permission) and "Evolution of a Model for Computer Integrity," in the October 1988 *Proceedings of the NSA/NIST Eleventh National Computer Security Conference*. A report by Dr. Marshall D. Abrams, et al. at the Mitre Corporation, also offers a good description of the model: "Report of an Integrity Research Study Group" (Elsevier Science Publishers, Ltd., 1993).

The CWI model represents generally accepted integrity and authenticity accounting controls. Its primary objective is to prevent the unauthorized modification of data in transactions to eliminate the incidence of loss from fraud or errors. The model does not include availability and utility or confidentiality and possession controls. It invokes the following mechanisms and principles:

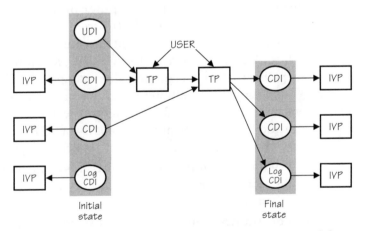

FIGURE 10.3 Clark-Wilson Commercial Integrity model.

- Mechanisms
    - Well-formed transactions
        - Provides double entry and balancing
        - Prevents erasure
        - Preserves audit records
    - Segregation of duties [and dual control]
        - Assures external consistency of data and procedures (validity)
        - Prevents collusion
- Principles
    - Data are usable only by a prescribed set of programs
    - The set of programs preserves well-formed transactions
    - Users are limited to executing subsets of programs that preserves segregation of duty
    - (Users have no open, read, or write usage of data and are not permitted to modify programs or the list of authorized users and their allowed capabilities [permissions])
- Additional principles
    - User authentication is controlled and audited
    - The audit log of program usage is protected
    - The computer operating system enforces the principles
    - The mechanisms are tamper-resistant

Although the figure shows only one or two items of each type, any number may appear in an actual transaction:

TP—Transaction procedure (computer program).　The purpose of a TP is to change a set of CDIs from the initial valid state to another valid state and take into account that a transaction took place. A TP transforms UDIs into CDIs, and it must reject unacceptable UDIs. In accounting, for example, the TP performs a double-entry transaction (e.g., recording the receipt of a payment in debit and credit accounts). The application owner and an auditor can determine the validity of a TP only by certifying it with respect to a securely held application specification.

UDI—Unconstrained data item.　A UDI is any data that a user or other source inputs to TPs (e.g., by keying data via a computer keyboard).

CDI—Constrained data item (output from TPs).　A set of CDIs may be, for example, the current balances of a set of accounts.

IVP—Integrity and authenticity verification procedure (computer program).   The purpose of an IVP is to confirm that CDIs in the system have validity and conform to the application's and user's intents at the time that the IVP is executed. In accounting, for example, this corresponds to balancing the accounting records and reconciling them to the external environment. The owner of the application and an auditor can determine the validity of an IVP only by certifying it with respect to a securely held application specification.

The rules of certification, which are performed by the application owner, and the rules of enforcement, which are performed by the computer system, are as follows:

- IVPs ensure that CDIs are valid.
- TPs are certified to perform correctly to preserve the validity of the CDI's.
- Only authorized TPs are allowed to change CDIs to ensure the integrity and authenticity of the CDIs.
- Users must be authorized for execution of specified TPs using specified CDIs to meet segregation of duties.
- The system authenticates each user who is allowed to use each assigned TP and to use no other unassigned program.
- The TPs are certified to write to an append-only secure CDI audit log.
- The TPs are certified to be valid for UDI inputs and to produce only valid CDIs and reject invalid UDIs.
- Authorization lists of users may be changed only by an owner or a security officer.

Figure 10.3 illustrates how a valid user may execute one transaction or one sub-transaction. The user would conduct additional, related transactions by inputting new UDIs to the final state shown, which then becomes the initial state for the next transaction. The final CDIs become the initial CDIs for the next transaction. There may be many more TPs and IVPs than those depicted in the figure. After the initial state of input and verification of constrained data items, the transaction system is unconstrained until all of the CDIs have been verified by the IVPs to reach the final state. Other segregated users may be executing sub-transactions that share some of the CDIs and UDIs to accomplish complete transactions. The model does not account for the possibility of two or more users engaged in the same transaction (dual duties) as an alternative to or enhancement of segregation of duties.

This model needs refinement and extension to be more generally applicable. We would be able to do more detailed security explication if we took into account and applied the differences between integrity and authenticity. But even in its present state, it should be useful to application developers and analysts for helping to assure the security of transaction application systems.

CONCLUSIONS

The current focus on computer systems security is attributable to the understandable tendency of computer technologists to protect what they know best—the computer and network systems, rather than the application of those systems. With a technological hammer in hand, everything looks like a nail. The primary security challenge comes from people misusing or abusing information, and often—but not necessarily—using computers and networks. Yet, the individuals that currently dominate the information security folk art are neither criminologists nor computer application analysts.

The security foundation and the framework models that I've proposed in this chapter represents an attempt to overcome the dominant technologist view of information security by focusing more broadly on all aspects of security, including the information that we're attempting to protect, the potential sources of loss, the types of loss, the controls that we can apply to avoid loss, the methods for selecting those controls, and our overall objectives in protecting information. This broad focus should have two beneficial effects: advancing information security from a narrow folk art to a broad-based discipline and—most important—helping to reduce many of the losses associated with information—wherever it exists.

11

Information Security Assessments

Information security assessment is the technique for determining how much money to spend to protect information resources, and how to spend that money. The most important and significant contribution to making these determinations should be to implement the same types of baseline security controls and practices as other prudent information owners in similar circumstances. There is no need to conduct extensive threat or vulnerability analyses until after you have installed the baseline controls, other than noting any unusual situation that distinguishes your circumstances. There are enough generally accepted baseline controls and practices to keep you busy for the next several years, and enough vendors selling effective security controls to strain your security budget—and possibly your tolerance for security constraints. You should "benchmark" your security status from time to time along the way, and consider whether your state of security is generally prudent and adheres to the current concept of best practice in view of known abuse and misuse.

While you are implementing the baseline security controls, you'll need to consider any threats and vulnerabilities introduced by new technology and/or new applications for which there are no generally accepted baseline controls. You may need to create new controls for these vulnerabilities or use controls that are not yet generally accepted. Such is the life of prudent security innovators.

In my experience, every organization that makes a serious effort to protect its information assets is in a perpetual state of catch-up. It may be well along in some areas of protection, especially those areas in which the staff is proficient or the organization has suffered some type of loss; and still developing, improving, or planning due care safeguards in other areas. For example, an organization may be well advanced in PC computer security, but not yet have started developing security for mobile computers. Or, it may have excellent security policies and standards, but few training materials to guide employees in implementing the policies. I am familiar with many organizations that have not yet made security an explicit requirement in job descriptions and annual performance reviews. Without this basic employee motivational practice and management commitment to make it meaningful, much of their security is likely to be cosmetic. This is because employees do not like the constraints of security that detract from their job performance, for which they do receive rewards. Therefore, for security to work, it must be a part of everybody's job performance.

In this chapter, I explain why (and how) organizations should avoid certain methods of selecting security controls, and how they can implement practical, cost-effective standards of due care to protect valuable information resources. In many respects, using due-care security controls to avoid accusations of negligence is often more important than attempting to directly reduce risk of loss.

RISK ASSESSMENT

The concept of risk of loss should never have been introduced into information security. Many years ago at SRI, we naively attempted to perform a quantified risk assessment for a bank that insisted that we do so. (All too often, clients know what they want, but not necessarily what they need.) Competent, experienced consultants performed the assessment; the costs were enormous and the quantitative results of annual loss expectancy were so ludicrous that we had to reject them. Fortunately, the qualitative findings and recommendations made sense, and the project was a painful success, but we learned an important lesson about the folly of risk assessment. (Although I did write favorably about risk assessments early in my security experience, I have long since rejected those opinions based on further research and experience.)

Most risk assessment (sometimes called risk analysis) methods focus on the operating systems and general applications in computers and networks, rather than on the people who cause information loss. These individuals may misbehave to intentionally inflict loss that they can convert to their own gain, or may simply be careless about protecting information and unintentionally cause loss. In either case, however, people are the underlying cause of the need for security. Assessment methods such as the NIST annual loss expectancy, CRAMM, Riskpack, and BDSS (which I describe later in this chapter) focus on technical controls to protect computers and networks in an organization and, as such, are inherently flawed. In addition, they concentrate on reducing the risks of loss and, except for CRAMM, ignore the objective of meeting standards of due care to avoid negligence. They employ quantitative and qualitative calculations of risk that require the use of loss experience data and loss predictions that cannot be determined, and are not applicable even if they could be determined. Overall, such methods are excessively costly to use, and require expensive experts to interpret risk. Simplified or abbreviated methods are generally inadequate because of the ingenuity of our adversaries and complexity of threats and vulnerabilities.

The highly structured risk reviews largely ignore rapidly changing storage media, systems, and organizations and many of the sources of loss caused by trusted, authorized people, such as embezzlers. They also tend to ignore the manual handling of information, such as interoffice mail, verbal communication, and information input to specific applications of computers and networks such as automated engineering design, payroll, and general ledger. Because most of these reviews rely on the simplicity of CIA and DDUM models of security, they are likely to overlook important control objectives such as avoidance, deterrence, proprietary protection, and transfer of accountability, and thereby fail to recommend specific safeguards such as the removal of unused information, use of double envelopes, segregation of duties, audits, job performance motivation, rewards and penalties, and insurance.

Performing a risk assessment implies that there are known and accepted security controls that can be applied to a risk situation. For example, the risk of a hacker intruding from the Internet into an organization's intranet may be very low because Internet connection and usage is limited to only a few minutes each day. In this case, based strictly on risk assessment, it may be difficult to justify installing a firewall. In a broader view, however, not installing a firewall may be considered negligent since a firewall is a generally accepted standard of due care—independent of the actual risk, as long as there is any connection to the Internet. A firewall is a low-cost control that helps organizations to avoid being accused of negligence and may save many hours of embarrassing confrontations trying to explain why baseline security controls were not implemented. In addition, the presence of a firewall may remind employees of the need for security when using the Internet. Risk assessment does not necessarily consider these factors.

A Study of Risk Analysis Methods

Professor Richard Baskerville at the School of Management, State University of New York at Binghamton, performed the only thorough analysis of formal assessment methods that I know of. Unfortunately, his analysis covers only computer systems security design, and not the holistic scope that I believe is essential. Baskerville's study is theoretical, based on published literature rather than actual experience with the methods that it evaluates. (To my knowledge, there has never been a test using two independent groups of experts doing the same review to see if they would draw the same conclusions.) The study is a valuable description of the history and development of methods, however. It does not attempt to evaluate risk assessment in terms of selecting security controls for information throughout organizations; rather, it assumes that the methods are to be applied only to security in the design of computer systems. In addition, Baskerville accepts, without question, all of the elements that the information security folk art generally accepts in risk assessment methods, namely, the CIA framework; detection, prevention, and recovery; and DDUM. This further limits the scope of his criticisms. But even within the limited scope of computer systems security, his theoretical conclusions question the value, if not validity, of much security risk assessment.*

Baskerville began his academic research into risk analysis methods by identifying three generations of methods. The first consisted of:

> **The checklist and basic risk analysis methods for selecting system security components.** The quantified *SAFE Checklist* by Len Krauss is an example of the checklist method. Krauss, an early EDP auditor, included 844 controls in his version pub-

---

*Baskerville's series of academic research papers started with "Risk Analysis as a Source of Professional Knowledge," which he wrote as a working paper at his university in 1991. He went on to publishing a paper "Risk Analysis: an Interpretive Feasibility Tool in Justifying Information Systems Security," in the *European Journal of Information Systems* (vol. 1, no. 2, 1991). He then published "An Analytical Survey of Information Systems Security Design Methods: Implications for Information Systems Development," in the Association for Computing Machinery *Computing Surveys* (vol. 26, 1994).

lished in 1972 and 1980 (New York: Amacon). In 1979 Peter Browne published another version, *Checklist for Computer Center Self Audits,* with 954 controls (a project sponsored by the American Federation of Information Processing Societies). These checklist methods offered discretionary rather than required controls.

The risk analysis methods that were developed in parallel with checklists, adding cost-effectiveness justification of controls. Examples include the NIST *Annual Loss Expectancy* method developed by Robert Courtney (FIPS PUB 65) in 1977 and *Securate,* developed by Professor Lance Hoffman and his students at George Washington University in 1978 (*AFIPS National Computer Conference Proceedings* 47). The NIST method uses a simple annualized cost and expectancy of loss formula that relies on rough estimates of orders of magnitudes, while Securate uses fuzzy set theory metrics (e.g., low, medium, high) for these calculations.

Baskerville characterizes the second generation of risk assessment methods by four fundamental assumptions common to all.

First, the requirements and impacts of the security system elements will be complex and interconnected. There is a web of assets, threats, and safeguards that must be partitioned for comprehension. Second, the exact controls could be unique and ideal for the system requirements. . . . This leads to a third assumption that the solution set is unlimited and impossible to capture in a single database or checklist. . . . Fourth, second-generation security methods inherit from the more general systems methods the assumption that a well-understood and well-documented security design will lead inevitably to more efficient security maintenance and modification. . . .

Analysts concentrate on detailed inventories of system assets and potential threats. This activity uses various analytical techniques to reduce the complexity implied by the assumption that security elements will be complex and interconnected. Second, analysts must enumerate possible controls. . . . Third, analysts conduct risk analysis. Fourth, they prioritize controls. . . . (There are no boundaries on the set of possible controls).

Finally, Baskerville adds a maintenance review step.

Second-generation methods include Will Ozier's Bayesian Decision Support System (BDSS), RISKPAC From Peter Browne, the British government's CRAMM, and Parker's Computer Security Program. Baskerville described the method that I developed in 1981, indicating that it consisted of five phases to be carried out by a task group. The first phase consisted of the identification and valuation of assets and identification of threats. This phase was followed by risk assessment using either the Courtney risk assessment method or a less costly alternative of exposure analysis based on the numbers of persons who could cause losses according to their occupations. After monetary values are assigned to each vulnerable asset, the task group can compute the risk exposure of assets. Management then applies the criterion of a "prudent person" in deciding the degree of implementation for the exposure list. Finally, the safeguard identification, selection, and implementation phase uses safeguard selection principles. At the end, the task group implements and advances the program through an ongoing update of the process and system adaptation.

Baskerville claimed that my method made important contributions by using a bottom-up life cycle and recognizing the importance of social aspects of security balanced against the technical problems. He also noted that my exposure analysis method of risk calculation fundamentally conflicts with other research that found no significant relationship between user privilege and system abuse. This may mean, he felt, that analysts would be distracted from controls that protect against outsiders and natural threats. He concluded, "Parker's program is among the first to incorporate a qualitative alternative to risk analysis (the prudent-person criterion)." In those early days of security assessment, I developed some ideas that did not work in practice, and my methods have evolved significantly based on experience which has caused me to reject the concepts of risk assessment and general exposure analysis.

Baskerville characterizes the third and present generation of risk assessment in two broad categories. He states:

> Logical models tend to express system needs and behavior in a functional or data-oriented sense. They sometimes begin with a physical model of existing systems. References to physical processing technologies or data storage media are then removed to create the logical model. New system design transformations are merged into this logical model. The logical model is translated back into a physical model by establishing technological boundaries around the processing and data elements. Transformational

models are a highly distinctive second class of system models. These models express organizational (not system) needs and behavior in a social or theoretical sense and are characteristic of methods that look beyond the functional information require- ments to focus on problem formulation, job satisfaction, and worker autonomy or emancipation. The term 'transformational' denotes an emphasis on work-force management, organizational theory, and social philosophy as a whole. . . . This generation of methods de-emphasizes cost-benefit analysis because the abstract modeling phase more closely links the system solution to the organizational problems. . . . Cost-benefit analysis is less important in determining the final selection of system elements.

Two methods have been published that approach Baskerville's third- generation criteria: the U.K. government (CCTA) Structured Systems Analysis and Design and CRAMM Method (SSADM-CRAMM) interface and the Logical Controls Design method. According to Baskerville, "CRAMM is the only second-generation method that has been rational- ized onto an overall information system development method." These methods go beyond the scope of this book and security itself, because they refer to general system design methods. However, they imply that security may finally be considered as an integral part of information sys- tems design.

CRAMM, the U.K. Government Risk Analysis and Management Method

I base my discussion of the Comprehensive Risk Analysis and Management Method (CRAMM) on an article in the August 1996 *DataPro Information Security Service* (Item 3215), "Risk Management" by Robin Moses. CRAMM is currently implemented by Version 3.0 of a software tool from the CRAMM Consortium—a group of companies that jointly provide support for CRAMM—and the CRAMM Users Group, which meets twice each year.

CRAMM incorporates three stages. Stage 1 scopes the organization to be analyzed and identifies and assigns values to assets based on their importance to the organization; stage 2 assesses the threats, vulnerabili- ties, and risks; and stage 3 defines security countermeasures or controls to manage the identified risks at an acceptable level. Assets may consist of current or developing information technology (IT) systems, software, and/or information. *Value of assets* is defined in terms of assessed levels of seriousness from loss of confidentiality, integrity, and availability from likely threats and vulnerabilities. *Risks* are broad types of adverse business impacts of disclosure and modification, unavailability and destruction. Levels of risk are assessed from a combination of asset values and levels of threats and vulnerabilities.

I believe that CRAMM has some inherent flaws that cause problems from the outset. Even with a broad interpretation of the CIA and DDUM models, it would not cover such common abuses as observation of information, stealing copies of information, misrepresenting information, or replacing information or hardware. It considers only likely threats and vulnerabilities, although the unlikely threats are the ones most likely to cause huge losses in practice. For example, no one would be likely to include in CRAMM the potential threat of an information security consultant using social engineering to steal $10 million, or anticipate an out-of-control trader in Singapore betting on the Tokyo stock exchange to a degree that his actions destroyed Barings Bank.

As far as I can tell, CRAMM does not accommodate different asset values for different types of threats. Modifying a data file, for example, may change its value quite differently than merely observing it. The CRAMM documentation instructs users to aggregate assets, threats, and vulnerabilities wherever possible to simplify the information gathering process. There is certainly good reason for doing this; a CRAMM assessment project would be very expensive otherwise. But aggregating assets and threats can make it difficult to distinguish differences in value, the likelihood of loss or partial loss, and the scope of appropriate countermeasures. A CRAMM assessment requires considerable skill and knowledge on the part of the users to avoid missing important details that may spell the difference between effective and ineffective solutions.

A close look at one aspect of CRAMM indicates other problems. CRAMM classifies the impact of the threat of modification into only three categories: small-scale errors such as erroneous keying; widespread errors such as programming logic errors; and deliberate modification. The coarseness of the granularity and inconsistent depth of these three categories boggles the mind. What about small-scale and widespread deliberate modification? The designers may not understand that the differences between errors and deliberate actions are unrecognizable in many cases, making it difficult to differentiate the countermeasures. Many keying errors are wide-scale in their impact, and many programming errors are extremely small-scale in their effect. Where do these examples fit into the CRAMM classifications? It is impossible to apply comprehensive lists or categories to peoples' irrational acts or to the highly variable consequences of their acts.

CRAMM does have some strengths. It offers more flexibility and features than other automated assessment methods, and provides for both subjective values of assets on a relative scale and the use of specific quantitative values. It also provides a baseline set of generally accepted controls that can be applied before the risk assessment is complete and situation-specific controls determined. In addition, it offers a complete solution, including recommended controls, if you are willing to accept the latest list of controls. Thus, there is no need to select controls and then repeat the analysis to show that you have selected the right ones to reduce the risk to an acceptable level.

CRAMM is unsuitable for many situations, however, because most organizations already have extensive controls in place and need to determine if those controls are adequate, and what additional controls or changes are required. This type of assessment is typically triggered by the introduction of new technology or by updating applications in the realm of security that has not yet been addressed. And many information systems vendors embed many of the generally accepted due-care controls into their products, often offering little choice of options, regardless of the situation-specific requirements.

PROBLEMS WITH QUANTITATIVE RISK ASSESSMENT METHODOLOGIES

In its simplest form, risk is the probability of an exposure of information to a loss occurring in a given time period (or at a rate of occurrence) multiplied by the cost of the loss from the exposure. For example, the risk of the modification of a document starts with calculating the probability that it may be modified and the loss from a single event. This is expressed in the number of times in a year that it might happen, for example, one-half (once in two years), times $2,000 (money that would be lost in one event), or $1,000 ($0.5 \times \$2,000$) per year. Of course, the same risk would result if the expected event occurred twice as often at one half of the loss. Practitioners must sort out the possibilities of many values of the two numbers that give the same product in reporting the results. They must determine expected frequency of loss by considering the ways it may occur, evaluating how many times it has occurred already, and identifying the circumstances and conditions under which it could occur in the future. If that sounds difficult, consider determining the value of the loss for each way in which the loss could occur. Some assessment methods use an even more complex risk formula that applies weighting factors and vulnerability variables. If these methods expanded the ranges of threats from the simplistic CIA and DDUM models to the expanded, realistic loss model that I proposed in Chapter 9, the users would soon be over-whelmed by the complexity of data gathering—even if they use computers for the calculations.

The units of measure are critical to understanding the risk. Because some threats result in a loss over time, risk is usually stated within a given time of loss occurrence, such as a year, a week, or a month. Therefore, risk is expressed as a rate of probable occurrence, such as the NIST unit of *annual loss expectancy* (ALE). Some high frequency rates and fluctuations (e.g., credit card fraud) are best expressed on a weekly basis, while others, such as less frequent funds transfer fraud in banking, are best quantified on a ten-year basis.

Risk assessment is based on probability theory, which is probably the least generally understood subject in mathematics since Pierre de Fermat created it in the early 1600s to help his friend Blaise Pascal solve a gam-bling game problem. Information security artisans should know by now that it is impossible to obtain adequate data on loss expectancy to estimate risk to any useful degree. It involves trying to estimate the future misbe-havior of unknown people, using unknown methods with unpredictable motives, against unknown targets that may cause unknown losses. There are no statistically valid samples applicable to specific vulnerabilities for use in information security risk assessment. Amateurs obfuscate the mean-ing of risk probability, and incorrectly assume that an event with low prob-ability is not imminent. In one case, a manager decided not to follow his security expert's advice because a risk assessment indicated the expected frequency of loss of the entire business was once in 20 years, and he was going to retire in ten. Because future event frequency is unknown and cannot be adequately estimated, we attempt to use data on past loss expe-riences. But past data consists of a series of known events; it is not a com-plete or valid sampling set of independent observations—as demanded by the laws of probability.

After Bob Courtney convinced the NIST that this risk assessment cal-culation was viable, I asked him how he actually applied risk assessment for his clients. He said that when the client identified information to be protected, he would observe and identify the threats and vulnerabilities based on his extensive experience. He would then calculate "on the back of an envelope" the likelihood of loss in terms of his estimate of frequency of occurrence and the possible monetary loss to the nearest $100,000 or $1,000,000, and multiply as I described earlier. That was the extent of his risk assessment. He thought the NIST had gone too far with the elaborate methodology published in their FIPS PUB 65 Manual.

Over the years, the U.S. government has wasted millions of dollars creating thousands of numbers in hundreds of pages of many reports. The U.S. Office of Management and Budget (OMB), which required risk assessments from every department during the 1980s, actually bragged (at a Civil Service Security Conference) about the flow of huge reports that they were receiving as the result of their edict. At the time, I commented that the OMB had produced a modern version of "The Emperor's New Clothes" and repeated my assertion that risk assessment is not a valid method. Some time later, the OMB changed its edict and allowed government departments to use whatever method they chose. In its statement, the OMB admitted, "Rather than continue to try to precisely measure risk, security efforts are better served by generally assessing risks and taking actions to manage them" (Revised OMB Circular No. A-130, Appendix III).

The information security literature continues to assault us with attempts to make us believe that comprehensive quantitative risk assessment is an accepted and successful methodology in information security. Risk assessment has popped up in NIST publications ever since Bob Courtney and Bob Jacobson convinced the NBS (as NIST was known then) and the OMB that risk assessment was a practical and viable method. Today, NIST publications, including its latest version of the *Computer Security Handbook,* continue to promote and describe risk assessment in the U.S. government. However, the organization, along with the NSA, has quietly halted efforts to further develop risk assessment.

New security technologists who are pressured by business management for quantification of the security needs of the organization seem to repeatedly reinvent this faulty method. Once they have tried to apply it, they discover how impractical and unnecessary it is and revert to the default process of baseline due care decisions for selecting new controls. But this admits to their failure, because management has come to expect those magic numbers once they have been promised.

Various efforts to slay the risk monster have signaled the hoped for final demise of the methodology. However, like the many headed serpent, the more heads we remove, more are there to replace them. Information security risk assessment is a fruitless and expensive attempt to quantify the unquantifiable.

The Work of the Information Valuation Committee

In my view, quantitative monetary valuation of information, at least for security risk calculation purposes, is impractical at best and probably impossible. From 1990 to 1992, I participated as the only dissenting member of the Information Systems Security Association (ISSA) Information Valuation Committee led by Will Ozier, which developed a *Guideline for Information Valuation.* I had two very important reasons for being on this committee. Firstly, I believed the committee was providing some extremely important insights about the essence of the information security field having to do with information assets that we are commissioned to help protect. Secondly, I believed that the results of the work of this committee would support my conjecture that it is not possible, or at least not feasible, to generally apply monetary value to information for security purposes. We can sometimes perform useful qualitative, relative ranking of the sensitivity of information for security and other purposes. We would presumably only need to assign a value to information when there is a lack of consensus about security, or when costly controls require that we try to get more explicit information. In other words, if the stakeholders agree on the best practice to protect information, then we have implicitly and sufficiently valued it for security purposes.

As I discussed in Chapter 2, information is, by nature, complex. So it follows that determining the market value of information during specific time periods is even more complex, and determining the value of information in terms of loss for security purposes is exceedingly complex. Buyers and sellers determine market value of any commodity by the decisions they make in a dynamic market where buying and selling occur frequently and are recorded, broadcast, and analyzed. We would have to determine the security value of information similarly in a dynamic market of criminals with shifting levels of security at times of interest, and consider related attacks by perpetrators in ways that can also be recorded and analyzed. The problems in attempting to do this are immediately obvious. We would need all of the various costs of all combinations of all types of applicable security controls, along with their effectiveness—measured in monetary terms of the losses prevented or mitigated in each case. We would also need to know costs of possible civil and criminal litigation, embarrassment, and increased insurance premiums that might arise from the loss. (How much are negligence and the loss of employee perpetrators worth?) This valuation is clearly not possible for security purposes.

Security has a weak-link dependency; theoretically, it is no stronger than its greatest vulnerability—assuming that adversaries have broad capabilities and intent. We are at the mercy of what we do not know about our vulnerabilities. Part of our job as security practitioners is to try to deduce what the weakest link is before our adversaries do and fix it, thus creating a new weakest link. A similar concept applies to security valuation of information. We can not know what value an adversary places on information, and the adversary's valuation may be quite different than our own. If the adversary places a higher value on the information than we anticipate, he may be willing to go to great lengths to attack it and thereby increase our vulnerability. I was hoping the Information Valuation Committee, which was composed of a group of very competent people, would provide some significant insight into this essence of our field. Although the committee produced some very impressive insights on the challenge of information security, it concluded (incorrectly, I believe) that it is possible to value information for security purposes.

The committee identified six value factors in its theory of information valuation: possession, utility, cost of creation and re-creation, liability, monetary convertibility and negotiability, and operational impact. It further defined three purposes of security for each of these six factors: confidentiality, integrity, and availability. (In my view, three more were required, but ignored: utility, authenticity, and possession.) For each of the elements in the resulting matrix, there are at least five different stakeholders, each of whom would have a different value of information for security purposes. And the stakeholders include our adversaries, whom we do not necessarily know. If we multiply these three numbers together, we get a three-dimensional matrix with 90 matrix entries. In addition, the committee identified 107 types of values or costs. If we multiply those figures (since there are 107 possible items for each of the 90 items in the three-dimensional matrix), we end up with 9,630 possible values and costs associated with the security value of information.

The committee concluded that these values could not be combined in any way. Their extremely complex relationship was already grossly simplified by the dimensions that I just described. The factors are probably incomplete, and the security purposes are undefined. (We blithely defined them in the committee. Despite the fact that the best minds in the security field have met at least twice to define the purposes, but have failed to agree on a definition of integrity alone, not even considering the other two purposes of CIA security.) The greatest concern is that there is no proof that there is not a 9,631st value that exceeds the other 9,630. We do not know what we do not know.

The Heisenberg uncertainty principle, very loosely applied here from physics, indicates that the valuation process alone can change the value of information by giving it so much attention. Applying or removing controls to information can also change the security value of information. If we increase the protection of information by applying controls to it, then it becomes more valuable—but possibly better protected. As a result, we may have to apply more or fewer controls. I conclude that the relationship of security values to information values is recursive. The committee never considered this.

The results of information valuation, and quantified risk assessment as well, are expressed in monetary amounts. Unfortunately, management people who make decisions based on the results may assume that the monetary units are the same as used for the value of goods and services, budgets, and profits and loss. Instead, risk assessment monetary units actually constitute a language in which the information security specialist is conveying his opinions, justifications, and recommendations about security. Unfortunately, many managers do not recognize or are not told the difference between this funny money and real money. (This problem applies to risk assessment as well.)

I should mention that the committee's conclusions have never been tested, nor has the work been reviewed by experts from other fields, such as law, accounting, economics, or statistics. Since there is no reported experience of anyone actually applying valuation in the real world, the committee's theory is untested and still incomplete. Although the *Guideline* contributes to the folk art, its theories and methodologies are unproven. To validate them, we would need actual cases with which to test the valuation methodologies or, failing that, we would need to develop fictitious cases. My own conclusion is that monetary valuation of information for security purposes, like that of risk assessment, requires considerably more study and validation. The committee's work, though important and interesting, is of little practical value so far.

Another View of Risk Assessment

Dr. Eugene Schultz takes a cautious approach to the issue of risk assessment in his recent collaborative book, *Internet Security for Business* (Wiley, 1996), applying significant caveats to the entire subject. For example, although risk assessment is "stylish" in business, Schultz warns that the process can be difficult, if not impossible. Further, Schultz questions the underlying motivation for risk assessment, stating (on page 59), "Although critics question the meaning and validity of any such [risk] numbers, they often have more impact and credibility in making the case to management to install security controls than do purely verbal descriptions." This statement provides insight into what is to come further in the book.

The book offers some good advice (on page 67):

> Actual methods of risk determination vary considerably. Many businesses that I work with do not invest a huge amount of effort in determining risk, in part because they typically do not have sufficient time and resources to do justice to this activity, and in part because risk is somewhat nebulous (especially with respect to estimating its likelihood). These reasons are especially valid in the complex world of the Internet, where services are constantly being modified, and new services and entry methods are routinely introduced.

Schultz presents calculation of annual loss expectancy as one viable method (described in the NIST FIPS PUB 65) but goes on to say:

> Although not frequently used within industry anymore, [it] nicely illustrates the complexities of several quantitative risk assessment methods. . . . Although assessing security risk can be useful, a growing number of information security professionals (SIC) have become increasingly skeptical about the utility of attempting to rigorously measure risk . . . [They conclude that] "risk" is too nebulous and that determining risk is at best an exercise of guesswork that consumes too many resources for the few benefits it produces.

How true.

Schultz then presents the baseline due care method, but concludes the description by advising that a risk assessment be done afterwards to: ". . . identify areas of particularly elevated risk, address security risk not covered in the baseline controls, obtain consensus when different sets of baseline controls are contradictory, and provide business justification . . . when justification is less than compelling."

The implied deficiencies of the baseline method may be justifiable if the baseline method is not expertly conducted or if quality benchmark input cannot be obtained from appropriate sources. After a baseline of generally accepted controls is chosen, however, we can—and should—do further research to advance security beyond this level. Or we can settle disagreements over the best choice of controls by considering special or newly derived controls for the few intractable vulnerabilities that are left.

Reducing risk is only a small part of the motivation in the due care process, except implicitly; loss has probably been reduced in the 25-year history of applying recorded knowledge of loss experience, identifying vulnerabilities, and devising controls. More importantly, the possibility of negligence for failure to choose due care controls has almost certainly been reduced. Reducing loss may be an explicit objective in the baseline method that I advocate but only after achieving due diligence. For example, in extreme cases of lack of management consensus or when a costly control with potentially marginally value is proposed, more analysis is necessary. Such analysis may be based on additional samples of loss experience, or on loss scenarios created to aid in sound management decisions.

Schultz ends his discussion of the baseline method by remarking on some experts' criticisms of the technique, "Critics [of baseline] claim that this approach is too blind—that understanding the real risks that are present is essential to controlling risk." The critics that Schultz quotes are wrong. They do not understand that avoiding negligence is more important than reducing risk. For example, you are more likely to be fired for negligence, but receive sympathy for a loss (at least the first time it happens). In addition, the critics fail to acknowledge that we already know many of the potential threats and vulnerabilities, and reducing them with known controls can keep a large staff busy for years. The baseline method relies on comparison with others' efforts under similar conditions, taking advantage of the fact that other organizations have already implicitly performed the risk assessment many times over attempting to meet due care standards and achieve best practices by their cumulative actions for all but the very latest technologies and newest threats. Nearly every information-intensive organization needs computer and physical entry controls, authentication of users, classification of information, audit logs, segregation of duties, warning banners on screens, filters and firewalls, and well-formed transaction controls. There will always be tough decisions to make based on when due care applies, such as when to switch from reusable passwords to one-time passwords and tokens. And, the security aspects of new technology will always be problematic and subject to a trial-and-error process.

According to Schultz, "Critics also argue that this approach produces a set of baseline controls that are quickly outdated; new security threats emerge constantly, but corporate information security controls evolve more slowly." Again, the critics are wrong because risk assessment takes far more effort and time than the baseline method, which produces direct and immediate conclusions about many known and lasting controls that can be implemented. None of the critics (or anyone else that I know of) explains how to directly proceed from a calculated risk to selecting appropriate controls to reduce that risk to an acceptable level. Once the control is installed, the risk assessment must be incrementally repeated to determine if the risk has sufficiently diminished. The baseline method is an ongoing process that updates control recommendations based on loss experiences, vendors' new security products, and others' control choices.

Schultz continues,

> Although the jury is still out concerning the baseline controls approach, substantial limitations inherent in risk assessment itself may convince you to try it. These limitations are sufficiently serious that many businesses in reality 'skim over' or bypass altogether the risk analysis process, especially with respect to assessing Internet security risk. The baseline controls approach provides an attractive alternative.

In my view, the jury is not "still out." Its decision is clearly in support of the baseline method; it is the default method that has been used all along and after failures of risk assessments have occurred. SRI has successfully conducted more than 250 baseline reviews for clients during the past 25 years.

A Summary of Risk Assessment Failure

Risk assessment methods fail because of the failure of each of the basic steps:

Step 1. Risk assessment requires determining the likelihood of future harm from people and/or natural forces involving the specific information to be protected, in its form and media; the type, time, and location of damaging activity; and particularly the environment and current controls that have been applied. We can not make this determination because we have insufficient (or no) loss experience in the specific circumstances we are assessing and on which to base valid statistical conclusions. Even worse, we would be trying to estimate frequency when only one or two incidents have occurred. One possible exception is credit card fraud, which often involves high frequency, consistent circumstances, and accurate and complete tabulation of losses. Alternatively, we may use actuarial data of many others' experience to determine risk. While this is applicable for setting insurance rates for fire, water, or earthquake damage for a large number of environments where the risk is spread, it is not applicable to any one environment. The one environment will not be sufficiently average, and the data can not be sufficiently timely in rapidly changing environments such as computer and communications systems. For example, if the likelihood of a payroll fraud were once in 20 years nationwide, that would have little bearing on a company that undergoes great fluctuation of staff size and turnover. Although to some extent this is also true in choosing due care controls, the choices are based on avoidance of negligence rather than the elusive likelihood of loss.

Step 2.   Risk assessment next requires that we make estimations of future loss from each type of incident involving information, even where we do not know that an incident with the specific circumstances has ever happened. The value of the information involved in the incident is often not material, since it is the unknowable consequences of the incident that determine the loss. For example, in a trade secret espionage case, it is what the recipient does with the trade secret information and when, such as quickly using information about the success of creating and selling a new product, that determines the size of the loss. The ISSA valuation study provided insights indicating a complexity far beyond practical limits to put a security value on specific information, and the proposed method for doing so remains untested, with no practical means of testing its success.

Step 3.   We must combine frequency and size of loss data collected from steps 1 and 2 in some mathematical or logical way to produce meaningful results. We can do this quite successfully by using simple multiplication to produce a timed expected rate of loss, Baysian statistical calculations to produce a range of loss, fuzzy logic, or relative loss estimates among events using abstract scales. This is the easiest, most appealing step for technologists not concerned with the validity of the data used. The value of results is limited by the quality of the inputs, no matter how elaborate the mathematics. Calculating the best possible results from limited data is commendable, but not necessarily valid. The successful prediction of future human malicious behavior based on limited (or no) experiences, each with different and unique circumstances, is not possible. Game theory might be a more successful tool here, but only when dealing with an intelligent adversary who plays by known rules. Unfortunately, we do not know the rules used by an irrational adversary.

Step 4.   Next, risk assessment requires that we select controls and effectively implement them. However, the risk assessment results presumably reveal only how much could be lost, and how frequently it would happen in the specific circumstances with a specific set of security controls in place and others missing. This guidance, however poor, identifies where to put controls, and the upper limit of how much to spend for them (not to exceed the value of the expected losses). But there is no guidance on what controls to use. We must still select candidate controls experientially or by use of some other method (such as applying the standard of due care). Then we must repeat the risk assessment with the new controls in place to conclude if the risk was reduced to an acceptable level. Finally, we have no guidance on what is an acceptable level of risk. That would change dramatically in today's fast-paced business and depend on many factors including what might be done with funds if not spent on the controls.

ALTERNATIVE TECHNIQUES

Qualitative risk assessment is one alternative to quantitative risk assessment. You can estimate and express the probabilities and asset values in more subjective ways than monetary loss per time period, as in using the NIST ALE approach. You can use the mathematical methods of fuzzy logic by measuring with the terms of *many, some, much, little, few, large,* and *small.* Use of numeric scales of abstract amounts such as from 1 to 10 is another method.

A number of other methods, such as focus groups, brainstorming, and polling information owners and experts, are sometimes useful for identifying threats, vulnerabilities, and information loss values. Will Ozier and others have suggested using the Delphi technique, which involves repeatedly polling experts who are given the results of previous polls before each input. Although the Delphi technique was never more than experimental and remains controversial since the Rand Corporation developed it in 1967, there is some indication that in long-range forecasting, opinions do converge. According to N. C. Dalkey, one of the original developers of the technique, "where answers can be checked against reality, it is found that the median response tends to move in the direction of the true answer." B. Brown, another one of the original developers, reported, "Choosing the panel of experts, whose expertise could be decided on various grounds, is one problem with the method; another is the questioning technique itself."

In 1974, Dr. Harold Sackman of the Rand Corporation, evaluated the Delphi technique in the light of contemporary standards for social experimentation, test design, sampling, use of experts, and interpretation of findings. He concluded that conventional Delphi is an unreliable and scientifically unvalidated technique in principle, and probably in practice.

> Except for its possible value as an informal exercise for heuristic purposes, Delphi should be replaced by demonstrably superior, scientifically rigorous questionnaire techniques and associated experimental procedures using human subjects. . . . Delphi should not be used until its principles, methods, and fundamental applications can be established experimentally as scientifically tenable.

To date, nobody has accomplished this, particularly for security risk assessment. We are warned to limit use of Delphi to informal inquiries, and to always rely on other means as either primary or corroborative methods of reaching consensus on security. The selection of experts is crucial here, because security loss involves so many unknown or obscure factors that may not be subject to controls. However, the very people who created the technique at the Rand Corporation have discredited this forecasting method for many applications, including the application to security. (See the Rand Report R-1283-PR, *Delphi Assessment: Expert Opinion, Forecasting, and Group Process* by Harold Sackman, April 1974.)

Exposure analysis, which I recommended at one time, is another possible alternative. This technique assumes that the relative measure of threats that harm information is proportional to the total number of people who use, or could normally obtain, the information within their authority. For example, software piracy would be twice as likely among 20 users than among ten users, other factors being equal. This is based on the idea that since we can not possibly determine probabilities of people misbehaving in specified ways, an asset has more or less exposure to loss depending on the total number of people having direct ability to cause loss, independent of motivation and reason. This is probably the best that we can accomplish in quantitative analysis of threats, but it is far from adequate in practice, since other factors will hardly ever be equal.

Scenario techniques are useful for obtaining stakeholders' observations of likely ways in which losses may occur, and to identify existing vulnerabilities. These involve creating scenarios in the form of one-paragraph, neutral, unemotional stories ending in losses that are fictitious or, ideally, based on real past loss experience. (The Threats-Assets-Vulnerabilities Model that I introduced in Chapter 10 can serve as a useful outline for creating scenarios.) We can play these scenarios theoretically against the assets, against the people who would be affected by the loss (with their consent and cooperation), and in the loss environments, to determine credibility of threats, identify vulnerabilities, and validate controls. With each playback, we can suggest various controls that might reduce the vulnerabilities, then repeat the scenario to determine possible improvements in security. I have used this technique quite successfully for a number of clients. In one case, I used about 30 scenarios based on my collection of computer crime cases, covering the range of possible losses determined from interviews and observations of the client's organization. Each scenario represented several different variations of the same general attack.

The scenario technique tends to draw ideas from the potential victims about vulnerabilities and threats that they might not otherwise perceive. It also tests the proposed solutions closest to real circumstances (except for anticipating the irrationality of real people misbehaving under stress). Finally, it is also an effective way to obtain management's buy-in to the solutions, because non-experts can so easily perceive some of the potential kinds of loss in this dramatic way. Denying the solutions becomes more difficult, because it requires denying the already accepted viable scenarios.

All of these methods are feasible alternatives to the NIST and CRAMM risk assessment methods, which I believe are far too elaborate, problematical, and costly. A fundamental problem with these so-called "quick" methods, however—in addition to a lack of valid data—is that they are often limited to using CIA, DDUM, and gross generalities and may miss many of the more important threats, losses, and vulnerabilities. Doing a valid risk assessment would require significant attention to *all* loss events and require the expertise and experience of qualified information security specialists and people who work in the target environment, since a missed event may represent the largest loss. After all, we are battling against an adversary who likely knows the environment and circumstances of his intended target better than anybody in the world. And, he is far more motivated to succeed than the defenders; if he fails, he is likely to go to jail, but if the defenders fail, they will simply try to do better next time.

THE BASELINE APPROACH

Information security has had more than 30 years to mature and gain experience, and information security specialists are aware of the generally accepted controls for protecting information from well-known threats. It is more important now than ever before to document the best-practice controls that contribute to meeting standards of due care. We can then turn our attention to dealing with new vulnerabilities. The baseline controls that we should use to measure our conformance are the ones that any well-managed, information-intensive organization under similar conditions of vulnerability should be using, or should have good business reasons for not using. This is the definition of baseline due care security.

Businesses are not interested in meeting only an average, baseline level of performance in their competitive pursuits. Rather than doing what everyone else is doing, they strive to achieve "best of class." Security, however, is a different arena. Unlike the competitive business or service mission of an organization, security is difficult to justify as a bottom-line expense. While there is no doubt that it contributes to the success—or very survival—of an organization, it rarely contributes directly to produce a profit or improve service (although we are searching for more ways to achieve this). And in some ways, security detracts from productivity and profitability—at least in the short run. A business goal is to have a prudent level of security that provides protection that is not too expensive, yet not too cheap compared to levels in other businesses, especially those of competitors. Baseline security is not a minimum level; it is the middle ground. It is a crucial position to achieve to avoid negligence, harmful litigation, and high insurance costs. As far as I know, however, no business or service organization has ever reached this ideal goal. This is because most organizations that are committed to using the baseline controls are also aware of the need for more advanced security controls. They may seek additional safeguards for peace of mind or because they recognize the strategic values of security for advancing their competitive position or for enhancing market share. For example, taking extraordinary measures to protect customers' private information may be good advertising, especially for commercial Internet transaction communications, where privacy is of particular concern to customers.

In a series of projects starting in 1980, SRI identified and documented many of the baseline controls and practices that aid in approaching standards of due care status. The selection of due care controls is based on the common usage of numerous organizations that are advanced in their protection of information. One such group includes more than 75 large corporate and government members served by the SRI Consulting International Information Integrity Institute (I-4). The less exclusive European Security Forum (ESF), modeled on I-4 by Coopers and Lybrand, and now owned by its members, also provides due care advice based on surveys from their 100-plus member organizations. The information security managers of member organizations can compare their organization's selection of controls and practices with other members' safeguards. They do this within specific topics, and anonymously through the service to preserve the confidentiality of their security status and choices. Confidentiality is important because revealing too many details of your security controls to outsiders, and especially to competitors, is in itself a gross violation of security.

The Standards of Due Care

Standards of due care (or *due diligence*) is a legal term that arises in liability and negligence civil and criminal litigation. The T. J. Hooper case (District Court S. D. New York, October 15, 1931, 53 f(2d) 107) was the first precedent-setting case in the United States to define due care. The T. J. Hooper tugboat company lost a libel action for failure to have radio receivers aboard to receive weather reports, a failure that resulted in the foundering of two coal barges off the New Jersey coast in March 1928. Two tugs were considered negligent in not anticipating the storm, which was reported by radio. While it was not the duty, statutory or otherwise, to carry radios, the court found that it was common practice for tugboats and barges to do so. Several other tugboat owners testified that they had radio receivers to obtain weather reports, and they did not venture out into the storm as a result of the information they received.

This court cited a statute that required steamers licensed to carry 50 or more persons to carry a radio receiver. In the tugboat case, the judge stated, "The standard of seaworthiness is not, however, dependent on statutory enactment, or condemned to inertia or rigidity, but changes with advancing knowledge, experience, and the changed appliances of navigation. It is particularly affected by new devices of demonstrated worth, which have become recognized as regular equipment by common usage. . . . The use of the radio was shown to be so extensive as to amount almost to a universal practice in the navigation of coastwise tugs." Clearly, each case of alleged negligence in meeting a standard of due care must be decided on its own merits. However, the general principle is well established that the standard of due care is predicated on two factors: that a practice has become common among prudent persons, and that the practice is particularly affected by new devices of demonstrable cost effectiveness, which have become recognized as regular equipment by common usage.

My definition of the standard of due care principle in information security (although not necessarily on legal grounds) is as follows: Due care is achieved when a security control or practice is used, or acknowledged as preferred for use, when it is readily available at reasonable cost or is in regular use by many organizations that take prudent care to protect their information under similar circumstances. In addition, the organization adopting a security control or practice should seek to verify that it meets these criteria. The justification for having such due care controls and practices should stem from common use and availability and prudent management rather than from the desire for explicit reduction of risk.

Examples of standards of due care provide more insight. The existence of a security policy and mandatory standards in an organization is a due care practice. If your organization has not adopted a policy and standards and does not have a good reason for not doing so, then you are not meeting a standard of due care. I conclude this, because other well-run organizations, including the 75 I-4 member companies, have a policy and standards and the information security management books and manuals recommend it.

Due care controls are different from candidate due care controls. For example, the use of secret passwords that are difficult to guess is a due care control for authorized logon to computers. The use of token devices and one-time passwords that work in conjunction with biometric devices such as fingerprint readers are, however, still candidate due care logon controls. They may become accepted as baseline controls as their use increases and costs diminish. Cryptographic protection of communicated confidential information is emerging as a baseline due care control, since it is readily available at reasonable cost and is coming into common use. It is becoming the equivalent of the use of radio receiver in the days of the T. J. Hooper. If you are not already using it, you should begin to—at least in pilot tests—or have a good, documented reason for not doing so.

A security control is the policy, practice, device, or programmed mechanism to avoid or deter, prevent or detect, mitigate, investigate and sanction, transfer, recover, or correct information losses. Controls have the objectives of preserving the availability and utility, integrity and authenticity, and confidentiality and possession of information. Implementation variants for a particular use are established in the detailed descriptions of the controls, given in the remaining chapters of this book. Best practice controls are the well-implemented baseline safeguards that meet the due care requirement among representative organizations (such as the I-4 members) that are advanced in the protection of their information. The goals of baseline due care controls are to reduce vulnerabilities and loss to avoid negligence, achieve an orderly and protected society with successful commerce, adhere to laws and regulations, and protect privacy and other rights.

A baseline control has generally had one primary set of objectives and several ancillary ones, but the way in which it accomplishes these objectives may differ depending on its specific implementation. For example, insurance companies, banks, and manufacturers have many of the same information and protection objectives, but they also have some that differ. They use some of the same baseline controls in different ways, as well as some different controls, for both like and unlike purposes. These businesses have similar accounting, shareholder service, payroll, human resources, operating system, database, and spreadsheet applications that require essentially the same security controls. Although security experts, auditors, and consultants may have differences of opinion over which controls to use in a specific case of a widespread vulnerability, they seldom disagree about the control objectives. This agreement on objectives is indicative of a well-formed art.

A baseline is a collection of control objectives selected by experts' opinions about common use. Organizations use a baseline to measure security status in meeting a standard of due care. There is no official or generally approved set of baseline control objectives; baseline control objectives may be official standards, or we may accept them only because they are readily available and in general use. And, we must continually upgrade baseline controls or control features and implementations to prevent them from becoming obsolete as technology and organizations change. Thus, we informally agree upon rapidly shifting concepts that would suffer from any attempt to wait until they are formalized as standards before use, since standard-setting, as practiced by professional societies and national and international standards bodies, is a long and ponderous process.

The success of the baseline concept lies in having sufficient numbers of information security specialists identifying, accepting, and reporting the best array of generally used controls and practices. Specialists use baselines to advise responsible business managers and owners of the need to adopt the best controls for protecting their information. Certainly, security experts have sufficient experience with the baseline controls that have been identified in security literature and used in commercial products in the past 25 years to agree on their due care value. Management should be willing to accept a recommended control if the security specialist can show that it is a prudent, generally accepted choice for the application at hand. Organizations that do accept due care controls benefit from the experience of other, similar organizations, and managers should achieve some measure of peace of mind from the knowledge that their organization is protected by the same controls that are generally used by other similar organizations—thus likely meeting a standard of due care. (There is no assurance of meeting a legal standard of due care except in a court of law based on the merits in the specific case.)

Opponents of the baseline method argue that the process resembles the blind leading the blind. Each organization may end up with the same wrong controls for the wrong (or unnecessary) purposes. In reality, there are organizations using baseline controls that are unnecessary; they may have these controls only because others have them, or the need for a control may no longer exist because the threat no longer exists. In my view, however, having unnecessary controls is far better than not having sufficient controls, since the latter situation can open the organization (and the security expert) to accusations of negligence. Some business managers and information owners, along with security practitioners, question whether the due care baseline gradually degrades as organizations collectively seek the least security possible to meet their objectives. My answer is that baseline due care aims at meeting or exceeding the practices of the most security-savvy organizations in each aspect of security. If, for example, we use a scale of 0 to 10 to represent the quality of each vulnerability solution and the baseline value is 5, organizations should seek to score a 6. This practice will inevitably lead to a stronger, rather than weaker, level of due care. Baseline, at least in my definition, does not—and should not—mean a minimum level of security.

Other opponents of the baseline method argue that since the controls are, by definition, well known, they are also well known to criminals who, armed with that knowledge, can avoid or neutralize them in their attacks. We should note that risk assessment, although a much more indirect and costly process, also results in using baseline controls. But, both methods (baseline and risk assessment) include the development and selection of special controls that provide an additional challenge of unpredictability for

A Brief History of the Baseline Development

I developed the concept of baseline standards of due care, and the original set of baseline controls, in 1982 as part of a larger project at SRI for the U.S. Department of Justice. In the development process, I selected several types of computer-dependent organizations to study their common security needs and controls. Due to budget constraints, we limited the study to seven field sites:

- A state department of administration
- A private law research institute
- A county government
- A state department of justice
- A city government
- An insurance company
- A university institute for social research

All seven organizations had at least one common need—that of maintaining the confidentiality of personal information. The insurance company was included specifically to contrast to the other six noncommercial organizations.

Three teams, each with two experienced computer security consultants, spent three or four days at each of the sites. They asked managers at each site to identify the best-controlled activities and most effective controls they had in place. The purpose was to find exemplary security measures, not deficiencies. They also asked managers to specify how they would like to improve or augment controls and to indicate their plans for future control enhancements. The teams focused on activities and areas where personal data existed. In this sense, the control objectives, controls, and control variants identified fell primarily within a selective baseline for computer centers that process significant amounts of sensitive personal data. Even so, many of the controls fit general baselines.

At the completion of the fieldwork, the project teams, field site representatives, and project consultants attended a two-day workshop at SRI. We reviewed the findings at each field site and identified duplicate or overlapping controls. We then classified each control as baseline, selective, or special, or rejected it. Rejection occurred because of inconsequential effectiveness, inappropriateness, or poorly or confusingly documented reports. Duplicate or overlapping controls at the field

(continued)

sites indicated common usage and reinforced their classification as baseline or selective. *Selective controls* were those that were appropriate for use in some kinds of organizations but not others. I documented the 82 control objectives that were agreed upon, and the Department of Justice published them in 1982 in a report titled *Computer Security Techniques*. This was the first collection of control objectives that had broad support in the art toward meeting due care status.

In 1985, SRI provided the 82 documented baseline control objectives to the SRI I-4 member organizations, and began to act as a clearinghouse for new baseline controls. We refined and expanded the original collection through surveys and reports from I-4 members, as well as from ongoing information security reviews for SRI clients around the world. We selected the original control categories after the controls were identified—the reverse of the usual practice that begins with determining vulnerabilities and then developing control objectives. The reverse process of finding the best control objectives first again emphasizes the baseline concept of identifying the best controls in use for reducing common vulnerabilities without particular regard to specific vulnerabilities. Letting natural groupings of control objectives determine the control categories resulted in less-than-comprehensive treatment of vulnerabilities. Important control objectives were missing from the study, because we found no commonly used controls to satisfy them. We left such control objectives for treatment as special categories or for further research of common controls among a wider range of computer centers. Therefore, the control objectives, controls, and variants presented in the original report were not intended as comprehensive or complete for all needs. In fact, the field organizations and project team and its members' sponsors did not necessarily all endorse all of the controls; majority ruled.

As distributed computing gained acceptance, a colleague at SRI and I documented new applicable controls. In 1992, we surveyed 192 I-4 member organizations to determine their use of the controls; then Dr. Douglas Webb of SRI compiled the I-4 baseline controls into a checklist of more than 300 control objectives. With help from a number of other consultants, we eventually produced detailed control specifications and a checklist of control objectives as a proprietary product for distribution to I-4 members. Other organizations, including the U.K. DTI Task Group, used information from the report in the early 1990s to simplify the control objectives and strengthen due care acceptance.

Today, despite risk assessment's failure to disappear, I stand vindicated in my efforts to introduce the due care objective into the information security art. Increasing numbers of organizations are using the baseline methods and convincing management of its viability. The information security literature is filling with databases of baseline control objectives (see the list of sources in Chapter 12).

the criminal. In addition, we must design and implement controls in ways that make them effective even though the enemy knows they exist and understands how they work.

Using Baseline Controls

The existing databases of controls include both baseline control objectives that are currently in use and candidate baseline control objectives to address the latest technological advances and applications. At SRI, for example, we maintain baseline control objectives at a step ahead of strict baseline due care. While there is significant redundancy among the controls to ensure that each category is complete, it is generally better to be redundant than to overlook an important control, since adversaries are continually seeking vulnerabilities to attack where there is an absence of controls.

Many controls are parts of other controls, and some can be used together to increase effectiveness. For example, the computer logon password control objective includes several practices and operational controls such as length of password, false password usage attempt limits, nondisplay of passwords, cryptographic protection of stored passwords, and initiation and termination administration. We choose sufficient fineness of granularity of objectives in the SRI collection to include one control in another's description (coarseness), or to break it out separately with its own description (fineness). We determine this on the basis of whether the control could be implemented without the presence of another control that might be inclusive of it under some circumstances. In addition, we may break out a dependent control separately if it is particularly important and might be overlooked if it were only a feature of an independent control.

Documenting Baseline Controls

It is important for organizations to document and publish their security controls and practices, and to incorporate a written record of all baseline and special controls in the internal security guidelines that are available to security implementers and information owners. Some controls should be mandatory, requiring formal exceptions if not implemented. Others can be discretionary, with implementation decisions left to informed information owners.

Organizations may need to rewrite or edit control documentation, finding the standard versions too detailed or too specific, too general, or too redundant. In the case of control documentation, redundancy is not necessarily a bad thing; it sometimes makes a particular control and closely related controls easier to find, and lends support to their due care status. You may wish to remove some control objectives that are not applicable or add new ones that support new technology. Control publishers include some controls that are embedded in information processing products (e.g., password logon controls) or are sold as separate products (e.g., secure modems, secure Internet browsers, security smart-card tokens, firewalls, and security diagnostics software). If an organization uses controls that are embedded in specific products, they may need to document them according to the vendor's specifications in the internal standards documents. In addition, it is advisable for organizations to document candidate baseline and special controls in discretionary guidelines, restricting the mandatory standards to the generally accepted baseline and special controls that are in some degree of use.

We must adapt many controls for a particular use to fit various threats and needs (in part to meet Bob Courtney's point concerning some degree of uniqueness of each organization). For this reason, in the I-4 collection, I identify the important variables for each control objective. Ideally, we should implement controls with changeable values, and even automatically changed values when used in automated systems. This can often provide significant added strength to the control because even though adversaries know the controls are in place, they cannot know the current settings. This makes the environment unpredictable, and much more difficult to attack. We must always assume that adversaries have our lists of the controls we are using, but that they will encounter a secure environment nonetheless. (We should treat detailed information about controls confidentially. It is not good practice to answer questionnaires from outside, untrusted sources that request details about security. Organizations should share such information and internal security standards and guides only with trusted peers, and only after obtaining permission from top management, and obtaining written assurances of confidentiality from recipients. Otherwise, these practices are gross violations of security.)

Using controls effectively and to make them fault-tolerant and resistant to failure requires a combination of skills and experience. It is important to remember that an adversary is likely to be familiar with most controls and will try to circumvent or overcome the controls in his path of attack. In Chapter 13, I describe 27 control guides that provide insights for making controls effective, such as instrumentation to know if they have been attacked and are still in good condition.

Benefits of Baseline Controls

Adopting baseline controls is a simpler, less expensive, and more effective way to select security safeguards than risk assessment. Once an organization follows the baseline approach and selects appropriate controls to ensure a level of due care, it can apply its remaining resources to the task of identifying and resolving new vulnerabilities or control problems. As organizations apply the baseline approach to select due care controls, they will further advance the baseline concept by encouraging uniformly high-quality security. The identification of generally used controls and their variants should help to stabilize and enlarge the security product market, leading to a wider range of less expensive control products that require fewer model types and options. For example, as we develop and accept procedures for the use of cryptography and key management, cryptographic products are likely to become more uniform and less costly.

Criteria for Identifying Baseline Controls

Baseline controls are not a minimum set of controls. In many cases, organizations never manage to achieve a full baseline level of security because it requires more resources and time than they can expend. Also, in some cases, implementing the full set of baseline control objectives would impose on the organization and negatively affect its ability to succeed. I suggest the following criteria for choosing a control to achieve a baseline control objective.

Either you have already selected the control as a baseline control in a previous security review, or several independent and respected sources identify a candidate control for you to consider. For your organization to have achieved a standard of due care, the following criteria for each candidate control should hold:

- The organization has the control in place, or has near-term plans to institute it, in essentially the same form as described.

Or, if the organization does not have the control, it can document one of the following conclusions:

- It does not need the control (for example, because it does not have the information or media to be protected, or the control does not apply to the organization's environment or mission).
- It has compensating or equivalent controls.
- It has considered the control, rejected it, and decided to accept the consequences of not using it.

I recognize the difficulty in specifying generally used controls for particular environments and circumstances. For example, preventing unauthorized computer or server room entry is a baseline objective, but the prudent controls to accomplish the objective and the values of the control implementation variables vary widely. To carry this example further, any good published security checklists of best practices include the following specific physical entry controls:

1. Physical barriers (sturdy walls, floors, ceiling, windows, locks, and doors)
2. Administration of entry control (accountability, authorization, and record keeping)
3. Contingency plans for failure of entry controls
4. Policy and procedure documents for entry control
5. Frequent testing and auditing of entry controls
6. Sign-in/out log
7. Procedure and notice (e.g., signs) to challenge the presence of a person
8. Presence of two or more people required during entry
9. Electronically or mechanically locked doors
10. Mantrap or turnstile doors (a pass-through isolation booth)
11. Guards at doors
12. Wearing ID badges required
13. Closed-circuit television monitoring of doors and areas
14. Microprocessors for entry monitoring
15. Biometric identification verification for entry (e.g., fingerprint scanning or iris scanning)

Controls 1 through 5 must be present to achieve baseline protection, but the use of other controls depends on traffic, security levels on each side of the barrier, alternative forced-entry possibilities, and exposure to unauthorized entry.

This list expands the one control objective to be met to 15 specific controls. An organization should have written specifications concerning strength of the walls, persons to administer entry control, frequency of audit, content of the contingency plan, explicit policy content, method and records for identification of authorized personnel, and specific constraints. The baseline of 15 controls has more detail than the typical checklist, but not so much as to inhibit selection of variants.

The control implementation variations accounting for whether windows are present, for example, would be beyond baseline specifications because the choice would depend on many factors such as the nature of the potential threats, the type of area adjacent to the windows, and the purpose of the windows. However, another variant, the type of window material, may fall within the baseline definition because of general agreement that high-impact-resistant plastic or especially hardened glass is always necessary. An organization would consider the advice of the vendor's sales staff, its own experience, and the experience of other organizations with similar circumstances. The considerations of (1) generally available products at reasonable cost and (2) what others are doing are the keys to ensuring that you achieve due care. Of course, to follow the baseline approach, any deviations from this advice are acceptable for sufficiently prudent reasons, but the deviations and reasons should be documented to avoid the appearance of negligence.

12

How to Conduct a Baseline Security Assessment

An information security review or assessment is the process of allocating security resources and selecting prudent controls. In a home or small business, this is a simple process. It is, however, somewhat more complex in a larger organization and may require assistance from security consultants. In this chapter, I focus primarily on the security assessment process for a large organization, although I do offer some guidelines for small businesses and home computing environments at the beginning. That way, if you're only concerned with security for one or two PCs in your home or small business, you need only read the first few pages of the chapter.

GOOD SECURITY IN A SMALL BUSINESS OR HOME ENVIRONMENT

If you are considering the information security needs of a small business or home environment, the process of selecting best-practice, due-care controls is quite simple. Begin by considering ways in which to avoid the need for security by removing any threats (e.g., a child who is into hacking), eliminating any vulnerabilities (e.g., avoiding untrustworthy Web sites on the Internet), or storing valuable information that you do not need for awhile in another secure location and/or medium. Next, establish a good recovery and correction capability. In particular, be sure that you use good backup practices and have a source of good advice for emergencies, such as your local computer vendor. You should back up important documents and any files that you modify on a frequent basis, and store copies and diskettes of each week's changed computer contents at some remote safe location, such as in your safe deposit box. (I use the Iomega Zip disks and store everything at a remote site after about ten sessions of use.) Be sure to install the most recent versions of applications software in your computer and use all of the security features that the software provides, because they usually contain the latest protection mechanisms.

If you are the only user of your information or share your computer and documents only with trusted family members, you are probably not concerned about the possibility of those in your household viewing or using your information. If this is the case, just be sure to lock the computer room doors and windows and keep the blinds shut as much as possible. Also, be sure to include the value of your computer and software in your homeowner's insurance policy.

If, however, you want to keep information in your office and computer confidential and protect it from anybody who has physical entry to them, be sure to use the operating system or application software to lock the information files. You may also lock the power-up process with a secret password and similarly secure your physical document containers. If you add software to your computer from time to time, you should have a good, frequently updated antivirus program in your computer. In any case, if you connect your computer to an outside network such as the Internet, you need antivirus protection.

Connecting your computer by modem to an Internet service provider (ISP) increases your exposure to risk. You should consult your provider regarding recommended controls, and be sure to keep your computer offline as much as possible, or turned off when you are not using it. Also, always be careful about the Web sites that you visit electronically, much as you take care in strange neighborhoods or in unfamiliar business establishments.

Do not release personal information (including credit card numbers) to others over the Internet unless you trust the recipients and are using communication protection that they recommend or your own encryption software. It is possible to suffer a computer virus infection (from a macro virus) when you receive e-mail, but only if you open a document enclosed with an e-mail message and your computer automatically executes infected macro formatting programs attached to it. Good, updated antivirus software will protect your computer from the known viruses, but you may be the recipient of a new one that the antivirus software does not yet recognize or neutralize. Be observant; look around occasionally to see that information, other people, and processing appear normal and as you expect. Question abnormalities and anomalies.

Because computers and the information they contain are especially fragile as compared to printed documents and filing cabinets, you may want to be super-cautious and have two computers. Reserve one for on-line use, and the other for critical computing, such as your financial or other personal applications. Then, use diskettes to manually move data from one computer to the other. If you follow this advice, or make conscious, prudent decisions not to follow it (and are willing to reap the consequences), you will have achieved a baseline due care level of best-practice security. This means that you have significantly reduced the likelihood of being accused of negligence under many circumstances, and you may even prevent a real loss. In any case, you should have sufficient security to feel confident, and not have any remorse about your level of protection if you do happen to suffer a loss.

A SUMMARY OF THE BASELINE SECURITY REVIEW PROCESS

Some organizations refer to the process of selecting prudent security controls as a review; others call it an assessment. The terminology is not important. Name it to fit the culture of your organization, but do not call it an audit, because an audit—by law and regulation—is a review conducted by professional auditors and has legal implications and liabilities associated with it. *Risk assessment* may be a good choice for a name; it is likely to impress management more than *security review,* but I prefer to avoid the word *risk* because of the resulting confusion regarding the actual methodology.

Most organizations rely on the default due-care method for selecting security controls, even if they call it something else—like risk assessment. This method is the least costly, best known, fastest, and most effective; it is also scalable, so it is suitable for organizations of all sizes. Before proceed-

The Difference between Audits and Reviews

It is important to reserve the word *audit* to describe what qualified and licensed auditors do, and not confuse those responsibilities with what information security specialists do. Auditors conduct conformance reviews in an adversarial relationship to those being audited. They then produce official audit reports, which go to the organization's Audit Committee and may also be submitted to shareholders and/or government or regulatory agencies. Information security specialists perform security reviews as consultants for organizational units. The reviews are generally based on the organization's own information security policies, standards, and guides. The results of the review may be distributed to several levels within the management structure, but the local organization unit may treat them confidentially and restrict distribution.

ing with the baseline due-care process, you may need to deal with a few contingencies to back up your information or deal with any losses that might occur while you are improving security. You also need to structure internal accountability and information protection authority to cover all kinds, representations, forms, media, and locations of the information, and determine who or what might cause losses. In some cases, it is advisable to obtain special insurance coverage for the period of maximum exposure, until the due care safeguards can be selected and implemented.

You also need to determine if your organization has sufficient in-house expertise to conduct an effective security review and select and implement appropriate controls. If the in-house talent is not sufficient, you will need to find and retain outside consultants who can bring the necessary level of skill, knowledge, and experience to the process. Then, the security specialists—whether they are in-house staff or outside consultants—need to become thoroughly familiar with the information owners and users throughout the organization to determine the organization's culture and attitudes, as well as the existing state of security, any special threats or loss experiences, and vulnerabilities. They can do this by conducting interviews, reading the owners' and users' own documentation as well as audit reports on them, and observing their environments and practices. Using that information, the specialists can work with organization management to establish security policies that are both necessary and likely to be followed. Once the policies are established, the security specialists can create a set of mandatory control objectives; these may be adapted from published security literature (see the list of sources further into this chapter) or borrowed from other, similar, well-run organizations. In most cases, organizations use a combination of sources, using their own existing policies and standards as a starting point and surveying other organizations to determine what they are doing under similar circumstances, then borrowing the parts that are applicable. (Most organizations have accumulated some body of security documents, typically including practices, policies, and guidelines. And, many organizations are quite liberal in sharing this information with others as long as it does not reveal details of their implementation of the controls.) The resulting documentation then becomes the organization's source of guidance about a baseline standard of due care controls and practices.

Inevitably, questions arise concerning the order or priority of implementing controls selected by the baseline method. What controls should be implemented first? Fortunately, there are some useful guidelines. First, address the immediate loss experience if one exists, to mitigate that loss and avoid negligence in case it happens again. Then make sure that there are adequate backup and recovery capabilities. A badly handled information loss could be disastrous to the security assessment and controls selection process (and to the in-house security expert's job). Next, consider doing the obvious things that show immediate progress and results, so that management will notice, to maintain their interest in, and support of, the security assessment effort. Start with the lowest cost, visible but least restrictive forms of security. Then, address the lowest cost and less visible ones, and gradually move toward the higher cost, more restrictive controls. Do not implement restrictive controls until the people who are going to be constrained by them fully understand the need for such controls and are willing to work within their constraints (see Chapter 13, "Good and Bad Controls").

Notice that I have said nothing about priorities of control selection based on risk of loss. Read the current news and trade press (especially the publications that your management is likely to read), and consider implementing the controls that are recommended or that address the losses being reported. Reducing the risk of loss is an indirect benefit of baseline controls.

Implementation priority may also be affected by circumstances within the organization, such as new systems development status, changes in staffing levels, or internal project priorities. Be sure to take these factors into account; they may indicate the appropriate order for implementing controls. In many cases, such circumstances can have a significant effect on the ultimate success of the implementation. While it is a good idea to have an implementation plan, it needs to be sufficiently flexible to deal with any contingencies that arise. (I always generate an implementation plan for clients, listing the order of implementation for each recommended control objective.)

Once you decide on the baseline control objectives to be implemented, you will need to identify any special threats and vulnerabilities within the organization that may not be addressed by the selected baseline controls. If such threats or vulnerabilities exist, you will need to develop or acquire new controls that are not yet included in the baseline, and combine these with the chosen baseline controls for implementation.

Organizations also need to establish an internal standards deviation process so that information owners can avoid implementing mandatory control objectives when good business judgment dictates that this should be done. It is generally advisable to create a form for this process, so that the information owners can obtain the proper authorization sign-offs, and document the reason for the deviation and its potential effect on other business units, and the justification for it. Such forms, when properly filled in and signed, can become valuable pieces of evidence for avoiding accusations of negligence and proving due care actions.

In addition to selecting mandatory baseline control objectives for implementation, you should consider discretionary controls and guidelines to supplement the due care level of protection within the organization. It is a good idea to provide information owners and users with documentation on discretionary controls and encourage them to consider using such controls on a regular basis, or occasionally, when additional protection may be needed. And, you will need to periodically update the security standards by eliminating obsolete control objectives, adding new ones derived by monitoring the practices of other organizations, and moving some control objectives from the discretionary controls guidelines to the baseline as they come into normal use by other organizations in similar circumstances. Of course, security specialists need to work closely with management throughout the security review and implementation process, obtaining agreement for the implementation and any changes in the existing security structure. Justification should be based on the concept of continuing to meet an advancing standard of due care, corresponding to (or possibly exceeding) the security practices of other well-run, similar organizations, so that if losses ever do occur, management is unlikely to accuse anybody of negligence or hold them liable for losses.

GUIDELINES FOR CONDUCTING BASELINE INFORMATION SECURITY REVIEWS

The proprietary baseline developed by SRI directly identifies control objectives and controls that meet management criteria and sound security practice based on many years of experience. The method is not new. It is based on Baskerville's first generation of assessment methods, with the added justification of due care. Once information assets and their uses have been identified, the next step in the process is to select the baseline due care controls that are missing from the subject environment or need updating. These controls are the well-known, obviously needed, and moderate cost ones that are used by other respected organizations with similar potential threats, assets, and vulnerabilities. For the most part, these controls are quite apparent in the current security literature and conferences.

Once you have applied due diligence efforts for due care controls, you may want to apply focused analysis, such as using scenario and exposure techniques, to identify the few additional new or special controls and practices that may be required but are not effectively addressed by baseline controls. You may also need additional analysis to settle any remaining disagreement over recommendations, or to further consider recommendations that are only marginally justified due to high cost or modest anticipated benefit. It is advisable to initially focus on implementing the relatively easy, routine baseline efforts, then concentrate on the more difficult vulnerabilities that are not well addressed by baseline efforts.

A METHODOLOGY FOR INFORMATION OWNERS UNTRAINED IN INFORMATION SECURITY

Do not expect information owners in distributed computing environments or users who have not been trained in information security practices to perform adequate information security reviews of their own information. The do-it-yourself practice will usually be of limited value, particularly in distributed computing environments where security experts are not readily available. Users typically want quick answers to security questions so that they can get on with their primary job responsibilities (for which they are rewarded).

To get started, however, users may assess their own information and identify the assets that require protection, then rank those assets in order by need for protection using a simple three-level scale (high, medium, and low). This type of self-assessment may be helpful for increasing the users' motivation and security awareness, and to serve as a guide for the information security experts to specify controls for them. But many information owners find such procedures bothersome and are willing to tolerate them only one time. In addition, the results may be questionable, since users are often naïve about potential threats and vulnerabilities and perform the assessment without the necessary insights and objectivity that experienced security artisans bring to the process. For example, some information owners may think of computer larceny in terms of the value of the stolen hardware, while in reality the most significant loss probably involves the information contained in the stolen computers along with the resulting embarrassment, or the staff time required to replace the hardware, software, and information. It is important to have security experts review these assessments, and to advise the users on methods for protecting their information.

Information security practitioners within an organization should help information owners to understand and practice proper security procedures by providing them with written standards and guidelines that explain the controls mandated by the information security policy. It may be useful to begin with a "starter" set of security controls and gradually move toward a more advanced, comprehensive set. In addition, various business units that require more or less security may need different sets of mandatory and discretionary controls and practices, all spelled out in different versions of written standards and guidelines documents. In an accounting department, for example, security controls and practices may emphasize threats from financial fraud; in a research and development department, controls and practices may focus on espionage; in a warehouse and shipping department, security controls focus on theft; and in a manufacturing department, security controls and practices target threats from sabotage. The written standards and guidelines for each business unit should use a style of writing consistent with the abilities and interests of the employees within that unit; while a brief general explanation of the control objectives may be sufficient for one unit, others may need a more detailed description of the actual controls, along with step-by-step guidelines for implementing controls. And, because information owners sometimes have good reasons for not implementing some of the controls or practices, you should have a formal procedure in place to allow them to explain their decision not to implement, along with a written explanation of possible alternative plans for protecting the information.

The U.K. BSI *Code of Practice* (BS7799) is an excellent resource for assisting in developing a security guide for information owners. The keyed items in the document form the basis for a good security starter set, which you can expand to produce an advanced set of internal standards. One large corporation seeks assistance from the vendors of computer and network products to help it write specific standards and guidelines. This typically delivers a high degree of technical expertise to the process, along with an outsider's view of the organization, which is helpful for determining which types of controls are likely to be most effective. Although the corporation pays for the assistance it receives, some computer and networking vendors provide this type of service free of charge in exchange for the right to share the information with their other customers.

THE METHODOLOGY FOR INFORMATION SECURITY EXPERTS

A security review intended to bring an organization to a level of due care controls and practices should include a complete, comprehensive analysis of threats and vulnerabilities or, in some cases, a targeted analysis of specific security issues. A complete review requires both management and technical skills. Information security is so complex and applies to so many different environments that no one security practitioner—whether an in-house security expert or an outside consultant—can be expected to have the knowledge and experience to do the entire job. Therefore, many organizations use a combination of specialized security and technology artisans in team reviews. For example, reviewing the technical aspects of information systems and networks typically requires special expertise. An expert on IBM MVS mainframe systems is likely to be of little help in a review of Microsoft's NT operating system or an analysis of Internet firewalls. (Although I am usually able to perform operational reviews of such items as password logon usage and false data entry for many systems and applications, I must leave in-depth reviews of systems that include analysis of firewall ports, routers, and switches to the specialists in those subjects.)

To identify current standards of due care controls, I suggest the following sources:

- ANSI standards (also includes other countries' national standards)
- ISO standards
- British Standards Institute *Code of Practice* (includes more than 80 control objectives)
- CRAMM Database of Controls

- *CobiT: Control Objectives for Information and Related Technologies* (includes more than 300 generally accepted control objectives compiled by the Information Systems Audit and Control Foundation)
- *GASSP* (available from Will Ozier, wozier@pacbell.net, (707) 762-2227)
- OECD *Guidelines on Information Security, Privacy Guidelines, Cryptography Guidelines,* 1991–1997
- U.S. NIST *Common Criteria*
- U.S. NIST *Computer Security Handbook*
- *Computer Security Techniques* (Donn B. Parker, U.S. Department of Justice, Bureau of Justice Statistics, 1982)
- *Information Security Policies Made Easy* (730 controls written by Charles Cresson Wood, Baseline Software, Inc. 1995)
- CSI *Alert* description of a new checklist, 1997
- MIS Training Institute publications
- Safeguard vendors' product specifications, manuals, and advice
- Trade journals, conferences, exhibitions, and books
- I-4 and ESF benchmark databases of controls and practices (proprietary and availability requires membership)
- National Computer Security Association (NCSA) firewall and antivirus product certifications
- ITSEC in Europe and TCSEC (The Orange Book) in the United States

In Chapter 13, I offer 27 control guide principles for implementing the selected controls.

A security baseline review should include the following five steps.

1. Identify the scope of the review and create a review plan.
2. Gather information for baseline decisions, including a review of any special security requirements.
3. Select baseline and special control objectives.
4. Recommend baseline and special controls.
5. Implement controls.

I explain each of these steps in detail in the remainder of the chapter.

Identify the Scope of the Review and Create a Review Plan

The first step in a security review is to identify the various physical, logical, management, and organizational elements to be included; in some cases, this may include outside services such as software development contractors, IT outsourcers, and advertising agencies. Once you've identified the domain and scope of the review, you need to develop a plan for observing the various facilities and interviewing the staff. This generally entails assembling a review team composed of security staff members and, if necessary, knowledgeable specialists from other departments or outside consultants. You'll also need to develop a target schedule and budget for the review and determine how best to report the results to management or designated department heads. Management support is crucial throughout the process, since top-level managers will need to approve the steps in the review and, ultimately, the implementation of recommended controls and practices.

The review may include any or all of the following domains:

Physical domain

Buildings and adjacent areas, egresses, roads, offices, laboratories, production facilities, storage

Equipment, objects, containers

Channels, media

Supplies, money, documents

Services

Power, water, air, external and internal mail delivery

Transportation, communications, guards, maintenance

Storage, suppliers, retailers, backup

Police, fire, emergency, disaster, repair

Logical domain

Computer systems, voice and data networks, peripheral equipment

Processing, communication, software

Living organisms

People, animals

Bacteria, viruses

The review team will obviously depend on the scope of the review, including its overall size and objectives, and the number of locations to be covered. In some cases, two consultants will be sufficient to conduct a general, management-level review. An in-depth technical review, on the other hand, may require a team of 10 to 30 specialists in the particular subject areas. One individual may be able to conduct a limited review, such as testing firewalls at one site or evaluating password use versus token entry for a computer system. (A typical complete review from my experience requires two to four experts and takes about three months, including four weeks of on-site observation and 50 to 100 staff interviews. Costs typically range from $50,000 to $250,000.) Results of the security review may be presented in both verbal and written reports, and must specify the findings of the review, a list of prioritized recommendations, a comparison of due care controls in similar organizations, and a detailed implementation plan. (The results of my reviews typically include about 100 recommendations and a written report 20 to 100 pages in length.)

Gather Information for Baseline Decisions

Experienced information security practitioners know many of the controls and practices that any organization should have in place for a due care level of security before they conduct a threat and vulnerability review. But they still need to know the current status of security, how much and what kinds of security the organization desires (and will tolerate), and any special threats and vulnerabilities that are not covered by the baseline controls. Much of what they need to know is the culture and the business of the organization, any losses that have occurred, the staff's views on threats and vulnerabilities, and the information and facilities that require protection. Security practitioners gather this information by reading the organization's documents, interviewing the appropriate people in the organization, and observing and testing the environments and systems. The information security foundations and framework models that I've introduced, along with the various lists in this book, all serve as useful checklists for the review team. In particular, I recommend reviewing the Threats, Assets, Vulnerabilities model (Chapter 10) at least once each day during the review until you are thoroughly familiar with it. In a complete, comprehensive review, it is crucial to cover all of the items in this model and the associated checklists; the failure of any review is the result of missing something important (especially if your client or security peers discover it first).

As I've mentioned before, management support is extremely important to conducting a successful review. Not only must top-level managers support the entire process, they need to make their support clearly known throughout the organization, especially to the individuals and departments that will be contributing information. One of the first steps in garnering such top-down support for the review is to send an announcement of the review to everyone in the organization before you actually begin conducting interviews or observing business activities. The highest-ranking, most influential manager in the organization—usually the president, chairman, CEO, owner, or equivalent—should sign the announcement.

After you have announced the review, you can begin to identify and collect the organization's relevant documents for study. This includes security policies and standards, forms used, organization charts, employee directories, current directives, organization newsletters, content of Web sites, products and services marketing material, information systems and services instructions, outsourcing contracts, guides, and manuals. Recent audit reports are extremely valuable for identifying security problems. Because the review also needs to take the existing security controls into account, you should inventory the controls that are currently in use. This will serve as the starting point for improvements and to identify new baseline or special controls. You should store all of these documents in secure places while they are in the team's possession, since much of the information is sensitive.

Obtain the help of the people closest to the review effort to identify the key people to interview and facilities to observe. This should include a cross-section of employees from different departments and at different levels within the organization. The interview process typically includes members of central staff, heads of business and operational units, the movers and shakers within departments, employees held in high regard and high trust, and employees known as troublemakers. The obvious people to interview are those intensely involved with the organization's information, including the information systems and security staffs. It is also advisable to talk to the organization's legal council, head of human resources, auditors (very important), plant security manager, marketing and sales staff, and insurance risk manager. (I also try to visit the local FBI, police, fire department, and city emergency response manager. In many cases, this is a chance to introduce the organization's information security staff to these individuals. I try to include the organization's information security manager or review liaison in the interviews and observations except in cases where my independent, unbiased position is of particular advantage.)

A typical review includes from 50 to 100 staff interviews; regardless of the size of the organization, interviewing more than 100 individuals is likely to produce redundant information. The first interviews are always the longest because there is more to learn than in subsequent interviews, when you are primarily trying to verify information from the earlier interviews. (A colleague and I generally interview about four people a day in the initial stages of a review, expanding that number to about six a day later in the process.) It is, of course, very important to document each interview and to cover all relevant topics. You can use handwritten notes or laptop computers to record information, but it is generally a good idea to keep the notes brief during the interview so that the subject does not become preoccupied by the amount of information that you're writing or keying, since this can give false signals. (I find that laptop computers are more intrusive than handwritten notes, and sometimes the noise of the keying is bothersome.) It is better to take brief notes during the interview, then expand them at the end of the day while the information is still fresh in your mind. Using written checklists can be intimidating to some subjects, and does not provide sufficient flexibility to discuss topics of interest to the subject. (I use a mental checklist that covers the ten security functions, the short list of losses, and the roles of computers in crimes. At the end of the interview, I review the six elements of information security to determine if we have covered all the points.) It is sometimes possible to combine interviews, meeting with two or more individuals from the same department or business unit. A sole subject may reveal more sensitive information, but a small group may stimulate conversation that reveals more, and more accurate information.

Never lie to or deceive any of the organization's staff in interviews or in testing for vulnerabilities. A security practitioner is in a position of trust, and should not violate this trust under any circumstance. Staff members need to understand that the security review is intended to help them, and the organization itself, to practice good security. It is not an adversarial situation. When interview subjects understand this, and trust the practitioner, they are more likely to be open and forthcoming with information. For example, I always begin an interview by telling the subject that at the end of the interview, I will ask him if there is any other subject or concern that we have not covered and advising him to keep these topics in mind during the interview. I also offer to let him see any portion of my draft final report that concerns him or his organization to get his feedback before I present it to management. In some cases, I will modify the report to meet his approval, but if there are any irreconcilable items, I offer to let him include his own exception report. In some cases, you may be able to recommend ways to reduce existing security controls or relieve constraints. In one situation, for example, I recommended to a manager who had an out of control software development project not to worry about limiting programmers' use of data files. I suggested that he should get his project under control before applying security constraints on his programmers.

Many information security consultants start an interview by asking the subject what she believes is the most sensitive or valuable information in her computers. In my experience, this is not a good starting point. I have found that it is better to ask about the business goals and objectives of the subject's department, and ask who (or what) could cause the most trouble or the greatest loss—not limiting the conversation specifically to information or computers. In answering these questions, the interview subject implicitly conducts a threat analysis, focusing on the areas that are of primary concern to her or to her department, without being led into the subject. Sometimes, however, subjects need to have "the pump primed" to understand what types of information you're looking for in the review. In these cases, I relate some of the crimes that have happened to others in similar circumstances and ask if the same crimes could happen to this organization. I ask what she would do if she became disgruntled or had a serious personal problem to solve. I suggest that we create one or more scenarios to describe her greatest security concerns, and then we act out the scenario in her organization to test for the presence and absence of baseline controls. (Some experts argue that this is dangerous, because it might stimulate users to engage in misbehavior. However, I find that the people we interview have already talked among themselves at times about what they could do, and the interview does not break any new ground. My being there puts a security spotlight on the user, and is likely to divert her from engaging in any misbehavior.) I ask about what would stop her, an expert, or me from causing a loss. This eases the transition from threats to vulnerabilities to revealing the present state of security. To get ideas about others to interview, I also ask who else could give me more insights.

During the interview process, I pick up some hints about the culture of the interview subject's organization, such as common attitudes about the organization and its current security practices, ethically strong and weak people, cooperation, morale, and what motivates people within the organization. I usually trust the subject to tell me the truth, and accept what she says without further or independent investigation. If, however, I find any discrepancies with other information, or with what she says at different points in the interview, I confront her with those differences and ask for further explanation and/or clarification of the facts.

There are a number of reasons beyond the obvious for observing and testing facilities. In addition to reviewing the physical and logical security of facilities, such observations often help to further understand the culture of an organization. Be sure to test the doorknobs of locked doors, watch traffic, check fire safety equipment and video surveillance, check communications closets and cable raceways, examine plenums and building materials, locate the toilets and rest areas, and use the stairs and elevators in all of the various buildings. Check badges, trash, and signs. The signs outside buildings and in public lobbies that indicate what is going on inside may help to direct criminals to their targets; in many cases, legitimate invited visitors do not need signs or detailed directions. Observations should include the facilities' immediate surroundings and neighborhood locale. It is important to know where the busy traffic streets are, and where the power, utility, and communication lines run. Finding and reporting security weaknesses in executive offices and facilities is always a good way to get management attention and support for the review.

During the observations, talk to people you encounter to check for possible vulnerabilities from social engineering. Finding violations of security during observations and testing can provide powerful evidence to support your recommendations. For example, I once found the complete payroll listing on a public loading dock behind a bank building, and at another time, a colleague and I found a client's five-year marketing plan stamped "confidential" in a trash dumpster in a public alley. In the latter case, we dramatically returned the planning document to top management.

I always visit key facilities such as accounting departments, research labs, car parks, loading docks, lobbies, and computer operations during second and third working shifts late at night. Day workers and night workers tend to be very different types of employees; night-shift employees are generally out of view of the primary decision makers in an organization and therefore are likely to take a far more casual approach to their job responsibilities than day-shift workers, who are accustomed to being observed. At night, secured doors are often left open because they offer the shortest distance to the coffee machines. Computer output listings may be left in insecure areas because everyone in the area is known. Visitors are rare. Cleaning staffs, who come and go at will in many organizations, do their jobs in the sensitive offices with workstations still logged on.

It is important to identify assets that are subject to loss, such as computer hardware and software, communications and transport facilities, employees (with their many, varied talents and stored knowledge), reputation, identity (e.g., signs and logos), and—above all—the organization's information. Information must include all kinds, representations, forms, and mediums, such as spoken, known, printed, displayed, and electronically and optically produced forms. In each case, you need to identify the location of information at all times, and identify the enterprise applications, client services provided, outsourcing, internal staff services (e.g., payroll, transaction systems, spreadsheets, and mail), and the business models used. In a security baseline review, unlike a formal risk assessment procedure, you need only identify these assets and determine their individual values to the extent that they are or are not significant enough to be included in the review.

You also need to identify the material threats and vulnerabilities within the organization. It is generally advisable to consider all threats to be intentional, since some acts or accidents that appear unintentional may actually be intentional, and controls that protect against intentional acts also protect against unintentional acts. You need to decide upon a reasonable level of abstraction to list the threats, to ensure that the list is comprehensive, yet manageable (i.e., not too large) and consistent. For example, avoid high-level descriptors such as fraud, espionage and theft, but be careful not to get lost in the details of attack methods such as eavesdropping or using Trojan horse viruses. The complete loss list in Chapter 10 is a good example of the best way in which to summarize threats, as is its order of presentation. Using this type of list facilitates matching the types of controls that are already in place with the new ones that may be required.

One effective method of identifying threats is to create brief, general threat scenarios to identify the major uncommon threats, or threats whose reality might be debated among the staff and managers. Scenarios ("What would you do in these circumstances to cause various kinds of loss?") provide a good vehicle for discussion and are useful for control testing at a later time. Reading audit reports and interviewing potential victims of threats are also good methods for identifying threats. But remember, you need only identify threats that might otherwise be overlooked, since the baseline controls that you select in the third step of the review process address the threats that are common to similar organizations.

Testing computer system facilities such as firewalls for vulnerabilities is generally useful, and may be conducted either as a separate project or as part of the security review. Regardless of how or when it is conducted however, such testing can not be exhaustive or realistic. Vendor security manuals often serve as guides for this type of testing and there are checklists available in some specialized technical books. Because security testing of real systems can be destructive, it should be undertaken only by experienced, trusted experts. To be safe, try to isolate systems as much as possible without destroying realism to minimize any damage that may occur during testing. Also, be sure to warn any employees who may be affected by the testing to avoid adverse effects on them. You are also well advised to have a management representative present during testing, particularly someone who can (and will) take responsibility for the outcome.

SPECIAL INFORMATION SECURITY REQUIREMENTS

In many cases, security reviews expose special threats and vulnerabilities that are not addressed sufficiently by baseline controls. Although there is great commonality of information security requirements in similar organizations, security practitioners must not fail to recognize the significant differences that exist among different organizations; individual organizations certainly face some special needs that correspond to their particular types of business and corporate culture. Bob Courtney and I agree on the existence of such differences; we disagree only about how far we can go in meeting common needs before having to consider special needs. Many special needs can be met with choices and variations of baseline controls. Outside of the baseline control database, however, special threats and vulnerabilities are challenges to even the knowledgeable information security artisans. For example, baseline controls do not yet address the use of voice recognition and response technology for processing customers' requests in the securities brokerage business. When we attempt to match new security controls to this application, we need to understand and acknowledge the tradition of trust between brokerage sales representatives and their customers—selecting controls that can preserve this level of trust while also allowing brokerage firms to improve their services by taking advantage of the new technology.

Information security generally plays a less important role in risk-taking businesses where profit making is the primary mission than it does in organizations such as the military, where the primary mission is security and risk-taking is minimal. In part, this may be because we commonly expect businesses to suffer some material losses or to fail at times, which is directly opposite to our expectations for the military, which is not allowed to fail. The difference in missions partially explains why organizations take different approaches to security, such as the use of discretionary information classifications in business versus mandatory classification of information and people in the military.

The information security differences among businesses, which can also be significant, are revealed by the finer-grained framework model of information security that I propose in this book (e.g., differences of confidentiality and possession of information). The differences may be profound even within a specific industry, such as banking. For example, a retail bank may have 80,000 computer users and 1,000,000 customers with small account balances, while an investment bank may have only 8,000 computer users and 1,000 customers with large account balances. The differences in scale may dictate different information security standards and different means for implementing them. At one time, I suggested to the information security manager of a large corporation that he send out a brief notice about a new computer virus threat to employees. He said, "Do you realize the effort required to create an appropriate message and send it out to 120,000 employees in 132 countries in six languages?"

Different business products and services have different security needs. For example, intangible intellectual products such as software and

Factors Differentiating the Security Needs of Organizations

Many factors determine whether an organization requires more or different security controls than the baseline level. While some of these factors are obvious, others are not. The following list presents a sample of such factors, all of which may need to be considered during the security review.

Industry or government function (e.g., where different concepts of possession of information prevail)

Mission (service, security, profit, nonprofit, research, education, etc.)

Ownership (e.g., public, corporate, private, partnership, government)

Geographic and legal jurisdiction, location, and business regions

Governing regulations and laws

Dangers of products or services and responsibilities for liabilities

Threats to information and information sources and destinations

Flows of information among organizations

Information as a product or associated with a tangible product

State of IT and communications advancement

Internal culture and management style

Extent of trust required among stakeholders

History, including history of losses

Owners and management perceptions of loss and security

Industrial security practices and state of advancement

Information security practices and state of advancement

Organization of functional, overhead, and outsourced units

Workers and professional unionization

Employee relations, practices, and appraisals

Rewards and sanctions practices

Employee benefits programs (e.g., pensions, health, advisory)

Public visibility, advertising, marketing of the organization and its products and services

Extent of field staffs (e.g., sales force, service providers)

Internal security policies, standards, and guides

Use and reliance upon external communications networks

books are considerably different—and have different security needs—than tangible products such as automobiles. The product of investment broker-ages is information, while for pharmaceutical firms, information may be used only to facilitate delivery and explain tangible products. We need to consider these different roles of information in creating special security controls for an organization.

Vendors are making information security an integral part of their computer operating systems, as well as networking and general applica-tions products such as in Microsoft Windows NT and Office. However, such security primarily addresses the threats of unauthorized computer use and attacks from strangers. Unfortunately, the operating system and applications products do little or nothing to address attacks by misbehav-ing authorized people engaged in unauthorized activities in specific appli-cation systems. Examples are accounts payable or payroll applications, where the largest losses occur. By default, information security experts have left this area of threat to the auditors and to the controls that busi-ness systems developers specify, but information security must address this area as well. Further development of this aspect within information security will result in security models, architectures, and practices that can carry security into the heart of the organization to provide truly compre-hensive, seamless protection against crimes.

Select Baseline and Special Controls

After you have finished gathering information, you need to analyze your findings to identify baseline due care security improvements and/or new special control objectives and the controls derived from the objectives to recommend. For choosing special controls or when recommending a base-line control is a close call, review your field notes to identify material threats and vulnerabilities. For each information security threat and vul-nerability pair to solve, there are eleven steps to follow, to accept it without action, eliminate it, or reduce it to an acceptable degree. You should apply all eleven steps to one or more scenarios that describe the threats, vulnera-bilities, and loss incidents that may result from each threat and vulnerabil-ity pair. This process helps to anticipate as many aspects of a vulnerability as practical. The topics covered by each of the eleven steps represent some of the usual categories of controls and practices found in the literature. For example, the detection step and the prevention step correspond to detection and prevention controls and practices. This simplifies the search for appropriate safeguards to recommend for reducing or eliminating the vulnerability.

Operating System versus Application Level Controls

In nearly any technical security review, questions abound as to who should identify and implement special controls and whether those controls should reside in the computer operating system or applications programs, or should be external to the computers. To what extent should application security such as transaction-limit checking and data reasonableness controls in a widely networked application be provided in the operating system using application program interfaces (APIs) as opposed to the traditional implementation of internal controls in the application itself?

Placing controls near that point at which information (and actions on it) may be exposed to losses is crucial to protecting it. For example, the validity of information from a transaction should be checked both at the point at which it is created and later, at the point at which it is to be displayed or printed. This technique ensures that changes have not occurred between creation and use. Such placement of controls should be reflected in systems architecture. Refer to the Clark-Wilson Integrity model that I introduced in Chapter 10. This model is an elegant algorithmic representation of common accounting controls and well-formed transactions, which are presented for the first time in a form that technologists are comfortable using in system requirements and design stages.

Follow the eleven steps, one at a time, in the specified order. Do not skip even a single step, and do not go on to the next step before concluding the previous one. After you have performed this method several times, going from step 1 to step 11, it becomes automatic and you do not have to think about it, much like hitting a golf ball or writing a letter. The following paragraphs define each step, provide examples, and describe the process. I'll explain the rationale for moving to the next step later in this section. Be sure to pay particular attention to the first step, because this one is frequently ignored in security literature and practice. Here are the eleven steps; they correspond to the functions of security as identified in Chapter 10.

1. **Avoidance.** Before you consider controls, attempt to remove the threat or information subject to the threat.
2. **Deterrence.** Stop people from developing the intent to misbehave.

3. **Prevention.** Stop a harmful incident from occurring, give alarm, and record it.
4. **Detection.** Observe or discover an anomaly, give alarm, and record it.
5. **Mitigation.** Stop an attack, give alarm, record it, and minimize or prevent a loss.
6. **Transference.** Assign the appropriate parties to deal with an incident.
7. **Investigation.** Find the causes and failures and the guilty party.
8. **Sanction or credit.** Punish and reward the appropriate parties.
9. **Recovery.** Restore or compensate for the loss.
10. **Correction.** Implement or improve on the actions in steps 1 through 9 as needed to prevent a reoccurrence.
11. **Education.** Document and learn from the experience of the incident.

You can *avoid* a vulnerability by removing the threat from the information or other threatened asset, or by removing the information from the threat. Examples include removing a disgruntled employee from a sensitive assignment or taking sensitive information away from him, thereby removing the means of misbehaving. Alternatively, you may be able to transfer the accountability for the vulnerability from your security review to another, more appropriate entity such as a party more expert in dealing with the vulnerability. If you cannot avoid a vulnerability, then at least discourage people from thinking about taking advantage of it by applying deterrence in the next step.

Deterrence is defined as discouraging from acting by fear or consideration of dangerous, difficult, or unpleasant attendant circumstances or consequences. *Fear* is the operative word here, and you can use it to great advantage for security. We generally think of fear as an unpleasant emotional state characterized by anticipation of pain or great distress, but it has another useful definition as well. Fear is also a profound reverence or awe. Both definitions can be used for security purposes by recognizing and using the things and authorities that we fear. We fear budget and schedule overruns, information that may harm or embarrass us, personal injury or sickness, guns, detection of our wrongdoing, and computers. We also fear (from both pain and awe or respect) management, police (especially in uniform), government, auditors, enemies, competitors, our peers, and God. Fear is also so powerful that we must be careful to avoid excessive or inappropriate use of it. You may be able to deter potential perpetrators by increasing the penalties or difficulties of their planned attacks, making the circumstances surrounding their acts unpredictable for them, or by focusing their attention elsewhere. For example, you may remove building signs or computer logon screens that attract unnecessary attention to sensitive information. If you cannot deter people from misbehaving, then you need to *prevent* what they attempt, such as by using cryptography, and *detect* what they have done.

Prevention is never totally possible, making detection that much more important. *Detection* can be quite complex, as well as powerful, in its application. This is particularly true in computers, where automated detection can be effectively, comprehensively, and inexpensively achieved. Detection controls have two sub-functions. First, the control must recognize that an anomaly has occurred. For example, a transaction limit control must detect when a transaction amount is excessive. Second, the control must record the event and activate or trigger an alarm or response by another control to mitigate, sanction, transfer, recover from, or correct a loss (most of the remaining functions in the list after *detection*). The detection control may be instrumented to alarm a security officer. The effect is to transfer detection to a human for response. In many cases in automated systems, informing an officer or administrator is insufficient to accomplish any of the other functions such as *mitigation,* and automatic triggering of another automated control is necessary.

Some of the remaining functions are often not the direct responsibility of an information security specialist; management has the ultimate responsibility, along with the information owners, who may delegate their accountability to others. In large organizations, qualified industrial security staffs (with police expertise) often *investigate* crimes with the assistance of information security specialists. Otherwise, investigative firms are contracted for this specialized work. Reporting suspected crimes to the police authorities for investigation is a public duty. However, management should do this carefully with the advice of legal council to minimize the impact on the organization. In my experience, investigations are sometimes a cost to the organization that far exceeds the value of the loss. Investigation should lead to identity of the perpetrators and others involved in the incident. *Sanctions* against the perpetrators and those accountable for negligence are a management prerogative, although the information security department may serve as behind-the-scenes advisors. Management is also responsible for *rewarding* staff members who perform exemplary service in any of the functions relative to a loss incident.

Transference, recovery, and *correction* are the next three safeguard functions. *Transfer* of accountability usually means purchasing insurance coverage or self-insuring, which is done by risk managers who specialize in insurance. Computer crime insurance and all-risk information insurance are becoming popular. *Recovery* from physical disasters is performed by information systems recovery experts in the information security department or by a separate specialist group. Otherwise, recovery is accomplished by restoring that which was lost or accepting and adapting to the consequences. *Correction* consists of updating and restoring information security after a loss incident to minimize the possibility of a repeat of the loss. In my experience, restoration is almost always performed in some fashion, often by repeating these eleven functions, but security experts rarely identify it as a specific function as I do.

You can *educate* stakeholders by fully documenting any losses that occur and publishing the results appropriately or using the documentation for training purposes. Documenting losses is important for justifying future budgets and security plans. You should keep a file of cases within the organization, as well as cases reported outside, which are useful to apply as examples of threats and vulnerabilities for future security purposes.

Recommend Baseline and Special Controls

Once you have finished identifying the controls or practices that are appropriate for eliminating threat, improving security controls or practices, or implementing new or specialized controls to meet due care criteria, you should review your findings and proposed recommendations with the direct stakeholders and the individuals and departments that will be affected by them, as well as the individuals and departments that will actually implement them. After making any necessary revisions, you can present your recommendations to management for approval.

My final reports typically consist of the following six elements:

- An executive summary (the last part to be written)
- The original review plan and directive
- A history of the project (including an appendix of sites visited and people interviewed)
- The baseline due care status of the organization relative to others (a benchmark)
- Each finding, along with the conclusion, recommendation, urgency, and relative cost estimate
- An implementation plan that sets priorities

Both you and the organization need to treat the report as highly confidential. Be sure to identify it as such on the cover and each page. To help control distribution of this sensitive information, number the report copies and keep a log of the recipients. In some cases, your final report may include multiple sections, with separate sections pertaining to different parts of the organization. This type of report organization enables management to direct pertinent information to the departments that are directly involved, eliminating the need to distribute information about specific vulnerabilities and security controls to organization units that do not need to know the information.

The organization's security position relative to other, similar organizations is often the highlight of the security review final report. That information, along with the organization's potential security position, generally receives much interest from management. I find that it is better to combine the findings (i.e., current position) with recommendations for improvement (i.e., security potential) rather than separating findings and recommendations into two separate sections, even though this arrangement sometimes requires repeating a finding that results in more than one recommendation. I also identify each recommendation as a baseline or special control, and explain its significance and cost range. The implementation plan lists recommended tasks in order, along with justifications for the order, suggested staffing, and a time schedule (i.e., Gantt) bar chart. Timing is often dictated or constrained by other activities in the organization, such as major software application developments or technology upgrades. Be sure to identify these factors in the chart.

I almost always make verbal presentations of the final report, using visual aids such as overhead slides to illustrate our findings and recommendations. I sometimes present the report to a broad audience of stakeholders or groups of stakeholders from various business units, then follow up with an executive version of the presentation for top management. Occasionally, during the verbal presentation, an attendee attempts to embarrass the review team or to win favor with her boss by claiming that there is a significant threat, vulnerability, or information asset that the team failed to discover. I attempt to avoid that type of situation by prefacing my report by indicating that we considered a broad range of threats, vulnerabilities, and controls during the study, then narrowed the field to include only the critical ones. I also emphasize that no review is likely to catch all possible problems. Distributing a copy of the draft report to information owners and interview subjects for their review and comment prior to the formal presentation also helps to avoid unpleasant surprises.

GAINING SUPPORT FOR BASELINE RECOMMENDATIONS

The objective of a baseline review is to achieve a level of security that compares well with other, similar organizations and approaches a standard of due care. (It is generally advisable to avoid using the term *negligence* in the presence of management). You can best illustrate the baseline security status of an organization by conducting a benchmark survey of several other similar organizations, then presenting management with the results, comparing the organization with the others in key areas of security controls. I have used a graphical representation of the benchmark status to illustrate a client company's position. Figure 12.1 illustrates one such graphical information security benchmark.

In the figure, we list each control area in the left-hand column and represent the ranges of the extent of adoption of controls as horizontal bars using a scale from 0 to 10, with 5 specified as the baseline due care target. This scale allows us to represent organizations as being below the due care baseline, down to having no security at 0, or being above the due care baseline, up to excessive security at 10. We estimate the comparison organizations' scores subjectively, based on a standard set of questions that we pose by questionnaires or by telephone to the information security managers. Ranges show the lowest to highest organization scores; in some cases we include only the middle half, or we discard the one or two extremes to reduce the ranges. The ranges shown for the target organization (i.e., the subject of the security review) represent the scores for each of our several business units or departments within the organization.

This graph provides comparisons at a glance and usually elicits vigorous discussion during presentations. Our goal is to make recommendations to the organization that will put it solidly within the upper middle range of other organizations' scores (i.e., a score of 5 to 6). A score near 5 does not necessarily mean that the organization has achieved a standard of due care, but that it is in a good position for an external audit, public scrutiny, or if it faced litigation as the result of a material loss. On occasion, we are able to explain to management that the organization is too advanced or is excessively constrained by too much security in a control area.

It is generally advisable to obtain the greatest management support for recommendations for new or modified information security controls. To do this, you can categorize controls by cost (i.e., high to low), or by resources required and significance for the organization in meeting due care and conforming to laws or regulations in addressing the potential loss they may avoid, prevent, or mitigate. Although it is relatively easy to derive cost estimates of controls, you need to derive each cost for each local environment. We generally present a rough scale of cost ranges based on staff time to implement and operate a control, which usually accounts for the largest portion of the control cost.

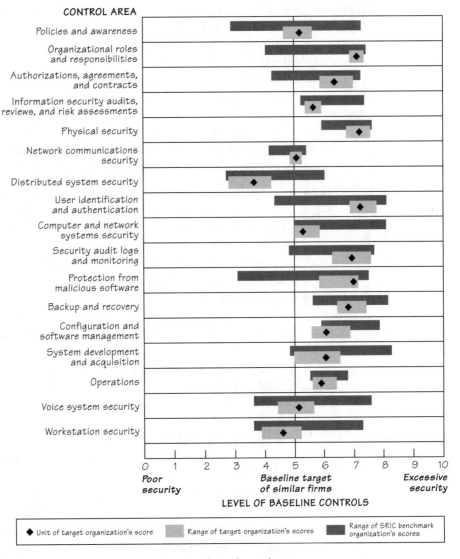

FIGURE 12.1 Information security benchmark.

One effective method of categorizing is to divide controls into four categories and present them to management in the following order:

- Low cost, high significance (easiest decisions)
- Low cost, less significance (easy decisions)
- High cost, high significance (more difficult decisions)
- High cost, less significance (most difficult decisions)

This arrangement places the most attractive options first, and puts management into a mode of accepting recommendations. Some presenters change the order to correspond with management's sensitivity to cost, placing the high-cost, high-significance controls in the second position. I find that cases with marginal benefits are the most difficult to present, and suggest that you gain approval for as much as possible before presenting management with the difficult decisions involving high cost.

There are a number of factors that determine a control's significance to the organization. Some of the factors that should be considered in prioritizing the implementation process include the following:

Obvious significance. The need for many recommended controls is obvious, and individual managers are likely to implement them even before you recommend them in the final report. This type of initiative should be rewarded! Be sure to include these controls in your final report, noting that they are already implemented or currently being implemented.

Visibility of controls. The significance of a control is determined, in part, by the extent of its visibility to management. The controls that are visible and can be implemented relatively quickly should be installed first to show progress and gain momentum. The organization should implement safeguards that are not directly visible or that may take considerable time to implement (such as internal software controls) as soon as possible based on other considerations. Such controls should, however, have minimal interference with implementation of the visible ones.

Loss urgency. Controls that can prevent the occurrence of a loss scenario or avoid recent types of organization losses should be considered significant. Some threats and vulnerabilities that are the subject of imminent loss may warrant immediate approval and implementation, even before the review process ends.

Management accountability. It is sometimes necessary to remind management that a failure to take recommended action in implementing a security control places them in the position of accepting the full effects and responsibility of the consequences. In some cases, however, a refusal to implement security controls or practices may be a prudent business decision relative to the organization's mission. In these situations, the information security experts making the recommendation should be sure that management understands the due care justifications and benefits and is making an informed decision to reject the recommendation. If that is the case, then the security practitioners need to accept and document the decision and rationale behind it.

Availability. The availability of controls, the resources to obtain controls, and the readiness and expertise of the staff to perform the necessary implementation tasks may all influence the order of implementation. Obtaining controls from vendors is often dependent upon schedules of delivery to others. Limited resources in budgets may require delays to accommodate budgeting cycles, sometimes extending months or even years into the future. And, if the computer operations staff is involved in a major project that requires all of their resources, control implementation may have to wait until the project is complete or until they hire and train additional staff.

Tolerance. The effect on people constrained by the controls may influence the order and timing of implementation. It is generally advisable to install readily accepted controls first to obtain cooperation and preclude resistance that may otherwise carry over from the implementation of disagreeable controls. Also, controls that impose severe constraints can generally be implemented in stages or in already-restrictive applications first to avoid cultural shock or drastic changes in work methods.

External influences. Some controls may be required by order of internal or external authorities such as auditors, regulatory agencies, or court directions. Even if they do not absolutely require controls, the authorities may strongly encourage their implementation. The order of implementation may also be dictated by the need to meet other obligations, such as waiting for new products that contain the controls, some of which may reduce costs or avoid negligence.

Contingency plans priority. Disaster contingency plans should have a high implementation priority relative to other security controls because of the potential for extreme loss in the event of a disaster. If there is no disaster contingency plan in place during the security review, it may be advisable to develop an interim plan to cover the review and implementation period.

The favored control priority. In some cases, an executive or auditor has a favorite idea about security or a specific control, which is typically revealed during the review interviews. This type of control may be among the most urgent to recommend as long as it does not interfere with the order of implementation of other more urgent controls.

Notice that risk assessment does not play a role in determining control significance. Instead, significance—and therefore, implementation priority—is based on achieving a due care level of security that will compare favorably with other organizations in similar circumstances and avoid negligence.

Implement Controls

The implementation plan should always include details about when, how, and by whom the newly selected controls are to be implemented or the current controls modified. The implementation effort typically requires a broad-based team approach, with a staff of information security artisans implementing the generally applicable controls (e.g., a new organization-wide policy or standards), and individual information owners and system administrators throughout the organization implementing the local controls. Implementation may take a long time. In one case, my team and I recommended 104 controls and management approved 102 of them. Five years later the company was still using recommendations and implementing the controls. In some cases, too, organizations delay implementation to accommodate other, ongoing changes in non-security policies or practices.

13

Good and Bad Control Objectives

This is a book about controlling cybercrime, not a book about security control objectives. I haven't included detailed control specifications or comprehensive checklists because there are many other publications that do that. And, many control objectives are obvious, such as authentication of computer users, segregation of duties, and application of a security policy. It is much more difficult to select appropriate control objectives and implement them effectively than to merely understand them. What is a good control design, and what is a bad one? In all too many instances, control objectives as they are implemented are worthless or even dangerous because they give the illusion of protection and actually aid the criminals.

In this chapter, I present the principles, guides, and do's and don'ts for selecting and implementing controls. In my experience, these are subjects that are rarely, if ever, addressed in other books, especially from the perspective of real loss experiences. In this chapter, I use some horror stories to illustrate cases of extreme poor judgment concerning implementation of control objectives.

Bob Courtney tells a story about a gung-ho information security officer, fresh out of the army, at a company with a computer center across the street from a college. The security officer had read about student uprisings and decided to be ready for anything. He started installing a bomb warning procedure, external video surveillance, 24-hour guards, and double sets of doors. Management barely stopped him in time as he started building a moat and berms around the property and installing two mean-looking cannons aimed across the street at the college.

Another company in San Francisco disguised its computer center. For security (and other) reasons, they installed the center in an old factory building in a rundown part of town and followed good security practice in not having signs to give any clue as to its purpose. Befitting the level of security, they decided to acquire a state-of-the-art building entry system. The security staff installed a mantrap (two remotely controlled, electronically locked doors with a waiting area between them), a weighing station to detect more than one person in the mantrap, and a biometric hand-measuring device to authenticate identities. They started it up for the first time at seven o'clock on a foggy Monday morning. Within minutes, they had a line of employees two blocks long waiting to get in at a rate of one every 40 seconds. Their well-hidden, low-profile facility trailed a highly visible long line of cold, irate employees. They solved the problem by throwing open both doors from 7:00 to 9:00 every morning and allowing people to stream through, checking their badges only.

Many years ago, I performed a security review for my employer, SRI International, in which I discovered and reported a terrible vulnerability. It was possible to enter the plenum space above the ceiling from areas outside of the locked and secure computer facility, crawl over to the secure area, and drop from the ceiling into the middle of the computer room. No one worried about this vulnerability until a burglar used that route to enter the computer maintenance area and steal tools. The following day, I smugly sent another copy of my report to the controller with the finding highlighted.

One urban myth describes a hacker who logged onto a computer system and destroyed the contents of the memory. After the police caught him, the judge let him go, because the initial logon screen said only, "welcome to the XYZ computer service." A similar story describes a diesel oil–powered electrical generator in a computer center on the 50th floor of a New York high-rise building. Every Friday, the company tested the generator for ten minutes using a small tank of fuel on the same floor. They never used this backup power supply for more than fifteen minutes, but for a real power outage, they had a motor that would pump fuel from a larger tank in the basement. When a real power failure occurred, however, they discovered that the pump motor was not on the same electrical circuit as the emergency power system. The pump ran for fifteen minutes and stopped; a 50-story bucket brigade began shortly after.

Many losses happen where there is an incredible lack of security, or even more common, a lack of understanding of the principles of good controls. With such limited and poorly planned protection, security practitioners often wonder why victims do not have many losses. Often, organizations initially had good controls, but they allowed them to deteriorate to the point of being "on the books" but nonexistent, or actually in place but not functioning in practice. I call these *negative control objectives,* and they are worse than none at all. At least when no controls are present, organizations know that they are exposed to loss. Negative controls are more dangerous, because they appear to be in place when they really aren't—giving a false sense of security.

The lesson that all organizations should learn from these negative-control experiences is to periodically review security policies, control standards, and documented and approved exceptions; then, to conduct compliance reviews in each part of the organization, or rely on the auditors to conduct thorough security audits to ensure that security in reality conforms to security as it is specified. Information owners must either comply with the policy and standards or obtain approved exceptions for good business reasons. Otherwise, organizations should change their policies and standards to conform to the reality of their actual practice. If they do not, top management, which is held responsible for security, may be declared negligent, and all Hell can break loose when a loss happens.

CONTROL EFFECTIVENESS STRATEGY

Although there is a lot of information available about what security control objectives to use, little of it offers guidance on how to make the control objectives effective against an intelligent adversary or even against people causing errors. Implementing a control, such as segregating employees' responsibilities or installing a local area network firewall, is merely the first step in protecting information. Malicious people who are sufficiently motivated and persistent are not likely to be stopped by the mere presence of a control in the deadly serious game that they play. The control must be effective.

Information security must protect against accidental losses as well as those that are intentionally inflicted. By considering all threats to be intentional, we also guard against the unintentional ones. The opposite is not true; the control objectives that we invoke against accidental losses and the implementation methods that we choose do not necessarily protect against intentional losses because they do not take into account an intelligent adversary intent on misuse. Using passwords for computer entry control is a good example. If we were dealing only with benign business circumstances, we would not need to keep our passwords secret. But, this is clearly unacceptable, given the nature of people with intent to abuse and misuse information. Besides, in many cases, we are unable to distinguish accidental losses from intentional ones.

In some security implementations, we may inadvertently make systems more vulnerable by installing an effective control. This can happen when an intelligent adversary looks elsewhere or avoids the control to accomplish his malicious objectives, and finds a vulnerability that we have not yet found or addressed. The result may be an even greater loss

---

Knowing the Enemy's Game

There are many examples of the lessons that we must learn to be smart about security. Playing a game in which we don't know the rules that our opponents play by makes the game tough to win. Consider the young man who was inducted into the army in a small, backward country. They had no arms, so they issued him a broom. "What do I do with a broom?" He asked. They took him to the rifle range and told him to practice aiming the broom at the target and saying, "bang, bang, bang." Next, they gave him bayonet practice, and they told him to stab with the broom and say, "stab, stab, stab."

Unfortunately, the war came along, and the new recruit found himself at the front of the battle with enemy soldiers running at him across an open field. He still had his trusty broom and did not know what to do, except for being guided by his training. He aimed the broom at the enemy soldiers and yelled, "bang, bang, bang." Some enemy soldiers fell down, but others got so close, he had to yell, "stab, stab, stab." More enemy soldiers fell down, but there was one enemy coming at him, and he yelled, "bang, bang, bang." It had no effect, and the enemy got closer. He yelled, "stab, stab, stab," with still no effect. The enemy soldier ran over him, knocked him into the dirt, and broke his broom in half. But as the enemy ran by, the recruit heard him muttering under his breath, "tank, tank, tank!" Moral: Know what the rules are before you play the game if you expect to win.

than the control was meant to preclude. Implementing control objectives effectively tends to cause vulnerabilities to change, but not necessarily to disappear. Eliminating vulnerabilities requires a system-wide view of control selection; locking the doors and leaving a window open merely shifts vulnerability.

Information security is a folk art because, despite many years of experience, we are unable to prove the validity of control objectives on demand and under specific circumstances. We learn about the effectiveness of control objectives only from very limited, poorly articulated experience when the controls are attacked by real perpetrators. Testing can never be more than a qualified success, since we can not test real loss experience caused by real, irrational, unpredictable adversaries. We define good security as nothing bad happening, but recognize that the absence of "bad" events does not necessarily indicate that our security efforts are successful. Instead, it may indicate that our adversaries are incompetent or we are just plain lucky. We can not anticipate all of the likely abuse, irrational behavior, vulnerabilities, or targets in order to effectively test our control objectives. We can only continue to search for, observe, and learn the right security practices by limited testing, from occasional losses, and by practicing due care prudence so that we can effectively protect our information and avoid negligence.

We can improve on the process to some extent, however, by designing, implementing, and operating our control objectives in the most effective manner possible. Way back in 1975, Jerome Saltzer and Michael Schroeder stated the eight principles of secure system design ("The Protection of Information in Computer Systems" in the *Proceedings of the IEEE* 63:9, pp. 1278–1308), which I have expanded during the past 23 years to 27 guiding principles for protecting information (listed at the end of the chapter). The original eight principles were:

1. Users (processes) should have the minimum set of rights and authority that are necessary (least privilege).
2. Use requires explicit permission (fail-safe defaults).
3. Design of the security mechanisms should be simple and brief enough to be verified (economy of mechanism).
4. Every use should be checked for authorization (complete mediation).
5. Security should not depend on the secrecy of the design (open design).
6. Rights to objects (processes and data) should depend on more than one condition to be satisfied (separate mechanisms).

7. Mechanisms shared by multiple users should be minimized (least common mechanism).

8. Mechanisms must be easy to use (psychological acceptability).

Throughout my career, I have collected ideas such as these eight principles for designing, evaluating, selecting, installing, and operating information security control objectives. I have conducted interviews with literally hundreds of victims and more than 200 perpetrators of loss, and I have learned continuously. For example, my study of the branch bank fraud taught me the danger of static controls and the importance of minimal sharing of the knowledge of controls in use.

Over the years, I also learned that we must not rely on the secrecy of our control objectives and their mechanisms for their effectiveness. In addition, controls must be instrumented to report their condition so that we know when they have failed or when they have been activated or attacked. Controls that are not tolerated by the people who are constrained by them or controls that do not have owners to care for them will likely be neutralized.

The guides that I present here are based on my years of experience; they can help you to decide on the best control objectives in given circumstances and the best control designs and implementations. Given two or more alternative controls to mitigate a particular vulnerability, the guides can provide a checklist to help you choose the best one.

USE OF ELEMENTS TO IDENTIFY AND SELECT CONTROL OBJECTIVES

In this section, I first present a sample of due care control objectives for each of the six elements (availability, utility, integrity, etc.) of information security. I have drawn the control objectives from a number of sources based on the loss scenarios that I developed and on the definitions of the six elements that I presented previously. It is essential to consider all six elements in a threat and vulnerability analysis, along with the list of possible threats that I presented in Chapter 10, to ensure that you do not overlook some necessary control objectives. I did not attempt to pair specific threats with control objectives here because each control deals with multiple threats, and each threat should be addressed by several control objectives. Thus, there is no one-to-one correspondence between the various threats and control objectives.

We can use several control objectives to preserve or restore *availability* of data files in computers. The control objectives include having:

- A backup directory with erased file names and pointers until the user purges the files by overwriting them with new files
- Good backup practices
- Good usage control objectives for computers and specific data files
- Use of more than one name to identify and find a file
- Utility programs available to search for files by their content
- Shadow or mirror file storage (a copy in the background)

Four types of control objectives that can preserve the *utility* of information are:

- Internal application control objectives such as verification of data before and after transactions
- Security walk-through during application development to avoid the appearance of unresponsive forms of information at times and places of use
- Minimization of adverse effects of security on information use
- Assignment of authority that does not allow unauthorized persons to reduce the usefulness of information

Control objectives that can be used to prevent the loss of *integrity* of information include:

- Using and checking sequence numbers and checksums or hash totals for series of ordered items to ensure completeness and wholeness
- Doing reasonableness checks on types of information in designated fields
- Performing manual and automatic text checks on presence of records, subprograms, paragraphs, or titles
- Checking for unexecutable code and mismatched conditional transfers in computer programs

A number of control objectives can be applied to ensure the *authenticity* of information, including:

- Confirming account balances, transactions, correct names, deliveries, and addresses
- Checking on genuineness of products
- Segregating duties or dual performance of activities
- Using double-entry bookkeeping
- Checking for out-of-range values

- Using passwords, digital signatures, and tokens to authenticate users at workstations and LAN servers

Control objectives to maintain *confidentiality* include:

- Using cryptography
- Training employees to resist deceptive social engineering attacks to obtain their technical knowledge
- Physically controlling location and movement of mobile computers and disks
- Controlling the use of computers and networks
- Ensuring that resources for protection not exceed the value of what may be lost, especially with low incidence. For example, you may be well advised not to protect against radio frequency emanations in bank ATMs. In a particular situation, consider the cost of shielding and usage control, the paucity of such high-tech attacks, and the limited monetary losses that are possible.

Finally, several control objectives are useful for protecting the *possession* of information. These include:

- Using copyright, patent, and trade secret laws
- Implementing physical and logical use limitation methods
- Preserving and examining computer audit logs for evidence of stealing
- Using file labels
- Inventorying tangible and intangible assets
- Etching identification on computer equipment
- Using distinctive colors and labels on disk jackets
- Assigning ownership to organizational information assets

Again, the effectiveness of these control objectives depends on how smart the practitioner is about implementing them. A good fisherman, for example, does not plunk a bare hook on the end of a string into any nearby water to catch a fish. While the technique may be correct, the implementation is sadly lacking.

HOW TO USE THE GUIDES
TO THE CONTROL PRINCIPLES

The best time to select control objectives is during and after baseline analysis. This allows you to base your selections on your recommendations, security demands revealed by the analysis, and/or the availability of the recommended due-care controls. In some cases, you may need to consider only one control, or one type of control with a choice of implementation methods; in other cases, you will need to select several control objectives to address one vulnerability. To make the appropriate selections, you will need to ask a number of questions concerning the application of the control. I suggest using the 27 control principle guides that I provide at the end of this chapter, along with the descriptions of them. The following twelve key questions to select control objectives and determine how to implement them most effectively summarize the evaluation.

Twelve Questions

1. Is the control reasonably priced, reasonably implemented, complete and consistent, and used successfully by others?
2. Does the control have an acceptable impact on operations for sufficiently long periods and with minimal adverse effects and human attention?
3. Will the people constrained by the control tolerate, fear, and respect it?
4. Are the consequences acceptable when activation, deactivation, reset, recovery, and replacement occur, and can an administrator securely stop the control with acceptable fail-safe and default capabilities?
5. Is the control instrumented for necessary and legal reporting of its activation and operation states, and resistant to repudiation?
6. Can it be effective without being kept secret, but capable of secret operation if desired?
7. Can the administrator apply the control with few or no exceptions and operate it independent of those people who are controlled by it?
8. Can it be more effective by making it unpredictable and by making it more tamper resistant?
9. Are their other independent backup control objectives forming a defense in depth, and can each be effective if others fail?
10. Is the control available from a trustworthy source, and is somebody accountable for its successful operation?
11. Will it effectively serve secondary functions as well, and are entrapment, deception, and personal privacy addressed?
12. Will it be positioned to be effective relative to the locations of threats and the threatened information assets?

You may have to make some trade-offs to deal with conflicting issues among these guiding questions. Achieving a satisfactory answer to one question may preclude achieving another. You may also want to use a scoring method to compare various control objectives and determine the best choices. These questions are also useful to apply in the requirements, design, and development stages of new control objectives and control products. I have done this for several commercial security companies that were developing new safeguard products.

DESCRIPTIONS OF THE GUIDES

In this section, I describe the 27 control principle guides and provide scenarios for each to illustrate how criminals may take advantage of a failure to follow these guides. These guides, which are grouped into 14 sets to facilitate comprehension, are actually updates and additions to the 20 principles that I originally described in 1985. This is not, by any means, an exhaustive list. I recently added the unpredictability principle and guide, and there are undoubtedly others that will be discovered and added in the coming years.

Using these guides does not necessarily guarantee that the control objectives will be effective, or that vulnerabilities will be reduced, but using them will certainly result in a better selection of control objectives, and a more robust security implementation. I believe that a control that adheres to many of the principles in these guides is likely to be more successful than one that does not. Some of the control guides are mutually exclusive; that is, total adherence to one guide may preclude (at least partially) the implementation of another, or weaken the effectiveness of another. Thus, the security practitioner's experience and good judgment play a major role in determining the successful application of the guides.

Guide 1: Cost Effectiveness, Due-Care Value, Completeness, Consistency, and Authenticity

As a basic rule of thumb, a control should cost less than the amount of losses that may occur without it. It should not cost any more than it is worth relative to the prices that others have paid for it, or would be willing to pay relative to their use of it in similar circumstances. In some cases, determining the cost/loss trade-off is in itself too costly to justify consideration of the control; in that case, it is better to suffer the potential loss or look for another control that you can more easily cost-justify. In other cases, you may be able to justify the control based entirely on what other prudent organizations in similar circumstances are doing, without regard to cost or by assuming that the others have performed the cost analysis in their selection of the control.

The total cost of a control may be difficult to determine. Some of the factors that you should consider in determining cost include:

- Cost of selecting and acquiring the necessary materials and mechanisms
- Construction and placement
- Necessary modifications to the environment
- Operation and maintenance
- Test, repair, and replacement
- Changes in insurance coverage
- Any reduction in productivity or performance caused by the control
- Cost of settling disputes for using or not using the control

Determining cost effectiveness is an even more difficult task. The controller for one international company that I know received a request for a $200,000 expenditure to install a fire detection and suppression system in a small computer center in one of the company's divisions in another country. Because the computer center had a book value of only $55,000, the expenditure for fire detection seemed outrageous and the controller denied it. However, he failed to understand that the computer center processed monetary currency trading, and routinely handled $50 million each day. The dollars passing through the center were the real issue, not the computer system. The decision was further complicated by the fact that the company maintained a duplicate center as a backup, and could quickly transfer currency trading activities to the backup center. And, the backup center had an elaborate fire protection system. So, was the controller correct in his original analysis and decision to reject the expenditure? Or did the company need two well-protected facilities? What about the issues of employee safety and the company's public reputation or the shareholders' trust? The question of negligence can rear its ugly head in this type of situation. How much is due care worth?

Many control objectives actually reduce operating costs by increasing employee performance and productivity and reducing errors. For example, office entry control can reduce employee idleness that may occur when employees wander at will into other areas for personal conversations or receive casual visitors. Similarly, you can use check digits to correct input data as the users enter data into a computer system, which is less expensive than making corrections after the data have been entered. Thus, to determine the real cost of a control, you may need to calculate the net cost of total expenditures less the savings from using it.

In many cases, however, it is just not possible to determine the real cost of a control and the material losses that it may preclude. That is why meeting a standard of due care should be the primary concern, using others' experience and practice to determine what control objectives are required. Many controls are relatively inexpensive and can be implemented without need for cost analysis. At times, using multiple, relatively inexpensive controls can produce the same level of due care protection as one or two more costly ones.

In addition to considering the cost and due-care value of a security control or practice, you need to ensure that it is complete and works as specified. For example, a fairly common security practice is to reserve test computers for programmers' development activities, restricting them from using production computers. I found that this practice was not completely followed in one organization that I reviewed. The production staff did manage to keep the programmers at bay during the day, but at night, any programmer could—and often did—wander into the operations center to use the production computers.

It is crucial to supply complete specifications, instructions, and training materials for each control that you select for implementation. In addition, you may need to provide a trained staff to operate the control. For example, classifying information for security requires clear instructions to help information owners discern various levels of sensitivity. To test the effectiveness of the instructions, you can ask two people to classify the same information using the instructions, then compare the results to see if they agree (or are at least reasonably close). Be sure to design, build, implement, operate, and maintain control objectives consistently and sufficiently according to their use. Do not, for example, try to apply to individual workers an entry control that is designed to segregate groups of workers. Also, test and document the identity of controls to ensure that they are approved and genuine. Adversaries, such as malicious hackers, may try to replace authentic controls with faulty ones.

Guide 2: High Performance and Sustained, Automatic Operation

A control should perform correctly over a sufficiently sustained lifetime at an effective level relative to activities with which it is associated. For example, you should update or replace an antivirus software package on a frequent basis to maintain protection against newly released viruses. While it is still necessary to detect the Michelangelo virus, it is also necessary to detect the sophisticated macro and polymorphic viruses that are delivered in today's data files. As a general rule, control objectives should function effectively for at least the length of time between audits.

You should be aware of—and willing to accept—the burden on system overhead and the constraints on data rates inflicted by encryption and decryption control objectives. Controls should be as automatic as possible to minimize their reliance on computer users to make control decisions during usage, and they should function effectively in the time scale of the computer environment. Users should not have to wait several seconds for decryption or be forced to make decisions about what to encrypt on a case-by-case basis. Ideally, they should be able to specify such decisions in advance, then allow the computer to encrypt automatically when necessary. Many information system and communication control objectives function in micro- or milliseconds to catch adversaries' automated attacks—much faster than any user could make an informed decision. In general, choose controls that avoid the need for the plodding decision-making of slow humans.

The people who administer and operate controls are clearly the vulnerable link in the chain. Violators can "spoof" or overload controls to wear down a human decision-maker—especially if the control function relies on a fragile human as an active component. Humans have short attention spans; they quickly lose patience or attentiveness without frequent reinforcement of motivation. Computers, on the other hand, perform at the same level continuously, without coffee or comfort breaks, almost forever. In one case, the repeated activation of a detection system caused by an unseen fire prompted the computer operations staff to disable the fire detection control, and the fire suppression system as well. Be sure to consider the human element in all control objectives, not only during routine functioning, but also when anomalies arise or they need special attention (i.e., when a control is violated or needs to be serviced).

Guide 3: Tolerated, Feared, and Respected

The people who are constrained or monitored by a control should tolerate, fear, and respect it. As a general rule, never install a control unless the individuals who are constrained by it will tolerate it; otherwise, they will neutralize it every time. People become frustrated when they see a control in place for one vulnerability but no control over other perceived vulnerabilities. They want to know why the control is necessary, whether it will be effective, and how they will benefit from its use. You must sell people on control objectives before installing the controls.

Gaining support for unpleasant security constraints is tricky. Dr. Mich Kabay, an expert on information security psychology and head of education for the International Computer Security Association, offers good advice. He won the best paper award at the NIST/NSA National Computer Security Conference in 1994 by explaining that you must achieve change in people incrementally by small amounts to accomplish significant attitude or cultural changes. People need reasons for constraints that you put upon them. For example, making respect for control objectives a part of employee job descriptions and annual job performance appraisals is an excellent way to obtain support. The installers of controls must deal with many human complexities and foibles. One company's security trainer told me that his company has a great motivation technique: If you support security, you get to keep your job. That is not exactly what I had in mind when I emphasized positive motivation.

Anyone who disables or neutralizes a control creates a particularly vexing problem, especially if she does it secretly or without notice. The control operators (or information owners) falsely believe that the control is still functioning correctly. In such situations, you need to sensitize the operations staff to be alert to any changes that may indicate that a control is not functioning, or not functioning properly, and, of course, you need to improve the control to prevent future occurrences. Think back to my experience with the COBOL programmers (in Chapter 1), which illustrates the lengths that managers must go to develop positive attitudes about acceptance of control objectives.

Control objectives can have significant deterrent value if violators fear and respect them. If violators do not fear and respect the controls, you may need to remove and replace them. Some criminals, especially hackers, view strong control objectives as a challenge to their skills—a view that can stimulate repeated attacks. Others attack when they encounter "Mickey Mouse" controls that they view as pitifully weak or contrived. Overall, the message from security experts must be, "Yes, we know that you can beat our control objectives with sufficient effort. These control objectives are barriers only to remind you that if you go any farther, you are engaging in shameful and possibly criminal activities." Simple password control objectives, dual-control constraints requiring two people to participate in actions requiring great trust, and simple cryptographic data scrambling are examples of such control objectives that require careful conditioning of people affected by them. I call these *confrontational control objectives,* because they merely confront potential interlopers with the clear message that they are violating the rules by proceeding. Such control objectives can be valuable in dealing with small groups of well-disciplined people. I find that many businesses, government services, and other institutions assume that people will behave themselves and can be trusted most of the time. While this may be true for the great majority of our population, juvenile hackers, career criminals, and extreme advocates often spoil this social trust.

Guide 4: Acceptable Consequences of Activation, Deactivation, Reset, Recovery, and Replacement

When an adversary attacks a control, or an event triggers a control, the control should react appropriately (e.g., detecting a fire and suppressing it). Similarly, a control should not react to any changes of status for which it is not set to activate. If, for example, a computer user accidentally enters an incorrect password, the control should not disconnect the user, at least not on the first occurrence. When you install a control, you need to understand the consequences of activating it, and ensure that it activates in an acceptable manner.

You should also be able to reset a control to its original condition, or reactivate it in a timely manner—all within the range of acceptable cost and effort. You should, for example, be able to replace a computer user's password and token card with minimal disruption to the user or the computer system. If a control is out of service for any reason (e.g., while it is being reset, replaced, or serviced), you need to have some method in place to counter the period of vulnerability; this may be something as simple as training the information users or operators to be especially vigilant or as complex as having a backup control in position to replace the nonfunctioning one. In any case, you need to anticipate such events and plan accordingly because adversaries are always ready to take advantage of a lapse in security. In one case, students in Palo Alto, California spent more than 100 hours monitoring a campus computer, waiting for a maintenance engineer to reset the control objectives after maintenance. Eventually, their patience was rewarded; while the control objectives were deactivated they swooped in and changed their recorded grades.

Individuals that are authorized to deactivate some controls, such as LAN administrators, need special passwords to perform the function. If an authorized individual does have to deactivate a control for any reason, the action should be logged in such a way that unauthorized individuals are unable to detect that the control is not functioning. In addition, it should be impossible, or at least very difficult, for unauthorized individuals to deactivate the control without detection. Control objectives that could cause harm should be reversible, and equipped with appropriate alarms to notify operators of any inability to maintain a fail-safe state. When activated or deactivated, the resulting state of a control should be acceptable with minimal danger to the assets being protected and with minimal adverse consequences. Vendors should deliver new products to customers with the controls activated and require specific deactivation if the controls are not needed or wanted.

If a control can easily be deactivated—particularly if it can be deactivated without detection—it is vulnerable to attack from a reasonably intelligent adversary. The default state of a deactivated control can be dangerous. For example, when power is shut off, should electronic door locks be in a locked or unlocked state? The safety of people on both sides of the door must be considered, as well as the possibility of using some type of notification device or installing override capabilities. No control should endanger humans unless violation of the control could cause them greater harm. Control objectives that restrict human entry to sensitive areas and those that protect from natural disasters are the ones that typically engender such concerns, and the decisions about how to implement them require consensus among the security experts and the individuals or departments likely to be most affected by them.

A violator may activate or subvert a control to distract the victims from observing his primary purposes. He may repeatedly activate a control to induce weary victims to think it is malfunctioning and remove it, or to reset it in a predictable state that the violator can more easily compromise. For example, re-initializing encryption may reset the encryption key to a starting value that the adversary knows or can easily detect. A violator may cause an event, then take advantage of the recovery period while controls are in a weakened or nonfunctioning state. In some cases, the violator can substitute his own Trojan horse control for a control that is being replaced or reinitialized.

Another example illustrates a related problem with controls. A fire started in a paper supply room adjacent to the computer room, and the computer operators did not detect it. The fire activated the ion detectors, a loud horn sounded, and the operators raced over to the control center and shut off the alarm. The operators had been conditioned to do this, because a false alarm had sounded several weeks earlier, causing a dump of costly fire-retardant chemicals under high pressure into the room, nearly splitting the operators' eardrums and blowing dust and everything that was not nailed down into the air. They were determined that it would not happen again. Therefore, when the new event occurred, they stationed an operator at the switch to repeatedly turn off the alarm until they could disconnect the electrical power to the fire detection control to shut it down permanently and avoid the chemical dump. The fire completely destroyed the computer center. If a criminal learned of this incident, he might conclude—accurately—that spoofing might be a successful technique for circumventing the company's control objectives. When control authorities tire of reacting to a control, they are likely to turn it off.

Guide 5: Instrumented, Auditable, and Conforming to Rules of Evidence

Many security controls are inherently instrumented. If you try to pass through a guarded door, the guard yells and calls for help if you do not stop; the control is instrumented. But what about controls that you can not see, like transaction limit controls, that are buried deep inside computers? These controls must be explicitly instrumented to give visible indications that they are working and have been attacked. They may do this by printing or displaying warnings or generating help messages, and recording the violations as evidence of the attack.

Every control must be instrumented in such a way that there is a timely, logged alarm or notice of its deactivation, malfunction, or activation by a change of detected conditions or circumstances. Otherwise, it is not a valid control. The computer recording of the alarm or notice should be acceptable as an ordinary business record under legal rules of evidence, so that it can be used in litigation if necessary. Control logs should be resistant to repudiation by violators of the control objectives. Reporting should be sufficiently timely to mitigate loss as much as is reasonable, and notice must be sufficiently effective to alert an administrator under reasonable circumstances. It should include date, time, administrator's identity, and pertinent circumstances, conditions, and actions taken.

Control administrators should be instructed to record extraordinary circumstances and sign their initials or digital signature in the recordings or logs when significant events occur, and at the beginning and ending of their duty periods. An independent auditor should be able to examine the record at a later time without the aid of an attendant to reconstruct pertinent facts of an event during a particular time period. We should design and install controls anticipating that auditors must test them for compliance and effectiveness at reasonable intervals and at times unknown to the operators or parties constrained by the controls. The tests should artificially invoke conditions that trigger controls, and result in observable consequences that auditors can verify against standards or specifications. In addition, our computer systems should also be designed to periodically test controls and in appropriate cases, to test them each time an application is executed.

With automated crime staring us in the face, we now need to go one step further in control instrumentation. The controls must take action, not merely to report violations, but also to mitigate attacks and possibly even recover from the loss before the administrators even know anything is wrong. Some antivirus software and credit card transaction systems are already doing this.

Guide 6: Design and Application Secrecy Not Required

A security control should not rely on the secrecy of its mechanism or of its presence to be effective. Knowledge of its existence and operation should, however, be limited to as few people as possible. The exception is when the control's primary purpose is deterrence (e.g., monitoring or logging control objectives), in which case, the more people that know of its existence, the better; its operation, however, should still be closely held. In designing and operating control objectives, we always need to assume that our adversaries know as much about the control objectives as we do, yet our control objectives must be effective despite their knowledge. The concept is much like a lock manufacturer who designs door locks to be effective despite burglars who may be among the first to buy one to identify vulnerabilities and design tools to break it. Even when we assume our adversaries know exactly how our control objectives work, it is never a good idea to help them in their quest for knowledge by unnecessarily revealing information about control objectives' operation.

The secrecy of a control objective's operation can be greatly enhanced if you can make it dynamic and variable. If you enhance a control by relying on its secrecy, the secrecy can be expressed in a variable that you can change frequently to make it difficult for adversaries to deduce (see the guide on dynamic control objectives). For example, the well-known DES cryptographic algorithm is public, as is the content of the S-boxes that contain the parameters used in the algorithm. The reasons for the choices of the parameter values are kept secret, however—thereby maintaining the control's ability to protect information.

The military has traditionally relied on the principle of least privilege, which is based on a practice of need-to-know. This principle dictates that the least possible amount of information about control objectives and their mechanisms should be provided to the least number of people or to other processes (i.e., computer programs) to carry out their necessary functions effectively. For example, when a main computer program calls a subroutine to perform a function, it usually must pass data to the subroutine as well. The program does this by passing the memory addresses to the subroutine that indicate where the needed data are stored, and then giving the subroutine use of that part of the memory. The subroutine can, therefore, obtain not only the required data, but also other sensitive data that it does not require. Security is reduced, because the subroutine has to be trusted to the same degree as the main program. The simplest solution is for the main program to impose least privilege by supplying the subroutine with only the data that it absolutely needs to perform its function. At first glance, the principle of least privilege may seem to conflict with the principle of nonreliance on secrecy. The methods and mechanisms of control objectives should indeed be kept as secret as possible, but should not rely on that secrecy to be effective.

Guide 7: Universal Application, with Independent Control and Subject

Always try to apply control objectives with the lowest possible number of exceptions. Controls that have, or require, many exceptions to their features and applications generally are not as strong as those with few exceptions and, therefore, tend to provide a lower level of protection. Exceptions to rules and procedures are probably responsible for a greater number of control failures than any other cause.

Control objectives should be imposed as uniformly and completely as possible over their entire application domain. The primary values of this principle are simplicity, fairness of application, and methodical treatment of exceptions. For example, an aerospace company where I once worked implemented the practice of wearing of badges. Although the practice was supposed to apply to everyone, the executives who worked on "mahogany row" would not be caught dead wearing a badge. As a result, the "worker bees" that made up the remainder of the company were equally reluctant to wear badges. After all, if the executives did not have to wear badges, why should they? Not wearing badges became a status symbol. Employees wore badges to enter the building, then removed them once they were inside. Gradually this practice eroded the badge system until it became unnecessary for anyone to use badges, even to gain building entry. However, the badge requirement was still on the books, acting as a negative rather than positive control.

An incredible impersonation occurred in this pleasant, anonymous, insecure environment. An unemployed engineer who had never worked for the company needed office services as he looked for a new job. He moved into an empty office between two sets of offices occupied by two distantly related departments. He told his neighbors on each side that he was on a special assignment for top management and reported to the department on the other side. Nobody bothered to check his credentials or ask to see a badge. He used telephone, fax, computer, copying, and secretarial services, in some cases borrowing them from a department other than the one he claimed to be in. He submitted lavish travel expense claims with unused employee ID numbers and reputed the few that were questioned, and he charged his meals in the cafeteria to various departments where they were treated as unresolved errors. The two managers of the neighboring departments did not know one another in this huge anonymous company. The scheme worked for several months until one fateful day when one of the managers asked the other to give up office space. You can imagine the conversation. "I thought he was working for you." "Who is that guy?" Embarrassed security and company officials asked the unemployed interloper to quietly leave and never tell anybody what he did. Universal badge wearing was promptly restored as an active control. The value of badge control is usually totally destroyed when even minor exceptions occur. If a badging system is used to control physical entry into sensitive areas, then it should apply universally to all people entering the areas. No one should be allowed to enter without an authorized badge.

In a different type of example, a software development department designed a computer operating system that was initially judged by many computer security researchers to be highly secure. But, when the engineers modified it during implementation to improve its performance and reduce development costs, they introduced errors that resulted in the delivered product being unable to identify exceptions to control objectives, thereby introducing security vulnerabilities. Compromises of this no-exceptions principle are difficult to avoid in practice. When you must make exceptions, you should keep them to a minimum, clearly identify them, and test them for practicality.

Control objectives that organizations do not apply to higher levels of management or that discriminate by level or type of worker, professional, or manager are particularly insidious. In contrast, some control objectives are acceptable at one level but not at another, and an organization is sometimes forced to implement differently at each level. For example, security staff should write security motivation and awareness material in different ways for use by accounting clerks and researchers. Clerks may accept checklists of violations to avoid, but researchers may reject lists of rules and want to know the principles to apply and reasons for constraints.

These are sensitive cultural issues that require careful consideration based on organization history, pilot testing, and evaluation before full-scale application in an organization.

The other part of this principle concerns independence of control objectives and the people they constrain. The people that the organization intends to constrain with the control objectives should not administer the controls. I find that many people do not like control objectives that constrain or monitor them, and if given the opportunity, they will shut off the controls or otherwise neutralize them. For example, it is difficult for organizations to enforce use of standard protocols for programs that activate (open) and execute subprograms if management allows voluntary compliance without consistent monitoring. Programmers are likely to ignore protocol standards if such standards add constraints, complexity, or extra effort to their jobs. Programmers know that the possibility of others discovering coding practices they have buried in their programs is remote. However, if the software that compiles their programs will not accept them unless correct protocols are used, then computer control of their insecure practices can be performed independent of the programmers' efforts, and the adherence to standards will have a greater chance for success. Programmers will often accept constraints imposed by computers more readily than those imposed by management.

It is sometimes impractical to separate the people who are responsible for control objectives from those who are subject to them, especially in small organizations. Multiple or dual control, a technique that requires two or more people to be involved in each control, is an alternative to separation and can offer some advantages over total independence. For example, banks control entry to safe-deposit boxes by using two locks on each box and assigning one key to the customer and one to an employee who is not allowed to be a customer and have a safe-deposit box in the bank. Thus, the bank maintains independence of control objectives from subjects of the control objectives. The same concept should be applied to cryptographic key administration. Two halves of a key are placed in the custody of the computers of two different parties, neither of whom is associated with, or affected by, the content of the messages that are encrypted. Dual control, in which two or more people control the same safeguard, is the other, sometimes-weaker alternative.

Guide 8: Unpredictability

Controls would be far more effective if they were unpredictable. When controls are unpredictable, our adversaries do not know how or when the controls might stop them, and they have difficulty planning or programming their crimes. I consider controls dynamic when we program and set their variable features to change. Even if adversaries know about the existence of the controls and know how they work, they do not necessarily know the current values. One way to accomplish such unpredictability is to change the values frequently under automatic control of a computer. An even better way is to use a random number generator and automatically change controls to use random values (within acceptable ranges) at random times so that no one knows the current values. Weaker static controls have values that are not changed or that remain constant sufficiently long to give adversaries a chance to discover them and plan how to defeat them.

Examples of values that can be changed to make a control dynamic include password values, the number of password entry attempts allowed, monetary value limits to trigger audit or additional constraints, ranges of acceptable values, timeouts, time limits, and authorization limits. Changing these and many other values makes controls far more effective. Credit card processors have become quite sophisticated in transaction pattern analysis where the types, sizes, and locations of transactions examined are highly variable. Credit card fraudsters can not examine enough transactions to predict their chances of being detected.

Criminals must be able to rely on knowing and anticipating the exact environment and circumstances for the crime to succeed. This means that the victims must act predictably, the environment and events must be predictable, and the assets involved must be exactly as predicted; otherwise, the criminal faces apprehension and possible incarceration. Criminals are also in trouble if they are surprised during a crime, as well as by unpredictable changes in circumstances. Surprise often has a disastrous effect on the commission of a crime, but less often an unpredictable event may work in the criminal's favor, for example, by revealing a favorable vulnerability.

Cybercrime is a particularly risky business because of the complexity of computers and their resultant unpredictability. In many cases, the benefits of cybercrime are simply not worth the criminal's effort to figure out sufficient details of the computer operation and environment. Unfortunately, criminals are not always rational about choosing their victims, and may take a chance and perpetrate the crime anyway. Criminals have told me that they would have chosen easier, less complex, and safer ways to accomplish their objectives if they had an option. A computer attack is often the choice of last resort. In spite of a negative cost benefit, irrational criminals may still go for it, and the victim can still lose. Thus, we need to defend against both rational and irrational perpetrators.

Two of the crime cases that I recounted earlier illustrate the value of unpredictable controls. The branch bank manager who stole millions by making sure that no single theft in the central computer exceeded the fixed transaction limit control was detected through his own careless error rather than the bank's predictable control objectives. Until the fateful day when he accidentally exceeded the $1 million transaction limit and triggered an audit, the manager was successfully plundering accounts and covering the thefts by moving funds among accounts. Although the bank's control objectives were working, they were ineffective against the nimble, knowing branch manager because he knew exactly what the transaction limit was. He had previously worked in the central computer organization that developed the control objectives. The controls merely constrained the amounts that he could safely steal at any one time. Of course, the value limit control was responsible for finally triggering the audit that caught the perpetrator, but only because he had failed to avoid it on that one occasion. Making the limit control unpredictable would probably have saved the bank 18 months of loss from the manager's use of this technique.

The case of the bank teller who stole $3 million in a year similarly illustrates the value of unpredictable controls. He covered his activities by distributing the shortages between two sets of accounts, taking care to move the shortages back and forth before the bank printed each set of monthly statements so that customers did not notice anything amiss. He was successful because he knew exactly how the system worked. The auditors always gave him two weeks notice of upcoming audits, always performed exactly the same routine in exactly the same orderly steps, and always asked him to assist them in the audit. The teller watched this routine for fifteen years before he finally took criminal advantage of it. Although the teller was caught, it was through no success of the auditors. Instead, another bank employee saw him placing big bets at the race track and reported it to the bank management. When the bank investigators confronted him, the teller admitted the embezzlement. He told me that he knew that he would get caught soon, since his record keeping was so complex that he was losing track of the amounts and accounts. He had records written on slips of paper stuffed in his pockets, his desk, and in the taxi he drove at night (in a fruitless effort to catch up on his debts). As we chatted in his prison cell, he agreed that the secret of his success was the predictability of the auditors and the accounting systems, as well as the nonchalance of the other tellers, his manager, and the customers he stole from. He also told me that the first thing an embezzler must do is beat the auditors. This is part of predicting the circumstances for the crime.

Here is one more case of a more personal nature. In 1912, the State of Minnesota convicted my grandfather of bank fraud for making unsecured loans to his farmer friends trying to save their farms in a financial depression. He had a secret means of knowing the day that the state bank examiners would arrive, and would "cook" the books the night before a scheduled visit. In the third year of the embezzlement, a new examiner popped in unannounced and caught him. He could not predict this surprise event. The state bank examiners were furious that he had deceived them for three years. He served two years of a ten-year prison sentence before his farmer friends, family, and townspeople managed to obtain his parole.

VARIABLE CONTROL OBJECTIVES

In each of these cases, accurate prediction was the primary means of criminal success, and unpredictability was the primary cause of criminal failure. There is a lesson here for us. Unpredictable circumstances and environments can discourage and stop crime more often than not. Unfortunately, computer technologists who design systems that are susceptible to crime may overlook this fact. Computer technologists deal successfully with the repeatable performance of computers, but do not understand misbehaving and irrational people. They try to make systems predictable, not unpredictable. Therein lies the fatal flaw, because security in computers is designed by technologists to achieve rational, predictable performance, and that is exactly what criminals who attack computers count on for success. So, is the solution to put security under the control of unpredictable people to make safeguards unpredictable, or to automate the safeguards to make them predictable? I believe that the best solution is to make automated safeguards predictable for owners and unpredictable for perpetrators.

Suppose an organization frequently changes the limit in a value limit control so that a potential criminal does not know what it is, can not find out what it is, and can not change it (at least not without great difficulty). This action has little or no effect on users making transactions, but it can disturb the surveillance process because of the increased frequency of checking that may be required. If auditors carry out surveillance, they can be overburdened at times if the limit is low, but be underworked at other times if the system raises the limit. Alternatively, suppose auditors change the surveillance strategy so that transactions are audited occasionally, even when they fall below any value limit. If the auditor does this, the criminal is foiled by the doubly unpredictable practices. In addition, we can make control changes occur very rapidly automatically. We can use a pseudo-random number generator so that no one ever knows the limits. We can also change the range of limits (although possibly not as frequently). Computer technologists, security people, and auditors may find such methods to be quite unsettling, since they are generally accustomed to predictability. On the other hand, such techniques can increase the effectiveness of computer controls, possibly by an order of magnitude or more.

We do, however, need to exercise caution in applying unpredictable values to controls. For example, if we vary the limits in transactions value limit controls by only small amounts, we minimize the interference with auditing practices while still achieving the goal of confounding the efforts of potential violators.

One obvious alternative for a criminal confronted by a powerful, unpredictable control is to incapacitate the control. Sometimes, criminals gain root or super-user privileges to an entire system and can incapacitate the control objectives even though this typically requires attacking the layer of safeguards that protect root or administrative privileges. If, however, the system itself were internally unpredictable, the attacker would find it difficult, if not impossible, to gain such privileges in the unfamiliar environment.

VARIABLE SYSTEMS ARCHITECTURE

Another powerful protection to consider in addition to dynamic controls is to make the programs in computers more variable, and to make certain functions nonrepeatable in the same way, as long as the results are correct. This adds protection from criminal modifications such as computer viruses and other Trojan horse attacks at the object program level. To make entire systems unpredictable, designers could force the computer program compiler to produce different object code each time the source program is compiled; the object code would, however, always perform exactly as specified in the source code. Criminals attempting to write programs to modify the code in the computer would have great difficulty and would need to seek out the source code to make changes, then wait for the next compilation. The designer could achieve dynamic object code by having the compiler reorder independent parts of the object program and use equivalent commands and algorithms. It could add B plus A instead of A plus B (using mathematical commutativity, the answer is the same), put program constants in different places, and use different coded names for subprograms. Unfortunately, this could make the contents of computers complex and unpredictable (even though the output would be the same) for everyone—good guys and criminals alike. The solution must be modified, therefore, to make computers less predictable for crooks, including malicious hackers and computer virus writers, and perfectly predictable for authorized users.

The solution to this is to have the designers provide tools to mask the unpredictability of the system "internals" by using conversion or transition tables. Unfortunately, a persevering criminal could also use those tools, unless they were made variable, thus requiring higher-level mechanisms, and on and on in never-ending cycles. The systems staffs would become exhausted or unwilling to participate in such a complex, time-consuming game. One or two layers of unpredictability might be sufficient to discourage attacks, depending on the perseverance of the adversary, the value of his criminal prize, his skills and knowledge, and the willingness and dedication of the systems staffs to create and maintain the more complex systems.

For practical purposes, let's assume that there are enough potential miscreants without the capacity or will to go beyond a system architecture with two layers of unpredictability. This might make it worthwhile to pursue the development of this unpredictable system architecture. Increasing numbers of people who are using and being served by computers do not have the skills and knowledge to modify the internals of the computers that they use to cause trouble. At the same time, malicious hackers can produce automated crime packages to do the dirty work and make the packages available through the Internet. But let us also assume that possession of such packaged crimes will be considered a criminal offense, which may discourage their use (much like the criminalization of possessing burglary tools). We probably need only two levels of internal unpredictability to make the application control objectives, file names and content, and the operating system and its control objectives unpredictable.

System designers and implementers are likely to be somewhat resistant to the changes required to make systems unpredictable because of the inherent complexity of such systems and difficulty in operating and maintaining them. Systems are so complex that they barely work now, without the added complexity of chaotic code and data, and the addition of complex code in the tools to decipher them. Alternatively, we can introduce some relatively simple, small changes that achieve an acceptable level of unpredictability, such as those that I suggested previously in the crime examples. The following suggestions can help to achieve automatic unpredictability in computers; some function within the operating system and application programs, while others function at the control level.

- Frequently change the names of internal data files, both in the directories and in the calling sequences in the operating system and applications. This requires differentiating externally used and internally used files.
- Frequently change the names of computer programs and subprograms or objects both in tables and in calling sequences.
- Change the locations in random access memory where programs are stored and executed. This requires location-independent programming, or recompiling and reassembling at different locations and in different orders.
- Change the locations of constants and variables and the addresses where they are used.
- Use equivalent but different mathematical calculations employing commutativity.
- Introduce dummy data, branch transfers, or instructions to change the lengths of programs, with matching changes in length parameters and hash totals.
- Use variable control values, for example, for password-attempt and timeout limits, value limits, and reasonableness test values, and then change the values frequently using random number generators.
- Introduce variable initial or pre-logon screen formats with minimal information except for inclusion of a "no trespassing" warning banner to confront potential intruders.
- Encrypt particularly sensitive programs or parts of programs and data until immediately before use, and encrypt again immediately after use. Keys can be generated on the fly and stored inaccessibly except to authorized users with secret entry codes.

We can also achieve unpredictability in procedural ways. One of the best auditors in information technology once told me that she could not audit the work of the 100-plus programmers in her bank. But she was very effective by conducting random examinations of program code at varying depths of detail so that the programmers were kept off balance by not knowing where and at what level she would look next. She also continued to periodically prove that she had the skills to effectively examine their code. The following items are suggestions for achieving unpredictability using procedural control objectives.

- Conduct unannounced audits or unexpected examinations of records using different methods each time.
- Use variable routing of communications to make eavesdropping and traffic analysis difficult.

- Require password changes at unpredictable times.
- Conduct unannounced searches for sensitive information that users have left unattended or in insecure form and location.
- Perform unannounced checks for pirated software or other information in the possession of people who may be unauthorized to have it.

In conducting these latter procedural practices, be sure to avoid overtly deceiving people. Unfortunately, some information security specialists use deceptive "tiger team" testing to identify security performance vulnerabilities. This type of deception destroys the trust needed between users and security practitioners to encourage reporting and mitigating loss incidents and poor security practices. In contrast, it is acceptable to withhold some information from people for security purposes, such as planned times of inspections, password changes, or reports of loss incident details, as long as it does not jeopardize their mental well-being or jobs. Management should always obtain the informed consent of employees to be subjects of surprise inspections. Good judgment and ethical treatment always have precedence.

Guide 9: Tamper Resistance

Tampering consists of methods that make control objectives ineffective to protect information. Less obvious tampering methods include replacing an authentic control with a modified, fake, or weakened control and repudiating control actions and logs. Tampering also includes delaying activation; overloading with violations (spoofing); and modifying or attacking during a control shutdown period (see Paul Baran's report, *Security Secrecy and Tamper-Free Consideration*, RM-3765 PR, published by the Rand Corporation way back in 1964). Criminals may also tamper with the vulnerable instrumentation of a control or its power source. If there is no one present to take action when a control is triggered and sounds an alarm, a criminal may be successful even if the control works correctly.

We can enhance tamper resistance by placing controls in protected domains, creating controls to secure control objectives, using cryptographic techniques, and requiring additional passwords to administer control objectives. Many criminals do not have the skills and knowledge to attack technical controls and must rely on other, more expert criminals to instruct them or provide crime scripts and tools, such as hackers do through their electronic bulletin boards and Web sites. Therefore, we should make control objectives resistant to analysis and neutralization by more sophisticated enemies as well. Control objectives, especially dynamic ones, must be sufficiently tamper-resistant to discourage adversaries' attacks or to convince attackers to pursue other targets. Making control objectives tamper-proof (in contrast to making them tamper-resistant)— that is, to make control objectives perfectly secure from attack—is either not possible or too costly. Avoid attempting perfection, and for reasons of liability and truthfulness, never claim that a control is tamper-proof.

The news and trade media, as well as the Internet, offer a great deal of information about how to successfully violate control objectives. I remember one article that appeared in the *London Sun* newspaper about how an enlisted army man had managed to cheat a telephone company using the popular Green cash cards used in pay telephones throughout the United Kingdom. The reporter of the story described the demonstration and how he participated in it, but purposely did not reveal the simple method until he published his second article. In the meantime, I called my friend Donald Davies, the top cryptographer in Europe, to discuss the case. We surmised that the perpetrator tampered with the card by freezing it to resist the heating unit in the telephone card device. (The heat deforms the code pattern pressed into the plastic card surface as service is being used, causing a subtraction of value from the impressed value that was paid for the card.) The head of security at the telephone company subsequently revealed that the perpetrator's tampering technique was to paint the back of the card with nail polish. This does not work, but the perpetrator had deceived the journalist into believing it.

Guide 10: Compartmentalization, Defensive Depth, Isolation, and Least Common Mechanism

Compartmentalizing controls is important. Do not think of each control as functioning in isolation. Control objectives should work in concert with other control objectives so that failure of one control does not result in a successful attack or loss of the others. For example, one control can be duplicated several times, and applied to various sets of circumstances or assets to accomplish compartmentalization. The analogy useful here is to the watertight compartments that designers build into a ship so that a leak in one or a few compartments will not sink it. We can compartmentalize the physical security of a computer system by installing dampers and exhaust fans in various air ducts within a building to limit the spread of harmful gases and smoke. Defensive depth is another similar tactic; the failure of one control causes a perpetrator to face another one before he succeeds in reaching his target.

We can achieve defensive depth by implementing a sequence of controls that will be serially encountered by a perpetrator who is working toward a specific target. An attacker may give up when he faces one control after another. The number of controls in the sequence should be consistent with the need for protection, since defensive depth can become costly. For example, physical entry to a sensitive computer operations area, such as the magnetic media library, should require passing through the highest number of entry control stations in the building that houses the data processing function. The violation of one control station should immediately alert a security administrator and result in reinforcement of the other controls. Adding controls for defensive depth alone may not be cost effective, but we can often replace one expensive control with simpler, more flexible serial control objectives.

When you apply this principle, be sure to analyze the role of control objectives in relation to other safeguards and their environments. Perpetrators seldom perform only a single act or violate only a single control in attempting to reach their ultimate goals. Violators often engage in many independent efforts at once, in which they embed sequences of dependent, sequential acts. For example, a violator may make simultaneous attacks on an organization's payroll and accounts receivable systems. If he is forced to encounter a sequence of control objectives, he may attack the controls by starting at the beginning of the series, within the series, or at the end. Thus, we need to evaluate each control relative to the other control objectives that are in the same environment or that protect the same target.

You should also be able to isolate a control in its environment in such a way that it can be individually tested, evaluated, and repaired or replaced. Finally, controls that must act in concert or serially should not be dependent upon the same source or resource for their functioning. If they are dependent on the alert actions of a single person, the same electrical power or communication source, or the correctness of the same calculations, they may be vulnerable to a single source of failure.

Guide 11: Assigned Accountability and Trustworthy Source

Each control should have an "owner," a trusted person whose job performance is measured, in part, by the correct functioning and effectiveness of the control. When I review a client's control, the first thing I do is identify it and ask whose job is on the line if this control fails. The "owner" of the control should be in a position to monitor and administer it. Dual or separated responsibilities may be advisable for major security tasks such as making large funds transfers more secure. In banking, the *maker, checker, signer* concept requires one person to execute a transaction, another to check its integrity and authenticity, and a third to watch and authorize the first two. I saw this control dramatically demonstrated at the money exchange desk in the Beijing Holiday Inn. One clerk received the money and counted it; another recounted and deposited it in a box and calculated the exchange amount. A third clerk recalculated the exchanged amount, counted out the new money from another box, and handed it to a fourth clerk; she recounted it and handed it to me. A fifth, sharp-eyed supervisor stood behind the four clerks watching, ever watching. Each clerk used both her own abacus and an electronic calculator. Labor is cheap, and crime is expensive, in China.

In many cases, we protect high-value assets with relatively low-cost but possibly complex controls, which can hide a multiplicity of vulnerabilities. We must put great trust in the suppliers of the controls. For example, a large corporation would not want to entrust its important information security to a control product developed by a two-person start-up firm of hackers working out of their parents' garage, no matter how good the product is. Security product suppliers should have employees bonded and carry insurance in favor of the customers (some vendors carry insurance but only to protect themselves). When purchasing controls, be sure that the vendor escrows any secret components of the product (such as software source code) and its specifications with a trusted third party, and check into the supplier's financial state, owners, other customers and suppliers, and background. Shun any companies that hire notorious hackers or offer their products publicly as challenges for testing attacks (see Chapter 7 on hackers).

Guide 12: Multiple Functions and Prudent Entrapment

We usually apply a control to perform one or two of the eleven specific security functions among the choices of avoidance, deterrence, prevention, and so on. However, the control may also serve other functions as well, which need to be considered and exploited as part of its value. Choose a control based on its primary functions, but also consider its value based on additional ones. For example, a prevention or detection control also has some deterrent value, especially if it is highly visible. We may also consider avoidance control objectives, which separate assets from threats or threats from assets, to have prevention or correction values. When evaluating two or more controls that have the same primary function value, choose the one with the additional value among its other functions.

We need to give the technique of entrapment special consideration because it can have strong negative, as well as positive, effects. An entrapment control objective entices would-be adversaries to engage in attempts to attack or cause loss in such a way that they may be more easily caught and proven guilty. Many people believe that entrapment is unethical in some ways. Going to extremes of entrapment is certainly unethical and probably illegal; some legal jurisdictions outlaw various types of entrapment. Victims have lured hackers into computer systems and given them harmless challenges in order to identify them for prosecution. They call this the *padded cell technique.* (We all know about the detective movie ploy of keeping a person talking on the telephone long enough to trace the call.) Entrapment becomes unethical when the bait is so attractive and the opportunity is so blatant that it tempts victims beyond a reasonable level of normal resistance. The presence of any control may have an entrapment value by luring attackers with the challenge of beating it. Therefore, you should consider the positive and negative entrapment values of each control.

Entrapment is useful for making computers more secure when a large number of known vulnerabilities can not be protected with available control resources. The strategy of passive computer entrapment is to make a few of the system vulnerabilities attractive to potential violators. These vulnerabilities are then heavily and regularly monitored to detect any attempts at compromise. Thus, a perpetrator attempting an attack is likely to choose one of the weaknesses and will be detected and stopped. (This is also called the *honey pot technique* and is described in the next chapter on tactics.)

Passive entrapment has several drawbacks. First, it is based on the assumption that the potential perpetrator is rational and has thoroughly studied a number of possible vulnerabilities before attacking. The violator must consider at least one of the vulnerabilities set up for entrapment in order for the method to work. And the success of this strategy depends on the perpetrator having at least latent motives, skills, knowledge, and authority presumed by the security designers (he is playing your game instead of your playing his game). This is not always a valid assumption. Do not inadvertently entrap an employee. Sound management principles dictate that a manager should never assign an individual to a position of trust that exceeds his capacity to resist the temptation to violate that trust.

Guide 13: Position for Effective Use

It is often necessary to position controls close to the assets to be protected, or to place the controls between the assets and sources of threats. For example, a bank stations its guard at the front door, close to the tellers and vault, not a block away. We must also place controls in positions where they can be defended. In a computer system, attackers may use the strategy of changing information after it is created or acquired in one place and before the time of its use in another place (this is called time of computation/time of use or TOC/TOU). In a series of processing activities, transactions, or movements of information assets, we should place controls in the best positions in the stream of events where they can do the most good.

We must protect information at times and in places where it is vulnerable. For example, we should apply a control both at the time of creation or entry of data into a system and at the time of use. The first placement is to protect the authenticity of the data, while the latter placement protects its integrity from the time and place of its entry to the time and place of its use. We may use the same controls in both places, or use different ones at either end of the process. Integrity and authenticity control objectives, such as reasonableness and sequence controls, are important in both input and usage locations, while utility and availability control objectives are most important at the time of data usage. We need confidentiality and possession control objectives throughout the life cycle of sensitive data. If we are free to place a control in more than one position, then other factors being equal, we should place it where it is secure from attack.

Guide 14: Transparency

One of the many desirable attributes of security control objectives is transparency. I frequently complain in security meetings about the speakers who say that controls should be easy to use. They should not be easy to use; they should be transparent, so that users need not overtly initiate them. It is acceptable for us to see them or sense their presence for deterrent purposes, but any interference required or extra efforts by those people affected or controlled should be avoided as much as possible. For example, it would be nice to dispense with passwords and authentication of computer users in some settings. We might put the trusted users and their computers in an isolated environment, and hold each user accountable for his own identifiable work in ways that do not require separate records. But we are unlikely to achieve this utopia in cyberspace—at least not until we have universal and invisible cryptographic protection. Security control objectives should be like the Cheshire Cat in *Alice in Wonderland*—the cat is there and functioning, but only the smile is visible.

CONCLUSION

Hopefully, by this time you realize that there is much more involved in effective security than selecting and implementing control objectives based on checklist items or control objective standards. Controls will only be effective if we carefully design, deploy, and maintain them using the 27 guides I described in this chapter. The control objectives are critical factors in the deadly earnest war that we conduct with information violators. We must think like our adversaries and constantly defend ourselves against them. As we gain more loss experience and technology continues to advance, we will have more insights and more ideas for adding to this list of principles and guides.

Checklist of Control Guide Principles

- ☑ Cost effectiveness
- ☑ Due-care value
- ☑ Completeness and consistency
- ☑ High performance
- ☑ Sustainable operation
- ☑ Automatic function
- ☑ Tolerated, feared, and respected
- ☑ Acceptability of consequences
- ☑ Secure override and failsafe
- ☑ Acceptable default
- ☑ Instrumentation and auditability
- ☑ Non-repudiation as legal evidence
- ☑ Avoidance of secrecy dependence
- ☑ Secrecy applicability
- ☑ Universality of application
- ☑ Independence of control and subject
- ☑ Unpredictability
- ☑ Tamper-resistant
- ☑ Compartmentalizable
- ☑ Isolatable
- ☑ Least common mechanism
- ☑ Accountability
- ☑ Trustable source
- ☑ Multiplicity of functions
- ☑ Control of entrapment and deception
- ☑ Positional for effective use
- ☑ Transparent

14

Tactics for Effective Information Security

The information in this chapter is derived from my findings during my many years of experience in performing information security reviews for large organizations around the world. My approach to security differs somewhat from that of other practitioners because, unlike most of the others, I can apply the knowledge that I have gained over the years from personal interviews with computer criminals. In this chapter, I apply that knowledge in recommending tactics for dealing with these adversaries. I focus largely on the topics of security during dangerous organization changes, the changing security needs for confidentiality and classification, good enough cryptography, and authenticating users. I also discuss the dangers of testing security, protection from social engineering and gullibility, limitations of technical security and other tactical values that are rarely if ever presented in security literature. I begin this chapter by addressing tactics for dealing with close-range topics, such as reacting to a loss, that are likely to face all information security practitioners—and most information owners—at some time in their career. Then, in the next chapter, I address the strategies that pertain to the goals of an entire organization.

From a tactics standpoint, information security is concerned with protecting information from accidental and intentional losses, and for achieving a standard of due care rather than trying to use security to add strategic value to the organization. We base the selection of security controls on threats, vulnerabilities, and loss experience that occur during our use of information, primarily while that information is in electronic form. Before automation, traditional industrial security specialists and auditors focused their efforts on protecting printed information in manual systems and documented their findings in the industrial security literature such as that published by the American Society of Industrial Security, the American Institute of Certified Public Accountants, and the Institute of Internal Auditors. Today, however, we focus on the vulnerabilities caused by advanced information technology.

INFORMATION SECURITY CONTROLS FOR ORGANIZATION CHANGES

Although information security is always important, it may play an even more crucial role at times of high stress within organizations. Businesses often have special cause for concern about an increase in information-related losses during periods of change because of the additional stress that change causes among employees and management. Stress occurs when there is uncertainty of job longevity, changes in management and objectives, and changes in productivity and profits. Such changes result from:

- reengineering
- downsizing
- upsizing
- mergers or acquisitions
- rapid changes in markets or the economy
- litigation
- organized labor actions

Changes in computer or communications services or computer equipment upgrading may also cause stress. Workers and managers react differently under stress—individually and collectively—but are often unpredictable, and sometimes irrational and potentially dangerous.

During these periods of change, information security practitioners need to take extra precautions against the increase in potential threats to the organization and its assets, particularly to the fragile information infrastructure. Disruption is sometimes a good cover for crime, and is always a source of errors, omissions, and accidents. Current and former employees may cause losses out of disgruntlement or in conspiracies that result in wasted work time, harassment, slowdowns and strikes, larceny and fraud, sabotage, privacy invasions, or espionage. Outsiders such as hackers, associates of employees, customers, suppliers, and professional criminals may take advantage of the changes and unrest to engage in attacks against the organization.

In some cases, changes and the resulting periods of instability may even reveal ongoing frauds or larceny, which are also disrupted by the changes. Successful crimes require predictable environments, and when those environments change, the crimes may fall apart. Thus, security practitioners should be particularly alert during periods of instability to detect signs of anomalous events that may be indicative of ongoing crime. For example, in a city government, a programmer added a control to a new version of an accounts payable system to detect and report payments of identical amounts in double payments. The next time that the city ran the system, the printer rapidly ran out of paper from printing the double payments in an ongoing fraud. The perpetrator was temporarily changing a payee address to his own in another city under the same name as the valid payee. He was sending duplicate checks to each address under a $13 million progressive payments contract. This unexpected discovery illustrates the security value of control changes that are unknown and unanticipated by perpetrators.

Periods of Instability Can Lead to Crime

Trusted people attempting to solve intense personal problems are the sources of much computer crime in the workplace. Greed and the desire to live beyond one's means, while often identified by law enforcement and criminal justice people as the primary motives, are rarely the reasons for business crime. (My interviews with more than 200 computer criminals and the research of the late Donald Cressey, a noted criminal psychologist, both support this finding.) Managers must be aware of motives in their treatment of trusted information technologists and computer users with authority to use the powerful and fragile computers in the organization. For example, this sensitivity makes providing confidential advisory services (to help employees solve their personal problems) an important information security control, especially under adverse organizational conditions.

We may produce significant upheavals and discontent when we change the way in which we use computers and communications, advance to new versions of systems, centralize or decentralize computers, change vendors, and outsource services. Converting systems to account for the year 2000, for example, may trigger unpleasant events. The case of a contract programmer that was terminated by a credit union illustrates the chaos that can result from a single personnel change. The credit union went through a nightmare when they terminated the programmer's contract. He changed the names of two files in the demand deposit accounting program and attempted to extort the organization to win back the contract ("What, your system will not work? If you retain me again, I can fix it."). It took a criminal prosecution and two weeks of downtime to find and correct the change. (By the way, the judge in the appeal overturned the programmer's computer crime conviction on the basis that simply changing two words could not possibly cause the damage that the victim claimed!) Management should have known how dependent the organization was on that single programmer and solved the dependency problem before taking the action to terminate the contract. Programmers are usually in very high positions of trust and must be treated appropriately.

In another case, an organization gave the entire second shift of computer operators two weeks' termination notice. The employees decided that the termination was unreasonable, so they piled the tapes and disks in the middle of the computer room and urinated on them just before they set the place on fire. As a result, the company invoked its disaster recovery plan, which delayed the layoff because management had more important problems to deal with. Normal intelligence gathering activities should have alerted company management to the fact that the second-shift operators were capable of violence and should have been extra careful in dealing with them, possibly by gaining their support to solve the problems that led to the need for the layoff.

Security Controls for Dangerous Times

In the following sections, I present a list of actions that may be warranted under circumstances of organization change.

PERSONNEL MEASURES

Participation.   It is often advantageous to engage key people in security functions or to make them part of the transition activity. This can improve employee morale, especially among highly trusted, indispensable employees such as systems programmers.

Informants. It is sometimes useful to engage informants, on both formal and informal levels, to assess the degree of discontent among employees and determine if any overtly hostile actions may be forthcoming. In most cases, an informal arrangement with trusted employees willing to report unusual activities in their work areas is sufficient, but some special situations may require the use of licensed investigative services experienced in this type of work.

Coordinators. Security coordinators within the organization's business units should be specially trained to be alert for any unusual activities or reactions among the staff and managers that may indicate extreme dissatisfaction and possible attacks.

Rewards. Offer rewards, such as bonuses, for special achievements or dedicated service. For example, many companies reward employees who accomplish required tasks before a layoff occurs or who remain in their jobs until job termination dates.

Termination. Extend or renew procedures for terminating employment such as conducting exit interviews, using formal termination agreements, and retrieving all keys, tokens, and company equipment. Also be sure to change passwords and other security codes as employees are terminated.

Counseling. Offer special job and career counseling and outplacement or alternative employment opportunities. Offer and renew notices about confidential employee services for personal problem solving.

Promotions. Engage in promotional efforts, emphasizing ethics, trust, self-esteem, and importance of preserving one's career as more important than current job changes.

Authenticity. Establish authentication procedures to verify the identity of outside callers and e-mail sources in order to resist possible social engineering. Such controls include callbacks and use of password or pass phrase exchanges. Train employees who interface to outsiders to be more cautious about deceptive practices.

DOCUMENTATION

Policies and standards. Organizations can design or modify their policies and standards to accommodate periods of change. For example, it is always advisable to review, and if necessary revise, and republish policy documents and employee guidelines. If the organizational security policy is based on the traditional CIA foundation, it probably does not cover a multitude of dangerous behaviors, such as stealing copies of information, misrepresenting information or people, and repudiation, thereby giving miscreants the opportunity to argue that their behavior does not violate organizational policy.

Monitoring.   Begin, or expand, the current policy of monitoring e-mail messages, paper mail, voice communications, and work areas. Be sure to obtain written informed consent from subject employees and managers prior to beginning or expanding the monitoring activities. Merely warning the employees that monitoring is imminent, without obtaining signatures, is not sufficient to avoid accusations of privacy violations in some legal jurisdictions. Also carefully consider the cost and liability of monitoring. You may find that sporadic or occasional monitoring is sufficient to maintain security, or that you need to monitor only when there is cause for suspicion of wrongdoing. In addition, you may want to use some automated methods, such as indecent-word searches of electronic documents, to sample electronic documents and e-mail messages.

Records.   Record, analyze, and file intelligence and loss experience information for future use. The information must be handled in ways that preserve it for possible litigation purposes.

Retention.   Establish standards and guides for retaining (and destroying) specific types of information. Remember that it is often very difficult to completely destroy copies of specific information in automated systems.

Possession.   Limit distribution and possession of sensitive documents such as telephone directories, addresses, organization charts, plans, manuals, contracts, and software to trusted employees within the organization, and keep track of such distribution.

Absence.   Be sure to enforce vacation and termination policies.

LOSS MITIGATION

Unpredictability.   One of the best ways for organizations to mitigate loss, as I discussed in Chapter 13, is to ensure that sensitive functions and conditions are unpredictable. You can do this by varying transaction amount limits, password entry attempts, workstation timeouts, and so forth.

Systems documentation.   You should be sure to thoroughly document systems operations and maintenance, and keep the documentation complete and up-to-date at all times. You can store one copy of the information in a secure on-site location, and keep a backup copy at a safe off-site location. Be sure that the identity, location, and availability of key software maintenance staff is available for reference when needed, along with contact information for hardware and software vendors. Back up copies of cryptographic keys for non-transitory ciphertext used throughout the organization, and put these functions under the direct control of high-level management. Take an inventory of your vital and timely data and software and make at least two backup copies. Copies should be under independent control and segregated from use by operational staff (at least two copies are needed to safely use one of them under emergency recovery circumstances).

Intelligence.   Establish or renew special hot-line telephones and staff to receive confidential intelligence information. Establish a procedure to process and react to confidential information while protecting the privacy of the source.

Response.   Establish or enhance an internal emergency response team, and increase contact with external intelligence services such as the Computer Emergency Response Team (CERT) (www.cert.org) at Carnegie Mellon University in Pittsburgh.

Support.   Renew or establish contact with local law enforcement and emergency response services and inform them about any special conditions in the organization.

Segregation.   Review your procedure for segregating duties and establishing dual controls over sensitive functions. If necessary, revise or develop procedures to meet new or changing conditions within the organization.

SYSTEM CONTROLS

Acceptance.   Before you install new security controls or practices, make a special effort to gain acceptance for them from the people who will be affected by them. In times of change or stress, employees may view the imposition of new constraints as a sign of mistrust or impending disaster. As always, avoid using a heavy hand in announcing the new controls or practices—for example, by warning about dire consequences for not following them.

Transparency.   When possible, make security controls transparent to the people affected by them or cast them in a positive light so that people view them as contributing to the organization in general, and to their job performance in particular. And, as much as possible, minimize the use of controls that constrain people's functions or job performance.

Isolation.   Minimize, as much as practical, communication among internal systems and networks and from public networks, at least during times of inactivity or crisis.

Administration.   Revitalize and establish procedures for terminating, constraining, and establishing user accounts and password and logon token administration.

Dormancy.   Cancel dormant user accounts and keep administrative actions current.

Accounting.   Extend or renew accounting controls such as monitoring of suspense items, outstanding balances, expense accounts, employee and other special accounts, and error accounts. Increase frequency of reconciling and exception reporting and shorten closing periods.

This list is by no means complete. You will also need to consider other measures for special circumstances. Examples include timing of security reviews, limiting telecommuting at critical times, increasing the security staff and budgets, and constraining contacts with the news and trade media. In some cases, you need only adopt a few of these measures, but adopting any of these measures at or before critical times of change should increase management's confidence that the organization is meeting a standard of due care and there is a strong likelihood of avoiding claims of negligence, independent of the vulnerabilities involved. The many dangers and frequency of short-term crises and upheavals seem to be increasing in today's dynamic business world. Information, as well as people, tangible property, and capital, are important assets worthy of protection.

Of course, your organization may find some that some of these actions are unacceptable due to cost or cultural or business reasons. Some controls may be too burdensome or costly unless they are highly automated, such as scanning employees' e-mail and Internet usage for objectionable or key words. Be sure to carefully consider the ethical implications and the impact on your organization before adopting or adapting any of these measures. Some organizations, for example, find the use of informants distasteful in some cases, but acceptable or warranted in others. Some of these measures, if applied without appropriate consideration for the employees and particular circumstances, may actually increase employee stress levels and dissatisfaction with the organization. For example, some employees consider monitoring to be an invasion of their privacy, even if they are forewarned, and strongly object to its use. Also be sure to consider liabilities and insurance implications.

Some organizations need significant security experience and skills that are not available among the existing staff in order to evaluate the current situation and make recommendations for strengthening security during times of stress. When this is the case, I advise discretely retaining outside experts. And, it is always important to consult with legal counsel, human resources professionals, industrial security, audit, public affairs, and other related functions before initiating any security contingency plans.

THE CHANGING NEEDS FOR CONFIDENTIALITY AND CLASSIFICATION

In general, we need to maintain confidentiality for fewer kinds of information in today's business practices than at any time in the past. This is partially because current knowledge management practices emphasize sharing the organization's information, and because it is increasingly difficult to control information confidentiality given the ease of copying and communicating and the mobility of people. These vulnerabilities contribute to a permissive attitude toward confidentiality. At the same time, government agencies are making more information available to the public and requiring many commercial businesses to do the same. Intensive media coverage also makes it more difficult to keep information secret today, and the societal concept of what is private seems to be eroding as people are more and more willing to share their personal views and information about health, finances, family, and many other topics previously considered private. While confidentiality is more difficult to maintain, however, the importance of ownership and control of information (i.e., possession), as well as its availability and utility, and its integrity and authenticity, is increasing. Possession is becoming more important because of the increase in software piracy, as well as literary, music, and video piracy.

The strict confidentiality model used in the military (unclassified, unclassified but sensitive, confidential, secret, and top secret), has largely failed in the business environment because organizations (other than the military and defense industry) do not staff the classification function. Clearly, business information is sensitive in some way, or it would not be kept, but we need to rethink our tendency to rely on the military five-level model and need-to-know principle, and adopt information classification schemes that are suited to business information and procedures, and that accommodate information stored in computers as well as printed on paper.

The Nature of Information for Classification Purposes

Information is not necessarily valuable in proportion to its volume and number of copies. For example, a fifty-page report is not necessarily more valuable than a two-page report on the same subject. Some articles on espionage assert that the volume of confidential information is an indication of its sensitivity. A larger amount of information may make confidentiality and possession of it more sensitive than would be the case for a smaller amount. But the amount of business information subject to espionage is minimal (e.g., the as-yet unannounced date for a product sale, or a proposed contract bid price). On the other hand, possession of a large amount of information, such as a computer program or mailing-address database, may be more valuable than possession of a small amount, such as a subroutine or single address. Volume may or may not be a sensitivity factor depending on the type of information involved.

Time, form, and location dependencies, as well as the sources and nature of losses, may or may not play roles in the security sensitivity of information. Quarterly financial reports can increase in secrecy value over time, until they are made public, after which only their integrity and authenticity are at stake. On the other hand, such information may be quite sensitive—and worthy of protection—early in the quarter, because investors would have more time to trade in a company's stock. The encrypted form of confidential information may have a different value from the clear text form, and the value may depend upon who has the encryption key and means of decryption. Similarly, information in a research laboratory may have different security sensitivity than an unidentified copy of it carried on an airplane, because the secret may be who is doing the research, not what the research is.

We need a new concept of two-level information classification—public and classified—that includes all six elements of security, and not just confidentiality. We should classify by specifying the mandatory and discretionary controls for the protection of information, rather than by subjective classification of its sensitivity into arbitrary levels.

Just-in-time Knowledge and Obsolescence Reduce Security Needs

If knowledge is sensitive to loss of confidentiality, then there is a security advantage to having to protect it for only a shorter time. There are increasing numbers of examples of electronic performance support systems that provide this type of just-in-time knowledge, such as the Microsoft Excel and Word applications, which provide help and explanations only at the time that such information is required. These systems are reducing the knowledge and training that must be delivered in classroom settings, books, and manuals in today's workplaces. Transitory knowledge is created from stored databases only when it is needed to instruct computer users (see "Just-in-time Knowledge Delivery," by Kevin Cole, Olivier Fisher, and Phyllis Saltzman in *ACM Communications*, July 1997).

Based on my interviews with business executives, it is apparent that their emphasis regarding security is changing. Relying on the rapid obsolescence of trade secret information, rather than trying to protect it, is one indication of this change. Silicon Valley firms often operate on the premise that by the time their competitors discover, steal, and try to use their information, it is already obsolete. In addition to having inherent security from high complexity, we now have security from rapid obsolescence.

Increasing automation can also increase the security of information because less information is exposed to the possibility of loss. Information that is simply entered into a computer by its creator, rather than having intermediaries handle it, is less subject to loss through abuse or misuse. Enforcing controls is also far easier with automation than with management edicts; computers simply will not let you proceed with incorrect or prohibited action, but people choose whether or not to obey management edicts. A great deal of business information is communicated electronically and processed in a computer, with only the necessary results of the processing available for use by the owner and designated users. Thus, sensitive information is not available for general observation, disclosure, use, or taking by any other, intermediate users. In addition, the computers can be instructed to destroy information immediately after processing or communicating it. Unlike people, computers are often programmed to have no hesitation in discarding information—even if it may be useful some time in the future.

As the intellectual property and services industry continue to offer more information for sale or barter, a number of companies are beginning to treat their trade secrets as information for sale, following the principle of "Do not try to keep it secret; sell it for a profit." For example, See's Candy Company responds to private requests for candy recipes by offering to sell the recipes for personal use at a high price.

CRYPTOGRAPHY

Cryptography is well suited for communicating and storing sensitive information that needs protection. All organizations have sensitive information, and we know from actual loss experiences that there are adversaries, including competitors, spies, and thieves, that want to take advantage of such information. Cryptography transfers the vulnerability of sensitive information from the communications channels or storage facilities to the cryptographic keys, which we can protect more easily and effectively. Criminals that I have interviewed generally tell me that they preferred to look for plaintext information to steal or modify rather than dealing with information in cryptographic form. Unfortunately, however, we can not rely on such reluctance; some criminals are willing—and able—to attempt cryptanalysis to obtain the information or, more likely, to try to steal the cryptographic keys to decrypt it. Or, if time is not an issue, the criminal may just wait until the information eventually appears in plaintext format—which it will when it is used—and try to steal it or modify it at that point.

Because cryptography does provide effective protection, you may want to consider routinely encrypting all sensitive information to reduce its vulnerability. Unfortunately, the rudimentary state of cryptographic technology has made this impractical because of cost, inconvenience, the complexity of cryptographic key management, and the required systems capacity. Routine cryptography is rapidly becoming practical. Today, however, we must consider trade-offs and decide selectively what information to encrypt and when, how, and where to do it.

Many factors govern encryption decisions, most notably the volume and location of the plaintext information. Other important factors include cost, performance, ease of use, and strength. In addition, we need to consider the potential threats to the information and the history of loss experience. And, the protection must be consistent. If information is ubiquitous, it makes little sense to protect it in one place and not in another equally or more vulnerable place.

Overall, however, we should be guided by the due care practices of others to avoid negligence. Some organizations purposely do not protect some of their valuable information with cryptography. For example, news magazines purposely do not encrypt the information they exchange with correspondents in other countries, so that authorities in those countries can easily monitor the information. This is a safety factor for the correspondents who might be endangered if the authorities in a foreign country concluded that the information might be harmful to them in any respect.

Information security experts have generally increased their interest in cryptography over the past fifteen years. This is partially due to the widespread use of the Internet for information exchange, a medium that is helplessly vulnerable without encryption. Companies such as Northern Telecom (www.nortel.com) in Canada, and RSA Data Security (www.rsa.com), PGP (www.pgpi.com) and Sybase (www.sybase.com) in California, as well as many cryptographers around the world have responded to the need for cryptography with a surge of new encryption methods and products. While certainly offering a powerful control that warrants our attention for reducing threats to information, cryptography sometimes seems to be driven by intellectual and technical interest more than a desire to resolve threats to information. I occasionally receive requests from start-up companies for advice and assistance to promote their new cryptographic products. The new vendors usually have some new secret algorithm devised by an obscure scientist. When I explain that few customers are likely to buy such a product unless it provides key management bells and whistles and offers a public algorithm that is already trusted, I seldom hear from them again.

Products with secret algorithms are theoretically more effective. In fact, their use was the practice of some of the old-line European companies such as Gretag and Crypto AG. However, interest in secret algorithms was effectively squelched in 1985 when the U.S. government introduced the 56-bit key symmetrical (one key) Data Encryption Standard (DES), which is backed by 18 man-years of testing by the National Security Agency. DES is publicly available and, according to a number of cryptographic experts including Donald Davies in England and Dorothy Denning in the United States, contains no secret trapdoors.

The Uses of Cryptography

Although encryption is probably best known for protecting information from spies, this application is probably overrated in business because of the colorful history of espionage, and military and diplomatic concern that spills over into business. We really have no way of knowing how much industrial espionage, whether carried out by private individuals, competing businesses, or government intelligence agencies, actually occurs. There are only a few publicly known anecdotes and no valid statistics. Most information owners associate cryptography with espionage, viewing cryptography as a means of keeping information secret. In reality, it also has advantages for protecting the other elements of information. For example, chain encryption (i.e., in which part of previously encrypted information is used in further encryption) is commonly used to protect the integrity of an encrypted file, because if one bit of ciphertext is wrong or missing, then the error becomes obvious when major portions of the file can not be decrypted into viable plaintext. Cryptography has a variety of purposes and requires different kinds of key management for its three applications to communications, storage, and digital signatures (as Whitfield Diffy, the noted cryptographer at Sun Microsystems, often emphasizes).

In the first of the three applications, communicators use cryptography to protect information in transit when it is particularly vulnerable (e.g., going through the Internet) because the senders and receivers typically do not have control over the communication routes (e.g., public switched communications networks). This application requires short-term protection by encrypting the information before it is sent, and decrypting it upon arrival. Senders' systems may generate keys or receive keys from the intended receiver for short-term use. The challenge is for the sender's and receiver's systems to securely exchange and coordinate use of the keys, ensuring that no unauthorized party could change the sender's key or has possession of the decryption key with which to decrypt the information. Security product vendors provide elaborate means of accomplishing this. In selecting an encryption product for a communications application, be sure to consider only well-known products from reputable companies. In general, you need not concern yourself with how the products actually function, just be sure that the performance claims are authentic by making due care inquiries.

The second purpose of cryptography is protecting information during its storage. Possessors of information require several different methods to store information securely. Storing encrypted information requires the secure storage, backup, and retrieval of keys and cryptographic mechanisms—presumably in ways that are subject to better protection than the stored plaintext information. This presents a potential adversary with a twofold challenge: obtaining the keys and mechanisms and obtaining the ciphertext. The authorized decryptors must be able to securely retrieve the keys and mechanisms, possibly after long periods of time. After 20 years, for example, an organization should still be able to find the necessary keys to decrypt stored information, and have mechanisms that operate in, or with, contemporary computer systems.

Obviously, key and mechanism security is crucial to effective use of cryptography. The strength of the cryptographic algorithm is of little importance at or above a prudent level (which I will discuss later in this section). Much of the literature on cryptography emphasizes the need for key management, but often omits mention of the important preservation of the mechanisms as well. Without the mechanisms, or at least possession of the algorithms used, it is virtually impossible to retrieve the plaintext, even if you do possess the keys. That is why I always mention the mechanisms along with the keys.

The third use of cryptography is to protect digital signatures to accomplish the same things that we accomplish with handwritten signatures; in this application, cryptography is concerned with ensuring the authenticity and integrity of people, documents, and transactions. In addition to proving the authenticity of a digital signature, cryptography permits us to prove that the entire signed message, whether encrypted or not, has integrity and authenticity. The cryptographic application accomplishes this by including a checksum or hash total of the entire message (called a *message digest*) in the signature before it is encrypted. A new business function, called *certificate authorities* or *trusted third parties*, is emerging to create and ensure authentic digital signatures for people to use in electronic communications and transactions.

Cryptography Threat Analysis

I find that the most vulnerable form of information is usually spoken, followed by less vulnerable forms of printed and displayed information, then information stored on removable computer media, and finally, the least vulnerable form of information, that which is stored in computers and electronically and optically communicated. This is directly opposite to the ordering of vulnerabilities expressed by some other information security technologists; but my interviews with criminals indicate that criminals who encounter any kind of ciphertext—even that created by simple data compression schemes or Captain Midnight decoder rings—simply walk away and look elsewhere for the information, preferably finding it in spoken or printed form.

As with any security safeguard, we must create and apply it with regard to who are adversaries are and how they are likely to react to the safeguard. Any intelligent adversary is likely to first attempt to steal the plaintext or convince someone in the organization to tell him what he wishes to know. If that fails, he may search for the encryption keys and mechanisms to attack the ciphertext. Finally, if all else fails, he may try to apply cryptanalysis using as much information about the key, mechanism, and samples of plaintext and matching ciphertext as possible to aid him in this pursuit. If the only purpose of the crime is to successfully decrypt information—for example, to embarrass the victim or prove to fellow hackers that he can do it—he is more likely to attempt cryptanalysis. Similarly, if the adversary's purpose is to continue information gathering and decrypt more encrypted information (from the same or a different victim), cryptanalysis may be worth the ongoing effort, particularly if the victim (or victims) rarely change the keys. Information security practitioners need to follow the same order of threats in protecting information: first safeguarding the plaintext version and "spoof-proofing" trusted people; then using cryptography and creating secure, valid keys and storing them, along with the mechanisms and ciphertext, in a secure location, and changing the keys frequently; and finally, using cryptographic algorithms and keys with appropriate strength.

The final point in the strategy is controversial. Algorithm and key strengths depend to a great extent on economics. How much cost, time, and effort are your adversaries willing to expend on cryptanalysis? Historically, the importance of brute force, exhaustive key searches and the strength of algorithms was not particularly important. Much of the famous code breaking during wartime was accomplished because of poor practices in keeping keys secret, managing encryption and decryption processes, and the choice of keys, rather than the strength of the algorithms and length of keys. It is important to remember, however, that cryptanalysis is becoming cheaper as technology advances. Consider how long you expect to need to protect your information.

Many businesses can probably protect their information adequately using the equivalent of a child's secret decoder ring or with proprietary data compression software utilities to achieve the equivalent protection of sealed paper envelopes. Even using bad grammar or words with coded meaning, as some banks and oil companies do, may provide adequate protection. In general, the strength of algorithm and key management need be only good enough to meet a standard of due care, as established by others' use of cryptography under similar circumstances. I believe that "good enough" encryption (not the strongest that we can obtain or tolerate) is perfectly adequate for achieving a due care level of protection in the three applications that I described in this chapter. Certainly, there is some vulnerability inherent in this level, but business involves balancing risk against profit with the least effort and a reasonable exposure to possible loss. Fortunately, the growing use of cryptography and acceptable cryptographic products will continue to make it easier and more cost effective to provide an adequate level of protection for sensitive information.

If your adversaries happen to include a major government or a big-time organized crime syndicate with significant cryptanalysis capabilities, and your information is worth millions of dollars in the wrong hands, then you are in a high-stakes game that differs considerably from the normal concerns of most organizations. You should be using the strongest possible cryptography available. In special cases, your government may issue licenses and assist you. However, keep in mind that if your enemies possess such significant capabilities, they are also likely to possess similar capabilities in other aspects of espionage as well. They may be willing, for example, to offer a million-dollar bribe to one of your information stakeholders to obtain the sensitive information, rather than dealing with concerns of encryption and decryption.

This is an appropriate place to review the motivation to use cryptography as protection from threat (rather than simply the due care practices of others). I have never found any publicly reported cases of business criminal cryptanalysis (criminals deciphering encrypted information to engage in a crime), so it is difficult to base business threat analysis of criminal cryptanalysis on actual experience. With no reported loss experience, we might conclude that the use of cryptography is the perfect protection. Unfortunately, that is like declaring that we have perfect protection from elephants attacking shopping malls, because it has never happened. Also, because one of the obvious objectives in cryptanalysis is to keep its success secret from the victim, there is little likelihood of having public knowledge of cases. There are, however, many reported cases of criminal eavesdropping on communication of plaintext information, such as credit card number theft over the Internet, as well as many cases of modification of information for criminal purposes. Clearly, we see a need for cryptography today, and can expect this need to increase with the successful commercialization of the Internet.

FEAR OF COMPLEXITY OF CRYPTOGRAPHY

The complexity of cryptography presents an area of concern to many businesses. Managers read articles about the potential security problems of secret and public key exchanges and conclude that running a business securely is excessively difficult in the light of such complexities. They do not understand that the employees who use cryptography do not need to know (and should not know) anything about what kind of cryptography they are using, and whether it is symmetric (uses one key) or asymmetric (uses two keys, one to encrypt and one to decrypt). In addition, they easily conclude that it requires memorization and manual administration of keys containing numerous characters. Literature that falsely describes how cryptography works is one source of these misconceptions. For example, cryptography may be described as: "Bob encrypts with his 128-bit secret key, and Alice decrypts with Bob's matching public key." The literature does not mention that Bob and Alice never do this manually; their computers do it automatically, and Bob and Alice never even know that encryption is taking place. People possess keys; they do not know them (possession as distinct from confidentiality). The computers also perform the key backup and recovery and the digital signature authentication service automatically.

Security practitioners should disabuse business management of these false notions about key management and heavy-handed security, emphasizing the transparency of security controls in computers. Choosing cryptographic algorithms and managing keys should be the business of the cryptography experts. They should advise users about what products to buy, vulnerabilities to avoid, and what few "externals" they need to know. Many business people that I have interviewed do not want to know the details of security; they just want security experts to tell them what to do and which information technology products they should use to achieve transparent, due-care security.

CRYPTOGRAPHY DANGERS AND INFORMATION ANARCHY

Cryptography is a powerful technical means of protecting information from loss of confidentiality and other losses. It is so powerful that information owners and users can cause significant damage to themselves and others by its misuse. Information can be lost in the event of a single software error or hardware failure. The same thing can happen if keys are lost or destroyed. There is an urban myth about an employee who went on holiday and was the only person who knew the key that was protecting vital encrypted information. When he returned from a few days of debauchery, he was unable to remember the key except that it was taken from Shakespeare's writings. Users can also lose critical information if they encrypt it incorrectly. The inherent dangers of cryptography often encourage users to make more plaintext backup copies of the information, but that only increases the exposure to loss.

Information anarchy, where employees use their own rogue cryptography mechanisms and keys without management control, is a nightmare.

And it's a nightmare that is all too common in many large companies. One large company that I know of prohibited the use of cryptography for several years because of management and users' lack of understanding of key management and the problems associated with generating, storing, and using the keys and mechanisms. In reality, modern cryptographic products are relatively safe and can be very effective, but management needs to be aware of potential problems with this type of safeguard and establish and enforce appropriate policies for handling it safely. In addition, organizations may need to consider implementing special backup, maintenance, diagnosis, and recovery capabilities, some of which may entail additional cost.

Cryptography can harm society as well as organizations and information users. For example, when criminals use sufficiently strong cryptography that results in absolute privacy of their communication, the government can not protect its citizens. An orderly society protected from abuse requires a strong law enforcement eavesdropping capability authorized by court order, which can be lost as unnecessarily strong cryptography products come into general use.

Unfortunately, other countries beside the United States have similar problems from uncontrolled use of cryptography. The U.S. government restricts export of strong cryptography (i.e., which uses unacceptably long keys), and installation of cryptographic products in U.S.-based businesses in other countries that do not prohibit its import is allowed on a case-by-case basis. Other countries place similar restrictions on cryptographic products. The new, stronger cryptography intended to replace current DES algorithms, such as triple DES, long-keyed RSA, PGP (Pretty Good Privacy), and IBM's elliptic curves, is particularly troubling for governments.

SENSIBLE ADVICE FOR USING CRYPTOGRAPHY

There are, of course, some ways in which to improve the use and efficiency of cryptography as a security safeguard. But before you apply cryptography, there are a number of steps that you can take to help ensure the general protection of your information:

- Train persons entrusted with sensitive information to resist deceptive and overt queries by untrusted parties who might be attempting to gather sensitive information or determine the ways in which you protect it.
- Use the familiar, well-known controls to safeguard printed and displayed information such as labeling its sensitivity, securely destroying it after use, avoiding display where others can see it, locking it up,

using double envelopes in mailing it, instituting clean desk policies, and numbering and controlling copies of documents.

- Control removable computer media such as disks and tape cartridges and portable computers as you would printed information.
- Apply the many operational and technical intrusion controls and other security features available in computer and communications operating systems.

After you have applied these safeguards, you are in a good position to consider using cryptography. The first step in using cryptography is to establish secure, effective key management. Then, apply cryptography to situations in which there are clear dangers, as demonstrated by your own or others' loss experience, which are not addressed adequately by the other controls and practices that you have installed. Next, focus on protecting vital information where it must be used in plaintext format, and encrypt it where you have the least control over it in other ways, such as when it is stored in portable computers or communicated by microwaves or other wireless technology and over the Internet. Finally, apply cryptography where it is practical to use in order to meet a standard of due care, and where good, proven cryptographic products are readily available.

WHICH CRYPTOGRAPHY TO USE

Any cryptography products produced by reputable vendors using DES, triple DES, RSA, PGP, and other popular methods with moderate key length are acceptable for the foreseeable future. The RSA algorithm, which is slower than DES, is commonly used to communicate small amounts of information, such as DES keys, while DES is used to encrypt long messages. As new cryptography products come into the market, we are seeing some shift from DES to newer algorithms such as DES triple encryption. Although DES will be discontinued as a U.S. government federal standard in the near future, there is no reason to stop using it for moderately sensitive information. Vendors are having serious problems in achieving international distribution of strong cryptography products from the United States because of U.S. government insistence that it have access to recoverable keys and because of other governments' constraints as well.

Remember that products implemented in software are only as secure as the operating environment in which they reside. Hardware implementation tends to be more tamper-resistant than software and may provide higher performance, but software is still the preferred form. Be sure to obtain cryptography products that have the capacity to upgrade to new and different algorithms as due care changes dictate. There will continue to be rapid changes in cryptography for some time as experience with its use grows.

Effective key selection and management and proper security for the information about your use of cryptography are actually more important that the choice of algorithms. These functions are largely automated and transparent to users in the current generation of cryptography products, thereby resolving many of the problems that organizations have faced in implementing cryptography in the past. The vulnerabilities of real-time human involvement in cryptographic operations is the largest concern. The best protection when people must be involved is segregation of duties,

The Need for Law Enforcement to Control Cryptography

For several years, I supported the U.S. government, particularly the Department of Justice and the NSA, in their attempts to slow the adoption of cryptography by criminals, terrorists, and rogue nations by restricting exports of strong cryptography and making keys available for use by court-authorized criminal justice agencies. At the time, I believed this was necessary for public safety and protection from privacy violators who might steal personal information and encrypt it to avoid detection of the theft. (I still believe that absolute privacy, which prevents the government from eavesdropping on its citizens even when necessary for public safety, can lead to information anarchy and the collapse of a democratic society.)

Having cryptography freely available to our enemies has now advanced to the stage where its unrestricted use for good purposes outweighs the potential harm from its use by criminals and rogue nations. Continued restrictions on export are impractical and ineffective. The attempts to slow the use of strong cryptography, which have been quite successful until recently, have now run out of steam. The best that we can do now is to make the use of "good-enough" cryptography popular to discourage the use of strong cryptography. We can also criminalize the use of cryptography in the perpetration of crime—but this takes careful wording of laws and limitations to avoid abuse. We must give law enforcement as much capability as possible to engage successfully in properly authorized cryptanalysis and key recovery. I believe that authorization to eavesdrop must be made stronger than the currently required approval by one judge.

dual control, and frequent changes of assignments with forced long holiday periods. This helps assure that abuse would require at least two people acting in collusion.

My final advice with regard to cryptography is to delay using it for as long as it is prudent to do so. This will allow time for others to perform the "shakedown" functions and encourage further development for its use in the business environment. When you do adopt cryptography, be conservative in its introduction to the organization. Use it sparingly in limited applications to gain experience on a pilot basis, then do not expand its use any faster than the staff can adapt to it and managers can control it.

AUTHENTICATED LOGON CONTROL

Information security is about protecting information that authentic owners, users, custodians, service providers, and information systems need to work with. It concerns the functions that we are allowed to perform, and those that we are prohibited from performing, and with sending and receiving information. Business, and more specifically, business transactions and interactions among people, require trust, which, in some situations, is the antithesis of applying security. Trust is elusive and always problematic. Security controls provide the means to both induce trust and reduce the need for trust. We use both positive and negative methods to achieve trust among people through:

- Experience in previous dealings
- Handshakes (or bowing in some societies)
- Direct eye contact
- Observation of demeanor and dress
- Visible signs of adequate resources
- Signatures
- Segregation of duties
- Dual control
- Independent multiple recordings of events (e.g., double-entry book-keeping)
- Third-party assurances
- Financial commitments, debts and credits
- Self interest
- Friendship, love, and faith

In the anonymous remoteness of cyberspace, we lose or seriously weaken many of these traditional methods of building trust. We cannot look the other people in the eye, or observe their demeanor or appearance (yet), so we need to find ways to replace the trust-inducing controls that we have lost. In our financial dealings, for example, as we gradually move from using cash to credit cards and electronic money, we implement controls to establish the necessary level of security and reduce our reliance on blind trust. We have already begun to establish these controls in cyberspace, but need to expand these controls as more and more individuals and businesses venture into cyberspace for more varied applications.

We need to begin by establishing effective controls for authenticating the identity of parties in remote transactions conducted over networks. This includes authenticating both people and systems to one another because system-to-system transactions without human intervention and people-to-systems and systems-to-people transactions (e.g., ATM use) are increasingly common. In addition, modern business includes trust entities represented by trustees. The trust entities in transactions are involved indirectly through the actions of their trustees. Some people have more than one personification, especially if they serve as trustees. For example, I currently exist simultaneously as:

- Donn B. Parker, trustee of my living trust
- Donn B. Parker, trustee of my mother's trust
- Donn B. Parker, employee number XXXXXXXXXX
- Donn Blanchard Parker, driver license number XXXXXXXXXX
- Donn Blanchard Parker, U.S. passport number XXXXXXXXXXX
- Donn Blanchard Parker, Social Security retiree and Medicare patient number XXXXXXXXXXXX
- Donn B. Parker, annuitant XXXXXXXXXXXXX
- Donn Parker, loving husband and father
- Donnie, son of Miriam B. Parker
- Dparker@sric.sri.com
- The Bald Eagle on some hacker chat boards on the Internet
- Donn B. Parker, CISSP in my speaking and writing engagements

I have different bank accounts, credit cards, and credit histories for some of these personas. This means that, using the anonymity of the Internet and creating trusts and bankruptcies, anyone can start over again with a new identity—a long-standing American freedom and custom. Therefore, we need to authenticate individuals in the persona that fits the purpose and role that they are playing at the time. As individuals, we need not, and indeed should not, include some aspects of our identities (e.g., our Social Security numbers) when establishing some personas or moving from one persona to another.

What does it take to authenticate that you are who you say you are? According to some security experts, authentication is based on only three factors: what you know (a secret password); what you possess (token or key); and what you are (based on a biometric characteristic such as a fingerprint). Unfortunately, this is a fairly simplistic view that omits a number of other important characteristics such as what you do (signature dynamics), where you are (location, as based on Global Positioning Satellite data), and what time it is (the time of your location and claimed identity).

Passwords

Your identity is commonly authenticated by what you know. Banks and government agencies typically ask for your address, telephone number, and/or mother's maiden name. In turn, they assign you an ID number, an account number, a social security number, or a personal identification number (PIN). Computer services require you to know passwords or sequences of secret words (pass-phrases). Today, any computer that is available to more than one untrusted user should require at least a password to meet a standard of due care. In fact, a best-practice password system requires:

- A user- or computer-selected password or pass-phrase of specified minimum length that adheres to content and aging limits
- An invalid entry attempt limit with penalties
- Suppression of display of the password at entry
- Time limit for entry
- One-way encrypted master copy stored in a protected password file (decryption not possible)
- Minimal exposure plaintext form
- A different returned password or identifier from the computer to authenticate the computer to the user
- Minimal instruction and prompting aids for entry

I can make these requirements clearer with an example. A new password user identifies and authenticates himself in person by being introduced to the password administrator by another, authorized person. The password administrator obtains from her computer and supplies to the user a permanent, non-secret user ID (the user's name or a contraction), an initial password, and a computer response password on paper in a sealed envelope. The first usage of the user ID and password entry triggers a display response of the computer's identity (to preclude spoofing). No other clues are provided as to the identity of the computer or service provider, and the user's password is not displayed. The computer does not perform any checking of the password until it is entered completely, and gives no indications as to whether the password and user ID are correct. If the password is correct, the computer prompts the user to choose a new password and enter it immediately to replace the initial, temporary password. The computer tests the new password to ensure that it is the appropriate length (usually six to twelve characters) and to make sure that it contains at least one non-alphabetic character that is not a beginning or end character. It also makes sure that the alphabetic characters (in forward or backward combination) do not form a word from common language dictionaries or any other common appellation. The computer then encrypts a standard message using the password as the cryptographic key (to produce a one-way ciphertext) and stores the result as the master for future comparisons. It also checks the new password to be sure that the user has not used it previously. If the user enters a false password or exceeds the acceptable password entry time limit during future logon attempts, the computer reinitializes logon and requires the user to start over, reentering his ID and password after a ten-second delay. The computer occasionally varies the routine to make sure it is not predicable; it may, for example, require the user to choose a new password with a different length limit, or with different time-out and entry attempt limits.

For additional security, the password system may impose a limit on multiple logons using the same user ID and password. This control, which is often debated among security practitioners, needs to be applied with care, because the capacity for multiple logons by the same user is a valuable feature in some systems. When the feature is available, the first screen after successful logon should display the date, time of day, and length of time of the last session so that the user can verify that no one impersonated him since his last logon. Some very secure systems also employ a duress alarm that allows a user to enter a secret alarm signal (e.g., interchanging two or more password characters) that would not be detected by an attacker who may be forcing the user to log on. The tricky part of this control is how to respond to the user without causing retaliation by the attacker.

Obviously, it is crucially important to protect the software that manages the password process from modification or replacement and protect the computer from deception. Malicious hackers use a number of techniques to derive others' passwords. One such method is an automated dictionary word search that encrypts likely words and compares them with the encrypted passwords in the master file to find a match. In another method, malicious hackers set up their computers to respond just like legitimate computers to deceive users into revealing their passwords (called *spoofing*). Password administration software is usually protected through a combination of encryption and checksums, as well as occasional checking by the password administrator.

It is necessary to authenticate the identity of computer systems as well as computer users, as a case from Stanford University illustrated long ago. Students set up their own on-line campus computer and distributed its telephone number to other users, indicating that it replaced the official campus computer number. They programmed the initial response to attempted logons to their computer to look just like logons to the official campus computer, and collected the unsuspecting users' IDs and secret passwords when the users entered them. Then their computer informed the users that the telephone number had been changed back to the original and instructed them to log in again with the old number.

Every computer should have a unique identifier that is strongly resistant to change and available by computer program inquiry. We need to know that we are communicating with the computer system that we expect, as well as with the user that we expect. Asymmetric public key cryptography, which requires one key to encrypt and another to decrypt, and third-party verification services, such as VeriSign (www.verisign.com) for public networks and Kerberos security servers in private networks are important aids for achieving two-way systems authentication and helping to solve the repudiation problem.

WRITING DOWN PASSWORDS: HERESY OR EFFECTIVE PRACTICE?

Since the beginning of computer time, security practitioners have tried to discipline computer users to avoid writing their passwords any place other than in designated logon procedures. Writing passwords anywhere else, especially anywhere in proximity to workstations, is a serious breach of security. Along the way, we have wrestled with idea for making passwords easier to memorize and to reduce the urge to write them down. But simple passwords are vulnerable to guessing by intruders, and complex passwords, which are difficult to guess, are difficult to memorize—prompting users to write them down. In addition, many users need to remember several—or even many—passwords and change them frequently. Although a "single sign-on," which requires only one password for multiple purposes, has long been the Holy Grail of information security, single sign-on introduces a vulnerability by placing trust in a single password.

There may be good reasons for information security practitioners to deviate from tradition in some circumstances and allow users to write their passwords someplace. This practice would, however, destroy one element of authentication by eliminating the need to know a password, since users could retrieve the information from the written source. If allowing users to write passwords in secure places encourages the users to select complex passwords that are difficult to guess, however, the net result is likely to be beneficial—especially for users who must remember two or more passwords. But, security managers must restrict the places in which users can legitimately store passwords to ensure that the storage locations are secure from observation and stealing.

If they permit users to write passwords, security practitioners should advise them to:

- "Keep your password as safe as you keep your money."
- Avoid using a predictable standard or common medium to write passwords. (Users should be encouraged to invent mediums and secure places to store their written passwords.)
- Keep written passwords on their persons.
- Report possible disclosures, observations, or theft of passwords immediately and take action to change passwords whenever a loss is suspected.
- Keep the practice of writing passwords a secret.
- Whenever possible, use a simple encoding scheme to record the password.
- Avoid writing the password on any token or device associated with their use of a computer or workstation.

Cryptographers may decry the use of simple codes to obscure passwords, but even simple encoding is far superior to plaintext and may discourage intruders, who generally find it easier to attempt to guess simply written passwords than to decipher encoded ones.

Weighing the benefits against the vulnerabilities is still problematic. Loss of what-you-know as a form of authentication weakens security—but so does choosing simple passwords. Replacing written passwords with the practice of remembering only a simple secret code to disguise the written password is a weak alternative. Encouraging users to select quality passwords, change them frequently, and refrain from storing them near the workstation is likely to improve information security. In general, I advise practitioners to allow, but not encourage, users to write passwords and keep them in secure places and to develop policies that spell out appropriate conditions for writing and storing them.

Tokens

No matter how secure a password system is, a clever, persistent hacker can beat it. That is why many system owners now require use of tokens along with passwords. Tokens meet the second aspect of authentication—what you have, thereby supplementing the user and system authentication of what you know, as provided by passwords.

A token is a hardware or software device carried by, or in the possession of, a computer user. The token contains an electronically recorded and encrypted password; alternatively, it may have an on-board processor that can store or derive such a password when needed. A token may be a plastic "smart card" similar to a credit card, or a program stored on a diskette; mobile computers or pocket calculators may also be tokens if they calculate passwords. Tokens authenticate identity in two ways: The user is required to *know* a secret PIN and to *possess* the token. Tokens also provide additional security for the "what you have" element of authentication by continually changing the passwords. They do this by calculating new passwords every few seconds in synchronization with the computer that the token holder wants to use. The user enters his PIN, then reads the current value of the password from a display on the token device and keys it into the computer; or the token may exchange the password information directly with the computer using an optical bar code and scanner on the screen. The use of such tokens, often called a one-time password method, is significantly more secure than traditional multiuse permanent passwords, since eavesdropping on password entry and communication is of little value.

A token system requires more effort by users, as well as significantly more administrative effort, than the use of permanent passwords. Tokens must be deactivated, replaced, and reactivated when batteries lose power; administrators must replace the tokens when they are stolen or lost. Organizations must provide alternate means of logons when users misplace their tokens. Users sometimes resist the additional burden of carrying tokens, viewing them as unnecessary unless there is an imminent danger of attack or significant loss experiences. One way of dealing with such complaints is for organizations to offer multiuse token devices that are valuable for purposes other than security, such as credit or debit cards, or to receive special services such as parking lot entry, access to personal records, or charging meals in the company cafeteria.

Biometrics

One of the most important ways to protect information is to hold people accountable for their actions with regard to information. To do this, we need to expand authentication beyond the what-you-know and what-you-possess elements provided by passwords and tokens. The what-you-are and what-you-do elements of user authentication fall into the realm of the art of biometrics. This is a specialized field within information security that, despite great attention over the years, has made only limited progress toward the practical application of ensuring information security. Venture capitalists have funded an impressive array of start-up companies offering new biometic products, but nearly all fail to get off the starting block. In fact, I do not know of a single company that has survived and succeeded well in the market for computer user biometric authentication products. While biometric products are enticing from an intellectual, engineering, and market view, they have traditionally been too expensive, have had unacceptable error rates and performance, and are generally hated by the users.

The most common biometric products in use—and none are particularly successful yet in terms of widespread application—are those that use fingerprints, retinal or iris eye scans, or hand geometry methods to verify user identity. Because all of these products are quite costly, their use is limited to controlling physical door access or in the check cashing market. The computer usage market has, at least thus far, proven impenetrable. Many types of what-you-are authentication products have failed along the way, including those using skull geometry, footprints, earprints, skin chemistry, blood vessel patterns, and brain wave analysis. What-you-do authentication product failures include signature dynamics, signature analysis, and voice recognition.

Microsoft is currently working with the National Registry, Inc. (www.mrid.com) of St. Petersburg, Florida, which has introduced a product called NRIdentity Secure Authentication Facility for use with the Windows NT operating system. To gain entry to an NT-based workstation or network, an authorized user enters an ID, then places his index finger (if he has one) on an NRIdentity Personal Authentication Scanner. This prompts SAF/Windows NT to verify the user's identity and automatically completes logon by delivering the user's password to the operating system. Microsoft and NRI believe that there will be a demand for this technology among financial services companies, healthcare providers, and govern-

Crazy Biometric Ideas

An inventor in Canada once approached IBM with an interesting device. It was a helmet containing probes that measured skull shape. The *pièce de résistance* was a set of clamps in the helmet that captured impostors until they could be incarcerated.

At one time, the director of the Brain Research Lab at SRI called me to tell me that he had the perfect biometric device. In answer to my obvious question, he said that it worked by receiving beta brain waves unique to each person in the world. I suggested that he still had not told me how it works. He said that it was simply a matter of having electrodes attached to your skull; when you said one agreed-upon word, the device recorded the beta waves thus created and compared them to a stored value. I suggested the obvious problem of having things stuck to your scalp. He counter-suggested a helmet with embedded electrodes (where had I heard of that before?). I told him that my wife has her hair done every week and will not go out in a strong wind, let alone put her head into a helmet (although it would work fine for me). I told him to come back when he had invented a gun to aim at a person's skull from three feet away to pick up brain waves, but I never heard from him again. Can you imagine the uproar the device would create among the privacy activists?

Researchers at SRI invented a biometric product that seemed to be the perfect solution to authenticate identity based on what-you-do. It was a low-cost software product that timed and analyzed a person's typing on a keyboard. The product was very low priced, did not degrade computer performance, and best of all, was totally transparent to the user. In the early days of biometrics, I thought they had achieved success. Unfortunately, the product was designed and produced by research engineers rather than product engineers, and it ultimately failed along with the company formed to produce it. Even its transparency became a problem because many individuals do not like to have their identity authenticated unless they know it is happening. I suggested that the product place a notice on the user's screen during the process. The primary problem, however, was that the effectiveness was variable. Security specialists were comfortable with controls that either accepted on rejected. The control was variably effective over time as a user's typing rhythm was gradually discerned by the learning technology employed. Unfortunately, there was also the little problem of different rhythms before and after the subject's first cup of coffee for the day. It seemed to be more successful in determining drug violations and general health than in authenticating identity.

ment agencies. The price, approximately $200 per enabled workstation, is quite reasonable but may limit market acceptance to some extent. In general, biometric products are decreasing in price, but there is still a question of how well users will accept them. In this case, the device takes up desk space, is likely to become dirty as users repeatedly finger it, and may imply suspicion of criminal intent. Future products will be built into existing devices such as keyboards.

Other new products, including Trueface Cyberwatch from Miros (www.miros.com) in Wellesley, Massachusetts and FaceIt PC from Visionics Corporation (www.faceit.com) in Jersey City, use video cameras perched on top of the computer monitor to take the user's picture as she uses secure files. The products, which cost anywhere from $200 to $300 per workstation including the cameras, scan the pictures using pattern recognition software and compare characteristics to those stored in a file copy of the user's digitized photograph. The comparison takes "a very few seconds" according to the product advertising. The products can also record a picture of the user in a log during each workstation transaction. Although the price is probably acceptable for most organizations, especially if the cameras can be used for other purposes such as video conferencing, the "few seconds" delay may be unacceptable for many users.

The next two elements of authentication after what-you-know, what-you-have, what-you-do, and who-you-are are the *where-you-are and when* determination of identity, which can be used in conjunction with one or more of the other methods. The where-you-are and when element, which is based on the concept that one person can not be in different places at the same time, was not particularly useful when we were all using computers that were tethered to the wall with cables. Now, with mobile laptop and palmtop computers and wireless computing, we can be anyplace—including places that we should not be—at any time, but only one person in one place at one time.

Mobile computers have introduced an entirely new dimension of user location vulnerability into information security. The security of information may change dramatically depending on user location. For example, a user performing a very sensitive application, such as using a spreadsheet to calculate future product plans, on his laptop computer in his office in his company's building has one set of security concerns. If he picks up his computer and walks out into the public lobby or boards a commuter train while still engaged in the same application, he has a totally different set of security needs. While management may accept his behavior in the office, the same behavior may violate security when he is in the lobby or on the commuter train, where competitors could be shoulder surfing to observe his work. Ideally, a computer could log the user off based on his current location, or at least warn him about his security violation.

There are several ways to detect where a person using a computer is located, corresponding to the location of the computer. One way is to use the GPS system to identify the three "tudes": the longitude, latitude, and altitude of his position. This requires "sky contact" and does not work in a building (or other enclosed area) unless the building is properly instrumented. Another way, which does work in a building, is for the computer to record the various doors that it moves through or the stations that it passes. The computer would have to contain a digital map that could record its location in the same way that a computer figures out where the icon on the monitor screen should be relative to the movement of the computer mouse. We may see special applications of these controls in the near future, but due care status is a few years into the future.

When we apply all six elements of identity authentication, we determine if the user is who he claims to be based on what he knows and possesses, what he is and what he does, and where he is and when. Should this authenticated person then be doing what he is doing where and when he is doing it? Information security practitioners and organization management must ask if this type of authentication is too frightening or too intimidating for users. Is it an invasion of their privacy, or will it be perceived as such? Should a computer record so much about the person using it? And what about identifying the users of other devices that have embedded computers, such as cars, ATMs, telephones, TVs, and toasters? Good security is often a cultural, social, and business process of balancing conflicting values of protection and possible harm.

Role-Based Authentication

When more than one person has entry to a container of information such as a computer, we may need to decide who gets use of what information. After all, we do not want one person reading, controlling, or changing another person's information. There are basically two ways to determine such use: discretionary controls, in which the information owner designates use by others, and mandatory controls, in which the information user must abide by rules set by some authority.

Business and the military have different ways of authorizing use of information. Business generally uses discretionary controls, allowing owners to make usage decisions guided by organizational policies. The military uses a mandatory classification system that requires presetting classification of information and people, and then matching information classification levels with personnel who are cleared for each level. Business often uses discretionary classification schemes for information, but has never adopted the clearance process for people because of the cost and regimentation required. I do not know of a single company, (other than military contractors) that has even one employee devoted to classification administration.

Recently however, some businesses, such as health care systems, have discovered that they need more than discretionary usage controls and are adopting a variation of mandatory clearances for their personnel. This method, called role-based, nondiscretionary entry control, provides flexibility at low cost. It allows an organization to specify jobs or roles to use protected information when necessary, rather than allowing (or disallowing) usage directly by specific persons. For example, a person assigned the job of night nurse may have authorization to read and append designated patient records for a particular hospital ward, but only during certain hours of the day, and he never has authorization to change patient records. In an automated system, the nurse logs on to the computer workstation as the night nurse and is given entry to the records under the authority assigned to a night nurse. No one else has entry during the assignment period except for a person in an overriding supervisor role.

Some organizations add another entry control; once a person is assigned a role, other roles normally available to that person are denied, because they would conflict with or compromise the currently assigned role. This is called a Chinese wall control. In this case, the night nurse would not be allowed to assume a prescription medication role at the same time as his night nurse role, even though he may be allowed that role at another time. Role-based entry security systems offer a great deal of flexibility for automated control techniques. Access control packages such as IBM's RACF have access control lists (ACLs) that assign use of files by name IDs of users. Role-based ACLs would be double tables indicating users assigned authorized roles and roles authorized to use files. To read more about this, see the U.S. NIST CSL report, *An Introduction to Role-Based Access Control*, published in December 1995 (also see the *CSL Newsletter* No. 55, August 1996).

TESTING SYSTEM SECURITY

Penetration testing of computer and network systems, referred to as a *tiger team* or *red team attack*, is a popular means of discovering system vulnerabilities. Testing the hardware and software, for example by attacking the computer firewalls, is useful as far as it goes. Testing the greatest potential vulnerability, namely the people who run or use the systems, is even more useful, but this type of testing may present problems and often smacks of unethical conduct.

Consultants sometimes employ avowed hackers to stage test attacks as part of a security review for clients. In my view, this practice is unethical and should be condemned, especially when it challenges the organization's security without alerting the security staff or affected employees of the impending test. Using tiger teams to attack hardware systems is, however, acceptable with the informed consent and full knowledge of the people involved. Aside from the ethical questions that such attacks raise, they are extremely dangerous and can lead to severe damage, including the mental anguish of deceived employees. In addition, such tests are expensive and result in limited additional knowledge of vulnerabilities; the same information can usually be obtained through safer, more effective ways such as threat scenario analysis sessions with operations staffs. I personally know of one testing situation in which two EDP auditors were forced to resign from their jobs because they successfully penetrated their employer's computer systems at the direction of their audit management. It embarrassed the information technology department's management and effectively ended the auditors' careers. In another case, employees believed that they were under real attack and called in the local police, FBI, and Secret Service, causing a shutdown of services and considerable embarrassment.

The author of a recently published paper on the threat of social engineering to victim organizations whose employees are deceived into revealing sensitive information, actually encouraged organizations to "Perform a Social Engineering Attack on Your Own Organization," claiming that it is the only way to "fully determine what are an organization's vulnerabilities with regard to social engineering." The author went on to explain that the attack should emulate an outsider's efforts to "determine how a Social Engineer might infiltrate your organization," and that "it is the only method to see how far an attacker might get, and what level of damage they [sic] can do."

In my opinion, the author's misguided advice requires security staffs (or hired consultants) to engage in lies, deception, and intimidation of employees in attempts to obtain sensitive information. It also exposes the targeted information to eavesdropping by real attackers. The potential mental damage to the employee victims is unknown, but the practice poses a serious threat that opens the company to civil penalties, lower morale, labor strife, and even physical damage or violence. It also destroys the trust in the information security function, and trust is crucial to maintain close working relationships with the employees who might be deceived. In addition, the types of people who engage in such social engineering may not be the types of people who should be trusted with security responsibilities. There is also no assurance that they would discover the greatest vulnerabilities, since they would probably stop after finding the first one. Such testing is artificial in that it does not employ real adversaries, who are often irrational and desperate and may have backgrounds, knowledge, values, and motives that differ significantly from those of the testing staff.

The author of the paper went on to say that he and his firm offer this kind of social engineering testing service. The firm's lawyer had approved offering the service and claimed to monitor the testing staff's activities. He said that the client agrees to each test and often has one of its own employees monitoring the test conversations even though the victim employees are not identified to the client. In some cases, local law enforcement officials are informed in advance of the tests, and the conversations in the tests are "non-confrontational" according to the author. He also claims that the testing team members are not the same people who do the other security review work. In spite of all these precautions, I believe that social engineering testing is an unsavory practice at best, dangerous at worst, and is likely to cause more harm than good.

Replacing tiger team testing, including social engineering attempts, with interactive sessions using role playing and adversarial scenario analysis, while not as dramatic, may actually uncover more vulnerabilities because the participants know the objectives of the sessions, many of the vulnerabilities, and the intricacies of the security system. In contrast, a tiger team must take time to learn the system, then find one vulnerability or a series of vulnerabilities in order to succeed.

Insiders and Outsiders

Information owners need to be aware of where criminals come from who abuse and misuse their information. However, in today's complex business environment, it is nearly impossible to distinguish between an "outside attacker" (e.g., a malicious hacker) and an "inside attacker" (e.g., an embezzler or disgruntled employee). Such differentiation is also largely meaningless in the face of employee mobility, contract employees, outsourcing, and business partnering. From this viewpoint, the only significant difference between insiders and outsiders is that insiders typically already have the knowledge to attack and are in positions of trust, while outsiders do not have these resources and must acquire them. "Outsiders" who are former "insiders," such as ex-employees, are potentially dangerous

Example of a Tiger Team Application

A recent mock "penetration attack" conducted by firm against a multi-million-dollar manufacturing company illustrates just how far some organizations will go to test their security. A team of security specialists launched a simultaneous assault on the company's headquarters and five other sites. "They wanted us to hit them hard, as if we were hackers, to figure out where their holes were," said the team leader. An *Information Week* article (October 21, 1996, page 40; © 1996 CMP Media Inc., reprinted with permission) offers a detailed description of the attack:

> The team leader walked into the main office and distracted a receptionist by asking for directions, while two other team members walked up to a third-floor conference room. "That was the first hole," according to the team leader. "The receptionist should not be responsible for security, but in that case she was."
> Later, the team leader joined the others, and the group spent eight uninterrupted hours wandering through the client's building. By nightfall, the leader had entered the president's office. The executive's computer monitor was off, but his CPU was on and he was still logged on to the network.
> "I read his e-mail, looked at merger and acquisition material, and sent an e-mail to the VP of IS complaining about the security and telling him he was fired," recalls the leader. "The point was, if I was someone else, I could have wreaked havoc on the organization."
>
> Even more telling is the fact that the president of the company and a handful of other managers knew about the mock intrusion in advance. "And yet they left doors wide open, documents and disks laying around with confidential information," the leader notes. "The VP of IS (who was not really fired) knew about a lot of the holes and had told senior managers, but to no avail."

because they may possess the requisite SKRAM if management failed to remove their user authority, which happens all too often. Rather than worrying about insiders and outsiders, we need to understand the attackers in terms of their skills, knowledge, resources, authority, and motivation (refer back to the discussion of SKRAM in Chapter 6 for more details).

Honey Pot Decoys and Padded Cells

The anonymity of the Internet that allows criminals to hide so effectively can also be turned against them. In his book *The Cuckoo's Egg,* Cliff Stoll describes how he effectively used decoy data files with exotic names to lure prey to his hacker-attacked computer. This type of enticement is generally referred to as a "honey pot" or "padded cell," and anyone with a network of computers and servers is well advised to use one to learn more about the sources of threats to information. The technique involves setting up a dummy server on the network, and assigning an intriguing name (e.g., *finance.com* or *executivecompensation.com*), then loading a security monitoring program into it along with a few nonsense data files, a copy of an important application program, and a pager service. Because there should be no reason for anybody to use the server, when the pager calls to indicate unauthorized use, you can begin a trace to identify the source of the intrusion. In many cases, the hits will be accidental, but if you identify one real intruder among one hundred false alarms, the honey pot may be well worth its modest cost. Law enforcement agencies are using this technique with increasing effectiveness to catch pedophiles and other nasty miscreants. In one case, the mother of an intended pedophile target played along with the pervert, setting up a meeting in the flesh, and the police readily caught him with enough evidence for an easy conviction.

There is a downside to this technique, however. Inevitably, network users will discover the honey pot, and its effectiveness will diminish; alternatively, they may use it for spoofing you with false attacks. You may wish to inform your trusted, legitimate users about the ruse with the intent of catching intruders, or you may wish to run a honey pot for a short period of time, then replace it with a new one with a different identity. Remember that for every sting there may be a reverse sting in the making.

PROTECTION FROM SOCIAL ENGINEERING AND GULLIBILITY

In Chapter 6, I identified social engineering as a common practice of criminals, and the gullibility of people in positions of trust as a major vulnerability. The following questions should be helpful for deciding when trusted people should keep information private and when they should feel secure in revealing it.

- Is the information generally known? If so, it is probably not sensitive (unless the source revealing the information makes it sensitive, even though it is already generally known). For example, a fence around a building is an obvious security measure, and it is not harmful to reveal its presence (unless a stakeholder admits that he knows about it when it is not in his best interests to be aware of it).
- Would the information give the enemy aid and comfort or violate the privacy of others? What would be the effect of giving information about your greatest vulnerability to your worst enemy? It is prudent to assume that anything you say that may be heard by a party who could use it could cause you or others harm.

If the information meets the first two criteria, then additional questions should be asked.

- Do you gain something by revealing the information to someone? There are ways to exchange information in confidence that benefit the parties involved.
- Can the source of the information remain anonymous? If so, then you may be able to reveal sensitive information to those with a legitimate need to know. For example, surveys are often conducted anonymously, so it may be safe to respond to them if you have assurances about how the survey results will be handled.
- Is it possible for you to obtain authorization to disclose the information? In order to avoid assuming the security responsibility yourself, it is important to obtain informed consent and organizational approval before presenting a public talk or submitting a report or paper on security.

In short, the test for revealing information flows something like this:

- Is the information generally known?
- Even if it is generally known, should I say it?
- Would the information give aid and comfort to adversaries or violate privacy?
- Is there a benefit to me and to my organization in revealing this information?
- Can the information be securely dispensed?
- Can I obtain authorization to dispense the information?

In general, the best test for determining the loss sensitivity of information is to ask yourself, "Would I want my worst enemy or trusted associate to know the information? Would I feel comfortable hearing the information broadcast on the 6:00 PM television news?" Most of us can resist social engineering involving personal information about ourselves, yet we are sometimes insensitive about revealing information about our business activities or personal information about others. There is a natural tendency to reveal information that is helpful to others, especially when it promotes personal or business advantages, flatters one's ego, or creates the expectation of receiving something in return. It is important to remember that you must make some information freely available, but other information must be held strictly confidential.

The following information items are often the targets of social engineering for criminal purposes:

- Computer users' secret passwords and user IDs
- PIN numbers
- Computer logon protocols
- Operational commands
- Utility functions
- Instructions for using computer applications
- Names and contents of data files
- Telephone numbers that provide entry to computers
- Information about security controls
- Information about other users' practices

Information that is the ultimate objective of theft or espionage includes:

- Personal information that violates privacy
- Business information that may change the value of shares in a corporation (e.g., pending mergers and acquisitions)
- Financial account and inventory level values that could be used to perpetrate business fraud or theft
- Location of valuable assets
- Marketing plans and sales information useful to competitors
- Scientific and engineering plans and progress
- Production data
- Any other trade secrets

Some social engineering is intended merely to obtain information that can be used to embarrass victims or reveal their gullibility.

Objectives of Protection from Social Engineering

Any program to reduce vulnerability to social engineering should focus on creating personal motivation and awareness to resist it. Controls to resist social engineering and reduce the chances that trusted people may be gullible enough to reveal critical, private information should meet the following six objectives:

1. The controls should establish authority to exchange or offer identified information.
2. Communicants must mutually establish the identity and authenticity of one another.
3. Communicants must establish the need for communicating the information between them.
4. Communicants must decide exactly what information to exchange and the limits of that information.
5. Communicants must exchange the information in such a way that other, unauthorized people will not obtain it.
6. The exchange should be recorded or documented as proof of what transpired.

There are numerous practical controls that can make social engineering more difficult, reduce the gullibility of potential victims, and minimize the unauthorized flow of sensitive information. While I could categorize some of the controls relative to the six objectives, many serve multiple purposes and can not be effectively categorized. Thus, I list the following controls in no particular order.

SAFEGUARDING SECURITY

Any program to reduce vulnerability to social engineering should begin with the information security staff, who should be "spoof-proofed" to ensure that they do not reveal unnecessarily detailed information about information security controls, either voluntarily or involuntarily. Ideally, an organization should classify information security controls to the extent that only the people responsible for implementing and administering them know any information about them. However, we should not base the primary effectiveness of a control on the secrecy of its mechanism.

Public reporting of information security controls may be reasonable if you gain something in return, such as support for information security within the organization. However, there is no acceptable reason to reveal detailed information about controls to outsiders. For example, it is generally acceptable to reveal whether an organization is using secret passwords, tokens, or other security protocols for logon. However, it is not generally appropriate to reveal the number of characters used in passwords, guidelines for choosing passwords, logon attempt limits, timeouts, product names, and other variable values associated with controls.

Each information security manager and employee should receive detailed written instructions concerning these matters and should be periodically reminded of them. Less detailed and less rigorous instructions should be provided to users concerning the information security controls that they use or are constrained by. Surely, information about the security controls protecting the sensitive information in an organization should be at least as sensitive as the information that is being protected.

PERSONAL AND VOICE TELEPHONE COMMUNICATION CONTROLS

Trusted people should be cautious in face-to-face and voice telephone communications. I suggest adhering to the following guidelines:

- Choose appropriately confidential locations out of the range of hearing of others for discussion of sensitive information (lip-reading from a distance is a consideration).
- Document the identity of communicants by verifying and recording complete names, titles, locations of workplace, and reporting structure of their organizations. Obtain business cards or other printed material with such information.
- When authenticating persons over the telephone, first discuss personal matters that would be recognized by both communicants from past personal contact or knowledge.
- Formally arrange for a secret spoken code and response code for regular communication, for example, from help desks to branch offices. This technique is commonly used in banking. You can distribute code words on a regular basis in paper reports, by e-mail, or by bulletin boards (defeating this requires that adversaries compromise two or more systems before they can engage in social engineering). Change the code words frequently by using a time-based algorithm (which requires changing the re-initialization codes only occasionally).
- To protect communicants in sensitive conversations, arrange to have a trusted third party witness the communication.
- Manual callback control for voice telephone communications is desirable when time permits.
- Schedule sensitive conversations for a specific future time; this allows you to check identities before the exchange.
- Consider requiring the use of voice telephone cryptographic devices. For example, you can install a telephone protected with cryptography in an appropriate office for people to use on a limited basis when necessary.

CLEARANCE FOR TALKS AND PUBLICATIONS

Implement policies and procedures to review presentations and publications slated for delivery outside of the organization, especially those to be made in public. The clearance procedure may be as simple as requiring the approval of one's manager before speaking or publishing. In other cases, particularly when very sensitive information is involved, you may require formal approval from a committee composed of individuals from several departments within the organization, such as a public affairs officer, a human resources representative, legal counsel, and a marketing or sales representative. Another alternative is to provide guidance about the kinds of information that may or may not be publicly revealed.

MOTIVATION AND AWARENESS

Information security motivation and awareness programs should emphasize the need for trusted people to be cautious about revealing sensitive information through personal contact, telephone, voice mail, fax, and e-mail. Using the World War II phrase "loose lips sink ships" is one colorful way of promoting this particular kind of security. Trusted people should be reminded that both voluntary and involuntary ways of revealing sensitive information exist.

You can also stimulate motivation and awareness by requiring signed statements on an annual basis to remind employees and contractors of their responsibility to protect their knowledge of business secrets and other sensitive information. You can also obtain signed statements from employees prior to their departure on business travel or their attendance at conferences and meetings with outsiders. In some cases—for example in an information security organization—briefings and debriefings are a useful means of issuing timely reminders to people. The military uses this technique for people who are cleared for military information before they travel to meetings, especially in foreign countries. Any time trusted people are victims or targets of social engineering, you should require them to document their experience and indicate the important information that may have been conveyed in both directions.

E-MAIL CONTROLS

E-mail represents an important medium for social engineering. However, perpetrators engaged in deception must be more subtle than when the target is spoken information, since the victim typically has more time to consider whether to reveal information, and more time in which to seek authorization. Because most e-mail systems are relatively insecure, they should not generally be used to transmit information of a sensitive nature. There are, however, some precautions that you can take to make e-mail systems more secure, such as using X.500 CCITT Standard secure protocols and/or cryptography and taking care to keep passwords secret.

In addition, you should always question the authenticity of senders of e-mail messages. People who regularly communicate by e-mail should include serialized codes or personal information in their messages for authentication purposes. You can also use formal code words, but you need to change them frequently and convey them in a different medium than e-mail. (It's generally a good idea to change codes for messages exchanged during lunch hours, since this is a popular time for hackers to try to capture e-mail messages.) Be sure to shut down e-mail message files when recipients are absent for long periods.

You should protect print servers, which are particularly vulnerable in e-mail systems where it is the practice to print out messages, since these servers are often located some distance from the senders and receivers. It may be common practice for unauthorized persons to monitor printer output for you.

You should question excessively inquisitive messages or those requesting that the receiver engage in unusual activities; they may represent a form of social engineering. Do not complete and return questionnaires coming from unknown or untrusted sources without first verifying the legitimacy of the survey requests and the adequacy of protection to be applied to the questionnaires. People who routinely communicate with one another by e-mail should occasionally meet in person to discuss the nature and limits of the information that will be communicated between them, so that they are more likely to question any deviations.

FACSIMILE SECURITY

You need to protect facsimile messages against social engineering, just as you protect voice and e-mail communications. Many of the controls that you use for e-mail are equally applicable to fax messages; in addition, it is advisable to assign a trusted person to control the security for each fax machine. Fax machines facilitate the use of existing documents created for one purpose for some other, unauthorized purpose. For instance, an industrial espionage burglar need not take physical documents away with him; he can merely send copies of the document by fax while he is on the victim's premises.

It is a good idea to install fax machines in secure locations, especially if they are going to be used outside of normal business hours and incoming fax messages may accumulate after hours. Also be sure to place warning signs about transmitting sensitive documents near the fax machines, and empty the wastebaskets in that area frequently, in accordance with the organization's secure trash disposal program. You may also want to consider placing a shredder close to the fax machine.

When sending fax messages, be sure to authenticate the receiver by verifying the telephone number on the fax machine display to reduce the chance of sending messages to an incorrect telephone number. And, when you are sending a fax containing sensitive information, notify the recipients of the approximate schedule for the transmission so that they can be present at the receiving fax machines when the messages arrive—thereby reducing the possibility that an unauthorized person will intercept the messages or observe them while they are being received.

Use standard cover sheets for all outgoing fax messages that clearly identify your organization by name and logo. Also be sure to list all intended recipients of the message by name and address. A warning banner on the cover sheet should indicate the proprietary nature of the information (e.g., Company Private). If the information is particularly sensitive, the same classification information should be repeated on the top or bottom edge of each page in case the pages get separated from the cover sheet during printing or distribution.

When receiving fax messages in person, it may be wise to refuse to accept any messages that do not include the telephone number of the sender, at least until you are able to verify the source. You should also erase the residual electronic image from printing the last incoming fax message from the machine to eliminate the possibility of someone reading it later. Finally, anticipate an increase in the use of fax technology for social engineering. Most personal computer modems can now send and receive fax messages just as easily as e-mail, and fax machines are steadily dropping in price, making the technology cost-effective for malicious hackers (along with everyone else).

VOICE MAIL CONTROLS

Call-back is an effective means of authenticating the identity of callers who leave messages in voice mail systems. It should be a common business practice, expected and accepted by users in sensitive situations. It is also useful, since voice mail messages tend to be cryptic and need further explanation in any case.

Malefactors sometimes use voice mail to intimidate or threaten recipients. It can also provide an effective medium for social engineering because requests for information left in voice mail messages often disarm recipients, who assume that people with malicious intent are not likely to leave recorded messages. Perpetrators may choose to use this medium to take advantage of this belief.

In businesses involving a high volume of sensitive telephone calls and voice mail messages (e.g., securities brokerage) an automatic tape recording device provides a useful safeguard. If you use such a device, however, you should establish policy concerning personal telephone messages to protect the privacy of those engaged in telephone communication.

Although voice recognition is important in telephone and voice mail communication, remember that voices can be easily disguised—at least to the human ear—because of the relatively narrow bandwidth of voice communication. Therefore, you should rely upon voice recognition less than in face-to-face communication. Diction and speaking peculiarities are also useful for recognition purposes if done with caution.

EMERGENCY RESPONSE TO SOCIAL ENGINEERING

Establish an emergency response team to combat social engineering, or expand the scope of teams established for other security purposes to include social engineering attacks. An individual who suspects that he or she may be a victim of social engineering should consult team members for assistance. Such assistance should be confidential to encourage victims who may be embarrassed to report such events. A victim can trap an individual engaged in social engineering by continuing to supply carefully chosen information, but on a recorded or monitored basis. A victim of social engineering may also play on the egos of perpetrators or promise more information later in order to gain time to take actions against the perpetrators.

PREVENT DISCLOSURE

The following actions can help you to effectively prevent voluntary disclosure of sensitive information. These actions may sound familiar because they are essentially the same safeguards recommended to computer users, but from a different perspective.

- Establish a policy for information security, and publish it widely. Make sure that people understand it, especially those on the computer security staff.
- Develop a code of conduct (i.e., a set of rules to safeguard security procedures). Be sure to include rewards and penalties in the code, because without them, a code is only a set of guidelines. This may be

difficult to accomplish across the board at some companies, but you can certainly do it on a limited scale to apply to security people.

- Make confidentiality agreements mandatory. Many organizations require consultants to sign confidentiality agreements; if the agreements are not required, consultants should voluntarily submit a signed confidentiality statement to their clients.

- Avoid revealing details in any disclosure of information. For example, do not provide details about the use of resource access control packages, passwords, user entry attempts, or similar elements of information management and security.

- Exercise extra caution in hiring and firing computer security specialists. These positions are more sensitive with regard to information security than nearly any other positions within an organization, and therefore warrant an additional level of caution.

- Report any losses that do occur to the proper authorities within the organization first, and then to appropriate law enforcement agencies. This is a social responsibility; if management fails to comply, auditors or the security staff should do so—even if doing so puts their jobs in jeopardy. On the other hand, reporting suspected crimes to the authorities must be weighed against the violation of security and harm to the organization that may result. Public revelation of vulnerabilities and the lack of specific controls can conceivably reduce security. These conflicting principles may lead to difficult problems, so it is essential to seek legal counsel before reporting losses.

Organizations need to "spoof-proof" employees in positions of trust to make them resistant to deception, and unlikely to reveal details of sensitive information in social or business settings. Instruct equipment operators not to reveal information over the telephone without following a procedure to verify a caller's identity. Segregation of duties in security work assignments is important, as is physical and logical protection from unauthorized use of information. The number of computer security programs that are designed to run on shared computers is increasing. Consider adopting the military practice of using a PC or minicomputer that is isolated behind locked doors to run computer security programs, because there is no adequately secure computer for the highest level of sensitive security information.

Some other precautions for protecting sensitive information include:

- Numbering, logging, and otherwise controlling every copy of each document concerning security.

- Using cross-cutting or pulverizing shredders. (Ideally, there should be as many shredders as there are computer printers. In a humorous vein, one might like to have the default practice of paper coming from the printer and going directly into the shredder.)
- Exercising care in revealing the names of the vendors that provide you with computer-related services. For example, few people need to know the name or location of the commercial company that provides an organization's remote data backup services.
- Locking sensitive information in the trunk of your car when driving and parking. Also avoid packing sensitive information in checked luggage when travelling.
- Being aware of unusual circumstances when removing information from protected facilities in public.

THE LIMITATIONS OF TECHNICAL SECURITY

When we have considered all of the possible security tactics, it is clear that achieving the Holy Grail of perfect security is fruitless. Every commercial operating system, whether it is a version of UNIX or Microsoft Windows, contains bugs or undocumented programmer "conveniences," and each bug or informal code is a potential security vulnerability. Dr. Peter Neumann at SRI International continues to preach that systems applications security is for naught until we have a secure operating system base with which to operate and control it.

Computer scientists have designed completely secure computer systems on paper, at least to the extent that after thorough testing, no one has found a security vulnerability in the design. However, no one has ever been able to build a secure system from the secure design. This is because commercial systems are sufficiently large and complex (containing from 1,000,000 to 20,000,000 interrelated instructions) that no individual can create one and comprehend it all. Further, a team can not create one perfectly without bugs, because two or more people can not work together with perfect and complete mutually shared knowledge and cooperation. And even if they could, the high cost would negate the commercial value of any such system.

Commercial computer systems are so complex that experts can not predict what they will do under all circumstances—even if the hardware is perfectly predictable. Systems will repeat exactly the same correct or incorrect results with the same input, but there are too many sets of differ-

As Good As It Gets

The Honeywell Corporation and the Massachusetts Institute of Technology attempted to create a perfectly secure multi-access computer system at MIT in the 1970s. They jointly designed and built the *Multics Computer System* with a secure architecture of concentric logic rings of increasing entry exclusiveness, with the inner circle protecting the key security mechanism. Everybody agreed that the design of Multics was perfectly secure. However, as part of the testing efforts, Air Force Captain Roger Schell and his small band of authorized hackers a few miles away at Hanscomb Air Force Base were compromising the security of Multics over in Cambridge at MIT about once each week during the final two development years. The computer scientists could design a perfectly secure computer; they just could not build it to be perfectly secure.

The delivered commercial Multics products manufactured by Honeywell were very secure (but not perfect), multi-access, supercomputers, which competed with the Cray super-computers from Cray Research in Minnesota. The only problem was that users found that it was almost impossible to use Multics systems for practical purposes with the security in place, so in some cases, they turned off many of the controls, and almost everybody was happy.

Management in the customer organizations and their shareholders were happy, because they had the most secure multi-access supercomputer in existence. The users were happy, because they turned off the security and had the easiest-to-use and friendliest computers in existence. And Honeywell was happy as sales soared. The only people who were unhappy were the auditors, who saw the insecurity of the systems and reported it to closed-minded management—who would do nothing about it.

Theoretically, a large enough number of brilliant people could spend enough time under sufficient discipline to create a perfectly secure system. However, making a large enough number of people work together, and attentively enough for long enough, each person knowing only part of the operating system logic, would not be practical or commercially feasible. Object programming, where standard, small pieces of code along with the data to be processed are created and fitted together in building block fashion, offers some hope for the future. Computer Scientists at Stanford University and SRI International know how to mathematically prove the correctness of the coded instructions in software, but no software or hardware company has found it practical and feasible to do it. They have not been able to find the customers willing to pay the price to do it on a commercially successful basis. Generally, you and I do not want computers that are too secure, because of the severe constraints that would be necessary. Close-to-perfect security costs too much and gets in the way of productive work, and we would rather take our chances, to some degree, with criminals and losses, than pay for the security up front. However, as Bill Murray at Deloitte and Touche has preached, we will pay the price one way or the other.

ent inputs to test them all. If we do not know what a computer system will do in all circumstances, then we can never prove that it is secure. Each change (even just one bit) that maintenance engineers make in a system raises questions about its security and requires re-testing to prove security. Only God can create a perfectly secure computer system, and God does not write computer programs—as far as we know.

At the very least, however, we should try to obtain reasonably secure software products. Unfortunately, the first versions of most new products generally have insufficient security because the vendors are anxious to push their products out the door and do not take time to worry much about including security features. In addition, most software vendors do not want to include security that would constrain users and reduce the program's performance. Most do eventually get around to adding security in later versions of the products, though, so we would do well to take some advice from hackers here. Hackers advise purchasers that the best protection against maliciousness is to keep their software up-to-date, installing the latest fixes, updates, or versions that have corrected the known vulnerabilities and added security. As Biffsocko, a tattooed hacker, said at a DefCon hacker conference in Las Vegas, "Pay attention and get the latest patches."

15

Strategies for Effective Information Security

Information security plays a well-recognized tactical role in support of information processing. It also plays an increasingly strategic role in business because of the strategic value of information, the vulnerabilities inherent in distributing computing resources throughout an organization, and the dangers lurking in the Internet.

In this chapter, I describe how information security contributes to the strategic values of goals, objectives, and success of business organizations—extending far beyond simply protecting information from loss. I suggest how information security managers can assist their organizations to better achieve the business goals of productivity, growth, and profitability as well as meeting the tactical objectives of reducing vulnerabilities and loss. Good security can make the information associated with these goals more valuable, useful, and effective. User confidence that information will be where it is needed, when it is needed, in complete, proprietary, valid, and useful form provides the strategic value for successful security.

The exploration of why information security impacts organizations so profoundly focuses on a number of key questions:

- What have organizations done, or what is different about organizations, such that information security plays a strategic role?
- How can an organization capitalize on the strategic advantages that a well-conceived and administered information security function provides?
- What is the value of information security for competitive purposes or for limiting product or service liabilities and loss?

The answers to these questions can help information security managers to play a more effective strategic role in their business organizations.

STRATEGIC VALUES OF INFORMATION AND SECURITY

My study of top management's view of information security reveals four strategic values of information security:

1. Security advances business effectiveness by enabling information technology; our information systems would be unusable without it.
2. Security advances and differentiates the competitive positions of businesses. One company, for example, prides itself on keeping secret the information about its customers (the quantities of raw materials they supply, where materials are delivered, and the processes used to form products from the materials). This is a specific competitive advantage, because the company's primary competitor does not seem to value this kind of confidentiality, but the customers do.
3. A demonstrable dedication to information security helps to enhance the public image of organizations. Businesses can gain public and shareholder trust and avoid charges of negligence for failure to meet the requirements of due care practices. (Consider how banks create a secure image by displaying their vault doors to the public.)
4. Information security nurtures and helps retain the talent assets of a business. Organizations nurture and retain their talent assets (i.e., employees' knowledge and skills) by protecting their employees' personal privacy and building their confidence that information about them will be complete, available to them and to those they authorize, and authentic.

I'll address each of these strategic values in detail in the following sections.

Advancing Business Effectiveness by Enabling Information Technology

We need to consider the strategic value of information security relative to the strategic value of information technology (IT) because information security is an integral part of IT functions in many businesses. In addition, the information security department often works through the IT unit in performing its advisory and standards-setting role throughout the organization and—thanks to the secure commercialization of the Internet—outside of the organization. The Internet would be almost completely useless from a business perspective if users could not apply sufficient security from within their domains before allowing transactions to enter the public switched network.

Information security is often viewed as an IT requirement rather than as a requirement for all information, in all forms. When anyone mentions information security, most business people immediately think of computers and networks; they view information security specialists as computer technologists first, and business crime fighters second, if at all.

An article by Walter A. Kleinschrod titled "Leveraging Technology" in the April 1996 edition of *Beyond Computing* provides some insights into the role of IT in business. The article was based on a survey of chief information officers (CIOs). Two-thirds of the respondents indicated that their companies are leveraging IT and one-third indicated they are not. The CIOs' primary goals were quite interesting:

- improving customer service
- speeding employee use of information
- streamlining operations
- lowering costs
- improving employee productivity

According to the article, the CIOs intend to use the following methods to achieve their goals:

- installing new IT systems
- training end-users
- expanding existing IT systems
- increasing the technology budget
- training the IT department

Most of the comments quoted in the article focused on improving IT services, not business services. Nothing indicated that the CIOs were working directly with business management to meet the traditional goals of productivity, profitability, and business growth. Instead, they were pursuing the goals indirectly through internal IT development. For example, the survey report said nothing about gaining a competitive advantage in the marketplace. Only one respondent indicated that part of the goal was improving the organization's image, which is a strategic value. And, no respondents directly expressed the enhancement of the business and its competitive advantage. And the article contained only one veiled reference to security. A CIO said, "An idea we're playing with is to post a Web home page where people can login through a secure connection and tap into design and manufacturing information."

This type of article is bound to be discouraging for the outward-looking information security departments that are usually embedded in the IT organizations. This positioning may suppress the role that information security can play in furthering the strategic interests of the business directly. Is it necessary for the information security managers to play a different role than the CIO in working directly with management in the business units? Information security managers should provide advice, encouragement, and support, to apply information security in such a way that security enhances the products, services, marketing, and sales in a competitive market.

Another, more general issue that my studies have revealed is the importance of the enabling value of information security. Without adequate security, we would not have to argue about Internet taxation legislation because it would be impossible to impose taxes without the security to protect the finding of the transactions to be taxed. (Internet taxation legislation is a huge political issue in some jurisdictions which believe that they have the right to tax transactions that pass through their "territory" even though the transactions do not originate or terminate there.) Internet packet messages can take various, unknown routes entering and leaving legal jurisdictions indiscriminately as they find their way from one available node to the next. Customs duty, excise, capital gains, sales, and property tax authorities all have interests in milking the Internet. Yet, how can we tax the billions of encrypted transactions that follow devious routes around the world through the Internet? Certainly, the Internet, as a source of huge tax revenue, is tempting. But the means for tax fraud is frightening without significant security constraints, and constraints may inhibit electronic commerce.

Businesses are excited by the prospect of reducing the cost of a manual transaction from several dollars to a few cents on the Internet. However, they may be lured into traps by taking the chance for big gains without considering the possibility of taxation or taking into account the cost of sufficient security to deal appropriately with this form of commerce.

While security may enable technology, it can also lead us into new problems of vast complexity. Security on the Internet requires extensive use of cryptography and key management on a monstrous scale. Dr. Bob Blakley at IBM has some interesting things to say about public key cryptography (two keys, one private key to encrypt a message and one public key to decrypt it):

> Public key cryptography tries to address some of the problems caused by excessive reliance on secrecy. But is it the devil's bargain? The false hope that public keys could be printed in the newspaper and forgotten has faded like a mirage, and in its place we have hundreds of pages of legalese outlining under what circumstances key pairs (and corresponding certificates) of various grades may be issued, what it's safe to use them for, and what obligations they impose upon their issuers and owners. Indeed, public-key pairs seem more and more like nuclear waste; their private halves are hazardous if anyone comes in contact with them, and their public halves need to be kept around in elaborately secure crypts for longer than their owners are likely to live.
>
> This metaphor is in deadly earnest. Before we as a society create huge numbers of these key pairs, we had better understand the management and disposal issues we will face down the road. Public-key certificates are essentially reified trust, just as cash is reified value. Mankind had no experience managing stockpiles of trust—especially stockpiles of misplaced trust. Ghosts of broken promises, echoes of failed relationships, the assurances of frauds—all these will be in the box, waiting for some modern Pandora to discover a private key, erase a CRL entry, or break an algorithm and let them out.
>
> While we're on the subject, when we create key pairs with 10-year lifespans, or use a private key to sign a 30-year mortgage, will we think about what percentage of the planet's wealth we're willing to bet on the proposition that our cryptographers are smarter than everyone alive today, *and* everyone waiting to be born? *[from The Emperor's Old Armor, ACM New Security Paradigm Workshop, Lake Arrowhead, CA, © 1996 ACM, quoted here by permission of the ACM and of the author]*

Lynn McNulty, an independent consultant based in Washington, DC, commented on security as a business enabler while he was serving at the NIST, where he was attempting to follow the lead of the experts at NSA. He emphasized that implementing cryptography key and certificate management structures that serve the interests of corporations and private organizations (as opposed to the interests of governments) is essential. He went on to say that replacing passwords with tokens actually provides some degree of real user authentication and identification that is desperately needed by business, and advised that we must manage risks in open networks and align security so that it is perceived as being a business enabler.

Protecting and Enhancing Competitive Advantage

The second strategic value is to advance competitive position in business, or, alternatively in government to satisfy the desires of constituents and legislators. The demand for information systems security is a strategic value that business and government recognize strongly today in the establishment of Internet and intranet Web pages. Marketing and sales departments as well as government bureaucrats are creating technical staffs to develop Web pages that offer services and public advice, advertise products, and provide communication with sales staff, agents, wholesale customers, retail customers, suppliers, and contractors.

Many Web page developers are relatively naive about security. If they consider security at all, it is as an afterthought and heavily influenced by what they read in IT trade publications focusing on the confidentiality of information available through Web pages. Many developers fail to understand that there are significantly greater threats than the disclosure of confidential information, including the loss of possession of intellectual property (e.g., software), which may not violate any confidentiality. They need to understand the seriousness of possible loss of authenticity or integrity of disseminated information. They also need to be concerned about loss of availability or utility of information, such as through the garbling of information and interruption or delay of service. One Web page marketing manager admitted that he never considered any security requirements for the information going out through his Web page, only the need for confidentiality of information coming back in. He failed to understand the potential serious loss of authenticity of his broadcast price lists or to consider how his price lists could be covertly or accidentally changed or replaced with obsolete ones to sabotage the company.

Web pages also require protection from intentional, accidental, or well-intentioned, unauthorized but harmful actions of the organization's own staff. They need protection as well from other, more obvious sources of threats such as those from competitors. Information security managers should play an active role in developing and maintaining electronic marketing services to ensure that the other participants understand the range of threats and potential loss that can result from a lack of security.

Some companies use a technique called just-in-time decision making, in part, to protect the confidentiality of their planning process. The technique involves simultaneously developing a number of alternative plans and carrying them forward as far as possible until, at the last possible moment, top management chooses one to implement. This type of decision making eliminates the possibility of competitors learning important plans in advance; they may discover the existence of one or more of the possible plans but can not know which will ultimately be chosen because not even the participants in the decision making process know—at least not until after it is too late for anyone to take undue advantage of the information. Competitive magazine publishers often use this technique to protect their cover story articles, and marketing departments use it to protect information about new product releases or test plans.

Many of the managers that I have interviewed over the years frequently overlooked the importance of information authenticity (validity, genuineness, and accuracy) until I brought it to their attention; they then had high interest. For example, preserving the authenticity of product safety information, warrantees, price lists, and product availability information are high on the security list. Managers need to understand that false data entry into computers and modification and misrepresentation after information leaves computers are probably the two greatest threats to authenticity. What happens to the integrity of information while resident in computers and squeezed through communication networks is the next greatest concern.

Enhancing Actual and Perceived Values of Products and Services

The third strategic value of information lies in its ability to enhance the value of products and services to minimize loss and to improve the public perception of the organization, its officers and shareholders, customers, and other stakeholders. I include both actual and perceived values in this definition to emphasize the inherent value of avoiding any appearance of negligence on the part of the organization's management and the related value of increasing public trust in the company and its products and services. In my study, I focused on three manufacturers of tangible products, none of whom produced any intellectual property products such as commercial software or publications. All three companies do, however, have products that include or are accompanied by information. One company places great value on the manuals that are distributed for promotion and support of their tangible products, and the company is well known for publishing these manuals. The greatest interest in the security of this information, now distributed in the form of Web pages, requires electronically achieved integrity, authenticity, availability, and utility.

The competitive advantage of information security can occur in subtle ways. One privately held company has a significant competitive advantage because it treats its manufacturing customers' information, such as quantities, contents, and locations of materials ordered, as secret and proprietary. The company maintains a relatively low public profile—especially compared to its competitors. This purposely low profile provides its customers with the opportunity to take full credit for the products and to optimize the advertising of the product values, opportunities which their customers view as a significant service because it emphasizes the customers' retail branding. The privately held company claims that their publicly owned competitors boast and advertise about the importance of the raw products that they supply to their manufacturing customers. The private company uses the importance of this competitive advantage to promote the need for security within the business.

Security is intimately associated with an organization's culture. Some publicly held corporations and high-visibility government agencies operate as "open books," continually keeping shareholders and/or citizens apprised of their plans and financial state. Conversely, some privately held companies and relatively obscure government agencies operate as "closed societies," disseminating remarkably little information to their stakeholders. Most businesses and agencies are, however, a mix of the two extremes. Security practitioners need to understand an organization's information culture, as well as the nature of the organization relative to other similar businesses and competitors, before advising on security.

One remark by a CIO demonstrated the power of the press in forming distorted perceptions about information loss. The CIO indicated that his greatest fear in IT was international commercial espionage. According to FBI studies, although this type of espionage may be a major concern for some types of spoken and displayed information, it often has little to do with computers or networks as sources of information. Espionage agents concentrate on obtaining knowledge from people, not computers. However, it is important for promoting the strategic value of security that information security managers be aware of and address the perceptions of information owners—even though the perceptions may be exaggerations or distortions. One major objective of information security is to provide adequate security to allay the fears of owners—whatever those fears may be.

Protecting Talented Employees' Privacy and Workplace Satisfaction

The fourth strategic value that I identified in my study is that of protecting the talent assets of an organization—the key individuals and their collective knowledge that are critical to the success of the business. Organizations must ensure that these individuals, whether they are the top executives, middle managers, scientists, production manufacturing specialists, or salespeople, are happy and productive in their positions, and must make every reasonable effort to retain them for as long as they can contribute to business success. To do this, organizations need to create environments that are conducive to creative and energetic work, with as few distractions and little extraneous stress as possible. In addition, the organization needs to ensure the employees' safety and security, which includes protecting their personal privacy. Such protection may entail authenticating their identities to credit their high performance, and protecting their identities when they are the subjects of criticism. Security should be as transparent and unobtrusive as possible to avoid distracting the employees and to optimize their freedom of thought and action.

SUBTLE ROLES AND STRATEGIC EFFECTS OF SECURITY

The four strategic roles that security plays in protecting business information are often embedded in current business practices, products, and services in unexpected but important ways. For example, in one company, employees update their own personnel files on-line, which increases their privacy and the security of the records because there is no intermediary who can divulge personal information or harm it in any way. In another company, top management and human resources (HR) departments specify a percentage increase for each of their manager's payrolls for the year; then each manager makes the specific compensation decisions and distributes the increase among his or her people. This system replaces the customary e-mail and office mail communications to negotiate staff compensation with the corporate human resources department, and eliminates exposing a significant amount of the private, sensitive information that managers typically exchange electronically and on paper, thereby providing a serendipitous strategic security advantage.

HR systems that provide direct employee input and decision processes without involving intermediaries are examples of removing confidential, personal information from unnecessary view and knowledge of data gathering and entry clerks. Authorized decision makers see only the pertinent information stored in the computers that automatically implement the final decisions. We can see the implicit security here, because we recognize that possessing information without knowing it is quite different from knowing information in order to process it. Different security vulnerabilities exist for possession and confidentiality of information. We can possess and process much information without exposing it to other people, which would require additional confidentiality controls.

Another company, which broadcasts its product specifications to individuals throughout the world via a Web page, demonstrates the strategic public-image value of information security. Management did run into some trouble in one country that prohibits releasing certain types of information to its citizens, but resolved the problem by inserting a screen before displaying the sensitive information. The screen asks the user to indicate if she is a citizen of that particular country; if the answer is affirmative, the company limits the information that she can view. Of course, this does not prevent the user from accessing the information, but it satisfies the country's legal requirements and shifts the responsibility for security from the company providing the information to the people receiving it. The company can use audit trails to detect any infractions on the part of the users.

One of a news magazine's practices is a good example of the strategic security of maintaining the confidentiality of competitively sensitive decisions. In selecting a controversial article for publication, they carry out the research, writing, and print layout for a number of candidate articles up until the moment the magazine goes to press. Executives travel to the printing plants and, at the last moment, make the selection of the printing mats to prevent competitors from discovering the final choice in advance. In addition, in many cases, organizations find that relying on the rapid obsolescence of information is just as effective as prolonging the secrecy of information, particularly in fast-moving technology businesses.

Confrontational and Voluntary Security Alternatives

My interviews with business executives revealed that a number of companies are transferring owner control of information security to the discretion of the user. This shift is in addition to the common default state of users controlling security when they are in command of it. Assigning information security to explicitly defined owners may not be an effective control in distributed computing environments and in organizations where knowledge management prevails. This is because it is difficult to motivate individuals to accept accountability in view of the complexity of identifying appropriate owners of shared information and the limited authority to enforce the necessary widespread discipline. In a situation like that of the company that needed to restrict information disclosure on its Web page, voluntary adoption of security accountability by systems users generally works reasonably well for much business information. Good motivation is always at the core of successful security. But, the need for intensive user involvement may be changing as vendors implement more security controls, like cryptography, and makes their application universal and transparent to users, thereby reducing the role of users in at least some aspects of security.

Because business transactions are based on trust and risk-taking anyway, organizations can often rely on users to support security on a voluntary basis and take voluntary action against imprudent practices. In addition to prevention, which is the primary technological control function, organizations need to address the other security functions: avoidance, deterrence, and detection. Some organizations give employees the responsibility for not acquiring indecent or pornographic information that is widely available through the Internet, rather than attempting to stop the providers of smut. In other situations, the users may feel satisfied that their employer relies on software packages to filter out unwanted information or implement other types of avoidance or deterrence controls. The use of computer "no trespassing" warning banners on initial logon screens can be an effective deterrence tactic in trust situations (though, of course, of limited value against dedicated hackers or spies). These are not technological considerations, but in business, people are required to maintain high ethical performance in which a warning or confrontation can tip their response toward support rather than violation of security and prudence.

ETHICS: THE ESSENCE OF GOOD SECURITY

People are fundamentally flawed. Therefore, absence of an ethics program in an organization is a gross security deficiency, and fails to meet a standard of due care, because many organizations have them. Some companies frame their ethics codes and hang them on the walls. While the exposure may make management and employees more continually aware of the ethics code, the code must exist in the minds and actions of trusted people in order to be effective. Ethics is rooted in the cultures of organizations, and we need to understand the cultures to effectively promote and advance ethical values. In some organizations, ethical values and practices need not be overtly promoted and brought to the attention of managers and employees, because they are already uniformly ingrained from the top down. In other organizations, especially large, diverse, multinationals engaged in sensitive activities that affect people's lives (e.g., the automotive industry), ethics requirements must be explicitly promoted and adherence required. Laws and regulation, as well as learned values from childhood and later experience, make many ethical practices clear to managers and employees. However, applying ethical values in new situations that organizations create by adopting new technologies may require explicit and detailed statements of ethical principles or rules of conduct. For example, information technology introduced computer programs as a new kind of valuable information that requires new rules for fair treatment of proprietary software.

Many organizations have codes of good practice, primarily for business ethics. They are usually part of organization policies or are expressed in special ways such as in elaborate documents, and are commonly included in new employees' orientation packets. Some organizations, especially financial institutions, require officers to read the code annually and sign statements agreeing to abide by it. This comes close to a standard of due care and is required in banking laws and regulations.

I see two common problems with these practices in many businesses: The code does not cover ethics concerning the protection of information (except for some confidentiality rules), and the code is not cast at the right levels of abstraction to be effective for the various types of people it addresses. In the first case, codes may not cover privacy rights, personal use of computer services, software ownership, or authentic self-identification. And in the second case, codes may also consist of long lists of *dos* and *don'ts* that insult the intellectual levels of highly educated people, or at the other extreme, may be too esoteric for others. For example, researchers often do not like to be told the obvious specific acts that they should avoid doing. I find that the best solution is to provide a high-level set of principles coupled with several lists of more detailed rules for various types of work. Good detailed codes relating to information processing are available from the Association for Computing Machinery (www.acm.org) in New York City; the Data Processing Management Association (www.dpma.org) in Park Ridge, Illinois; and the IEEE Computer Society (www.ieee.org) in Washington, DC.

The high-level ethics code should start with the Golden Rule (or its equivalent) and be accompanied by stated principles. Individuals usually need guidance when they are faced with difficult decisions that affect people; these decisions generally involve conflicts of values, and the choices are likely to be beneficial to some people and harmful to others. My two earlier books, *Ethical Conflicts in Computer Science, Technology, and Business,* published in 1977 and a second version in 1987, identify more than 100 ethical dilemma scenarios and present the opinions of leaders in computer science, business, and technology. I have reduced those findings into five ethical principles that apply particularly to processing information in the workplace. These principles and examples of their application may be helpful as part of a periodic review of the decision-making process within your organization, or for use as a checklist in a methodical approach to problem solving and decision making. Although you are not likely to remember these principles on every occasion, reading them now and then or having them handy when making a decision may help you in going through difficult decision-making situations.

1. **Informed consent.**   Try to make sure that the people affected by a decision are aware of your planned actions and that they either agree with your decision, or disagree but understand your intentions.
2. **Higher ethic in the worst case.**   Think carefully about your possible alternative actions and select the beneficial necessary ones that will cause the least, or no, harm under the worst circumstances.
3. **Change of scale test.**   Consider that an action you may take on a small scale, or by you alone, could result in significant harm if carried out on a larger scale or by many others.
4. **Owners' conservation of ownership.**   As a person who owns or is responsible for information, always make sure that the information is reasonably protected and that ownership of it, and rights to it, are clear to users.
5. **Users' conservation of ownership.**   As a person who uses information, always assume it is owned by others and their interests must be protected unless you explicitly know that you are free to use it in any way that you wish.

Examples of Application of the Ethical Principles

Now consider some practice examples, and make your decisions on whether the people described in the scenarios would be acting ethically or unethically, without considering any other unidentified factors that may change the decisions you make:

Informed consent.   An employee gives a copy of a program that she wrote for her employer to a friend, and does not tell her employer about it.

Higher ethic in the worst case.   A manager secretly monitors an employee's e-mail, which may violate his privacy, but the manager has reason to believe that the employee may be involved in a serious theft of trade secrets.

Change of scale.   A teacher lets a friend try out, just once, a database that he bought to see if the friend wants to buy a copy too. The teacher does not let an entire classroom of his students use the database for a class assignment without first getting permission from the vendor. A computer user thinks it's okay to use a small amount of her employer's computer services for personal business, since others' use is unaffected.

Owners' conservation.   A vendor who sells a commercial electronic bulletin board service with no proprietary notice at logon, loses control of the service to a group of hackers who take it over, misuse it, and offend customers.

Users' conservation.   A hacker discovers a commercial electronic bulletin board with no proprietary notice at logon, and informs his friends, who take control of it, misuse it, and offend other customers.

Attempting to train people in the appropriate application of ethics is often difficult, boring, and unpopular. No one wants to attend classes to learn how ethical they should be. However, I find that people are fascinated with the unethical things that others do and with conflicts that arise (that is why I named two of my books, *Ethical Conflicts* . . . rather than *Ethics* . . .). I find that classes that I conduct are quite successful by offering scenarios of ethical dilemmas in pertinent subjects of interest for discussion, debate, and balloting.

LEGAL CONCERNS

Another information security issue of strategic importance in business concerns litigation and the related rules of evidence. Legal departments in many organizations are concerned with evidence disputes and the requirements imposed by court orders, as well as regulations governing the retention and destruction of electronic information. The tobacco industry legal liability battles are prime examples of these concerns. Corporate lawyers are asking how to totally destroy information and prove that it no longer exists and, conversely, how to perfectly retain information for as long as the company wishes or is required to do. Information security managers can help the legal departments to wrestle with the difficulties inherent in retaining information in readable form for 50 years or more, and in completely destroying all copies of electronic information very quickly. One company that I know of centralizes the retention of information, recording the locations of originals and copies, and tracking the destruction process to maintain consistent control for the entire corporation.

Legal requirements to retain information in readable form for long periods of time pose some very real difficulties for information owners and business management. The hardware and software needed to read electronic media may become obsolete and be replaced and, if the information is encrypted, the keys required to decode it may be lost. In fact, cryptography is having a major effect on information retention and destruction, since it, along with key management, require organizations to implement controls for retaining and recovering cryptographic software and keys, as well as the encrypted information. Such controls are necessary, not only because of the legal requirements for retaining and destroying information, but also to prevent information anarchy resulting from employees' independent use of cryptography and their personal keys.

Unfortunately, destroying information is no easier than retaining it. Destroying all copies of electronic information in all of the backup files, shadow files, magnetic media residue, buffers and storage areas that retain residual data, as well as printed copies, is a formidable task. (In many cases, the first thing that a computer operator does when you tell her to destroy information on a disk or tape is to make a backup copy of it.) Information systems operations staffs have strong inclinations to preserve information; these inclinations and practices are deeply ingrained and not likely to be easily changed because of legal requirements or requests from the legal department. Overcoming these habits is, however, necessary to accomplish effective information destruction.

To ensure achieving the objectives for preserving and destroying information, we need to focus separately on the issues of possession and confidentiality. Possession and confidentiality controls are different, and we need both kinds for their intended purposes. In addition, businesses need to have a single policy that facilitates uniformly controlling, destroying, and preserving strategic information consistently throughout the entire organization. The best way to control information preservation and destruction is to log all copies of information and track their use and storage throughout their life cycle—from creation and backup through destruction.

Lawyers face an incredibly complex array of legal issues in the commercialization of the Internet and often call on security experts to help them understand the inherent security requirements and limitations. For example, the International Organization of Securities Commission, the help from the U.S. Securities and Exchange Commission (www.sec.gov), is urging international securities regulators in 134 countries to strengthen Internet surveillance to combat securities fraud, especially across international boundaries. This requires security technology to make monitoring feasible as well as the introduction of secure personal and corporate electronic identity certificates, which are only now beginning to be generally available.

How to Destroy Electronic Information

We generally think of security with the objective of preserving information. Destroying information can, however, be just as important as a security control. Destroying obsolete information helps to ensure that no one reads it, or depends on it for decision making. It also helps to avoid the problems related to contaminating new information with obsolete information and makes room to store new information securely. Destroying information also gives us the additional advantage of no longer needing to protect it. Thus, we should always destroy unnecessary copies of information to reduce its loss exposure and the need to protect it.

In the ancient times of Greek city-states, a king would use a slave as a form of storage and communication medium to relay a message to another king. The sending king would print the message on the slave's shaved head, to be secured in transit by the hair that grew over it. The receiving king would shave the slave's head to read the message. Unfortunately for the slave, the only proper erasure method involved scalping or death. Ed Hetsko, an engineer at the Joint National Test Facility at Falcon Air Force Base in Colorado, summarized the standards of due care of destruction nicely in the January 1997 issue of the Boston-based MIS Training Company trade journal, *Infosecurity News* (©1997 MIS). I paraphrase his instructions by permission and add a few of my own.

We can easily destroy information printed on paper by destroying the medium. Destroying knowledge remembered by people gets messy, but is sometimes doable. Today there are three accepted means of erasing electronic information without destroying the media: clearing, purging, and degaussing. We can also get rid of information by using the computer operating system command usually called *erase* or *delete,* or by moving the name of a file from the file index to the trash icon. These two methods do not erase the information; they just remove it from view. Emptying the trash icon frees up the memory space that the information occupies, but it is still there and may still exist in buffers, caches, shadow files, and who knows where else. The information resides in memory until the system needs that memory space for new information, which is written over it. Various utility programs make it possible to find any remaining information that has not been overwritten yet, and there are laboratory methods using special equipment that can still retrieve it after several overwrites.

We can *clear* information by properly overwriting unassigned system storage space. A single overwrite is satisfactory to ensure that the information can not be retrieved by using software diagnostic tools such as Symantec's Norton Utilities (www.symantec.com). We can clear information from removable media (e.g., magnetic tapes and diskettes) by using a *degausser* (commonly found in computer centers) that subjects them to a reverse magnetizing field. This reduces magnetic induction to zero. Degaussers should be installed some distance away from where magnetically recorded information is stored. This allows some time for an individual to think about whether he really wants to erase the information as he walks over to it. Clearing will probably not protect the information from a laboratory attack (using powerful equipment), but if the storage media remain in the same protected environment, it will not be recoverable if attackers are kept out by physical entry controls which prevent them from removing the media to a laboratory for a stronger attack.

Now suppose that the media containing the information to be erased reside in an unsecured location, or will be outside of the control of those protecting it. We need a stronger kind of erasure called *purging.* We can purge some forms of memory, which enables us to reuse them. Users can purge EPROMs, EEPROMs, and EAPROMs, the three common kinds of programmed read-only memory, by pulsing an erase gate and then writing zeros or ones to all locations seven times. We can purge UVPROMs by exposing them to an UV-light eraser (following the manufacturer's directions). RAM, battery RAM, and static RAM as well as cathode-ray tubes are types of volatile semiconductor memory that we can purge by removing power for a minimum of 30 seconds. However, if information has been burned into them, destruction of the glass tubes is the only sure way to purge the contents. We can purge removable magnetic storage devices by overwriting seven times as well. However, it is often easier and cheaper to just destroy them.

We cannot normally clear or purge other forms of memory such as nonvolatile semiconductor memory, ROMs, or PROMs; therefore we must subject them to destruction, the ultimate form of erasure. I received a telephone call from a client who said that his hard disk drive had failed, and he needed to send it away for repair, but it contained highly sensitive information. I advised him to simply destroy the drive and the disks. Saving the cost of a drive was not worth the preservation of information so sensitive that he felt the need to call me about it. Destruction methods include disintegration, incineration, pulverizing, shredding, or smelting. It is a good idea to teach computer users how to destroy tapes and disks by having them practice on old ones. They may not be emotionally prepared to destroy media after having the concept of preserving information so intensely ingrained.

Your Legal Liability

In our litigious society, corporations, their officers, and their board members are often exposed to potential liability lawsuits—not only for failure to exercise "due care" in the protection of shareholder assets, but potentially even for the misbehavior of employees. While the officers of non-U.S. corporations may feel that such legal threats are remote, a global corporation is vulnerable to the laws of each country in which it operates.

In the United States, the legal constraints that apply are founded in tort law (concerning negligence), criminal law (statutes concerning stealing, destruction, and so forth), civil law, and the "law of agency." The latter makes a corporation liable for the acts of employees when the employees act as authorized agents or appear to others to act in this manner.

The adequacy of information security occasionally arises in civil litigation. In one case (*Schalk v. Texas*, 1991), the defense successfully argued that the plaintiff had not taken sufficient due care to protect information that was stolen from a computer system. Both Texas and New York have computer crime laws that require, or at least strongly urge, the presence of security for successful prosecution of an attacker.

A study by the Wyatt Company, a San Francisco consulting firm, indicates that in 1994 the average settlement of a suit against a corporation hit $4.6 million. This represents a 44 percent increase from the 1993 average of $3.2 million. About 25 percent of these claims involved settlements of more than $5 million. Not only are the settlements getting larger, the legal defense costs have also risen to an average of close to $1 million per case. Shareholder suits against directors and officers represented about 40 percent of the cases and averaged $7.7 million per settlement. While the proportion of these cases involving information systems is unknown, I presume that such cases were a large part of the total because it is almost impossible to do business without information systems involvement.

For a closer look at how an organization's use of information systems can make it liable to lawsuits, I have outlined some pertinent concepts from U.S. business law in the following sections.

DUE CARE

Due care lies at the heart of the legal responsibility of corporations and officers charged with the preservation of shareholder assets. The due care requirement involves:

- foreseeability of harm to the plaintiff
- closeness of the connection between the defendant's conduct and the injury incurred
- degree of injury received
- moral blame attached to the defendant's conduct
- policy of preventing future harm

In addition to due care related to the "prudent person" principle, liability may be increased if the action or event that caused harm was similar to a previous occurrence or if the organization did not take economically feasible steps to provide reasonable protection against such an event.

NEGLIGENCE

According to *American Jurisprudence* 2d, Sect. 135, "foresight of harm lies at the foundation of the duty to use care and therefore of negligence. The broad test of negligence is what a reasonably prudent person would foresee and would do in the light of this foresight under the circumstances." Negligence is defined by four concepts:

- A legally recognized duty to act with due care
- A breach of the duty by failing to live up to standards

- A reasonably close causal connection (known as *proximate cause*)
- Actual losses or damages

Shareholder suits arise from losses or damages incurred by reduced share value due to negligence on the part of corporate management. If, for example, an organization has failed to provide for business recovery for an activity located in a flood area, and the organization experiences major information systems outages as a result of a flood, it is liable to a lawsuit by shareholders, in addition to the costs of recovery.

CRIMINAL AND CIVIL LAW

Federal and state laws in the United States starting in the mid-1970s (and recently in the European Union) have made certain actions relating to misuse of computers a criminal offense. In addition, shareholders may sue if an employee commits a criminal act against the company's property and they can prove that management exercised insufficient care to prevent the act. Conviction of the employee could be *prima facie* evidence that the act occurred. Furthermore, if an employee commits a criminal act while acting as an agent of the company, the "law of agency" may impose a potential penalty on the employer. For example, if an employee slanders or defrauds someone while acting as an apparent agent of the company, the company may be liable. For this reason, companies have been reviewing their policies and controls regarding employee use of e-mail and computer bulletin boards.

Violation of civil rights can also result in suits for damages. In the United States, for example, violation of an individual's right to privacy may result in a suit against the company and its management. This is another good reason to review corporate policies relating to the use of e-mail and other computer applications. You may be able to mitigate the potential for lawsuits by providing adequate notice. "Notice" in this context means making others who might be harmed aware of the likelihood of harm.

What You Can Do about Information Systems Liability

First, consult your organization's attorneys to understand your potential liabilities. Then call on your Information Security staff to assist in developing appropriate policies and procedures to protect your organization and its officers from this exposure. Your Information Security staff should compare your policies to the policies and practices of other companies to aid you in establishing corporate practices that can be considered as exer-

A Management Case Study

No matter how far down in the organization structure the controls may be or how mundane or minuscule their effect, top management is ultimately accountable for the adequacy of the protection of the assets. My team and I performed a security review for one of the largest corporations in the world, and recommended more than 100 controls in the final report and presentation to the CEO and his top management staff. It had to be fast, because they grudgingly scheduled only 30 minutes of their valuable time. I knew from past experience that this was the only 30-minute slice of their time that the company's security staff and I were likely to get for an entire year.

Top management greeted us warmly in a mahogany-row conference room. I started the presentation in the classical way by telling them that terrible things would happen if they did not follow our advice. The CEO, always with a smile on his face, gently told me that nothing terrible had happened to their information so far, so why should they spend money on more security? (Good security is when nothing bad happens. And when nothing bad happens, who needs security?) At that point, waving my long skinny arms in the air in response to compensate for this setback, I sent a full glass of water that I had set on the beautiful polished lectern flying through the air and splashing over the final reports. My associates dove for cover. At least one terrible event had just happened, and it did wake up one of the senior managers. At that point, I had their undivided attention, and a miracle happened. The senior manager of the Singapore operations (who had awakened) said, "Don't you remember that we had a $2 million fraud last year in that inventory loss? That was a big computer problem for us." The rest of the executives grudgingly, but still smiling, admitted that was so, and the CEO said maybe they had better hear me out. Saved by the bell.

After each of my major recommendations, the CEO pointed to one of his underlings and said, "You go do that." Finally I interrupted his smiling countinence, and said, with some fear and trembling, that no, that would not do. For security to work, it has to work downwards in the organization but must start at the top—the very top. We needed him to personally go tell the troops to perform some of these remedial actions, and give just 15 minutes of his time twice each year to review the progress on our recommendations. They agreed to implement most of them, and even six years later they were still at work implementing the recommended controls under the occasional, brief gaze of the CEO, who might have remembered that dramatic moment of flying glass and water in the boardroom.

cising due care. (For a more complete view of the concepts of negligence and due care, see the September 1993 *Computing & Communications Law & Protection Report,* Paul Shaw, editor. Several points made here are paraphrased from his report by permission.)

Avoiding Liabilities in Failures of Information Security

Every organization should consider what it must do to reduce its liability when information security fails (and be assured that it will). Hopefully, by now it is clear that no computer, data network, or application can be made absolutely secure. Although security policies and practices are intended to meet a standard of due care relative to other organizations under similar circumstances, these policies and practices may not be sufficient to thwart either the dedicated hacker or (more likely) the employee about to make some unusual, unforeseen error or omission. If the loss is to your own organization alone (possibly shared with your insurance company), you may be willing to live with it. (You may be making a reasonable business decision not to spend the money or impose the constraints on users to make a computer or network more secure in some ways at some times— thus deciding to absorb any loss.) But if the loss injures a third party, such as a customer or the public, then liability for the loss may be attributed to the organization as a whole or to an individual manager or owner. That is what executives' and officers' liability insurance is meant to protect you from—if you have it, or have enough of it, but many organizations do not.

Legal reformers continue pressure for legislation to assign responsibility for this liability. For example, a proposal in California calls for a change in the *Computer Crime statute 502C* to make any person liable, with civil penalties, for recklessly storing or maintaining data in a manner that enables a person to commit a felony computer crime. This type of legislation is troubling and needs revision. Recklessness is a form of criminal negligence and belongs in a different category of crime, not in a law on crimes against or with computers. Reformers may propose or enact Legislation of a similar nature in any country; those people concerned about excessive statutes should be prepared to examine and possibly to defeat them.

The vulnerability of companies to liability for losses resulting from breaches of security was brought to light recently in U.S. federal sentencing guidelines that became law on November 1, 1992. According to the *Wall Street Journal* (November 1, 1991, page B1), under these guidelines, companies convicted of business crimes must comply with certain crime-prevention steps. The crimes include violations of antitrust, securities, employment, and contract laws, as well as crimes such as mail and wire fraud, commercial bribery, kickbacks, and money laundering. Although these sentencing guidelines apply only to companies that have been convicted, they should be considered *de facto* standards of due care for computer-using companies at any time. Here are some ideas taken from the guidelines that would apply to crimes and the suggested means to avoid liability suits:

- Firms should establish crime prevention standards and procedures for employees and agents. Large companies should have documented programs.
- High-level employees with substantial responsibility should be assigned to enforce standards.
- Companies might be able to take steps to prevent employees in high trust positions or with an apparent propensity to engage in criminal activity from exercising discretionary authority, e.g., by segregating duties or requiring dual control.
- Companies should communicate anticrime standards to employees and agents either in writing or through training programs.
- The anticrime program should include strategies to prevent and detect crimes. Hotlines could be set up, and whistle-blowers should be protected from reprisals.

Paul Seader, the Assistant General Counsel at American Express Company, says that his company has been beefing up procedures that fall short of the federal sentencing guideline standards. He also says that a requirement calling for a high-level employee to oversee the anticrime program creates a challenge for companies such as American Express that have several units involved in various businesses. In some situations, the guidelines may be difficult or expensive to fully implement.

Here are some actions that you may wish to take:

- Make sure your state of information security is well determined (ignorance is no excuse when it comes to liability).
- Make sure your company has a plan and an implementation effort under way or scheduled to improve security where you are vulnerable—even a long-term plan is useful.
- Reduce your policies and standards to include only the actual controls and practices being used and enforced—it is worse if you are caught without security that is required in your own policies and standards and you have no good business justification for it.
- Follow the U.S. *Federal Guidelines for Preventing Corporate Crime*—it makes good business sense to do so.

RECOMMENDATIONS FOR SECURITY ADVISORS AND CONCLUSIONS

Security practitioners and business executives alike can benefit from my findings about the strategic values of information security. Given the distortions in the business news media, security advisors must address the perceptions that upper-level managers commonly hold about security before tackling the reality. In their efforts to identify and place security of strategic value within their organization's operations, these specialists should seek support and approval from the CIO and management committee as they go through the chain of command. They can use the "walking around" method to learn the business culture, become better known, and build trust, and they should cultivate an interest in the business and its history. Keeping the four strategic values of information security in mind, along with the kinds of strategic business information that require protection, helps to focus on the important security issues.

A security advisor should be sensitive to the vulnerabilities of various situations encountered in any business organization. Application of the well-known controls and practices does not necessarily produce the many more subtle benefits of security. For example, security advantages come from having employees personally update their personnel records and managers make compensation adjustments locally. These practices can offer some very real security enhancements, but are not identified as specific controls in any security literature.

The often overlooked avoidance of vulnerabilities by removing assets from potential threats or by removing potential threats from assets is another subtle way of increasing security without adding constraining controls. Organizations can design application systems to make automatic, simple decisions so that fewer people need to know the information used in the decisions, since most only need to know the final results. For example, if an extra copy of information is never created and is not needed, then it is not exposed to threats, and the need for security is decreased. The security practitioner may see only a need for more security, but a businessperson would see beyond security to the advantage of one less copy. Information security advisors should understand the value of avoidance of vulnerabilities as possibly perceived by business managers.

The motivation and desires for prudent security must come from business management rather than from information technologists alone. The security advisor's job is to effectively create awareness of the broad dimensions of security among these key people. The information security imperative for the security advisor is that "you only get one chance to aid a business manager; your advice must be correct and acceptable the first time." The business management information security imperative is to develop the motivation for prudent security beyond the reaction to losses and avoidance of negligence, by selling the strategic values of information security that enhance business.

16

Organizing for Security

Two factors in information technology are dramatically affecting our need for information security, as well as the way in which we implement it: distributed computing, in which information owners and users have their own computers and networks throughout the organization; and the ever-increasing reliance of business on the Internet. The ubiquitous nature of computing throughout organizations puts information security into the hands of these owners and users who typically place a much higher priority on performing their assigned jobs than on making their use of information, networks, and computers secure (since security is not an explicit job performance requirement in most organizations). They do, however, need to learn some of the basics of information security and apply them to their local computing and networking environments. In large organizations, the central information security group must provide guidance and direction to these users, as well as to the operators of the mainframe legacy systems that still exist in many businesses. This task requires the information security specialists to be expert in writing, communicating, motivating, and teaching about information security. In many large, geographically dispersed organizations the security specialists may have no direct contact with some of the computer users and operators, making the task even more challenging.

In today's fast-paced business environment, where information users and the information security specialists are often separated, we must find effective ways to emphasize the need for adequate safeguards and practice more formal methods of conveying the necessary information for achieving prudent, due care levels of security to employees and management. We also need to make security transparent, or at least diaphanous (with few constraints), and balance it with the goals of the organization. My studies indicate that the greatest change brought about by the distribution of computing is the recasting of the information security department into an organization whose main activities are writing, publishing, training, and promotional. The technical security work is done primarily in the information technology (IT) and business units.

In meeting a standard of due care and avoiding negligence, the information security strength and posture of the entire organization will be measured by the weakest sub-organization if material losses should occur—and the weakest unit is where losses are most likely to occur. For example, the branch of the bank in California, that gave a beach bum hacker with a millionaire lifestyle sole responsibility for computer operations brought shame and raised customer doubts about the entire bank and all of its branches. The information security department must, therefore, help to raise the entire organization's security awareness, motivation, and effectiveness to the level of those parts of the organization that meet a standard of due care. Another bank branch, this one in France, had a massive steel shield that dropped with arm-shattering force onto the countertop to protect the teller and his computer in case of attempted armed bank robbery. However, the plenum area above the ceiling was wide open—giving entry to the teller's computer terminal, which was continuously left active. It would take these organizations at least five years at present average rates of progress to bring their security up to a baseline due care level—even without further advancements in technology. And of course, technology is racing ahead at bewildering speed. No organization that I have seen is at a baseline due care level across the board, although many are doing well in some aspects. In other aspects they are deficient, and in some others, security is nonexistent, or worse, they have negative security (a state that attracts and encourages loss).

My purpose in this chapter is to suggest ways of organizing information security in a distributed computing environment to achieve prudent, consistent levels of security throughout the organization. I try to give examples of the best security implementations that I am aware of, and recommend their application to other organizations to achieve the objective of a consistent, due care level of security.

FITTING SECURITY INTO THE ORGANIZATION

The advice that I give here must appeal to, and be understood by, a wide range of large and small organizations. *Organization* designates the largest entity or enterprise in a business or service capacity (e.g., a corporation, partnership, or government department) that succeeds or fails independently of others. A *unit* is a part of the organization that has its own hierarchy of management (e.g., a business unit, government agency, division, subsidiary, or department within a division). Most organizations refer to their information technology units as IT, or sometimes as information systems (IS), or management information systems (MIS). Because it is easy to confuse *IS* (information systems) with information security, I avoid using it altogether.

The information security unit in an organization is usually a directorate, department, or section in the IT unit; alternatively, it may be an administrative unit similar to the legal, accounting, audit, industrial security, and human resources groups. Information security may be referred to as data security, computer security, ADP security, or systems security, although any of these names may apply to only a part of the information security unit. *Industrial security* is the name of the unit responsible for administering physical security of tangible assets. Organizations often refer to this as the security unit, with no other delimiters. Industrial security, audit, and/or legal units conduct loss investigations—sometimes with assistance from the information security unit, which does not typically possess investigative skills. Rarely is the information security unit a part of the industrial security unit, because information technology is usually not sufficiently understood by the traditional industrial security staff, which often has a police or military background. Similarly, information technology is rarely a part of the audit unit (and I strongly advise that it not be), because the audit unit needs the independence to objectively audit the performance of the information security unit. I identify the audit unit as one of the most powerful security controls because of the fear it has produced among many of the criminals that I have interviewed. Any organization that incorporates the information security unit in audit has a serious problem to solve.

Information security policies, standards, controls, administration, practices, procedures, and guidance documents are collectively called *information security safeguards.* Security experts recognize the following documents for use in information security:

Policy. Broad principles, scope, instructions, control objectives (optional).

Standards. Mandatory control objectives and descriptions and implementation principles to be applied.

Guidelines. Discretionary implementation aids and control descriptions at vendor and computer levels.

Training and promotional materials. Manuals, workbooks, handouts, slide copies, videos, and artifacts.

Forms. Response and request documents (paper or electronic).

The information security units and stakeholders within a typical organization include:

Management Council. Executives with top management oversight of the information security unit.

Information security unit. The primary provider of information security policy, standards, and guidance.

Computer or data security units. Units of technologists that develop and maintain security in computers and networks.

Information security coordinators. Full- or part-time administrators and consultants within the units and under the dotted line management of the information security unit.

LAN, network, system, and platform administrators and managers. The local computing and communications services providers in the business units.

Information and application owners, providers, custodians, and users. People in the units accountable for the organization's information.

THE SIZE, NATURE, AND LOCATION OF INFORMATION SECURITY UNITS

The size, talents, and location of an information security unit depend largely on the nature, culture, location, and size of the organization that it serves. Today we see many information security units with combined technical and administrative responsibilities located at a relatively low level in the IT unit. The unit often reports to a manager who reports to the chief information officer (CIO). There are, however, many variations on this organization theme. In one company, a senior vice president heads information security and reports directly to the CIO. In another case, the unit reports to the legal department, and in another to the controller. In one company, the information security officer alone reports to top management, with a large technical staff of information security practitioners reporting to IT, and smaller units located in some of the organization's largest operational units in various parts of the world. In one electrical utility company, the head of industrial security also heads the information security unit, but he originally came from the IT unit. When he transferred into industrial security, the company moved information security into the IT unit. Whatever the reporting structure, information security units tend to be heavily staffed with IT specialists because of the intense need (and inherent difficulties) to build security into complex information systems and networks.

In one airline company, management moved the technically talented information security unit from IT into the industrial security department, which was headed by an ex-FBI agent, and deeply engaged in ticket fraud detection, shipping thefts, union violence, and air piracy. The two disparate staffs shared the same offices—computer programmers cheek by jowl with detectives. The arrangement survived for only about two months before management restored the original organization. In another company, management transferred computer technologists, one at a time, into industrial security every two years with the promise that they could go back to IT in a better job position than when they left. After about 12 years, a sufficiently technical capability was built up in the industrial security unit, and it was able to continue its information security function without the technology staff transfers.

Many of the information security budgets that I have reviewed are based on discretionary (i.e., overhead) funding that is not related to the organization's products and services. Therefore, the units tend to fluctuate in size depending on the amount of funding that is available—a situation that can change dramatically in good and bad times. Generally, organizations do not expect to spend much money on security, and are not forced to spend as much to comply with laws or regulations as they are to carry out the auditing function, for example. Many would just as soon take their chances with the costs of information losses, since they are unable to measure the changes in losses relative to the money spent on security to reduce such losses. Many organizations are only now beginning to understand that it is easier and more important to copy the practices of other well-run organizations to achieve a standard of due care to avoid negligence than it is to make security funding decisions based on reducing loss (refer back to Chapter 11).

The sizes of information security units are highly variable because of the vagaries of budgets and limited interest in security. A unit may consist of only two people who are primarily technical writers and trainers, but who obtain significant support from other specialists in other units. Or there may be several hundred information security practitioners with a wide range of talents in their information security units, with that number temporarily increased during major security projects. The sizes of the units sometimes depend on how many information security coordinators and administrators are located in other units that are heavily dependent on information systems. Occasionally I find a CEO who is highly motivated to have a significant information security unit. In one instance, this was because he had a terrible business crime experience in his former organization. There really is no trend or common pattern other than heavy focus on IT association and staffing.

Small organizations often do not have an information security unit per se, not even a single individual whose function includes a concern for information security. They often leave this function to an external auditor to worry about. For example, when small start-up companies populated Silicon Valley, many of them had no interest in information security or even backup (except for protecting their products from piracy), because they were advancing and expanding so fast that management believed their information was obsolete before it became sensitive to loss.

Ultimately, I believe that many large organizations will break their single information security units into two or more units. The technical unit is likely to remain in a central IT unit under the CIO, while the policy and administrative unit will be installed in the organization's administrative unit along with the industrial security unit, or become a part of it. Organizations will begin to view the tangible assets, talent, and intangible information simply as assets that need to be protected with the assistance of a single type of holistic protection expert. The current specialist breakdown of talent into former law enforcement officers in industrial security and former computer systems technologists in information security is likely to continue, but will be led by generalists in security. There will always be the need for the computer and network technologists to maintain the security within the systems and networks, and they will identify with IT, although they will be buried deeply within the central IT unit and have a relatively low visibility.

General Methodology for Distributed Computing Security

In the following pages, I outline my suggested methodology for managing information security indirectly through managers of information users and IT administrators and coordinators throughout the organization.

1. Form an *information security management oversight committee* with representatives from the top management of the organization's units in which most distributed computing takes place. Take organization-wide actions in the name of this committee to convey to people in the organization that their management directs the actions. The approval of the committee will also tend to maintain the principle of top-down order of information security decisions. (See the following section for more detail on organizing this committee.)

2. Create *awareness and motivation* for information security by tying security to job performance, informing distributed computing and information users about the threats and vulnerabilities, and making available to them particular valid safeguard solutions and vendor-supplied controls to avoid negligence. I do not recommend introducing the concept of risk of loss, since the users and business units untrained in security can not correctly evaluate it (see Chapter 9). The following four methods are effective in motivating people to support information security:

   ■ Make security a part of job descriptions and include it as a requirement in salary and performance appraisals along with providing rewards and penalties. (Managers need training and motivation to administer such appraisals.)
   ■ Indicate the need to avoid negligence by meeting a standard of due care relative to other similar organizations such as competitors and within the organization among similar units. Make sure that the organization treats negligence seriously.
   ■ Illustrate the consequences to the organization of security failures by case studies of losses.
   ■ Demonstrate the effectiveness and ease of use of many of the security controls that can help avoid and reduce loss.

   Address risk of loss only as a benefit of exemplary security performance, not as a motivator. Risk is not generally calculable, and not appropriate as a motivator or a measure of security. Management must encourage each member of an organization to achieve security as a matter of self-interest, without the constant presence of the information security unit staff—otherwise, security is only cosmetic and largely limited to lip service. Self-interest through the avoidance of the appearance or accusations of negligence, and the rewards and penalties associated with job performance, are the key motivation and awareness objectives.

3. Appoint *distributed information security coordinators* in local user units and subunits. (A subunit may include all of the users of a local area network, salespersons in a local sales office, a Web site development staff, or an accounts payable staff.) The coordinators are to:

- administer internal systems and Internet usage controls
- identify and authenticate users for assignment of passwords
- initiate and monitor physical and system controls such as clean desk practices and system logs
- report unusual events and losses to management
- submit standards exception requests
- provide security guides
- arrange for training
- convey the procedures for security from the central information security unit
- identify by policy definitions the owners, service providers and custodians, and users and their responsibilities

Coordinators are in high trust positions. To assure segregation of duties, they should not be the same individuals that are responsible for providing or administering distributed computing or network services such as LAN and firewall administrators. In small operations where segregation of duties may not be practical, you may want to assign two people to the coordinator duties on a part-time basis, thereby instituting dual control and reducing the possibility of errors or collusion to cause loss. Coordinators should convey safeguard standards and lists of approved products to be used by implementers and acquirers of systems and applications.

All too often in my security reviews I find small units with intense LAN usage in which the LAN administrator controls the network and its security. He performs the backup and often carries backup disks around with him in the trunk of his car. He has so many passwords that he can not remember them all, so he writes them on a Post-it and sticks it to the ceiling above the computer. He owns the LAN, and the entire unit depends on it—even if it is the executive personnel and payroll department. He is in a total position of trust and can do anything he wants to, and no one is likely to find out about it. This arrangement is not fair to the executives; it is not fair to the LAN administrator who is put into such a high position of trust; and it is certainly not fair to the organization stakeholders who have a right to expect better security with a security coordinator who has some independence from the LAN administrator.

Many organizations already have local coordinators to assist users of central computing services. These individuals may not, however, be qualified for distributed computing purposes. If this is the case, they should either be retrained or replaced by others that are familiar with distributed computing. In some cases, local PC consultants offer a resource for appropriate people. In large units, some coordinators will probably have enough to do to make the position a full-time job. Newsletters, electronic bulletin boards, special hot-line services, training courses, and conferences should be used to train and communicate with the coordinators. A coordinator-of-the-month program to honor and reward exemplary service is useful. You may be able to recruit writers of new security materials from among coordinators.

4. The organization's information security unit should select *discretionary and mandatory baseline controls* to be used for meeting the standard of due care, as well as special controls required for particular units and/or users. The unit should publish safeguard instructions in the form of *policies, standards,* and specific computer platform and operational *guides,* and provide help desk services, consulting, and training for information security. Instructions should be prescriptive directions in the simplest possible terms because few people (other than the military) wish to dwell on security. (The British Standards Institute *Code of Practice for Information Security Management* (BS 7799) is generally a good starting point for developing such documentation.)

   Units should be constrained to select and acquire new hardware and software products from approved lists. Such products must have appropriate security characteristics, and vendors should be instructed to deliver them to users with security and optional controls in activated states. Users should begin using new computer and communications products with all security functional, and turn off any controls only on a documented exception basis. Ideally, products chosen for the list should have controls that have limited constraints and do not detract from performance. Owners, service providers, custodians, and users of information should not be asked to make unaided decisions about control selections other than to request necessary exemptions. Exemptions should be considered only when the standard controls or practices can be shown to interfere in some way with business objectives. It is generally advisable to simply tell subjects what they must do to comply with security regulations, then deal with any problems in meeting the standard of due care on an individual, documented exception basis with approval from upper management.

5. Provide for *deviations from mandatory and special controls* when business needs require it. Design and use forms for this purpose and provide instructions to local managers for obtaining approvals from their higher management and the information security unit (and possibly from audit and legal units, as well). The information security unit can then devote its follow-up time to these exception cases.

6. You need an *accurate inventory* to determine what must be protected. Perform surveys on a regular basis to ascertain the status and growth of distributed computing and security. Such information will help to ensure that management decisions concerning resource allocation, due care, and budgeting fit the current needs of the organization. Surveys are also useful for updating inventories of computers, software, major databases, and networks as well as security controls in use. One of the first actions that I take in performing a security review is to ask for a complete description of the client's networks. I have never found any large company that could do this, and it brings forth my first question, "If you do not know where your networks are or what is attached to them, how can you ever know that they are secure?" One large company conducts a survey every 90 days and rewards managers who submit their inventory results by allowing them to attend important review meetings. Auditors spot-check the completeness of the inventories, especially of the security products in use.

7. Follow up with *audits of the organization units* conducted by the audit unit to check on and enforce compliance with mandatory safeguards. The audit unit should function as the enforcement arm by writing reports of failures in compliance, while the information security unit should function as the consulting and assis-

tance arm (although some auditors may view this advice the other way around). The information security unit should not develop a reputation as a policing organization when its primary functions are as advisor and consultant. Provide rewards and penalties through line management, and handle any serious violations through a management oversight committee. An organization should be able to determine if documented policies and standards are being complied with, or are about to be complied with, and that any exceptions are prudent and duly approved.

Discretionary controls and practices are those that units may voluntarily apply. The information security unit should describe these in the guidelines and encourage business units to apply them when they are appropriate. Mandatory controls and practices are those that business units are required to use, and which they can avoid only through documented, approved exception procedures. Baseline controls are those that have been found by experts to be necessary to meet a prudent standard of due care, or which have been considered and rejected for good business reasons. Technical baseline controls should be embedded in approved products to the extent possible.

OPEN AND CLOSED DISTRIBUTED ENVIRONMENTS

Information security can be implemented on an open or closed basis in a distributed computing environment. In a closed security system, every user, application, piece of equipment, and connection and location is known and inventoried, and has a security profile. Identification and authentication (I&A) are applied universally throughout the system. In an open security system, fewer inventory records exist, at least on a centralized basis, or those that do are less complete. I&A is handled as a discretionary, local function. Corporate standards and approved products may represent the only central control constraints in an open distributed computing security system.

Many distributed environments use an open security arrangement, relying on local information owners and periodic audits to ensure that assets are adequately protected. This type of arrangement makes awareness, motivation, communication of security policies and standards, and training efforts crucial to effective security. Regular, periodic surveys of system components and networks, as well as the associated security controls, are also important, but it is often difficult to enforce such surveys on a local level. Once again, this emphasizes the need for motivation and voluntary compliance. If local units do conduct such surveys, they need to report the results to central management to keep it aware of the security status and advancement toward a standard of due care. In some organizations, the information security department surveys are the only valid and complete inventories of information on IT systems in use.

POLICIES AND MANAGEMENT SUPPORT

I consider many of the policies and standards that I have reviewed over the years to be woefully deficient, but my view is probably biased, since the organizations whose documents I see are ones who call me in to help improve their security, which includes their policies and standards. The documents are often out of date, unclear, poorly worded, and limited to CIA and DDUM terminology, or worse. Policies, standards, guides, and training materials that are obsolete and not enforced are particularly dangerous to an organization because management is often deceived into believing that security does exist and operates at a higher level of effectiveness than is true. All organizations need to periodically review, test, and discard unenforced and otherwise obsolete rules, controls, and procedures to avoid this false sense of security. An alternative to periodic reviews is to specify a time limit for applying policies and standards, and assign limited life span to mandatory controls, specifying when they should become effective and when they should be nullified or replaced. This technique is generally referred to as applying *sunset rules*.

Negative value security is security that is thought to be in place but is not, a situation that is generally worse than having no safeguards at all. Negative security fosters complacency and diverts attention from the assumed secure, but actually insecure, information assets, making the information doubly attractive to adversaries or more vulnerable to accidental loss. Fortunately, cybercriminals are not motivated to misbehave by opportunity alone. Otherwise, we would have had to give up using computers a long time ago, because they are so vulnerable in their natural state—the condition I often find them in.

Management Commitment

An article by Daniel E. White and Mark H. Farrell of Ernst & Young (www.eyi.com) in Chicago that appeared in the Spring 1994 issue of the *Computer Security Journal* (published by the Computer Security Institute (www.csi.gocsi.com) in San Francisco) reports that management support for information security is the most important factor in a successful security system. The article, "Reengineering Information Security Administration," reported on the authors' information security survey of 870 CIOs. Nearly 80 percent of the respondents viewed information security as extremely or fairly important, with about 20 percent perceiving it as unimportant. The latter group may be the most important, since it represented the organizations with the greatest number of user groups of distributed computing.

Management commitment and support for security is essential to motivate information owners and users, because there are few natural motivations for it other than loss experience. Management support for security requires that the information security unit have high visibility and good rapport with top managers, particularly the top managers of information-intensive units. If those individuals do not support security, the employees that work for them are also unlikely to support it. The best time to obtain visibility for information security is when a loss occurs, especially if it occurs in the organization or unit with the most resistance to security or the greatest need for it. Emphasizing the negative effects of a loss experience on the whole organization is one means of applying peer pressure to motivate all units to improve security. Some organizations even publish lists of units in order of the quality of their information security. This offers positive reinforcement for the units that take an active role in information security and applies peer pressure to those that do not; it can be very effective if it fits within the culture of the organization.

In a distributed computing environment, local managers can demonstrate their commitment to security to end-users and systems staff through their own practices and in performance reviews. If an outside unit prepares security training materials and/or guideline practices, the authoritative local source—typically the managers who decide on and issue rewards and penalties—should sign off and approve it.

Management Oversight Committee

Many organizations already have a management oversight committee for information security. Others include information security issues in general oversight committees for technical or administrative concerns. In either case, however, the constituency of the oversight committee often reflects central IT services or industrial security, but does not apply to information security for distributed computing. If this is the case, the organization may need to reorganize or expand the existing committees to represent the new order of distributed computing needs. Members should include the top managers of units actively engaged in distributed computing, as well as managers concerned with external communications (e.g., field sales and services) that rely heavily on data communications. This type of committee, which is crucial for ensuring ongoing management support for distributed computing security, should be responsible for authorizing, reviewing, approving, and distributing corporate policies and standards.

Policy Writing Responsibilities

Either the information security staff or an IT policies and standards group under the direction of the information security staff should be responsible for drafting appropriate policies and policy updates. As an alternative, some organizations assign the responsibility to a task group under the auspices of a management oversight committee; this is a common arrangement when the policies are being written or updated in conjunction with a reorganization or more drastic reengineering of the information security unit. It is not generally a good idea to assign the policy writing task to outside consultants since the style and form of policies should be consistent with existing ones and should reflect the culture of the organization. (Recognizing this need for consistency, I recommend topics that should be addressed in policies later in this chapter, rather than supplying actual wording.) Prior to drafting new policies however, you may find it helpful to review the policies of other, similar organizations and use them as models for your own.

Types of Policies

Establishing policy is very much a cultural issue. Management support, wording, and distribution depend upon history, loss experience, type of business, personal philosophies of top management, previous policies, and other factors in the organization. If the culture supports specific written policies on various subjects such as IT, various internal services, and ethics, then it is likely that a written policy on information security will exist. Some organizations have a policy of not having written policies. Attorneys often do not like policies because they can be turned around and used against an organization that violates them, and many units in many organizations violate their policies occasionally as a means to achieve short-term objectives for resolving business problems or achieving goals. Information security policies should be flexible, and should permit exceptions, when appropriate.

If an organization has a written policy and distributes it throughout the organization, it should be mandatory and reflect top management's requirements for organizational behavior. When policies are written at a sufficiently high level of abstraction, they do not need to be changed as the IT unit and organization change—for example, shifting from centralized to distributed computing or toward the use of knowledge management and global information infrastructures. And organizational changes such as mergers, acquisitions, reengineering, or the adoption of total quality management can occur with little or no need to modify the policies.

When policies are written at the highest level of abstraction, they are only a few pages long—generally less than five. Some organizations include operational requirements in the form of control objectives with their policy statements. Others combine brief, high-level policy statements with more detailed standards, creating a document that contains both policies and standards. This type of document may create problems, however, if you want to show anyone your policies and, in doing so, must also reveal your standards—or vice versa. It is generally good practice to separate high-level policy from specific standards (which I'll describe a bit later in this chapter).

Operational policies are typically longer than high-level policy statements; some organizations refer to these as *standards documents*. An officer of the organization usually signs off on such a document to give it the proper authority. Some organizations publish it in a brochure and include a picture of the CEO or president (auspiciously sitting on the edge of his or her desk) and quote a personal message from this individual.

Importance of Policy

Policies are significantly more important in a distributed computing environment than a centralized environment because of the increased challenge of constraining activity from a remote location. Such policies must also be complete and clearly stated to reduce the amount of explanation and instruction that the organization needs to undertake to be sure they are understood. Policies should include general descriptions and identifiers for business units and functions rather than the names of individuals, so that they can transcend organizational changes, and should be confined to general concepts rather than specific controls (if you must include specifics at all). For example, a policy stating that "Each computer user must be authenticated by an acceptable method" rather than the more specific "Each computer user must be authenticated by a six-character password" does not need to be changed when tokens replace passwords.

Checklist of Topics for Information Security Policy

An information security policy should address each of the following items, or have a specific reason for omitting it, in keeping with notions of standards of due care.

- Importance of assets
- Need for security (GASSP or the OECD Guidelines on the Principles of Information Security may be useful)
- Governing laws and regulations
- Adherence to laws, regulations, industrial standards, and standards of due care
- Applicability to staff and contractors
- Elements, functions, and scope of security
- Kinds, representations, forms, and media of information covered
- Losses defined
- Strategic and tactical value of security
- Classification of information
- Privacy (the OECD Privacy Guidelines may be useful)
- Accountability, motivation, rewards and penalties
- Reporting suspected and attempted losses
- Emergency response, disaster recovery, and business continuity
- Information security management council and staffing
- Assignment of security implementation
- Specification of standards, guidelines, training, and awareness
- Deviations, exceptions, and changes to policies and standards
- Specification and enforcement of ethical behavior

It should also include a glossary, an appendix containing GASPP or OECD Guideline documents, and optionally, a list of control objectives:

- Security administration
- Segregation
- Standards exceptions
- Physical security
- Administrative and operating controls
- Monitoring, using agent software
- Identification and authentication
- Audit trails, diagnostics, and violations reporting

- Information availability and utility
- Information integrity and authenticity
- Information confidentiality and possession
- Commercial software registration
- Application development
- Use of test data
- Internal application controls
- Transactions
- Use of the Internet
- Network operating and management systems security features
- Network security
- File server, firewall, router, switch, bridge, hub, modem, line, and gateway controls

  - Communications
  - Status
  - Warning banners
  - Dial-up

- Business resumption planning and testing
- Personnel security
- Development and acquisition security
- Customer, contractor, and outsourcing security
- Product evaluation and testing
- Security reviews

Policy is also important in distributed computing environments as a means of establishing security discipline for a large, disparate group of users and business units that are generally only reached by formal communications and audit. It is particularly important when the organization relies heavily on contract or temporary personnel. Policy should adhere to the accepted practices of an organization, yet take advantage of all practical methods for influencing behavior and disseminating information within the distributed computing environment.

You may wish to include a code of ethics as part of the policy or refer to a separate code in the policy. I recommend a separate code that accompanies the policy. In any case, the policy should specify a code and its enforcement (refer back to Chapter 15 on Strategies for more details on the code).

STANDARDS AND DISTRIBUTED INFORMATION SECURITY ADMINISTRATORS

This section discusses only internal standards, those that apply only within an organization and among its business units. It does not address public standards that are established by formal standards bodies, except to the extent that they are incorporated into internal standards in an organization. External standards often have a long lead-time for adoption and should be recognized or incorporated in internal standards as appropriate.

Internal information security standards are mandatory controls and practices applied across the organization to the extent that deviations require explicit management approval. Some business units may be so unusual or distinct in their information processing activities and needs that they require specialized security standards, but these should be standards that are recast differently (e.g., for salespeople) and considered as additional requirements. In a distributed computing environment, the functional units should review and approve standards established by a central unit for applicability and practicality, since it is not possible to be aware of all implications outside of the functional units. Some units have a front office (dealing with customers) and a back office (dealing with processing customer information and administration of the unit). A local securities brokerage office is a typical example. I would consider these to be two separate units for security purposes, because of the need for segregation of duties and different wording of the standards to convey them to different kinds of people (e.g., researchers, salespeople, service people, and back office people).

While a policy may be only one or two pages in length, an internal standards document can range from ten to more than 100 pages, depending on its scope and details. Length also depends on how much you intend to communicate in the form of guidelines that support the standards. (Guidelines are considered discretionary rather than mandatory. I discuss them in more detail in the next section. Some organizations, through long practice or tradition, do not follow these definitions. One organization may make its guidelines mandatory, while another makes its standards discretionary. For example, the U.K. Department of Trade and Industry named its published guidelines, which represent nine organizations' collective opinions of best practices, "A Code of Practice for Information Security Management." It is not a code by any correct definition of *code*. The *Code of Practice* is now a British standard, which is discretionary [rather than mandatory, which *code* implies] and not enforced by law. Ultimately, considering the ease and frequency of communicating information internationally, it will be of great benefit if organizations move closer to agreement on these meanings. The independently sponsored *Generally Accepted Systems Security Principles* (GASSP) is a major step in this direction.)

Distribution and implementation of standards is important in a distributed computing environment to achieve uniformity and consistency across the organization, especially where there is extensive connectivity of data communications among units. Standards are also important in situations where security is usually set by the lowest common denominator for technical compatibility between nodes in a computer network. Development units that are intent on meeting deadlines and controlling complexity nearly always reduce higher security on one side of a coupling rather than increase lower security on the other side. In some cases security just disappears altogether. Since an organization is likely to be judged by the level of security for its greatest vulnerability, you should hold units to a common standard, one which can account for variations of threats and vulnerabilities. One unit with 100 users and ten LANs may be more than ten times more vulnerable than one with ten users and one LAN, assuming that other factors are equal.

The level of abstraction of standards (i.e., control objectives at the high end and detailed specifications of each control at the low end) is also important. To maintain a high level of stability and longevity, it should be just above the vendor product level of specificity to avoid standards obsolescence as security products and technology change. For example, you may specify passwords and tokens in standards, but you should document the specific features and products to implement and administer them in discretionary guidelines.

Examples of Standards

Standards vary widely among organizations, demonstrating the diversity of corporate cultures and their use of terminology. Many of the standards are not consistent with regard to discretionary and mandatory applications, differentiation of policies and safeguards, or their means of promulgation. There are formal, detailed control descriptions including strengths, weaknesses, costs, and auditability that are useful for security practitioners; there are also brief, informal expositions that may appeal to end-users. A NIST or industrial standard is an example of the former, while the British Standards Institute *Information Security Code of Practice for Information Security Management* is an example of the latter.

One large multinational manufacturing corporation divides its *Guidebook* into two sections: one on *Risk Assessment,* which requires 200 pages; and one on *Security Policies, Standards, and Guidelines,* which takes another 100 pages. The Guidebook also includes several self-assessment forms, some coverage of social engineering vulnerabilities, and—in the second section—a useful discussion of U.S. law including the *Computer Security Act of 1987* and summaries of other pertinent laws. Policies, guides, and standards are not distinguishable in the *Guidebook* except for implicit enforcement clues in word usage such as *must, should, be sure to, not permitted, if at all possible,* and other degrees of imperatives. The style is a mixture of formal bulleted text and informal prose that appeals to users. The document provides advice and instructions such as *How to Report an Incident* in the description of the internal *CERT* unit. It also provides names, telephone numbers, and office locations of security advisors, which requires frequent updating.

Another large manufacturing corporation summarizes its standards document into 13 pages using a highly structured outline format (and a small type font). The document includes forms for reporting loss incidents, approval of exceptions to requirements, and a mailing list for the document. It also describes a risk assessment process, and provides a long list of risks to consider.

The standards manual of one communications company is a very thorough document that intermixes policy and standards. It also includes an extensive index and a unique diagram (which is repeated at the head of each section) with shaded areas to describe section content relative to the rest of the document.

Another large corporation has two sets of standards, one for U.S. defense contracts and one for general business. Both documents include outlines and tables as well as extensive indexes. Both also supply forms for submitting changes to the manuals, along with a detailed self-assessment questionnaire. The manuals make extensive use of diagrams, with shaded boxes to highlight important items.

Finally, an electronics company has three standards. One is a generic network security manual that is highly structured. The second is a memo for *Evaluation Criteria for Workstation Access Security* that states the criteria that must be met to qualify a workstation security package or device for approved use. It uses a questionnaire format, which users must complete. The *Standards of Internal Control* is excerpted from a slick-covered 100-page manual on accounting systems controls and is an example of how security can be inserted into a more general document on internal controls.

Coordinators and Administrators

Many organizations with multiple sites that are geographically dispersed appoint information security coordinators on a full- or part-time basis to administer security services on a local level. For example, one security coordinator may serve one LAN, which in turn serves 20 end-users. Security coordinators convey messages, policies, standards, and guides to the end-users and provide assistance and advice from the central information security unit. In some cases they administer passwords and tokens locally and establish information file usage authorization through LANs to a mainframe that uses a central security program such as IBM's *RACF* or Computer Associates' *ACF2*. The central unit trains the coordinators and holds regular meeting to update their knowledge base to accommodate changes in technology or security practices.

In some cases, even the most successful of these coordinator programs may deteriorate over time, and all too often, unit management replaces the original coordinators with individuals who lack the necessary training or security background. In other cases, the coordinators or administrators leave their units, and the central information security unit loses contact with them. If the coordinators are oriented toward central, mainframe computing, a shift to distributed computing may require reengineering their role in information security. The reengineering process should be implemented gradually to ensure a continuation of effective security. One securities brokerage, in shifting from a central computing environment to distributed computing, laid off its entire twelve-person information security staff—advising the manager to cancel his own passwords and turn off the lights on his way out. When the firm finished the conversion process—without seeking assistance from security specialists—it hired a new information security staff and told them to start securing the newly installed systems.

Management must often appoint new individuals to administer security in a distributed environment, or retrain existing mainframe security specialists to work in the new environment and technology. Unit management may downgrade the technical and management reporting level of these positions based on business demands, downsizing, and the reengineering that significantly affects the organization. Although such changes are IT-oriented, they involve far more than strictly technological concerns—a point that management may fail to recognize.

Management could supplement or replace the existing mainframe security coordinators in each business unit with local PC consultants and network mavens. If I&A administration is not an extension of the existing mainframe I&A, it needs to be established on a local level. For example, one company developed its own software to facilitate local administration of passwords and user IDs.

In any case, clear segregation of duties is important to separate the LAN administrators, database administrators, network management systems operators, and supervisors, from the security administrators. Whenever possible, management should carry over the segregation of duties from legacy systems to the distributed computing environment, but the smaller scale systems and staffs may preclude this. The LAN administrator who also administers the security of the LAN may present the biggest problem in this regard. This jack-of-all-trades typically has applications modification and use authority, as well as the ability to impersonate other users by using their passwords or using system utilities to bypass the usage controls altogether. Many LANs are too small to have different people administering these functions, and some organizations do not have tools to remotely administer some critical controls. Besides, the local managers see an advantage to having a single individual administering LANs on a local basis; that is, after all, the way that vendors promote LANs.

The solution to this sticky problem may be to appoint information security coordinators who can administer security locally for several LANs, and make sure that they are fully trained and administered by the central information security unit. PC consulting firms are frequently good sources for security coordinators, and may be able to perform the local password administration and other security duties. Gateways to public networks such as the Internet require special attention and security staffing. The security advisors need to have expertise in setting filtering parameters in firewalls and performing extensive firewall audit log analysis. It may not be practical to require local coordinators to perform these duties. Filtering communications requires extensive knowledge of the unit's business to know what information to let pass through and what to reject.

Guides for Implementing Standards

Information security specialists need to describe controls in uniform ways. The standards, or less commonly, the guidelines, should also provide assistance for selecting, implementing, and operating controls. Many standards describe safeguards but do not define the characteristics or features that they should have. In a distributed computing environment, it is crucial to give people who are often inexperienced in security, guidance on what constitutes a good safeguard, and to explain how to install and operate it. For example, a standard that requires a control to be properly instrumented, auditable, safe to shut off, not reliant on operating secretly, and backed up with in-depth protection is as important as requiring the control itself. (Refer back to Chapter 13 to review my list of 27 guides for implementing good and bad information security controls.)

GUIDELINES AND TECHNICAL SUPPORT

There are many types of guidelines, including ones that are technical and specific to platforms, that address management and methodology, that deal with awareness and motivation, and that are intended for training. Some organizations confuse the subjects by using the name *guidelines* interchangeably with *policies* and *standards*—even within the same document. Because I have already described all of these subjects except for platform-specific technical guidelines, I will focus on that type of guideline here.

One of the primary roles of information security practitioners is to write the material needed to communicate security to the distributed computing users. But since they probably can not become sufficiently expert in all of the necessary technical subjects, other experts must develop the technical parts of the material for security guidelines. The documents should possess integrity and authenticity, be self-explanatory, useful, and not dangerous—even if used without expert on-site advice. They may be written in just-in-time mode for on-line use, as encouraged by good knowledge management.

One company creates task groups of experts to write draft guidelines. The central information security staff then converts them into standard, edited form. Professional editors are not used, but a publications department does the makeup and printing. Sharing guidelines among organizations is often very beneficial to all parties because many guidelines are oriented to particular IT systems rather than specific applications; although many guidelines are platform-dependent, they are not organization-dependent. Electronic forms of guidelines make them easier to share and modify, even when they are organization-dependent. Vendors may also supply guidelines that, in some cases, are developed in cooperation with their customers.

Some organizations distribute their documents electronically, but many recipients print them before reading anyway because they do not like to read text from screens. This makes printed paper guidelines still the popular form. Guidelines also include methods for achieving security such as baseline due care reviews, system security testing, and using business recovery plans. Some guides are printed full size; others are in booklet or brochure form. Organizations should distribute them with the signature of some authority and a message about their use in a cover memo or letter. They should note their proprietary status on the cover.

One example is *Guidelines for Keeping Your UNIX Systems Secure: Using Raxco Security Toolkit* (www.raxco.com) *and Other Methods.* It addresses the generic UNIX platform but describes use of a specific commercial security tool. The author's name is specifically identified, allowing readers to go back to the source for further assistance. It was written for system administrators and security administrators of UNIX computer systems within a business unit, and acknowledges—but does not condone—the practice of staffing these two positions with the same person. The author references the applicable standards in the foreword material and clearly indicates that this document supplements, rather than replaces, those standards. The author includes several sections from the primary standards at the end of the *Guidelines* document, and addresses the topics of management, general system integrity and security controls, network security standards, and workstation and LAN standards.

Novell NetWare 3.x Security Guidelines (www.novell.com) is another good example. The document applies to one organization, which sponsored the *Guidelines.* The document openly discusses likely security vulnerabilities, in keeping with the philosophy expressed that local management must understand the ramifications of various security exposures. The document defines the terminology that it uses. *Must,* for example, means to implement immediately; *should* means to follow the recommended action unless there is a significant reason to do otherwise; and *could* means that a control item or practice may be optionally used to further enhance the system security. It also includes sections on security terminology, staff responsibilities, physical security of LANs, auditing, and disaster recovery. The Appendix includes an assessment checklist, sample screen warning banner, and confidentiality statement, and there is an index.

Training and Instructors

Training materials need to take into account the subjects being covered, the capabilities of students and instructors, and locations and frequency of training classes. In most cases, teaching the instructors is more important than teaching the students. Training is essential for new employees, end-users, and especially for information security administrators and coordinators, as well as LAN managers and supervisors. The organization's training units should offer the training directly or indirectly through the information security unit. Some organizations outsource the training and invite guest speakers to lecture.

The training needed for distributed information security may differ somewhat from that of a centralized environment and may require changing the staffing in the information security unit. Instructors as well as technical writers generally play major roles in a distributed environment. One company that I know of has a formal training department to train instructors, who then train the end-users in the company's locations around the world. The company provides general guides for the trainers, along with specific instructor materials for various individual modules (e.g., Access Control) and student guide materials—all coordinated to facilitate off-site training.

In one example of training material, each subject is addressed by a set of overhead projector transparencies, two to a page, followed by reference text such as published guides, reports, policy, and standards. Popular trade books, such as Cliff Stoll's *The Cuckoo's Egg*, are sometimes included. One *Information Security Education Guide* introduces a "toolkit" from which an information security education campaign may be tailored to local needs. The campaign is adapted and used in conjunction with locally produced information security education material, and comes with a questionnaire from the central information security unit to evaluate the effectiveness of the annual training. Business units can order the toolkit materials, which include posters, a video, and manuals, separately. The development of this material is an excellent example of a small central information security staff attempting to educate large numbers of end-users and managers dispersed around the world.

In planning information security training, remember that most people hate security and resist having to endure training on a subject that takes time from their primary working objectives. In such circumstances, training may become a snooze session to rest up before returning to the real world of business. Producing an effective training program for this subject is a challenge. Humor, human and personal interests, controversy (such as privacy issues), outrageous loss experience in real cases, playing out dispute and opposing teams scenarios, and using classy videos and interesting guest speakers help. Still, as the old saying goes, you can lead a horse to water, but you can't make him drink. You need to create a fundamental motivation to support security to overcome the cosmetic application of the security folk art. This is where treating security as a part of job performance and rewarding it in annual job appraisal should help.

MOTIVATING END-USERS
FOR INFORMATION SECURITY

If information security can not be made transparent to users, it must, at least, be made easy to endure. This often entails minimizing the constraints that it imposes and finding ways to motivate people to use it. The three most important motives in business to support security are: reacting to loss, avoiding negligence, and enhancing strategic business values. Nearly all of us are more amenable to security after we have suffered a loss. And we generally gain peace of mind by having security that is comparable to (or better than) other, similar organizations. Finally, if security enhances our business, for example by giving us a strategic advantage over our competitors, we are motivated to continue or enhance it (see Chapter 15 for more on this topic). A fourth important motivator that I have identified is, unfortunately, not yet accepted in business. It involves providing rewards—financial or otherwise—and penalties in annual job performance reviews. I call this latter motive the mother of all security controls, and I address it in detail further on.

Motivation Factors

An organization that is serious about security recognizes the need for motivators and takes pains to develop some kind of security motivation program. Such a program should employ the following employee motivators:

- Anticipation and receipt of rewards
- Fear and experience of sanctions
- Ethical, honesty, work, social, and religious convictions
- Personal loss experience
- Others' loss experience
- Gratefulness and dedication to employer and profession
- Protection of investment of effort, money, or other asset
- Protection or furtherance of reputation
- Competitive desire to excel beyond peers
- Expediency and convenience

An extreme example of motivation would be to require an employee or, more practically, a contractor to pay a deposit or bond to indemnify the employer against loss from the individual's acts. Another would be to use loss experience to reinforce the need for security. However, the two universal, basic motivators—and the ones that I recommend—are rewards and sanctions. Rewards usually involve job advancement, financial remuneration (often in the form of specific bonuses for exemplary security behavior), and the satisfaction of a job well done. Rewards may also be prizes or recognition for exemplary security performance—for example, winning a competition among groups for the fewest guard-reported or auditor-reported security lapses or for the highest number of continuous days without a lost-time accident. Rewards can be recognition plaques to hang in offices, TVs for rest break rooms, or special car parking privileges.

Sanctions typically involve loss of position or remuneration, but there are many other types of sanctions that organizations may apply. One group publicly posted the name of anyone revealing a password and required everyone in the group to immediately change their passwords when a lapse occurred. This produced peer pressure to keep passwords secret, because no one liked having to learn a new one. Dismissal and legal action are the most severe types of sanctions.

Motivation for Security Through Self-Interest

I see poor security in every organization I visit—regardless of how good the information security unit and technical controls may be—because of the lackadaisical, unsustainable performance of the organization's users and system administrators to ensure that the controls and practices work effectively. They give lip service to security; they have bursts of security efforts when they are being watched or have suffered a loss; but the security ultimately deteriorates for lack of a natural, ongoing motivation in the face of the overpowering pressure of job performance. In contrast, computers maintain security, because it is built into their performance (if users and administrators do not tamper with it). We need to build security into the performance of people. Many information security experts complain to me that it can not be done, because the security performance can not be measured, yet they are eager to attempt to measure the unmeasurable risk of information loss. They complain that managers will not be able to sustain the explicit discussion of security in appraisals of their staffs year after year, because of the pressures of motivating staff job performance, which counts towards the managers' success.

If employees know that observing security measures will inhibit their ability to achieve work objectives specified by management, how motivated will they be to carry out these measures? The primary motivation for information security must come from rewards and penalties directly associated with job performance; otherwise, members of the organization view security as being in conflict with their job performance. Employees know that they can improve their performance and receive position and income advancement in their jobs by avoiding the constraints of security. For example, an employee can work faster and better without having to pause to make backups, use pirated software, avoid securely storing sensitive information, and get more information about his competitors by secretly sharing his organization's sensitive information with them over the Internet. We can remove these conflicts between job performance and security constraints by making security a part of job performance. And, we will not achieve real progress in security until we do this. The self-interests of job advancement and financial compensation are the primary motivators in employment, and security of information must be included in determining them to avoid being in conflict with them. The organization must do three things to satisfy this fundamental need for security to really succeed:

1. Include specific assignments to protect, and be accountable for, the employer's assets—including information—in job descriptions.
2. Include specific evaluations and discussions of the employees' support for, and practice of, security in annual job performance appraisals. Note any exemplary efforts in behalf of security, as well as any security violations, that have occurred.
3. Motivate managers from the top down to ensure their support for security and their sincere emphasis of it in the appraisals of their employees' job performance. Employees generally follow the lead of their managers, who must be good role models for information security.

Managers can consider a number of factors to evaluate security performance in annual job performance appraisals, including, but not limited to:

- Actions causing or resulting in protection from information-related losses
- Faithfulness and effectiveness of performing security assignments
- Endorsements of good security performance of employees by security coordinators, security staffs, customers, and peers
- Rewards and awards provided for exemplary security performance
- Security violation citations
- Commendations and criticisms included in audit reports to management
- Reporting suspected vulnerabilities and loss incidents
- Using effective security controls, such as antivirus software
- Attendance at training and awareness presentations
- Possession of, and familiarity with, up-to-date security documents

In some appraisal procedures, the process begins with a manager stating his or her expectations, followed by the employee stating his or her goals in writing. Ideally, this should include a general statement on protecting the organization's assets, identifying specific assets to be protected, controls to be maintained, and new controls or modifications of controls to be made. This requires clear identity of owners, providers, custodians, and users of the assets and controls, since the control "owners" or operators need to be differentiated from those who are constrained by the control.

Another useful tactic is to develop job description and appraisal practices that address security, then apply them on a trial basis in a few particularly suitable units before rolling the concept out to a larger number of units. You could, for example, begin with IT and the security units to demonstrate the viability of the experiment. Security specialists in any organization should be the first to have security job performance motivations incorporated into their reviews. Although their job titles may not identify the security aspects of their positions, they generally possess much of the sensitive information within an organization and have sensitive duties. The security of security requires extra security motivation and awareness.

I have witnessed significant resistance in attempting to institute security in job descriptions and appraisals, and do not know of any organizations—other than military organizations—that successfully carry out this crucial motivational practice. In many organizations, the resistance comes from the human resources (HR) units. HR usually strives to keep the appraisal process from being diluted with too many evaluation subjects, especially those that lack tangible means of performance measurement—like security. In one response to my plea, an HR manager said that security should be treated the same as smoking, using the Internet and telephones for personal purposes, and parking regulations. The rules are posted, and if you do not follow them, you suffer penalties—possibly even loosing your job for a serious breach of the regulations. He failed to see the significance of information security for the organization, its strategic value, and possible conflict with other job performance. We need top management support to convince HR and line managers to incorporate security in the ways that I recommend. Information security unit management councils should continue to include these motivational techniques in security plans and present them to top management until they are recognized and implemented.

MOTIVATION AND AWARENESS MATERIALS

Promotional materials can also be used to motivate good security among users and managers, particularly those in organizations that are widely dispersed. After all, security is in their hands, and it is difficult or impossible to monitor their performance with regard to security. Many organizations use some combination of the following materials:

- videos
- newsletters
- brochures, booklets
- signs
- posters
- coffee mugs
- pens and pencils
- printed computer mouse pads
- screensavers
- logon banners
- note pads
- desktop artifacts
- tee shirts
- stickers

Promotional materials should be consistent with the cultural practices of the organization and designed to appeal to the appropriate audiences. Some organizations sponsor an information security promotion week every year to raise employee awareness of security (although some security experts argue that this type of event causes people to ignore security during the rest of the year). One CEO believes strongly in a clean desk practice at the end of each workday. If the security monitors find any non-public company document on an employee's desk or a computer still running, the employee must visit the CEO to explain how it happened.

I have seen some promotional efforts that users interpret as bad jokes. These efforts are likely to have a negative effect on security. Instructional videos are especially vulnerable to rough treatment. Because most people are accustomed to high-quality (in terms of production, not necessarily content), high-priced programming, their standards of acceptable video training materials are very high. Soap opera-style episodes loaded with unrealistic concentrations of obvious security violations and solutions are the worst offenders.

But no matter how effective our promotional and training materials are in increasing employee awareness of the need for security, awareness is not enough without the motivation of every person in a position of trust to protect the assets of the organization. (See Dr. Mich E. Kabay's paper "Social Psychology and Infosec: Psycho-Social Factors in the Implementation of Information Security Policy." He provides an excellent guide and includes 35 recommendations, including limiting cultural changes to small incremental steps. This paper won the best paper award at the 16th U.S. National Computer Security Conference, sponsored by NIST and NCSC in 1993.)

Information security newsletters are particularly effective for presenting the image of security as a sustained, supported function. They also build credibility for the information security unit and can provide motivational benefits. In some organizations, for example, the information security newsletter is sent out on a very selective basis; receiving it is considered a status symbol. It can, for example, impart special knowledge to security coordinators and administrators, giving them an advantage over their peers and employees. It also provides the medium for announcing the results of security award programs for exemplary security performance. One company awards the outstanding security coordinator each year with a check for $500 and a TV set at the annual company information security conference.

The posters used in one company convey the security message in text, graphics, and cartoons in color and black and white form printed on letter-size poster board and heavy paper. This is an ideal size for gaining attention on bulletin boards and sending through the mail. The posters are often printed in wall-poster size as well for viewing at a distance. Posters should not, however, be displayed for long periods of time because they quickly become commonplace and are easy for employees to ignore or overlook. Many companies stamp a removal date on the bottom of the posters to ensure that they are removed or replaced on a regular basis. The innovative information security manager of a large bank on Long Island sponsored a poster design contest that drew a great deal of attention to the entries, which were mounted in elevator waiting areas. Although posters will probably never become obsolete as a communication medium, many organizations are supplementing them with their electronic counterparts—Web pages, bulletin board systems, display banners, screensavers, and e-mail messages—all of which can be useful for reminding users and managers about the importance of security.

Using a cartoon character, logo, or standard distinctive design on the promotional materials, and carrying the design on all security-related documents and promotions, is very helpful for creating and maintaining an identity for the subject matter. Such a design can, however, have a detrimental effect if it is used excessively or for too long a period of time. Publishers of this type of material should periodically survey their constituents to determine their acceptance of and attitudes about the materials. The timing of publication is important relative to the timeliness of the subject matter covered (e.g., a new virus), or for tying the information into other promotional efforts, such as an annual information security week.

Tying security motivation and awareness messages into new technology is important to increase employee interest in security. For example, the word "key" as used in "The Key to Security" is becoming important as cryptography with secret and public keys comes into use. The replacement of passwords with tokens, the use of servers and firewalls, the occurrence of LANarchy and computer larceny, and Internet usage are opportunities to use new jargon, themes, and plays on words. Extending the elements of security from CIA to confidentiality and possession, integrity and authenticity, and availability and utility provides another opportunity to advance awareness.

SECURITY AGREEMENTS

Some organizations require employees to sign a security agreement upon initial employment and on an annual basis thereafter. This is an excellent way to achieve accountability, because it ensures that the members of the organization (and contractors) review the policies and understand that they will be held accountable for their execution. Agreements could also include nondisclosure of trade secrets, a code of ethics, and privacy issues. Many banks use security agreements for their officers; low-level employees are usually not required to sign such agreements—although they should if their duties involve high-trust stewardship over assets.

Organizations often require security agreements only for outside consultants and contractors, assuming that the standard employee agreement which stipulates adherence to the organization's policies will cover their own employees. The motivational and accountability issues that arise, however, may affect both employees and contractors when appraisals, rewards, and sanctions do not accompany these agreements. Signing agreements is not enough; people need to be motivated as well. (For more on this subject, see Charles Cresson Wood's "Annual Compliance Agreement Signatures," in *Computer Security Alert Newsletter* of the Computer Security Institute, July 1994.)

Management Plan for Awareness and Motivation

To be effective, motivational tools, rewards, and penalties must be consistently applied over time. If nobody is *ever* sanctioned or rewarded, or if this occurs only sporadically, the motivational value is lost. Policies and standards that are not carried out represent severe security vulnerabilities themselves and should be periodically reviewed and/or eliminated.

In the commercial world, the goal is to put capital and labor at risk to advance profits, growth, and productivity. Applying security to reduce risk is antithetical to, and inhibits, these objectives except under rare, unpredictable circumstances when a loss is reduced or subverted. Optimally, an organization applies only enough security to facilitate its objectives and avoid disasters. Security, therefore, is not a naturally motivated effort. The organization must determine how much security it needs and then explicitly motivate people to perform at that level. Unfortunately, much positive security performance is not rewarded, whereas security failures are sometimes punished—a negative, one-sided reinforcement. One security training specialist told me that his company offered a "You get to keep your job!" reward for effective security. This is not the type of reward I advocate; security must be motivated with both real rewards and real sanctions liberally applied.

Clearly, linking security performance to job objectives and appraisals gives the information security unit some additional responsibilities because it then needs to develop and sustain an effective security program—including all of the necessary documentation (e.g., policies, standards, and guidelines) to clearly define security requirements, and promotional and training materials to motivate and educate users. In some respects, the users would be unable to meet the critical performance objective of security without a high degree of support and guidance from the information security unit. And, proposing annual performance appraisals would be certain to invite discussion of the organization's effectiveness in providing means and guidance to achieve effective security.

Summary and Action Plan for Motivation

The following action items tie together the various aspects of motivation for information security:

- Develop practical organizational policies and standards and offer guidance and resources to help members of the organization implement and maintain adequate security of the organization's assets.
- Require members of the organization and its contractors to sign a security agreement.
- Approach and attempt to gain support from the human resources department to add security accountability as an explicit work objective with rewards and sanctions.
- Establish security as a specific objective in job descriptions, to the extent that management allows. If management resists universal

An Example of Poor Motivation

A good example of poor motivation in action is the enactment by the U.S. Congress of the Computer Security Act of 1987 (Public Law 100-235). This ineffective legislation requires each agency to have a documented security plan for every computer that processes sensitive but unclassified information (Section 6), and every civil servant who handles sensitive but unclassified information to receive training in computer security. The stated objectives are "to enhance employees awareness of the threats to and vulnerability of computer systems and to encourage the use of improved computer security practices." These requirements, however, carry no specific sanctions or rewards, and consequently they have probably brought little or no advance in security, yet have wasted huge amounts of resources and money (according to the General Accounting Office's many agency security reviews).

During the hearings on the Computer Security Act bill, I wrote letters and visited the House of Representatives committee, urging them to introduce the motivational provisions that would make the requirements work. Committee staff members reassured me, saying that the Office of Personnel Management would add the motivational aspects. Those provisions that would include security in job performance criteria were never included in the bill. Therefore, they were never implemented, except possibly in the Department of the Treasury, where security was added to job performance reviews. The act is still in effect and its congressional author continues to praise it—in spite of its sad record. Business in general shares this failing of applying security only cosmetically because job performance appraisals do not include it. I have yet to uncover examples of organizations that do link security performance to job performance effectively.

application of this tool, first implement it on a limited basis for some job descriptions.

- Establish security as a specific objective in periodic appraisals. Implement this for members of the organization whose job description requirements include security elements. Measurement can be accomplished through peer evaluations, managers' evaluations, absence of security violations, recognition of advances in security controls attained, loss reporting, attendance at training sessions, etc.

- Specify a program of rewards for exemplary security performance and sanctions for inadequate performance, and implement it to the degree that management supports and applies this program. Rewards could include plaques or desk ornaments, public recognition, prizes, parking spaces, bonuses, job advancement, or remuneration increase. Penalties may include loss of computer privileges, change of password, loss of employment privileges, loss of remuneration, criminal arrest, or civil litigation.

OTHER INFORMATION SECURITY MANAGEMENT ISSUES

It is important for all products acquired by or developed in an organization to adhere to an established level of due care security, particularly as LANs, workstations, networks, and their various connections proliferate in distributed computing environments. We can ensure that products comply with our security requirements by restricting purchase to the latest approved products available from reputable manufacturers. If units must obtain products other than those approved through the normal security review and approval process, they should certify that the products meet the equivalent baseline of adequate security. (This includes the possibility of allowing noncompliance when supported by an approved business rationale.) This type of product acquisition policy can be effective in organizations with a strong, centrally controlled purchasing unit, but is difficult to enforce in a distributed computing environment where business units often acquire their own computing resources and are accustomed to relative freedom in regard to selection and acquisition. In any case, highly competitive, fast-moving businesses generally do not want to discourage the acquisition of new products that can be helpful in achieving the organization's objectives—even if the products have not yet been reviewed or approved for security capabilities.

One large company established a *New Technology Security Certification Procedure,* which defines a new technology to be any externally purchased computing hardware or software that is not pre-approved for security. It specifies a procedure for identifying control objectives, roles, and responsibilities, and provides a Security Certificate form for users to complete. After certification is accomplished, the product may be added to the pre-approved list if other purchases are contemplated.

Exceptions to Information Security Requirements

Organizations should have a security exception policy, even if the exceptions are limited to extreme conditions or emergency situations. Even the basic security controls, such as authentication of users, should be subject to exception to, for example, preserve anonymity or segregation of duties. The information owner and at least one level of management above the owner should be jointly responsible for authorizing any exceptions. Such authorization may be extended to higher levels for significant exceptions. The information owner should be responsible for informing the custodians, service providers, and users of the information, as well as the information security unit, about the exceptions. The audit and legal units may play roles in the process as well.

One example of an exception form includes the following topics: alternative method to be used, control of dial-in entry to a microcomputer not connected to a network, peer-to-peer communication controls, control of communication of sensitive information without encrypting it, and a category of *other* for additional exceptions. This list demonstrates the broad range of exceptions that an organization may need to cover, and demonstrates emphasis on particular issues that may frequently arise. The category of *other* covers situations where a specific safeguard standard is to be totally or partially ignored without an alternative substitute.

Loss Incident Reporting and Emergency Response Unit

Most information security policies state the duty of members of the organization to report "security incidents." An incident is typically understood to mean any anomalies or suspected anomalies (deviation from normal conditions, states, or events) that result or could result in loss. This duty is particularly important in distributed environments that are out of view of security practitioners. The challenge is to develop a sufficient level of sensitivity and alertness among staff, motivation to report sometimes embarrassing and unpleasant incidents, threshold levels of incidents requiring reporting, and what should be reported about incidents.

Information security units should maintain a central repository of internal incident reports and reports from outside sources such as CERT, which it can use to compile demographics and statistics; this is crucial for determining the effectiveness of security and monitoring trends over some period of time. Incidents can easily be overlooked if they are recorded only locally in the units where they occur, but local security coordinators need to be continually aware of incidents in their own, and others', areas of security responsibility. A designated hot-line or e-mail address can be very useful for reporting incidents, and the central information security unit can use bulletin board services and/or newsletters to disseminate incident reports to the appropriate individuals in a distributed environment. Rewarding employees for reporting incidents and protecting their confidentiality are very important for encouraging such reports.

The Security of Security Information

Detailed information about the specific safeguards installed in an organization, names of employees responsible for them, detailed security plans, and loss experience documentation are particularly sensitive kinds of information that the organization owns. This type of security information can reveal how to violate or find vulnerabilities in the organization's information systems. All security documents should be classified and labeled according to their sensitivity and should incorporate instructions for prudent handling. Some materials should be sent to recipients in secure mode (e.g., using encryption or double sealed envelopes through internal mail). Internal standards and guides are usually not particularly sensitive, but any information about specific implementations of security may be very sensitive.

17

Doing It Right and Preparing for the Next Millennium

There are increasing attempts by a number of eminent security experts such as Dr. Bob Blakley of IBM in Austin, Texas, who is calling for a new computer security foundation paradigm, to make information security—or at least the computer component of it—into a science. In my view, the entire subject of information security is a folk art, and will continue to be one, because it is not possible to prove that information security controls are effective against adversaries or that information is adequately secure. Thus, a control's merits are left to its self-evident features, recommendations by recognized experts, and its acceptance and use by other prudent users. Information security experts have almost 30 years of accumulated experience and knowledge in support of the viability of at least 300 well-known control objectives, and only rarely have we been able to demonstrate a control's success based on an actual number of foiled loss experiences. Adequately documented loss experience, including the identification of controls that worked and did not work, is minimal and certainly not sufficient to demonstrate effectiveness in many real situations against often irrational criminals. The SRI Consulting files, which house the largest collection of loss documentation in the world, include fewer than 200 documented cases (from among 4,000 reported cases since 1950) that provide sufficient information for use in scenario testing of controls to demonstrate their effectiveness.

Deterministic testing that would conclusively prove or disprove the effectiveness of a control does not work. Effective testing of an entire set of security controls, or testing even one control in place, as would be required to meet engineering standards, is a rational activity. Engineering deals with rational forces that can be tested in the laboratory and under controlled conditions. However, real attacks that can prove the value of a control are infrequent, irrational, and harmful acts by people in real, often stressful, circumstances. By definition, irrationality is not testable under controlled conditions. We can not wait around long enough for sufficient real experiences to accumulate to gain the necessary insights into all of the ways that controls and control systems are supposed to work to determine whether or not they are effective.

In information technology, computers are the adversaries to be tamed to do our bidding. They are rational in that they repeat themselves exactly under the same circumstances, and it is possible to predict their repeated behavior. The same set of inputs always produces the same set of outputs under frequently achievable normal circumstances, so that we can test conclusively within a known set of expected inputs. In contrast, people are sometimes irrational and rarely repeat themselves exactly, especially when misbehaving and under the stress of engaging in abusive activity, and are likely to put unanticipated data into computers, program the computers imperfectly, and use them in unexpected ways, making the computer's performance unpredictable. By definition, irrationality is not predictable or repeatable. Thus, security controls intended to constrain the abusive actions of often unknown people cannot be deterministically tested because of the unpredictability of people and consequently of the computers they use.

As I have emphasized, our security efforts are incomplete. For example, we must engage in avoidance of loss as well as deterrence and prevention. Although avoidance is frequently overlooked, it is a desirable objective (or should be) of our security efforts. We should focus on removing information from danger and removing danger from the information—and ultimately eliminating the need for some specific security in the first place. Otherwise, we must protect all copies of information in all media and locations. How can we prove that information is secure? How can we prove that we can successfully avoid loss? There are no scientific techniques to measure these vital aspects of our security efforts. We cannot predict what our intelligent, irrational, unknown adversaries are likely to do, and we can not predict with a sufficiently documented degree of accuracy how our controls that are operated by fallible people are going to respond to attacks. Rather than achieve a science, I would be happy to see information security become at least a well-developed and articulated art.

Failures and Successes of Testing Controls

Consider testing a computer usage control such as requiring secret passwords for computer entry and use. When use of permanent passwords is enhanced by use of smart cards that automatically produce additional temporary passwords that must be entered from the cards to obtain entry, an obviously stronger control is in place—assuming similar effective administration for both kinds of entry authentication. This is likely, because permanent passwords authenticate users by only what they know, but smart cards authenticate users additionally by what they possess. But we can not prove by experience that one control is better than the other, because we do not know about enough unauthorized attempted intrusions under the old and new controls in the applications under scrutiny. And the applications and their environments are constantly changing, and under the control of people who sometimes act irrationally. This adds to the difficulty of testing.

Testing old and new controls reveals little that we did not already know about the improved strengths of the new controls over the old ones. We must assume that there are unknown people with unknown methods of making unauthorized computer entry or use such as using a new powerful password guessing tool or some kind of unanticipated attack on the smart card or its software. They might also use unknown social engineering deception attacks on authorized users and administrators to gain their passwords or cards, or to gain knowledge about programming errors that allow intrusion with unexpected combinations of input data and commands.

By contrast, credit card fraud offers a possible exception to my claim of lack of experience to prove effectiveness of controls. There is a high frequency of known, and accurately recorded, credit card fraud. The industry has found that when more intense checking of stolen cards is performed, fraud goes down, and when it is relaxed, fraud goes up. Therefore, the value of experience is somewhat useful in a few isolated cases of high incidence losses, but not enough to advance from art to science.

MOVING INFORMATION SECURITY FORWARD

Our almost 30 years of experience with computer crime and security has given us great insights. Just because some of us long ago poorly articulated an incorrect, limited concept of the folk art of information security is no reason to perpetuate those wrongs or allow them to affect us adversely today. The old original foundation and framework model was wrong then, and it is still wrong today. But we did not know it or care enough to change the old model in the intervening years. We repeated the old information security foundation so much in our writings, policies, and standards that changing it would be a major chore, and cause significant embarrassment, thereby admitting that we were so wrong for so long. The old model seemed to work well over the years; there were no complaints and security advanced significantly in some ways because of such a great void of insecurity, unlimited vulnerabilities to fix, and obvious needed safeguards, despite the old incorrect framework and foundation.

Today, however, we must solve more difficult, and more complex, security problems. Information owners now assume the responsibilities for security, and security experts must impart the capabilities to them in rational and articulate ways. Effective solutions must start with the sources of loss—not just with the technical vulnerabilities. We can easily see that the old simple framework does not work. Many articles, papers, and books dutifully mention CIA elements and the DDUM losses, but then ignore them in the remainder of the writing, where their shortcomings might be revealed. We can no longer do without the advanced model that reveals the new challenges such as automated crime and computer larceny. We have been too busy putting out the fires and keeping up with advanced technology and the vulnerabilities associated with our complex information systems to change and fit our old model to today's practice. And there is a lack of interest, support, and money from business and government and information owners to fix it. In the meantime, our adversaries get smarter and more successful, while security gains strategic value with the commercialization of the Internet. The old model just does not work to meet current and future challenges.

Time marches on for all technologies. Medicine gave up bleeding the sick, removing ovaries to cure depression, and using electricity as a general cure-all. Physicists and chemists gave up trying to change lead into gold, and expanded the four elements of fire, air, earth, and water into today's Periodic Table. The military gave up the Maginot line, fortresses, and great walls. Fire, water, earth, and air are not sufficient on the elements chart, and preserving the confidentiality, integrity, and availability of information is not sufficient to meet today's challenges from irrational but intelligent criminals.

It is time for us to use the correct words, and to be precise, complete, and consistent in presenting a seamless protective wall that separates our information and systems from the peccadilloes of increasingly intelligent adversaries engaged in unpredictable mayhem. Our foundation and framework model must have integrity and authenticity in the full and correct meaning of those words as they apply to today's world. Advances in distributed and pervasive computing demand this. Mobile workstations, Internet communications, knowledge management, and virtual businesses are new challenges for adequate protection of the information they process. We must use all six of the foundation elements with their correct meanings that fully define information protection. We must be aware that there are many other ways than DDUM for information loss to occur, such as misrepresentation or stealing copies without violating confidentiality. We must recognize that the security risk of irrational enemy attacks is not generally calculable and that the new baseline due care guidance is the best way to protect us from negligence, let alone actual loss.

A Summary of What We Must Do

As we move information security forward to face today's challenges, and those of tomorrow, we need to overcome a number of harmful forces.

Errors and omissions. Security that is addressed to intentional loss will apply to this category.

Disasters. A security specialty field deals with this problem.

Pirates. The ease of software piracy makes thieves, counterfeiters, and robbers out of otherwise honest people. Industrial associations are tackling these enemies through the courts.

Hackers and virus writers. Malicious hackers and security technologists are locked in unending battle of one-up-manship that will never yield a decisive victory for either side.

Career criminals. They are controllable by law enforcement.

Trust violators. Better management of personal problems can help solve this threat.

Organized information warriors. Governments and industrial infrastructures must deal with information warfare and terrorism.

Risk assessments. Management must be made aware that business risk and security risk are different and the latter is not determinable.

I recommend several specific solutions for dealing with these challenges:

- We need to develop holistic new models and practitioners to convert information security from a folk art to a disciplined art.
- We need to create new laws to control the use of cryptography, clarify positions with regard to civil litigation and sting operations to catch computer criminals, and improve privacy through self-interest.
- Adding security to job performance appraisals will work miracles for raising management awareness and motivating individuals—managers and end-users alike—to practice good security.
- Building unpredictability into our information systems will help to foil our adversaries.
- Making our computer applications similarly unpredictable, and advancing formal internal control models (e.g., the Clark-Wilson model) can further foil attacks by our adversaries.
- We should replace the concept of risk assessment with the concept of due care to avoid negligence, which is more important and practical than avoiding risk, and accomplishes the same ultimate goal of protecting our information assets.
- We must divert youngsters from the hacker culture by making it socially unattractive and unacceptable.

We must update several aspects of information security if we are to achieve adequate protection for information. First, we must redefine confidentiality, integrity, and availability of information and expand these elements by adding utility, authenticity, and possession.

What you can do: Change your organization's written policy to include all six elements. Organize your control standards and guides by identifying controls under each of the six elements. Simplify your classification of information to two levels of sensitivity and expand classification to all elements and types of loss, and do not limit it to confidentiality. Expand your awareness training and materials to reflect the more fine-grained and complete and correct view of information security that is needed today.

We must expand the list of losses of information from destruction, disclosure, use, and modification to an all-inclusive one that reflects today's challenges.

What you can do: Remove these DDUM words from your documents and threat analysis and replace them with a general description of *information-related losses,* and refer potential victims to a new list that explains abuse and misuse in more complete and correct detail.

We must replace risk assessment for security planning with due-care selection of good-practice controls to avoid negligence.

> **What you can do:** Convince management that control selection decisions based on security risk calculations are unworkable. Introduce a new security review and controls selection methodology that is based on the standard of due care concept of using the advice, experience, and practice of others under similar circumstances.

We must replace the three functions of information security—prevention, detection, and recovery—with the eleven functions starting with avoidance and deterrence and ending with correction and education.

> **What you can do:** Establish a new mission for the information security unit in your organization to engage in, and promote, all eleven functions. Acquire the broader range of skills and knowledge of holistic practitioners who transcend computer technology to deal with the whole information security effort.

We must motivate employees and managers to practice good security by offering rewards of job advancement and financial compensation, rather than merely teaching the need for security awareness.

> **What you can do:** Work with human resources and top management in your organization to add information security to annual job performance appraisal forms and instruct and train managers (motivating them with rewards) to evaluate their employees on security performance with rewards and penalties.

We must determine the security-sensitive locations of users and their mobile workstations, as well as determining their authenticity. This adds another dimension to the need for computer usage controls against the changing threats and vulnerabilities of advanced technology.

> **What you can do:** Introduce the location of logons as a security factor along with user IDs, passwords, tokens, and biometrics, and urge vendors to include location in their logon product features.

Provide information owners with reasonable security advice that does not interfere with their primary business objectives of service, productivity, growth, and profitability.

What you can do: Emphasize achievement of prudent security and transparent controls that minimize real-time attention. Do not blindly recommend the most security that can be tolerated; business needs only prudent security that meets a standard of due care with the least constraints and lowest cost—not the maximum security that employees and the enterprise can tolerate. Much of the security literature opts for maximum robustness in security because security has military origins. But whereas the military requires a high level of security, business must weigh security against the mission of profitability.

SOLVING THE HACKER MENACE

We must stop the irresponsible, anonymous malicious hacker threat that is leading us into information anarchy. While we are building technical security barriers against their juvenile attacks and prosecuting the hackers that are apprehended, we also need to initiate a large-scale effort to stop the practice where it begins—with the young people entering into this dead-end culture. We need to convince the nine-to-twelve-year olds, before they become addicted to hacking, that there is a more exciting and rewarding path for them to travel into information technology. And we must look with disdain upon those who do follow the malicious hacker path, rejecting them as peers in the information society. Only in this way can we finally decrease the hacker population as the older hackers leave hacking to get on with their lives. Although there are some limited efforts currently underway—like that of Murt Daniels, when she was at Bell South (404-321-8000, Atlanta, Georgia), who produced a rock video on the perils of hacking, and Gail Warshawski at Lawrence Livermore Labs (www.linl.gov), who developed a puppet video—we need to do more in this direction, and on a larger scale.

Malicious hacking leads young people to engage in pseudo-professional work without achieving the solid foundation that is necessary to fully understand what they are doing. Learning how UNIX, LANs, bridges, routers, hubs, and gateways work from reading manuals and computer exploration does not prepare anyone—with the possible exception of a few already gifted individuals—for a successful career. We must inspire young people to stay in school, obtain a well-rounded education, and prove that they can be trusted to be responsible contributors to information technology. It is truly distressing to see young people who have been convicted as computer criminals and abusers of the technology, attempting to become information security consultants. They have proven from their malicious hacking that they are untrustworthy, unethical, and limited in their knowledge of the world, and are poorly prepared in their organizational communication skills to be successful in consulting.

The persistence of hackers, combined with the vast amounts of time that individual hackers are willing to expend in attacking systems, will ultimately win the day against any system. The people protecting the information and communications systems are engaged in productive work and cannot spend all of their time and energy defending systems from hackers. When they let their guards down to meet their work obligations, the persistent hackers are there to take advantage of the brief window of vulnerability—and they are likely to succeed. Workers operating and using computers and communications will never have the continuous motivation, alertness, and high level of skills maintained over a sufficiently long period of time to beat the numerous hackers and their continual challenges. Likewise, our technological controls will never be strong enough to stop persistent hackers, especially as we strive to make computers and communications easy, convenient, and effective to use. In the future, building hacker tools and automated crime packages will make it possible for only a few competent hackers to multiply their attacks through many other less skilled wannabes.

The computer virus problem is also inherently unsolvable unless we find ways to stop hackers from creating the pesky programs. My call for reducing the hacker population applies here as well. Infrastructure systems will become more vulnerable as hackers create macro viruses that gain cross-platform compatibility as a result of macro language compatibility and as document formats become richer with more embedded executable code. The virus threat grows worse as victims inadvertently spread them by sharing data as well as programs. Malicious code can enter your computer when you browse the Web and click on links. Potentially, information in the systems and networks is a breeding ground for viruses and Trojan horses. Push technology pushes the bad with the good. We will be unable to safely download software, rely on the Internet for processing via network computers, use net-based agents and push technology, or communicate and store information without extensive use of cryptography, which requires that we develop elaborate cryptographic key management. My personal solution to the hacker technology threat would be to have two computers, one for vital computing (such as my book manuscript work and financial system), and the other for vulnerable connection with the outside world.

The Technology Solution

The first part of the solution is to raise the information security barriers against hacker activity to a comprehensive and consistent level of confrontational security controls (the equivalent of locked doors) such as firewalls, resistance to social engineering deceptions, and use of "no trespassing" logon warning banners. Rather than trying to prevent attacks, confrontational security makes violation sufficiently difficult to make it obvious that violations are unacceptable. Although we would be irresponsible if we did not pursue this part of the solution, we cannot expect to win the war against malicious hackers, or even prevent their attacks, through technological and procedural security controls alone.

The complexity of our computer systems assures that there are always vulnerable paths into systems that we have not anticipated. Thus, we can not provide sufficient security against all vulnerabilities because we do not know all of them. This is clearly an inherent insufficiency that we will never be able to overcome; indeed, the problem is only likely to get worse as our systems and networks become increasingly complex, fragile, and open to attack. Idealistic hackers do not understand this immutable law of system complexity, and continue to taunt us by saying that we can design sufficiently secure systems and at the same time make them friendly and usable. We must make hackers understand that among practical business environments, we will never have adequately secure computer systems. Therefore, beating the system is a game that can always be won with enough effort.

The Prosecution Solution

In addition to pursuing technologically based controls, we need to make effective laws against malicious hacking, and enforce them with stringent prosecution. Overall, we need to make the laws more effective by improving the quality of criminal codes and increasing the penalties to match the seriousness of loss. Laws will be effective against the hackers who are deterred by criminal law and frightened by the prospect of incarceration; however, there will always be malicious hackers who are motivated to engage in hacking in ways to overcome these laws and the efforts of the criminal justice community. Thus, laws are likely to have a strong, positive effect on some hackers, but not on all of them, and probably not against the most malicious hackers, who may do the greatest damage by developing hacker tools and automated crimes for others to use.

In addition, hackers are learning to take advantage of the limitations of the law, and are more effectively resisting law enforcement and the criminal justice system. Hackers who have been apprehended are sharing their experiences with young hackers through the hacker bulletin boards. The Bedworth case in the United Kingdom provides one example of how hackers are taking advantage of the legal system. The case involves Alistair Kellman, a brilliant hacker defense lawyer, who was successful in defending an introverted young hacker by claiming that he had become addicted to hacking before it became a crime in the United Kingdom. Conveniently, an expert witness psychologist testified that the arrest and indictment of the hacker was sufficiently traumatic to break him of his addiction, so that he no longer suffered from addiction. This caused great consternation of the hacker's two conspirators, who pled guilty to the hacking charges and received sentences of six months in prison. Fortunately, this type of "addiction to hacking" defense is unlikely to become very popular or successful; Kevin Mitnick tried the same ploy in Los Angeles with considerably less success.

The Interdiction Solution

The best overall solution to the malicious hacker problem is to carry out an interdiction program by deterring young people before they enter the hacker culture. Once captured by the hacker culture, they are addicted, and lost to any kind of interdiction efforts short of forced removal from the use of information technology. Nine-to-twelve-year-old children should be resisting the temptations put forward by such hacker publications as *2600 Magazine*. I believe it would be irresponsible of us not to attempt this solution. This approach could ultimately depopulate the hacker culture to a manageable few who can then receive the appropriate attention of the criminal justice system to control the problem.

An interdiction program must convince young people that there are better ways to achieve challenging, interesting, profitable, and satisfying lives. We know that many hackers start down the dead-end path as pre-teens and ultimately progress through the malicious hacking culture by the time they are 18 to 24 years of age. (In the United States, malicious hackers start to get cautious when they turn 18 because they know they can be prosecuted as adults.) Our treatment of hackers has deluded them into believing that challenging, interesting, and profitable professional careers await successful hackers who are sufficiently outrageous in their activities to draw the attention of potential employers. Ultimately, most find that their malicious hacking experiences and practices lead to joblessness or routine, boring, repetitive work. Then, often when it is too late, they realize that formal education and job experience are essential. An interdiction program requires the cooperation and support of a broad range of the business community, in particular, the communications industry, which probably is the major target of malicious hacking and suffers the greatest losses. And, the effort needs to be worldwide and multilingual, because the culture extends to virtually all countries in the world and is closely tied through electronic communication. Reducing the hacker culture in the United States alone will have little effect on reducing it in the United Kingdom, Bulgaria, Russia, or Italy, all of which pose threats to the international business community.

An interdiction program must target preteen and early teen science and technology students, and focus on the times and locations where they ini-

---

Proposed Actions for an Interdiction Program

- Sponsor an annual Responsible Computing week, concentrating interdiction activities in that week.
- Sponsor computing professional and law enforcement authorities' presentations to schools, student groups (e.g., science and computer clubs), the Scouts, 4H, and YMCAs. Make similar presentations to parent organizations (e.g., PTAs), business service clubs such as Rotary and Lions, professional information technology associations (the sons and daughters of professional computer users and computer technologists are potentially dangerous hackers because of the ready availability of systems), and teachers' groups, providing them with motivational materials to share with their students.
- Work closely with the management of computer game companies to get the anti-hacking message out to young computer users. Many young hackers enter the culture by starting with an addiction to computer games, then try to extend their game playing to other peoples' systems.
- Promote the anti-hacking message through all forms of popular media, including television, radio, newspapers, magazines, comic books, and videos. Also use electronic bulletin boards and Internet sites to present alternative challenges to young computer users and computer user groups.
- Schedule an international conference of opinion leaders to gain support for the interdiction program from business, education, and technology groups around the world, and make joint plans to divert potential hackers' attention to other, meaningful activities.

- In ways that children understand, write and publish codes of practice and principles of computing ethics and etiquette, promoting an appropriate system of rewards for practicing responsible computing. Such rewards may include plaques, prizes, and scholarships, as well as visits to the computing environments that these young people might be attacking if they were to enter the hacker culture. This could dramatically demonstrate the harm that their hacking activities could cause.

The interdiction program would need to produce and use the following promotional materials:

- Booklets, brochures, posters, and bumper stickers with anti-hacking messages
- Advertisements in the periodicals that young people read, as well as advertisements and articles in PTA magazines and other materials seen by parents
- Videos, such as those produced by Murt Daniels and Gail Warshawski, targeting the appropriate age groups and interests
- Learning and teaching kits to accompany the hardware and software used in schools
- Inserts for computer game products to attract youngsters' attention and interest from computer game playing to legitimate positive use of computers
- Articles, press releases, and prepared talks by responsible professionals in computer manufacturing companies and in the businesses that are targets of malicious hackers to establish proper role models for young people
- Electronic bulletin boards and chat rooms frequented by people explicitly engaged in producing this kind of communication
- Publications and explanations of computer abuse and crime cases, explaining what really happens to malicious young hackers in courts and prisons
- Reading lists of appropriate material to counter the *2600* periodical and hacker's handbooks
- Classroom exercises using computers and data communications to engage in role playing
- Movies with positive views of computer use, and reviews and explanations of the negative movies
- Testimonials from hackers who have suffered the addiction of malicious hacking and are willing to explain its negative aspects

tially interact with information technology—and form their first impressions. At that impressionable age, I believe that many can be diverted by appropriate warnings, promotional efforts, mentors' role modeling, and providing more attractive substitutes for their intellectual energy outlets. The program would need to make them understand that it is impossible to eliminate the vulnerabilities of information technology, and emphasize the harshness of the criminal laws that we use to compensate for the vulnerabilities and lack of security. And finally, the program should apply peer pressures, provide the support of role models, and offer a challenging and satisfying life of legitimate technical pursuits through academic achievement. The secondary targets of an interdiction program should be the parents, teachers, and youth leaders, as well as the computer product vendors who can apply their capabilities and opportunities to help solve the problem.

This interdiction program could promote the anti-hacker message to young people around the world, using an integrated, coordinated approach that is likely to gain their attention. It could divert youngsters from the dead-end malicious activities that are bound to lead more of them into lives of crime and ruin the bright minds that are so desperately needed in information and communications technologies.

DEALING WITH THE PRIVACY PROBLEM

A reasonably skilled investigator can find amazing amounts of information about you. It is a revealing and humbling exercise. You quickly learn that you have few personal secrets anymore. You have traded, bit by bit, information about yourself for the conveniences of today's advanced personal services that contribute to our high standard of living. We enjoy an ease of life that delivers nearly any type of goods and services that our hearts desire. To receive these benefits, though, we make our lives open books, and keep private an ever-shrinking body of knowledge. Our privacy concerns are changing from what, and how much, others (and their computers) know about us, to a concern about their ability to retain the integrity and authenticity of that information, and to use it with care. As we take increasing advantage of push technologies on the Internet and use automated bill paying and collection services, and payroll deposits, computers will have more information about us than people do. This shifts the privacy issue from concern about other peoples' knowledge of our personal information to concern about unseen data about us in computers; we begin to worry that people may program computers to make decisions that may effect us adversely.

Privacy requires that we consider both knowledge and noledge (information that is not knowledge, which I described in Chapter 2). Confidentiality applies to knowledge, while possession applies to both knowledge and noledge. This difference is important for security. Is our privacy violated if noledge is misused or abused by computers and causes us to lose control of our personal information? Or are these violations— such as fraud, theft, espionage, or sabotage—separate from the issue of privacy? Privacy no longer pertains only to what people know about us.

The other disquieting aspect of the change in privacy concerns violations of our identities. Criminals are escalating their efforts to violate our identities, and security specialists are working furiously to develop techniques to prevent such violations. Our efforts to authenticate identity have progressed over the years from using names alone, to using names and addresses, then names and Social Security numbers. We have added mothers' maiden names, one or more credit card numbers, and PINs. This type of escalation is likely to continue as crooks find more ways to steal our identities to defraud us.

We are currently answering the challenge of identity theft with smart cards that contain more secret information about us, third-party authenticators, cryptography, and the ultimate identity verification using biometrics. Advances in solving this problem will move toward increasingly powerful forms of biometrics that may be followed by implanting identity devices in our bodies. I know, we have an understandable revulsion for this type of extreme, but in a few years, as our values change and our demand for personalized and transparent services increase, so too will our acceptance of implanted body ID devices, especially when we suffer enough losses to make us desperate to protect our identities. After all, body piercing is already popular among our youth, and we are accepting embedded car identity devices. (Remember, we were revolted by the use of fingerprint scanners only a few years ago but now accept them routinely.) There is already a new chip available for such implants; it is called the *FRAM* (ferroelectric random-access memory), and is capable of storing large amounts of information with no power requirements; reading devices can interpret its content from a distance of one meter.

We should take into account that the preservation of privacy is aimed at a moving target of changing values. This should caution us not to move too quickly with draconian legislation as the European Union, Canada, and some European countries have done. The ubiquitous Internet, with millions of files containing personal information zapping around the world, has wiped out the practicality and cost effectiveness of national privacy commissions with their registers of personal information files. I predict that costly bureaucratic dinosaurs such as the ones in the United Kingdom, Canada, and a number of European countries will fade away as the original one in Sweden now seems to be doing. The United States has wisely constrained its use of privacy legislation, applying laws narrowly in limited areas of concern such as control of credit and health information where victims of harmful practices have redress through the courts to correct violations when they occur, and using ombudsmen to help the victims of such violations. Self-interest and outraged privacy advocates in the marketplace, rather than heavy-handed bureaucratic government regulation, seems to be effective for protecting the right of privacy.

SOLVING THE CRYPTOGRAPHY INFORMATION ANARCHY PROBLEM

I believe that our democratic form of government and civil rights requirements will not survive uncontrolled absolute secrecy of communications afforded by cryptography. The government should always be able to eavesdrop on any form of communications of its citizens, and to obtain information in plaintext under sufficiently justified and authorized circumstances. We must encourage and support the government to develop the capabilities to use technology to eavesdrop on, and search for, any information in any form. Properly authorized law enforcers with proper jurisdiction should have the means to decrypt or successfully engage in cryptanalysis of ciphertext without needing the cooperation of cryptography users who are the legitimate subjects of investigation. I realize that many civil rights, privacy, and libertarian leaders strongly disagree with this, and it does pose serious dangers. We must, therefore, restrict law enforcement and intelligence authorities from abusing their eavesdropping and deciphering capabilities. A single judge's authorization is not enough protection considering the powerful eavesdropping and searching capability within today's communications and computer technology. We could, however, develop the necessary oversight for such activities by creating panels of expert judges, or grand juries, to electronically communicate their considerations and decisions for timely authorization. Without a balance of privilege and safeguards, information anarchy and loss of our means of controlling abuse and misuse will prevail. Given the choice of criminals abusing my information in absolute secrecy and the FBI eavesdropping on my information, I choose the FBI.

We should also enact laws to criminalize the use of strong cryptography when it is used with explicit intent to commit or further the commission of specific crimes, and provide harsher penalties than those crimes would otherwise merit. We already do this with the criminalization of firearms in some jurisdictions by increasing the penalties if a firearm is used in the commission of a crime. However, we must carefully word such statutes to require strong proof of direct criminal intent of the encryption, and involvement of the use of strong cryptography directly in the crime for the purpose of trying to avoid law enforcement eavesdropping in the enactment of a crime. We must avoid prosecution abuses if innocent parties use encryption routinely or inadvertently for other purposes. For example, a taxpayer may use authorized strong cryptographic protection for routine honest tax calculation and communication purposes. She may suddenly start engaging in tax fraud and still be inadvertently using the cryptographic protection. Has she additionally violated the use of strong cryptography law? Legislators will have to sort this out.

Solutions to information anarchy and absolute secrecy afforded by strong cryptography are possible. Within organizations, solutions include having the backup and recovery or otherwise strict control of cryptography keys, control over the means of encryption, and secure independent backup of the information being encrypted. Trusted third-party key recovery services as suggested by the Information Security Business Advisory Group (IBAG) advisors to the European Union may become popular, but business may be unwilling to trust third parties with their secrets. Governments should facilitate recourse to litigation for harm done by key recovery and decryption.

In business, properly authorized management must always have line tapping and encryption override capabilities with the informed consent of employees. (One large bank prohibits the use of encryption, except for specific, limited purposes, because management believes that cryptography is too dangerous to use in informal or end-user circumstances.) While management has the right to monitor and control business information communications, as well as the private communications of employees in the workplace (with informed consent of the employees), it should exercise this right only for due cause and not routinely. For example, private labor union business communications should continue to be privileged. Our governments should encourage, or possibly require, business to develop internal key recovery and to preserve the availability and utility of mechanisms to decrypt.

Governments should take an indirect, rather than heavy-handed, approach to solving the absolute privacy problem. Perhaps government should encourage the use of "good-enough" cryptography for the purposes at hand (such as gaining the equivalent of opaque envelopes for e-mail) and discourage the use of strong encryption. Our governments could do this by supporting the commercial development of attractive good-enough cryptographic products with attractive key backup and legal protections that would make them more desirable than strong cryptography. Then, law enforcement agencies (and admittedly others as well) could engage in cryptanalysis with a minimum of effort and time. Governments could then endorse (not license) the use of strong cryptography where it is needed, such as for funds transfer in banking. This requires uniform policy on an international basis, however, which is part of the whole challenge of appropriately controlling the use of the Internet.

The obvious solution is to make good-enough encryption attractive, and strong encryption only selectively attractive for some purposes, rather than trying to use the force of law and export control, and to offer tax incentives and disincentives, encourage attractive cryptography products, and, most effective of all, encourage good and cheap cryptographic key management enterprises with effective intellectual property and liability insurance coverage.

Information Security Research

The state of applied research in information security is abysmal. What little money is available in the United States comes from the government, with its military agenda, and goes directly into computer and communications operating systems research in university computer science departments, at government contractors, and at the DoD and NIST. I was able to obtain small research grants from the National Science Foundation and Department of Justice in the 1970s and 1980s, as well as a small amount from the National Communications Service (a project jointly run by the Armed Forces), which allowed for field investigations of real loss experience on a modest scale. The U.S. Air Force Intelligence Agency conducted interviews of malicious hackers (in a project called Slammer) in 1996. In addition, there have been a number of commercial studies, including ones by the Computer Security Institute, Ernst and Young, and the MIS Training Institute, but these have largely been informal surveys and not statistically valid. Much of the applied research literature consists of shallow ruminations, without substantive fieldwork. There are few objective case studies or comparison reports of applying specific methods of security, review methods, and controls. Many of the articles are theoretical plans of how something should be done, without any attempt to report how such plans actually work in practice.

Sound applied research in information security is difficult to achieve for several reasons, most of which stem from a lack of funding. The audit field does a little better with well-funded research foundations in conjunction with their professional associations (e.g., the American Institute of CPAs (www.aicpa.com), Information Systems Audit and Control Association (www.isaca.org), and Internal Auditors Association). The audit and information security fields are similar in some ways, since both are staff functions in business and government, make significant use of accounting firms, and deal with controlling and protecting organizations. However, audit receives greater support, because audit is placed high in the management of organizations and generally reports to the board of directors. This makes money more readily available to the auditors, at least in comparison to information security. The latter is usually buried in the bottoms of the information technology divisions of organizations, where it receives only grudging small amounts. This occurs because management often views information security as an inhibiting function in the delivery of computing services, one that is often imposed as an afterthought in attempts to make computing responsive to the needs of the organization's business.

As far as I know, no one is doing research on the differences in information security requirements among different types of organizations—particularly with respect to government and business. Also, no one that I know about, other than Dr. Bob Blakley and a few colleagues, are doing research on finer-grained information security models that would extend beyond CIA. (I have, however, received requests for such information from individuals at the U.S. Central Intelligence Agency, from a defense contractor, and from the Trusted Information Systems Company (www.tis.com). Although a number of security consultants including Dr. James Anderson, Robert Courtney, and Edward Heinlein have publicly challenged some of my earlier, incomplete work on the subject, I believe that the framework model that I present in this book deserves their attention.) We must continue to engage in efforts to refine information security and apply it to the differences among organizations, and we must give broader attention to stay ahead of our adversaries who cause information losses. We need to engage in research to create, or find new or more effective controls that go beyond the baseline controls and address the uniqueness of organizations and their adversaries. We can do this by analyzing the special threats or situations that are not commonly addressed. This is breaking new ground in advancing the common body of knowledge, and may be necessary when vendors introduce new technology and business engages in new ventures that are threatened by automated crime.

Applied research is also inhibited by the nature of information security, which is—and must remain—secretive. Organizations do not want to reveal their embarrassing experiences of abuse and misuse of information, and it is a violation of security for them to reveal much in detail about their internal efforts to achieve security. How would you like to have the details of your security successes and vulnerabilities revealed to potential adversaries? Or to make your organization vulnerable to civil suits by publicly identifying those whom you suspect of having abused and misused your information? Without adequate funding, and without subjects willing to respond to applied research inquiries about the results of their experience with controls, little of experiential value can be accomplished or reported.

This partly is why information security is still a folk art with no substantive body of quality knowledge except on the antiseptic technology side, where there is little need to reveal actual loss experiences. We have endless articles, papers, books, and conference reports on security architectures, firewalls, entry control subsystems, and cryptography—most of which are dominated by the technical aspects of systems. They generally end without revealing any demonstrable value, sufficiency, or implementation experience.

Legal research to support legislation is likewise based on hearsay, urban legends, and the distorted trade and public media reports about cybercrime. A Senate committee recently tried to force the financial industry to appear and testify about their loss experience at hearings on new legislation. With good reason, the financial community refused to participate, and the hearings produced only the often-repeated generalities of consultants who are protecting the confidentiality of their clients. I receive several requests each year from television magazines asking me to identify businesses that have been victims of crime. I hear regularly from *20/20, Prime Time Live, 60 Minutes, Nova,* Canadian TV, the BBC, and even personal appeals from Dan Rather. They ask, "Tell us the names of banks and criminals who will let us do interviews with them and film simulated attacks." No way would I do such a thing, and no way would the banks and criminals that I know subject themselves to such public scrutiny. I advise my business clients to never reveal their security and loss experience. It is a matter of prudent security to keep quiet and not expose themselves to other criminals, embarrassment, and lost public trust. Moreover, they do not want more government control and regulation over their internal operations.

So how do we proceed to transform information security from a poor folk art of urban legends with a modicum of technological whizbang into an engineering and business discipline? I do not have a good answer except to adopt reasonable foundation and framework models, promote standards of due care for selection of security controls, and emphasize the strategic value of security.

The President's Commission on Critical Infrastructure Protection

In 1997, the President's Commission on Critical Infrastructure Protection (PCCIP) examined major threats to eight critical infrastructures of the United States, including transportation, electrical power systems, banking and finance, and telecommunications. I asked the chairman, General Tom Marsh, why they totally ignored an important part of the whole problem by failing to study the adversaries themselves, such as criminal organizations, terrorist groups, and rogue states. Many individuals from these groups are in our prisons, easily accessible for interviews. His answer was that it would be an endless quest, and the focus of the study was on computers and networks. I am sure that the PCCIP got some useful input by hearing the testimony of various law enforcement people. However, the failure to address the adversaries that are at the root of the problem indicates to me that technologists dominated the commission and its sources of advice. We can not adequately study a problem without an in-depth study of its cause. Starting with the vulnerabilities of computers and networks is starting in the middle. Actual interviews with the adversaries would have added much needed authority, validity, and insight to the study. I suspect that the senior policy people on the commission did not want to have to confront nasty people, or perhaps they failed to fully understand that they were studying a nasty problem. Many information security technologists seem to suffer from a similar failure to recognize that they are in a nasty business full of nasty people and not just dealing with the pristine, clean-room environment of computers.

The commission was also hampered by a lack of international perspective. Unfortunately, the bureaucrats in Washington do not see beyond the United States to the borderless cyberspace. Admittedly, the water supply systems, electrical power systems, and emergency services infrastructures are not primarily international (except near Canada and Mexico), but other systems such as transportation and banking are largely international—and they are increasingly dependent upon the (international) Internet. And, the adversaries at the root of the problem often have strong international ties.

On a large scale, the important but often unrecognized part of the solution to international commercial espionage is the creation of multilateral agreements between countries that would outlaw espionage against non-military business, much as treaties have outlawed the use of poisonous gases in warfare. This will obviously not stop all commercial espionage, but fear of outlaw nation status and loss of favored nation trading status could be strong deterrents. International corporations must convince governments of the countries in which they do business that it is not in the best interest of these governments to conduct business espionage for or against them because of the chilling effect it can ultimately have on their own commerce. The refusal of one aerospace company to participate in the Paris Air Show in protest against the French government's alleged industrial espionage practices is one small example of actions that are possible.

Espionage agents and other criminals have a great advantage over legitimate law enforcement agencies because they are able to operate internationally with impunity. Conversely, law enforcement agencies are mostly limited to their own national jurisdictions that do not extend to worldwide computer communications—which knows no bounds. We need an *Internetpol* operating parallel with Interpol, or as a part of Interpol, with broad new powers, standardized laws and rules of evidence, and international agreements for quick extradition and collection and export of evidence. The $10 million international funds transfer fraud from St. Petersburg (prosecuted in the United States) was apparently perpetrated by the former KGB and Russian organized crime. It is only one example of an expected proliferation of big-time international crime that we must deal with effectively without the limitations of national legal jurisdictions. The U.S. government has at least started efforts to gain international cooperation in the war on cybercrime by sponsoring meetings with prosecutors and the judiciary in Europe.

The PCCIP concluded that government research and security standards funding should be doubled. The bad news, however, is that the funding will probably be channeled mostly through NSA and NIST rather than the regulatory and law enforcement agencies and trade associations that deal with, and represent, many of the vulnerable infrastructures. NSA and NIST, while deserving of some of the funding, are both dominated by computer technologists whose focus is the needs of government and military systems. The commission also concluded that a joint industry and government center for the anonymous reporting and confidential recording of vulnerabilities and losses should be established. Unfortunately, it failed to recognize what most security practitioners already know, that industry will not voluntarily—or even by force of law—report such embarrassing information. The Department of Justice and the regulatory agencies are more likely to learn such information through their normal responsibilities and the "old boys network" of retired agents and policemen now working in business security jobs.

Although I concur with the recommendation to establish a center for the study and reporting of loss experience, we need to rely on sources other than victims' reports for case studies. Instead, the center should rely on the news media. (There are already enough cases reported in the news media to exhaust the resources of the center.) Rather than calculating statistics, the center should study incidents on a case-by-case basis in an effort to determine trends—identifying the adversaries' tactics and revealing new methods of attack. The center should engage in, and fund, in-depth studies of selected cases by interviewing the convicted perpetrators, witnesses, and victims and examining evidence to discover the real circumstances and events beyond what may be reported in the news. This is likely to be expensive and usually must await the completion of prosecution, but, in my experience (based on many years of collecting and investigating reported cases), more value will be obtained by in-depth study of fewer cases than shallow investigation of many cases.

Overall, any attention paid to the needs for more support for information security is welcome. The PCCIP recommendation to develop a curriculum for grade schools through graduate schools to teach the importance of information security is also a good idea if it is directed at creating respect and care for information rather than on ways to defeat security.

Security Architecture of Systems

According to Professor Hal Varian at the University of California, Berkeley School of Management, we underestimate the probability of rare events and overestimate the probability of common events. We think in terms of large-value fraud in large systems that deal with high finance, rather than small-transaction fraud in small businesses that use small computers. These perceptions distort the proportionality of our system controls needed to deal with threats. The designers often fail to understand that applications of computer systems mostly perform independently of transaction size, computer size, and frequency. They also fail to understand that security architecture in systems makes no sense unless it includes the people who operate, own, use, violate, and are affected by the systems, and takes into account the laws, insurance, regulations, and environments within which the systems function.

When viewed in this larger context, credit card systems are examples of poorly defined security architecture. The customers, who could control fraud, lose $50 at most. The banks, which offer credit cards, can not control who gets cards or what they do with them—yet they must foot the fraud bill (actually the banks just pass the losses back to honest customers who pay for credit). The merchants who accept the cards for transactions lose little from card fraud (the merchant banks swallow much of the loss), yet they are also in the best position to control fraud. As a result of this cockeyed failure to match liability with the capacity to reduce loss, some store chains have trained their salespeople to accept cards from customers even when they know that the customers are engaged in fraud. The stores are more fearful of lawsuits from customers and salesclerks, and the salesclerks more fearful of physical and mental harm that may result from confrontations, than they are of the losses that may result—especially since they are not liable for the losses anyway.

To be complete, information systems and networks security architecture for an organization must consist of a flexible security perimeter, an external security domain, and an internal security domain—but not in the image of a fortress. Within the perimeter, controls must protect the subject information and applications from known and trusted people and successful intruders also within the perimeter. When the information is external to the perimeter where the environment is more hostile, secure pipelines and other secure island bastions must be established. The purpose of the security perimeter composed of physical barriers and secure physical and communications gateways is to allow controlled passage in and out by approved people, materials, and information with no unapproved gateways. Firewalls as filters at the approved gateways must be viewed in the context of the entire perimeter—not as individual safeguards, and the perimeter and bastions must be viewed in the context of the external and internal domains. When I start performing a security review for a client, I discover or ask for a description of these three elements of the security architecture.

Some pundits say that we must protect infrastructure (entire industry) systems relative to changing roles of our basic institutions. The *BNA Daily Report for Executives* (September 6, 1996, A14, www.bna.com) quoted Michael Nelson, a leading Clinton Administration official on information security and cryptography matters. He said that traditional notions of sovereignty, national security, and warfare will be undermined by the year 2020, when the whole world is "wired" and e-cash is the norm. The result will be less powerful governments in relation to criminal organizations such as the Mafia and international drug cartels. He added that organized crime members are already some of the most sophisticated users of computer systems and strong encryption technology. In addition, computer attackers will pose a more significant threat. Nelson advocates resolving the issue of whether unauthorized use of a computer is an "act of trespass" or an "act of war," and then prosecuting accordingly. I suggest that the intrusion often starts as a personal problem or privacy violation, and only when perpetrated by a sufficiently strong organized enemy that intends to escalate the intrusion to utterly defeat and subjugate the computer owner does it become an act of war. Perspective is everything.

SOME FINAL THOUGHTS FOR BETTER INFORMATION SECURITY

Ultimately, we will no longer view the Internet as the provider of information services. Instead, we will recognize only the value-added Internet service providers and services such as AOL or virtual banks. As a result of this change, brand name recognition of types of Internet services will evolve, and each vendor of services will accept the liability and provide much of the security—just as the credit card industry does today. End-users will rely on the service vendors for security, rather than trusting the security of the Internet as a whole. The information service providers will use technical safeguards such as cryptography, authentication of user identity, and digital signatures, making the controls eclectic, transparent to the end-users, unpredictable to their violators, and automated. Ideally, much of information security will become Cheshire-cat transparent, and only the smile will be visible.

Many information security practitioners have apparently decided (I assume, judging from their inaction and refusal to accept the added responsibility of all information security) to leave the fate of our society to others. Who will take charge of protecting society? Some governments and individual business enterprises are starting to recognize the need for assuming the responsibility, but they are barely beginning to provide the money to do it. More importantly, however, they need the expert specialists to actually do the job. The specialists who understand the basic technological aspects of the problem are busy eliminating vulnerabilities from operating systems in one-upmanship games with hackers. The auditors are busy doing their important compliance job with little documentation standards to comply with. The information owners are busy making the world go around and telling us, "Solve my security problem. Tell me what I must do, but do not get in my way." Law enforcement is still trying to get up to speed, but they only offer solutions of catching and prosecuting the perpetrators after they have already caused the losses.

We need the holistic generalists who can take charge of achieving the total solutions. They must know enough about the nature of information and information technology, the adversaries that pose the threats, and the cyberspace environment of commercial transactions, to integrate the work of security specialists into total solutions. The generalists must be willing to take on the challenge of the entire information security model that I have presented in this book. They need to engage in all of the strategic functions of security, including stopping people from becoming criminals in the first place. Crime only diminishes when there are fewer people doing it.

We must totally abandon the concept of risk assessment in information security. It is not practically measurable, and it is not possible overall to know if our individual security controls or our system security architecture actually reduces risk. Risk deals with predicting the future. We can deal with threats and vulnerabilities that we know reasonably well, but we do not know what the future ones will be. We can deal with the criminals that we know, but we do not know who the future criminals will be, and we do not know what they will do, when they will do it, where they will do it, or why they will do it. Risk is unknowable. There is only one practical defense left for us to use, and that defense is meeting a standard of due care as prudent stewards of our information assets and others' as well to avoid negligence. We have almost 30 years of loss and security experience to use in determining the standard of due care. Meeting a standard of due care is not just solving yesterday's problems, because past problems continue to recur; it is doubly negligent to suffer from the same problem that we already experienced and should have corrected.

Meeting a standard of due care frees us from the waste of relearning the past and allows us to spend more of our limited discretionary security resources in anticipation of some of our future problems (such as automated crime) and to use new safeguards to work toward achieving exemplary security. But the basic defense for many of us is to make sure that we are effectively using the controls that we know about, to achieve due care protection to avoid negligence. In other words, it is not wise to begin using biometrics, security tokens, and other advanced controls until you have enforced security policies and standards, achieved segregation of duties, initiated office security, and properly motivated people with rewards and penalties to practice good security using the basic controls.

To repeat for the last time, the Information Security Imperative is a fact of life that security practitioners must deal with: When recommending security controls to others, you get only one chance because users generally hate the constraints of security and will find any excuse they can to ignore your advice. If your advice fails, they are likely to say, "We tried, but it did not work." And they will likely never listen to you again. Your advice, therefore, must be both practical and correct. Never recommend security solutions unless you are convinced they will work and be accepted in the environment and among the people constrained by the controls.

I N D E X